Mothers, Mammi
and Old Maids

ALSO BY AXEL NISSEN

Actresses of a Certain Character:
Forty Familiar Hollywood Faces from the Thirties
to the Fifties (2006; paperback 2011)

Mothers, Mammies and Old Maids

Twenty-Five Character Actresses
of Golden Age Hollywood

AXEL NISSEN

Foreword by Siân Phillips

McFarland & Company, Inc., Publishers
Jefferson, North Carolina, and London

LIBRARY OF CONGRESS CATALOGUING-IN-PUBLICATION DATA

Nissen, Axel.
Mothers, mammies and old maids : twenty-five character actresses
of golden age Hollywood / Axel Nissen ; foreword by Siân Phillips.
p.   cm.
Includes bibliographical references and index.

ISBN 978-0-7864-6137-0
softcover : acid free paper ∞

1. Women in motion pictures.
2. Motion picture actors and actresses — California — Los Angeles — Biography.
3. Character actors and actresses — California — Los Angeles — Biography.
I. Phillips, Siân, 1934–
II. Title.
PN1998.2.N58   2012   791.4302'80922—dc23   [B]   2012003910

BRITISH LIBRARY CATALOGUING DATA ARE AVAILABLE

Front cover image: *from left* Isobel Elsom
and Ida Lupino in *Ladies in Retirement,* 1940

Manufactured in the United States of America

McFarland & Company, Inc., Publishers
Box 611, Jefferson, North Carolina 28640
www.mcfarlandpub.com

To Storm

Table of Contents

vii

Foreword
by Siân Phillips

It is the lot of stage actors to write on the water; once the curtain comes down, their performances become the stuff of imperfect memories and within a generation or two even the memories dim and then are extinguished. Film outlives flesh, so performances treasured by our parents and grandparents are there — somewhere — for us to enjoy.

Are they, really? Alas, no. For one thing, taste and fashion intervene and the great performances in the great movies of the past lie neglected in boxes in storerooms. It seems hardly worth the trouble to track them down, even if we knew how.

We nod respectfully towards the most renowned titles, we vaguely recall some names of some stars that once were part of everyday life. So what of the people below the title, the supporting players, the character actors? Surely, they are consigned to oblivion. Not quite.

By the slimmest and strangest of chances they have been recalled for us. Not just that; from the pages of two books by Axel Nissen they sing out in their valiant, eccentric, imperious, comic and tragic selves; some downright homely, comfortably sagging into (often profitable) old age, others strained and corseted, anxiously measuring their chances of work by the degree of svelte good looks they are able to maintain.

Yes, this is the second roll call (the first: *Actresses of a Certain Character*, McFarland, 2006, paperback 2011) of supporting actresses from the films of the '30s, '40s and '50s. They are welcome on many levels, not the least of which is that they will silence the chorus of complaints which followed the appearance of the first book: "How *could* he have left out Miss X?" "No book on this subject is complete without mention of the *divine* Y and Z!" And so on.

There's happy reading for people on both sides of the Atlantic.

But, I ask you: What are the chances of these books being written at all? Is it at all likely that a Scandinavian academic with the bounding, affectionate enthusiasm of a golden Labrador, a mind like a rat trap, a gift for the acid putdown, the persistence of a tax inspector, the patience of a saint, and the looks of a teenage dilettante should decide to take up as a hobby the study of the lives and work of neglected character actresses?

Books about the movies are usually heavy on secondhand opinions, unconfirmed gossip and unsourced stories. It is such a treat to read a show-biz book which conforms to the comfortable standards of "proper" books. There are "Notes" — and "Sources" — and a proper index!

This is fun. This is useful. This is a joy.

Siân Phillips is an acclaimed actress whose stage work has ranged from roles in classics such as Hedda Gabler *and* The Three Sisters *to the musicals* A Little Night Music *and* Pal Joey. *Her films includes* Dune *and* The Age of Innocence, *but she is best remembered for her role as Livia in the classic BBC television series* I, Claudius.

Introduction

*We may love character actors because their scenes tend to tell
the story — as opposed to suffering from it.*[1]

"Pick me! Pick me!" Even after having profiled no fewer than 40 Hollywood character
actresses in my 2007 book *Actresses of a Certain Character*, I found there remained more
than enough female supporting players deserving of attention to fill another volume. The
result is in your hands. My main concern in the original book was making a representative
selection of actress types, backgrounds, career developments, and roles. This time I've
allowed my own personal taste to guide the selection to a greater extent. The actresses portrayed here range from the easily recognizable (Marie Dressler, Ethel Waters) to the long
forgotten (Esther Howard, Evelyn Varden), from the prolific (Clara Blandick, Mary Forbes)
to the "one-work wonders" (Jane Cowl, Queenie Vassar). All have in common, though, that
they have made an indelible contribution to American film history in at least one signature
role. Who can forget Juanita Moore in *Imitation of Life* or Josephine Hull in *Harvey*? On
the other hand, why have we forgotten Marjorie Rambeau as the long-suffering mother in
Slander and Helen Westley as the grasping mother-in-law in *Splendor*?

   Mothers, Mammies and Old Maids retains the alphabetical structure of *Actresses of a
Certain Character*, making it possible to dip into the book or read it straight through. As
in the former volume, too, each actress's profile is meant to be a "partial portrait" in which
I attempt to capture the essence of the subject's on-screen persona, unique talents, and popular appeal. But the present study needed its own individual identity as a book, separate
from *Actresses*. While clearly a complementary volume to the original, it differs from it in
two important ways (beyond dealing with a new selection of players): In addition to giving
an overview of each actress's career, the focus in each profile is on one definitive performance;
and the book as a whole focuses more on the *function* of typical character actress roles in
classic Hollywood films, something I said little about in the first volume.

   The films and roles selected are not necessarily the actresses' most familiar, but rather
the performances in which they are given most screen time and are most central to the plot.
Thus, I discuss Clara Blandick's role in *Shopworn*, rather than *The Wizard of Oz*; Constance
Collier in *Shadow of Doubt*, rather than *Stage Door* or *Rope*; Louise Closser Hale in *Another
Language* rather than *Dinner at Eight* or *Shanghai Express*. In the films selected, character
actresses run the gamut of classic types from aunts to housekeepers, dowagers to landladies,
confidantes to society women. There are mothers here, of course, of all sizes and descriptions:
good mothers, bad mothers, warm mothers, cold mothers, and especially those palpitatingly
possessive mothers. Not to mention the mothers-in-law and grandmothers.

   To ask about a character's function is to ask what a character is *doing* in the film, both literally and metaphorically. To ask about function is to ask: How does the character contribute to the plot and advance the action? Does the character also have other functions, such as providing comic relief or commenting on the unfolding events? How do character roles differ in function depending on the film genre? How does the film relate to its source material? What may changes in the supporting cast from the stage or the page to the screen reveal?

The American critic Gilbert Seldes observed in 1934 that "minor players are allowed certain human qualities which the major ones forego": "They are rude, violent, ironic, mean, brutal and mocking. They say what the audience often feels, pricking the great bubble of pretensions which floats through the morals of every movie. They are disruptive elements." He added that "they are very good company."[2] If you are reading this book, you are probably already a fan of supporting players, so I'll let you get on with it and won't preach to the converted. I do believe, though, that you will find one or two surprises here: an actress, a film, a performance that you need to know about. You will find, too, plenty of opinions to agree or disagree with. Either way, I'd love to hear from you. You can reach me at axelnissen@hotmail.com. We old movie buffs are a dying breed and need to stick together!

All the persons I thanked in the acknowledgments to *Actresses of a Certain Character* can consider themselves thanked again. My friend Siân Phillips has graciously provided me with a foreword, which I will always cherish. My husband Storm needs to be thanked for all the things he does to create a perfect home for Miss Universe, Mango Surprise, Minx Cocoa Cream, Viola Prima, and myself. I am also grateful for all the new friendships I've formed in the fascinating world of the cat fancy, first and foremost with the breeder of three of our Sacred Birmans, Synnøve Blix Henjesand.

Mother, May I? Clara Blandick in *Shopworn* (1932)

Are mothers always right? Don't form a conclusion until you see Shopworn.

If it is the essence of the character actress's persona to have a face more familiar than her name, then Clara Blandick is the quintessential character actress. She worked for more than 20 years in the movie industry and lent her talents to more than 100 films, yet all that remains today of her efforts in popular memory is a single role: Auntie Em in *The Wizard of Oz* (V. Fleming, MGM, 1939). "Everyone in that was touched with immortality," the authors of *They Had Faces Then* observe.[1] Last time I checked the votes at the Internet Movie Database, *The Wizard of Oz* was 30 times more popular than Blandick's second most popular film, *Heaven Can Wait* (E. Lubitsch, Twentieth Century–Fox, 1943).[2]

Clara Blandick both came into and went out of the world in an unusual way. She was born Clara Dickey on June 4, 1880, on board her father's ship the *Willard Mudgett*, which at the time was docked in Hong Kong. Her father was ship's captain Isaac B. Dickey and her mother Hattie, *née* Mudgett. Clara was raised in Quincy and Boston, Massachusetts.[3] By 1900, we find her in New York, where she debuted on Broadway in a play called *If I Were King* the following year. The huge cast of this often revived four-act drama by Justin Huntly McCarthy, which ran for 56 performances at the Garden Theatre in its original production, included E.H. Sothern and the author's wife, Cecilia "Cissie" Loftus.

Until the late 1920s, Blandick would make regular appearances on Broadway and was for a time under contract to legendary producer David Belasco. Among her 20 shows on the Great White Way were *Raffles* (1903–04), *Widow by Proxy* (1913), *No. 13 Washington Square* (1915), *The Wanderer* (1917), *The Enchanted Cottage* (1923), and *Applesauce* (1925). Her most distinguished and critically acclaimed role was as Meg Hunt in Hatcher Hughes's Pulitzer Prize–winning melodrama *Hell-bent fer Heaven* for 122 performances at the Klaw Theatre in early 1924. By then she had graduated to the mother roles that would become the staple of her film career; participated in a handful of silent movies (circa 1911 to 1917); performed overseas as a volunteer working for the American Expeditionary Force in World War I France; and seen something of marriage firsthand. On December 7, 1905, she married mining engineer Harry Staunton Elliott. Apparently, the couple separated by 1910 and divorced in 1912.[4]

A series of flops in the late 1920s may have been instrumental in convincing Blandick that the future lay in the West, even though she also had her biggest commercial hit on Broadway at this time: The comedy *Skidding* played for 472 performances at the Bijou

Theatre in 1928 and '29. At any rate, in 1929 Blandick moved to Hollywood to begin the long final chapter of her acting career. She lived in an apartment at 1830 North Cherokee Ave.[5]

In her youth, Blandick was a comely, dark-eyed, brown-haired lass, described in one review as "a dainty, petite, graceful heroine."[6] Yet her screen image is so fixed in frumpy middle age, that it is hard to imagine her ever having been young. In one of those brief glimpses in the autobiographies or biographies of the stars that are all a supporting actress can hope for, Ruth Gordon recalled that Blandick was known among her fellow players in the touring company of Booth Tarkington's *Clarence* (1919–20) as "Constipated Clara."[7] Her screen presence was distinguished by her "Everywoman" quality. Blandick was of average height. She had coal black eyes, that she could use to sympathetic or the opposite effect; exuding warm, maternal benevolence or sour, spinsterish sternness. Her graying hair was usually side-parted, wavy, and gathered at the back in a pristine bun. She commonly affected round glasses or pince-nez. Her voice and diction were as ordinary as her basic look.

Quite a few of Blandick's most salient screen qualities come out in *The Wizard of Oz*,

This faded photograph shows Clara Blandick in *So Goes My Love* (1946), a Myrna Loy–Don Ameche vehicle from Universal Pictures in which Blandick played Ameche's landlady. This was the last of her many pictures for Universal. Studio portraits of Blandick are surprisingly hard to come by, which may be due to her relatively modest position in the film industry or because all the *Wizard of Oz* aficionados are hoarding them.

despite the relative brevity of her most famous role. Auntie Em is "just plain folks"; conventional, yet delighting in small acts of rebellion, such as standing up to insufferable Almira Gulch; strict yet loving, hiding a heart of gold behind a forbidding exterior. In their rustic simplicity, both Charley Grapewin's Uncle Henry and his wife look just about ready to pose for Grant Wood's painting "American Gothic." Indeed, Blandick donned her fair share of sprigged muslin, lace collars, and bonnets in films set in the rural, nineteenth-century American past; two early assignments were playing Aunt Polly in the first sound versions of *Tom Sawyer* (J. Cromwell, Paramount, 1930) and *Huckleberry Finn* (N. Taurog, Paramount, 1931). Yet she should equally be identified with her roles in urban, contemporary settings. Just a few examples from her extensive repertoire are her spinsterish and devoted secretary to Lionel Barrymore in *The Girl from Missouri* (J. Conway, MGM, 1934); her portrayal of Robert Young's hard-tried mother in *The Wet Parade* (V. Fleming, MGM, 1932), the victim of deadly domestic violence at the hands of a drunken husband; the rich, bedridden dowager and murder victim in *The Nurse's Secret* (N.M. Smith, Warner Bros., 1941); Joan

Crawford's concerned, working-class mother in an early scene in *Possessed* (C. Brown, MGM, 1931); and a similarly proletarian, though more extensive portrayal as "fallen woman" Constance Bennett's mother in *The Easiest Way* (J. Conway, MGM, 1931). This partial list is also a reminder that, despite her spinsterish image, Blandick played mother to a wide range of stars during her career. Her most surprising entry in this category, perhaps, is the veteran child-bearer she plays in *Life Begins* (J. Flood, First National, 1932), a melodrama set in a maternity ward. With close-ups emphasizing her warm, dark eyes, Blandick looks both youthful and Earth Mother–like in *Life Begins*, where she supports Loretta Young as pregnant convict Grace Sutton.[8]

Like scores of older film actresses, Blandick worked for decades in relative anonymity. Yet unlike most of them, she has staved off oblivion, at least for the time being, through her involvement in a fabled film. She only secured the role of Auntie Em after May Robson passed on it as being too insignificant.[9] Talk about a bad career move! Sarah Padden and Janet Beecher also tested for Auntie Em, but the part finally went to Blandick. "It was too minor a role to cast from our contract players," recalled casting director Leonard Murphy, "and we really had nobody under contract who fit the part."[10] Blandick worked for one week

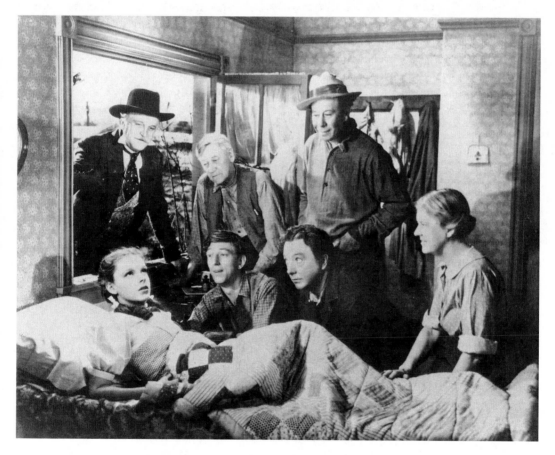

An unusually benign-looking Clara Blandick (right) in this famous photograph from *The Wizard of Oz.* During her forty-year career, Blandick played her share of aunts — maiden and otherwise — but nothing to compare with the exposure and recognition value of her Auntie Em in MGM's 1939 classic. Judy Garland is easily recognizable, but how many of her male companions can you name?

and was paid $750.[11] In comparison, Margaret Hamilton was paid $1,000 a week and worked for four months.[12]

Blandick was no stranger to MGM by 1938. Her sound film debut was in the MGM film *Wise Girls* (E.M. Hopper, 1929) and that was followed by films like *The Girl Said No* (S. Wood, 1930) with William Haines, *Inspiration* (C. Brown, 1931) with Greta Garbo, *Laughing Sinners* (H. Beaumont, 1931), *Possessed*, and *The Gorgeous Hussy* (C. Brown, 1936) with Joan Crawford, and *The Girl from Missouri* with Jean Harlow and Franchot Tone. She had worked for *Oz* director Victor Fleming at MGM as early as 1932, in the aforementioned *The Wet Parade*. She played Miss Watson in *The Adventures of Huckleberry Finn* (R. Thorpe, MGM, 1939) with Mickey Rooney at the same time as *Oz* was shooting. In fact, Blandick worked for Metro her entire career, racking up 25 roles (if not credits) between 1929 and 1950, the greatest number of her films for any one studio. Despite her ten-year track record at MGM, Blandick was credited below "Toto" in *The Wizard of Oz*.[13] About 25 percent of her screen appearances were uncredited.

Suffering from increasingly poor health, including severe arthritis, Blandick went into retirement and seclusion at the Hollywood Roosevelt Hotel in 1950. On April 15, 1962, after attending Palm Sunday services, she returned to her apartment at 1735 North Wilcox Ave., off Hollywood Boulevard. She lovingly laid out pictures and other mementos of her long career, swallowed a handful of sleeping pills, and reclined on a sofa with a plastic clothes bag over her head. Her landlady and friend, Helen Mason, found her dead from suffocation later that day. She had left a note that read: "I am now about to make the great adventure. I cannot endure this agonizing pain any longer. It is all over my body. Neither can I face the impending blindness. I pray the Lord my soul to take. Amen."[14] Clara Blandick's ashes were interred in a tiny niche of the Great Mausoleum at Forest Lawn Memorial Park, Glendale, with Franklin Pangborn nearby for company.

"There's no place like home...." Dorothy's incantation from *The Wizard of Oz* might well serve as a touchstone for our ongoing consideration of the function of the character actress in classic Hollywood films. As we have seen, Blandick played her share of homemakers, but none of them were quite like the upper-class matriarch we encounter in a film that started shooting at Columbia on December 8, 1931.

Shopworn, as it would be called, had a difficult birth. Columbia's original plan had been to adapt a novel by Charles G. Norris called *Zelda Marsh*, which had been published by E.P. Dutton in 1927.[15] *Zelda Marsh* is very much in the tradition of Theodore Dreiser's *Sister Carrie*, though published much later, and is even set during the same period: the turn of the last century. The plot of the novel, which traces the resilient orphaned heroine's rise from humble beginnings in Bakersfield, California, to the pinnacle of Broadway stage fame, included such unconventional behavior as living with a much older man without the benefit of marriage and aborting a child conceived *with* the benefit of marriage. This "dangerous material" caused strong objections at the Production Code Administration (PCA) in the spring of 1931, when Columbia first sought approval for the project. The draft screenplay submitted by the end of the year bore little resemblance to the novel, though the PCA still found it a "very grave problem." The storyline called for the female lead to become a prostitute after being sentenced to a reformatory and to lure her love interest away from his wife. To gain PCA approval, Columbia ultimately had to eliminate all suggestions that the heroine, now called Kitty Lane, had ever been a prostitute. Somewhere along the way, the hero's first wife also got cut. Further cuts had to be made to get the PCA to approve a re-release in 1938, bringing the film down from 72 to 66 minutes.[16] It is this shorter version which is shown on Turner Classic Movies.

Lila Lee was originally slated to star in the film, which finally became a vehicle for Barbara Stanwyck, still in the hard-boiled, hard-working, "woman of the people" phase of her career. Since her previous film *Forbidden* had wrapped on November 3, 1931, Stanwyck had spent two weeks performing a skit at the Palace Theatre in New York with her then husband, comedian Frank Fay. The couple were having marital problems; Stanwyck biographer Axel Madsen imagines that a return to Hollywood and the *Shopworn* set in the first week of December provided the star with a welcome escape.[17] Al DiOrio, on the other hand, calls the film "one of Stanwyck's least memorable pictures and one of her least favorites."[18] Her leading man Regis Toomey recalled that she was "aloof and very unhappy" during the three-week shoot.[19]

By the time *Shopworn* premiered on March 25, 1932, the storyline was so far removed from *Zelda Marsh* that no mention of the novel or its author was made in the credits. Screen credit for the story ultimately went to Sarah Y. Mason, known as the first continuity girl, who would go on to win a 1934 Oscar for her adaptation of *Little Women*. Mason also wrote screenplays for *The Little Minister*, *Magnificent Obsession*, *Stella Dallas*, and *Golden Boy*. Jo Swerling and Robert Riskin wrote the dialogue. They were closely associated at the time with director Frank Capra through films such as *Platinum Blonde* and *The Miracle Woman* (both 1931). Capra directed Blandick in two films — *The Bitter Tea of General Yen* (Columbia, 1933) and *Broadway Bill* (Columbia, 1934) — but not in *Shopworn*. The latter was helmed by journeyman director Nick Grinde, active between 1928 and 1945 and married once upon a time to delightfully daffy comedienne Marie Wilson. The film was produced by the big Columbia boss himself, Harry Cohn, which may explain what the PCA called the company's "stubborn refusal ... to take advice."

Shopworn in its final incarnation is a movie without a middle; those 30 minutes or so that would make it a full-length feature. It's as if the body of the film has been gutted; gone are all those complicating twists and turns that sustain suspense and keep us guessing. What remains is the bare bones of one of the most traditional plots in Western literature — capable both of a comedic or tragic treatment — where the union of two young lovers is opposed by one or more parental figures. There are only two possible outcomes in a story of this kind: either the authority figures give in and approve the union; or they don't and one or both of the young lovers are doomed to an untimely death.

The parental antagonist in *Shopworn* is the upper-class hero's widowed mother, Mrs. Helen Livingston. This is where Blandick comes in. At age 51 she was cast in this pivotal role in what was her first of 10 films at Columbia between 1932 and 1949. As we have seen, for all her ordinariness Blandick was a versatile actress, who could convey a wide variety of types. What nearly all her parts had in common, though, was just that: They remained types. She was seldom given the opportunity to develop any individuality or depth in her screen portrayals. Despite the bare bones quality of the film, indeed maybe because of it, *Shopworn* provided her with a dramatic role that in screen time, centrality to the action, and character development would remain unparalleled in Blandick's career.

Mrs. Livingston is imperious, snobbish, spoiled, hypochondriac, and overly protective of her milquetoast son David, played by Regis Toomey. In the film, Blandick gets to wear a series of elegant outfits, including a gorgeous beaded and barebacked evening gown with matching diamond earrings for a dinner party scene. She is also provided with a co-conspirator (though not a love interest) in the form of a local judge. Played by Oscar Apfel, Judge Forbes's relationship to Mrs. Livingston remains largely unexplored and unexplained beyond his evident closeness to her and her family and his willingness to do her dirty work. The latter includes a scheme to have Stanwyck's waitress heroine falsely accused of violating the "public morals act" and sentenced to 90 days incarceration in a "State Home for the Regeneration of Females." It is from the point she is released from the reformatory till she is reunited with David Livingston that the storyline gets sketchy, as the six years of Kitty Lane's meteoric rise to show business fame and fortune are given only the skimpiest of treatments.

Though there is evidence that Mrs. Livingston may have been built up in response to a suggestion from the PCA that the heroine "be made to struggle against the injustice of other unscrupulous characters in the story,"[20] the character also has some basis in *Zelda Marsh*. As a young girl, Zelda gets sexually and romantically involved with a classmate and promising young musician, Michael Kirk. His mother does all she can to break up the relationship and finally takes her son off to Europe, just as Mrs. Livingston does in *Shopworn*. Though the basis for Mrs. Kirk's disapproval is more subtle than the class snobbery Mrs.

As the well-to-do matron Helen Livingston in *Shopworn* (Columbia, 1932), Clara Blandick (second from left) has her steely gaze riveted on her only child David, played by Regis Toomey (far right). She is seconded in her attempt to prevent a misalliance between David and Kitty Lane, a young girl from the wrong side of the tracks, by her friend and lawyer Judge Forbes (Oscar Apfel, far left). Kitty is played by Barbara Stanwyck in one of her early starring roles as a brunette.

Livingston suffers from, there is a suggestion of the mothers' unhealthy preoccupation with their male offspring in both stories. Towards the end of the film, Kitty says to Mrs. Livingston, "It's a queer, selfish kind of love, but I'm beginning to understand it." Earlier, Mrs. Livingston's friend the judge asked her if she has considered consulting a psychoanalyst, adding that mother love turned inward can be dangerous. To this query, Mrs. Livingston responds: "Am I abnormal because I want to protect my son?"

We see in *Shopworn* a fairly primitive example of the significant "silver cord" theme in films of the 1930s. As I discuss in detail in the chapter on Louise Closser Hale and *Another Language* (1933), this period was rife with portrayals of domineering, obsessive mothers, who were increasingly being seen as warped and dangerous. Despite a superficial attempt at suggesting psychologically deep and dark waters, Mrs. Livingston is basically a figure straight out of melodrama with lines like "I'll die if you get involved with a common person like that." She refers to her son as "the only one I have left in the world"; avers in reference to Kitty's return to town that "I'm not going to see my life's work spoiled now"; and threatens: "David, if you marry that woman you are no longer my son."

We can only wonder how Stanwyck and Blandick got along in real life. Their scenes together were certainly the most riveting in the film, particularly the climax where Mrs. Livingston, in a final desperate bid to keep Kitty away from David, seeks her out in her luxurious hotel suite and threatens her with a gun. The two actresses were briefly reunited on the set of *The Bitter Tea of General Yen* in the summer of 1932. This time Blandick was cast in an uncredited role in the opening scene, as the hostess at Stanwyck's Shanghai wedding to fellow missionary Gavin Gordon. The two were also together in *Ever in My Heart* (A. Mayo, Warner Bros., 1933) for the third and final time.

Largely because of its hackneyed plot and butchered editing, *Shopworn* did not meet with a friendly reception from the critics. The *Hollywood Herald* thought the film was "tawdry and cheap."[21] The *Times* of London found it "a dull and characterless study" in which Stanwyck "does what she can with a thankless part."[22] The *New York Herald Tribune* wrote: "It happens, you see, that the film is not Shopworn in name only. That unfortunate, but descriptive, title provides, among other things, a pretty good critical estimate of the work."[23] Under the title "Notorious Kitty Lane," *New York Times* critic Mordaunt Hall called the film "a lot of fuss about nothing": "It is beyond the powers of such capable players as Barbara Stanwyck, Regis Toomey, Clara Blandick and Zassu [*sic*] Pitts to make their action in this film convincing or even mildly interesting." He particularly found it unconvincing that while " Mrs. Livingston "did not wish her son to have a waitress for a wife," she was "quite content to have him marry a musical comedy star whose reputation is not unsullied."[24]

Today we can afford to be kinder to this amputated classic of the rags-to-riches, "waitress-turned-star" genre. An engaging film with an authentic atmosphere and a classic conflict, it offers Stanwyck several opportunities to speak on behalf of the "little people," railing against the rottenness of the establishment and insisting on her worth and dignity as a working woman. Granted, Regis Toomey is as interesting to watch as a dripping faucet (and just about as wet), but there are entertaining turns by Zasu Pitts as Kitty's sympathetic, fluttery aunt and dresser and Oscar Apfel as the dastardly judge who "done her wrong." Above all, *Shopworn* gives one of Hollywood's most eminently ordinary actresses an extraordinary opportunity.

What a Pal: Helen Broderick
in *Top Hat* (1935)

"You know, I wonder if you've seen something
in Horace that I've never seen."

In comedy, as in tragedy, it helps to have a friend along for the ride, someone to share the ups and downs, to smooth the way, to provide a running commentary on the action, someone to *care*, so that the audience can be convinced that they should care as well. In a couple of classic musical comedies from the 1930s and dozens of less stellar productions between 1931 and 1946, that friend was Helen Broderick, worldly and wise, elegant and sophisticated, tall and svelte, but with a face that clearly wasn't going to launch a thousand ships (maybe a tugboat or two...). Moss Hart once described her as "part vitriol and part my favorite person in the world."[1]

Broderick was the daughter of an actor, the wife of an actor, and the mother of an actor. Her father was William Broderick, her husband was Lester J. Crawford, and her son was William Broderick Crawford. She was born in Philadelphia on August 11, 1891, and educated there and in Boston in public schools.[2] She married Crawford at age 18 in 1909 and their son, known as Broderick Crawford, was born on December 9, 1911. He would go on to a long and varied acting career and is best known for his portrayal of Southern political boss Willie Stark in the original film version of *All the King's Men* (1949), which garnered him an Oscar, a Golden Globe, and a New York Film Critics Circle Award.

Broderick began her stage career as a chorus girl at age 14. Alfred E. Twomey and Arthur F. McClure observe in their book *The Versatiles* that her parents "did not want her to follow the theatrical tradition of the family, but she never considered any other career."[3] In 1907, she made her Broadway debut in Florenz Ziegfeld's first *Follies*. Broderick was in the chorus then, but developed by stages into one of the country's leading comediennes. She teamed up with her husband in vaudeville while performing in a total of 15 "legit" shows on Broadway. "Male/female comedy teams were popular in vaudeville at the time," notes Melissa Vickery-Bareford. "Crawford would play the straight man as Broderick developed her trademark 'caustic, wisecracking style.'"[4]

Broderick is often said to have film-debuted in *Top Hat*. Actually, her first feature film role was in an adaptation of her own hit show *Fifty Million Frenchmen*, which premiered at Broadway's Lyric Theatre on November 27, 1929, and ran for 254 performances. The show had lyrics and music by Cole Porter, but the songs were not included in the film version (L. Bacon, Warner Bros., 1931). In this "musical spoof of American tourists," Broderick played Violet Hildegarde, "a bored spinster in Paris who sends risqué French postcards

We can assume that Helen Broderick is relaxing at home in this artificially natural candid issued by her first home studio RKO in 1936. There are a lot of floral patterns in competition here and the view leaves something to be desired, but "love's young dream" is evident in what is probably a wedding photograph of Broderick and her husband Lester Crawford.

home to her family and friends and buys copies of James Joyce's controversial *Ulysses* to give as gifts to kids."[5] With her both on stage and screen was her husband Lester Crawford. The couple also starred in a handful of comic shorts at this time, before returning to the East Coast. Broderick would star in three further successful Broadway shows before placing all her bets on her film career: *The Band Wagon* (1931–32) with Fred and Adele Astaire; *Earl Carroll's Vanities* (1932) with her husband and Milton Berle; and last but not least, Irving Berlin and Moss Hart's smash hit revue *As Thousands Cheer* (1933–34), in which she starred with Marilyn Miller, Clifton Webb, and Ethel Waters for 400 performances at the Music Box Theatre. According to John Springer and Jack Hamilton, Broderick "of the big bug eyes and acid tongue, did a lot for Broadway revues ... with her dry, economical way with a putdown."[6] At this time, *Who's Who in the Theatre* tells us, she was living at 37 Madison Avenue on the island of Manhattan.[7]

During her years in films from age 44 to 59, Broderick was most closely associated with RKO. Among her 14 films for that studio between 1935 and 1942, we find her in supporting roles in high-profile films such as *Top Hat* (M. Sandrich, 1935) and *Swing Time* (G. Stevens, 1936), and getting top billing in the less illustrious ventures *To Beat the Band* (B. Stoloff, 1935), where she was teamed with Hugh Herbert; *Murder on a Bridle Path* (W. Hamilton, E. Killy, 1936) with James Gleason; and *We're on the Jury* (B. Holmes, 1937) and *Meet the Missus* (J. Santley, 1937) with Victor Moore.

In the first half of the 1930s, the "senior" RKO comedienne had been Edna May Oliver, who hailed from Massachusetts and was eight years Broderick's senior. Oliver was lured away to MGM in 1935 after *Murder on a Honeymoon*. According to Springer and Hamilton, RKO "seemed to want to turn [Broderick] into an Edna May Oliver replacement."[8] Clearly though, Broderick was a different cup of tea from Oliver; in fact, she was an Irish coffee: "Whereas Edna May was the very personification of a persnickety old maid, Broderick was much more 'with it.'"[9] The differences between them also related to physical appearance and voice quality. Oliver's famously long, horsey face contrasted with Broderick's round face, saucer eyes, and weak chin. Oliver's voice was deep, resonant, theatrical, and almost British in its inflections, while Broderick's was lighter, more natural and modern in tone, and distinctively American. Yet there was a timelessness to both actresses. Oliver's timelessness was an ancient one, which made her suited to roles in classic film adaptations such as *Romeo and Juliet*, *David Copperfield*, *A Tale of Two Cities*, and *Pride and Prejudice*; while Broderick's timeless quality was strictly modern. We can imagine her playing much the same kind of best friend roles had she been alive today.

Broderick's most illustrious cinematic creation is in the best friend category: a middle-aged, fun-loving, stylish, filthy rich, and oh-so-worldly lady of leisure and society dame called Madge Hardwick, who lives in the wonderful world of RKO's biggest hit of the 1930s. *Top Hat* is a luscious, scrumptious banana split of a film, built on solid star bananas, piled high with whipped cream decor, garnished with tart maraschino character actors, and lathered in rich, creamy chocolate dialogue. Oh, yes, there's singing and dancing, too. Thirty-four-year-old Mark Sandrich directed what would prove his most popular film. Astaire and Rogers teamed up for the fourth time, as song-and-dance man Jerry Travis and model Dale Tremont. Art director Van Nest Polglase and his team delivered the whitest of white sets imaginable, in an architectural style hitherto unknown to man. Hermes Pan developed the celebrated choreography in collaboration with Astaire, and the legendary songs were the work of Irving Berlin.

In addition to newcomer Broderick as Rogers's older and more experienced friend and confidante, the stars were supremely well supported by *Gay Divorcee* alumni Edward Everett Horton, Eric Blore, and Erik Rhodes. Horton plays Broderick's straight-laced, slack-jawed, weak-kneed, and limp-wristed husband Horace, while Eric Blore is Horace's valet, the both servile and obstreperous Bates. It is one of the film's many ironies that Horace and his "gentleman's gentleman" seem more like an old married couple than do Horace and Madge. The latter couple, as Roger Ebert has observed, "spend long periods living separate lives of luxury."[10]

The *Top Hat* plot revolves around Rogers thinking love interest Astaire is Broderick's husband, which creates supreme situational irony and a lot of conversations at cross-purposes. To further complicate matters, Rogers is involved in an outwardly ambiguous relationship with an Italian fashion designer, Alberto Beddini (Erik Rhodes), though it turns out their relations are purely business. "That [Beddini] is gay goes without saying," quips Ebert, "and in 1935, it did."[11] As in *The Gay Divorcee*, Rhodes manages a terrific send-up of Latin machismo. According to Alan Vanneman, Rhodes "both cornered and exhausted the market for Italian sissies" in *Top Hat*.[12]

The character of Madge Hardwick has a threefold function: to move the plot forward by contributing to the complication of the action; to provide humor; and to act as a foil to the female lead character, the younger, more physically attractive, but also less experienced and sophisticated Dale Tremont. By a foil, I mean a point of comparison contributing to our understanding of the heroine through similarities and contrasts in character. These three different functions are, of course, closely interconnected.

Though Madge doesn't appear in person until 40 minutes into the film, we hear of her from the first as a matchmaker who wants to bring together her producer-husband's new star Jerry Travis (Astaire) and her friend Dale (Rogers). Madge has one goal throughout the film and that is to see her friend as happily married as she is herself; only then can she rest easy. Little or no background information is provided on the roots of Madge and Dale's friendship. We simply have to accept that they are close friends, though the entire plot is built on the premise that Dale has never met nor so much as seen a picture of Madge's husband, which would have made the misidentification on which everything depends impossible. The humorous effect is created by the incongruity of Madge seeming to be pushing her best friend into her husband Horace's arms. It is Dale who must try to come to terms with this contradiction, the climax of her quandary coming in the famous "Cheek to Cheek" number, which is surely one of the most ambivalent love scenes in musicals. While Madge looks on approvingly from a "ringside" table, the man Dale believes is Madge's husband whispers sweet nothings in her ear as they dance "cheek to cheek" and ultimately proposes to her, leading to one of several acts of physical violence perpetrated by women towards men in this film.

In Rogers's recollection "Helen Broderick would pull laughter out of mannerisms, rather than lines of dialogue"[13] — an oversimplification of Broderick's technique certainly,

All the major players are included in this gorgeous still from *Top Hat* (RKO, 1935). From left: Edward Everett Horton, Broderick, Eric Blore, Ginger Rogers, Fred Astaire, and Erik Rhodes. All eyes are riveted on elfin Astaire, while he stares blankly outward in typical star fashion.

in which the deadpan delivery of tart observations was key. Madge's urbanity in the face of her husband's potential infidelity is particularly droll, as revealed by the following exchange between Madge and Dale after the latter has joined her friend on the Lido in Venice. Dale is in a dither about whether or not to reveal she is being pursued by a man she believes to be Madge's husband. She finally tells Madge that Horace "chased me in the park":

MADGE: Really? I didn't realize Horace was capable of that much activity. Did he catch you?

DALE [*Pause*]: Yes.

MADGE: Good for Horace!

DALE: But Madge, you shock me.

MADGE: Oh, Horace flirts with every pretty girl he sees. It doesn't mean anything.

DALE: Well, that's a funny way to take it.

MADGE: My dear, when you're as old as I am, you take your men as you find them — if you can find them.

Ebert suggests that "Madge is elated by the news [of her husband's infidelity], the latest in a series of dalliances by Horace that result in payoffs of diamonds and furs for her."[14] Madge's attitude more likely reveals relief that her husband is showing an interest in the opposite sex at all, especially if we take into account that Horace is being portrayed by famously fey and old-womanish Edward Everett Horton.

At any rate, nothing can faze Madge Hardwick. She stays calm, cool, and collected throughout the film, as the other characters chase each other around, panic and fret, and generally go to pieces. Vanneman describes her tellingly as "a middle-aged Betty Boop, staring out at the world with impassive saucer eyes that have seen everything and are shocked at nothing."[15] Madge's whole attitude is also symbolized by her body language. Her most characteristic stance is holding her upper body slightly leaned back with her hands on her hips thumbs forward, ready for all comers. The actress's then 44-year-old body is slim and trim in a series of gorgeous gowns more form-fitting than even Rogers wears. Thanks to costume designer Bernard Newman, Madge is the height of middle-aged chic, except when first seen on the Lido wearing a white flattened tea cozy on her head. Both she and Dale have variants of the same German-inspired, braided twist hairstyle, emphasizing the subtle similarities between them, despite the more striking differences. What Dale and Jerry may well become, in time, is Madge and Horace Hardwick. The Hardwicks certainly represent a dubious endorsement of marriage.

Top Hat premiered in New York City on August 30, 1935. The critics for *Variety* and the *New York Times* both felt that Broderick had been given too little to work with. André Sennwald in his review for the latter organ wrote: "Miss Broderick, that infamously funny lady, has too little support ... from the script.... If the comedy itself is a little on the thin side, it is sprightly enough to plug those inevitable gaps between the shimmeringly gay dances."[16] Roger Ebert delivers the verdict of posterity when he writes, "Because we are human, because we are bound by gravity and the limitations of our bodies, because we live in a world where the news is often bad and the prospects disturbing, there is a need for another world somewhere, a world where Fred Astaire and Ginger Rogers live."[17] Let me add on my own account, that we still need a world where Helen Broderick lives. Though she died more than half a century ago, in *Top Hat* she will always be available to keep us in the best of company.

After a retirement of more than a dozen years, Helen Broderick died of natural causes on September 25, 1959, at Beverly Hills Doctors Hospital at the age of 68.[18] She was buried in Ferndale Cemetery, Johnstown, New York, where her husband joined her in 1962 and her son in 1986. Her gravestone reads "Wife of Lester Crawford," an apparent final act of assertion from her less famous spouse.[19] The epitaph construed by the author of her entry in the *Dictionary of National Biography* reads: "Through her work on the stage and screen, Broderick helped raise the quality of musical comedy, often turning two-dimensional characters into comic figures of depth and substance."[20]

Funny woman Helen Broderick looks unusually pensive in this 1943 studio portrait from Universal, taken when she was fifty-two and nearing the end of her film career. Without being anyone's idea of a striking beauty, she was quite the clotheshorse and carried herself with the easy, angular grace of a Rosalind Russell or Eve Arden.

Lady Detective: Constance Collier in *Shadow of Doubt* (1935)

Beyond the shadow of a doubt,
I want to know your love is mine...

Constance Collier's 21 films from the 1930s and '40s were only a small part of an extensive acting career dating back to her childhood. By the time she debuted in her first sound film in 1935, she was 57 years old and had been acting for more than half a century. Her parents, Cheetham Agaste Hardie and Eliza Hardie (*née* Collier), were professional actors in a modest way and their daughter, Laura Constance Hardie, was born in a theatrical boarding house at Windsor on January 22, 1878.[1] Known during her professional career as Constance Collier, she belonged to that talented generation which included actresses as various as Sara Allgood, Ethel Barrymore, Laura Hope Crews, Jane Darwell, and Lucile Watson. Not as prolific or versatile in films as most of these women, Collier nevertheless turned out several memorable performances during her 15 years in Hollywood.

Beginning as a child actress and later performing as one of George Edwardes's "Gaiety Girls" in London in the 1890s, Collier was a star from her breakthrough role as the gypsy Chiara in *One Summer's Day* (1898). Her signature stage roles give a more vivid impression of the variety of her talent than her film work, and include Mrs. Cheveley in *An Ideal Husband;* Nancy Sykes in the dramatization of Dickens's *Oliver Twist;* the Duchess of Towers in *Peter Ibbetson*, a play she co-wrote, produced, and directed (based on a novel by George Du Maurier); the Duchesse de Surennes in Maugham's *Our Betters;* Judith Bliss in Noël Coward's *Hay Fever;* and many roles in Shakespeare, including Lady Macbeth, Gertrude in *Hamlet*, Portia in both *Julius Caesar* and *The Merchant of Venice*, and Mistress Ford in *The Merry Wives of Windsor.* Always at her best when portraying an actress, Collier's last major stage role was creating the marvelously self-involved yet deeply human Carlotta Vance in Kaufman and Ferber's *Dinner at Eight.*

It is regrettable that with the exception of a silent movie version of *Macbeth* (J. Emerson, Fine Arts, 1916), Collier was not able to reprise any of these roles on the big screen. She did also take part in a film version of *An Ideal Husband* (A. Korda, London Film Prod.) which premiered in 1947, but by that time she had to relinquish her lead role as the charming blackmailer Mrs. Cheveley to Paulette Goddard and find herself relegated to playing Lady Markby.

Among the film roles for which Collier is best remembered today, we find the desperate, down-on-her-luck actress turned drama coach, Miss Luther, in *Stage Door* (G. La Cava, RKO, 1937); and the doughty dowager and amateur astrologer Mrs. Atwater in *Rope* (A.

Ralph Forbes (left), Frank Reicher, Constance Collier, and Jack Rice rally round Katharine Hepburn, as she receives news of the suicide death of a friend and housemate in *Stage Door* (RKO, 1937). Based on a play by Edna Ferber and George S. Kaufman, *Stage Door* is second only to Alfred Hitchcock's *Rope* in current popularity and critical acclaim among Collier's films. In *Stage Door*, she plays Miss Luther, an aging, down-on-her-luck actress turned drama coach, who zeroes in on budding actress Terry Randall (Hepburn) like a shark smelling blood.

Hitchcock, Warner Bros., 1948). In *Stage Door*, it is fascinating to watch Miss Luther moving in on wealthy wannabe actress Terry Randall (Katharine Hepburn) like a shark in the water. "It takes more than greasepaint and footlights to make an actress, it takes heartbreak as well," Collier intones in her distinctively throaty, mellifluous voice. In flowing aesthetic dress with long arty bead necklaces and her crocheting always at hand, Miss Luther is the type of self-reflexive, overtly theatrical role particularly well suited to Collier's maturity. In *Rope*, her portrayal of Mrs. Atwater, an unsuspecting guest at the home of two gentlemen murderers, is a less successful effort, because the silly, superstitious society woman she portrays is more conventional. The film reveals that Collier never became quite familiar with the minimalist technique required for subtle, naturalistic screen acting, as opposed to the flamboyant "acting out" she was so adept at.

Playing a self-appointed stage mother to Hepburn in *Stage Door*, Collier became a delightfully down-market parody of herself. She had been working as a drama and voice coach in the United States since the late 1920s. Among her more celebrated pupils we find actors from several different generations, such as Douglas Fairbanks, Mary Pickford, Norma Shearer, Mae West, Shelley Winters, and Annabella.[2] *Stage Door*, then, was full of personal resonances and a foreshadowing of her future real-life role as one of Hepburn's closest friends and most valued mentors. According to Hepburn biographer William J. Mann, "No one influenced the second half of Hepburn's life more than Constance Collier." Mann writes further that in her youth, Collier was "considered one of the great beauties of the early–twentieth-century stage": "In fact, her appearance was quite masculine, with heavy eyebrows, an imperial nose, and a prominent chin. During her heyday, most every photograph taken of her was shot from below to soften her imposing features. Tall and broad-shouldered, she had the hands of a man, which were nonetheless incongruously graceful when she spoke, gesturing as she made a point. People said Collier had the air of a duchess."[3]

At the turn of the twentieth century, Collier had been rumored to be engaged to the writer and artist Max Beerbohm. During the teens of the last century, when she shuttled back and forth between engagements in London's West End and on Broadway, she had been married to fellow actor Julian L'Estrange, born like her in 1878. Theirs was a liberated and unconventional marriage. L'Estrange had his own establishment on W. 52nd St. When in New York, Collier preferred to live at the Algonquin Hotel. In the fall of 1918, while Collier was playing Mrs. Cheveley to her husband's Lord Goring in *The Ideal Husband* at the Comedy Theatre, he succumbed to influenza. Collier spent the last 30 years of her life with fellow Englishwoman Phyllis Wilbourn, who was her live-in secretary, companion, and possibly lover. They had met in London in 1925, when Wilbourn was a young woman of 22 and Collier 47. Collier was diabetic and Wilbourn catered to her every need. "They came as a pair," observes Mann, "and everyone respected that."[4]

When Collier settled in Hollywood for good in the mid–1930s, it was after two previous, brief sojourns in Tinseltown. The first was as early as 1915, when at the behest of

Constance Collier looks mildly deranged in this portrait from *Whirlpool* (Twentieth Century–Fox, 1949), her final film. She died in New York City six years later.

D.W. Griffith she went west to participate in his film *Intolerance* (1916). This and other experiences in the early days of the fledgling film community, where she befriended Charlie Chaplin and was reunited with her former mentor and London leading man Sir Herbert Beerbohm Tree, are amply documented in often quoted passages from her autobiography *Harlequinade* (1929). The year the book was published, she returned to Los Angeles to coach Douglas Fairbanks and Mary Pickford for the sound version of *The Taming of the Shrew* (1929).[5] That stay ended when she secured the starring role in the Broadway production of G.B. Stern's new drama *The Matriarch*, which ultimately had only the briefest of runs in New York. It had originated in London, where the role of the matriarch Anastasia had been created by Collier's arch-nemesis, Mrs. Patrick Campbell.

As fate would have it, Stella Campbell's brief and unrewarding stay in Hollywood ended just as Collier's began.

Constance Collier looks regal and surprisingly youthful in this candid from her dressing room during the filming of *Anna Karenina*, starring Greta Garbo and Fredric March (Metro-Goldwyn-Mayer, 1935). Publicity shots of actresses with their pets are always amusing. Here we also note the picnic basket, lunch box, and other accoutrements of an approaching meal.

Though Collier was relatively little-used in front of the camera compared to her extensive work as a coach, she certainly fared better than Mrs. Pat. Between 1935 and 1949, Collier acted in more than 20 films and worked for most of the major studios. Twentieth Century–Fox appears to have been the only studio to have had her under long-term contract.[6] Noël Coward wrote to a mutual friend on March 19, 1935, after a visit to Los Angeles: "Constance has definitely fallen on her feet and has a fat five-year contract. Isn't it lovely for her? She was practically down and out when she arrived."[7] John Gielgud observed in a letter to his mother a dozen years later: "Dined with Constance Collier, who is in great form, with her appearance considerably renovated by the arts of Hollywood!"[8] In 1948, towards the end of her tenure in Hollywood, she was described by a newly arrived Englishman, who met her at a party, as the "elderly doyenne of the British colony with rasping voice and heart of gold."[9]

The *New York Times* observed on Collier's death in 1955 that she was "a helpful friend of John Barrymore, Noël Coward, Katharine Hepburn, Eva Le Gallienne and countless other theatre folk." Not many could say they were a close friend of both Charlie Chaplin and Queen Mary. According to Daniel Blum's *Great Stars of the American Stage*, Collier was a "very beloved figure in the profession."[10] "The story of Miss Collier's ventures and triumphs in England and the United States," her *Times* obituary noted, "was like a history of the theatre from Shakespeare to the scenarists of Hollywood, from Sir Herbert Beerbohm Tree to Bob Hope."[11]

By the time of her death at the age of 77, Collier had given up acting, but was still working as a coach.[12] Among her last pupils was Marilyn Monroe, whose film career was just beginning as Collier's was ending, but whose fame was still in the future.[13] Collier had moved back to New York after completing her final film *Whirlpool* (O. Preminger, Twentieth Century–Fox) in 1949 and shared an apartment at 157 W. 57th St. with her longtime companion Phyllis Wilbourn. It was there she became ill on the morning of April 25, 1955. She was brought to Lenox Hill Hospital, where she died the same day.[14]

Among the speakers at Collier's funeral two days later at the Universal Chapel, Lexington Ave. and 52nd St., was Cathleen Nesbitt.[15] During the early days of World War I, Collier had helped Nesbitt prepare for her wedding to the poet Rupert Brooke, but he died before it could take place.[16] Collier was cremated and her ashes brought by Wilbourn to England for burial.[17] Wilbourn observed to Hedda Hopper: "I spent my life with an angel."[18] One wonders if she would have said the same of the 40 years she would spend at the side of an even bigger star. When Collier died, Wilbourn went on to become Katharine Hepburn's personal secretary and remained so until her own death in 1995.

———— ∞∞∞ ————

Shadow of Doubt (1935) was a relatively modest offering from Metro-Goldwyn-Mayer in the year they released such high-profile films as *Anna Karenina*, *David Copperfield*, *Mutiny on the Bounty*, and *A Tale of Two Cities*. The film was helmed by George B. Seitz, whose 30-year directing career included other golden opportunities for older actresses such as *Kind Lady* (1935) with Aline MacMahon, *The Thirteenth Chair* (1937) with Dame May Whitty, and *My Dear Miss Aldrich* (1937) with Edna May Oliver. Best known for directing nearly all the "Andy Hardy" films, Seitz was also a writer, producer, and sometimes actor. *Shadow of Doubt* was based on a novel of the same title by Arthur Somers Roche, who died of pneumonia in Palm Beach two days after the film opened on February 15, 1935. Top billing in the ensemble cast was given to Ricardo Cortez and Virginia Bruce. Cortez, who was born

Jacob Krantz in Vienna and was about as Latin as apple strudel, took his new name on arrival in Hollywood during the height of the Valentino craze. Cortez played Sam Spade in the original 1931 version of *The Maltese Falcon*. Virginia Bruce, one of the 20 original "Goldwyn Girls," was being groomed for stardom at MGM by boy wonder producer Irving Thalberg. Frances Marion once said of her that she was "so pink and white and golden that she reminded us of an old-fashioned Valentine."[19] Bruce was briefly married in the early 1930s to John Gilbert. Collier was billed third in this, her sound film debut and her first of three films at MGM.[20]

Shadow of Doubt is a contemporary murder mystery set in New York City. Cortez plays suave, sophisticated advertising executive "Sim" Sturdevant, who is hopelessly devoted to fast-falling movie star Trenna Plaice (Virginia Bruce). Also participating in the film's game of romantic musical chairs are an unsavory producer and murder victim played by Bradley Page; his fiancée and equal in charmlessness, spoiled debutante Lisa Bellwood (Betty Furness); a young nightclub singer (delightfully played by Isabel Jewell); and her madly jealous boyfriend, reporter Reed Ryan (Regis Toomey). This is a world of swank art deco apartments, chic nightclubs, and liaisons more or less "dangereuses." The atmosphere of the film is decadent and thoroughly unpleasant. The characters are unsympathetic and their affairs and attractions completely inexplicable. Sharp-nosed, canary blonde Bruce, for one, is about as attractive as a large icicle looming above a sidewalk. Cortez is so persistently cheerful despite the many indignities he has to suffer from selfish Trenna, you want to slap him.

Among all these signs of the brave new world gone sadly wrong, Collier plays Cortez's moneyed, meddling maiden aunt, Melissa Pilson. Costume designer Dorothy Tree has her decked out in regulation dowager garb: a mostly black, floor-length, flouncy and lacy gown; large jewels; wavy white wig; cane, and lorgnette. Later, when Aunt Melissa goes nightclubbing with reporter Reed Ryan, she is dressed like a faded belle of the 1890s and is hardly able to fit her fur coat over an ostrich feather boa worthy of Mae West. Throughout the film, Collier resembles not so much a drag queen, as a not very convincing, handsome, middle-aged transvestite. She could make even Judith Anderson look feminine by comparison.

The reclusive Miss Pilson loves playing cribbage for money with her butler, listening to the radio in bed (regulation long hair in a braid and more lacy garments, now white), playing the organ for her pet parrot (with a harp in the background), and using salty expressions like "the impudent little hussy" (Trenna) and "Why, I'll thrash the brazen creature!" (Lisa Bellwood). As the story develops, Aunt Melissa feels compelled to venture forth from her palatial home for the first time in more than 20 years to prevent her nephew and heir from marrying Trenna, whom she has discovered is penniless and a murder suspect to boot. Why the romantic leading lady is named for a fish is as mysterious as Miss Pilson's sudden conviction on meeting Trenna that her feelings for Sim are genuine. Up until this point, Aunt Melissa's chief function has been to provide the necessary opposition to her nephew's plans, a role she fills ably, if predictably, by having Trenna investigated, threatening to disinherit him, and finally seeking Trenna out to buy her off. The scene in which she first meets Trenna, changes her mind about her, and is transformed before our eyes into a hulking Florence Nightingale at her bedside is unsettling to say the least. Collier leering like a lunatic while nursing Bruce with cold compresses is about as terrifying a sight as you're likely to see. Her sudden liking for Jewell at the nightclub, too, takes on all kinds of queer resonances when we consider Collier's Sapphic reputation.

Shadow of Doubt takes a considerably more amusing turn when the reclusive spinster

Constance Collier (center) looks like King Louis XV in drag in this still from her first sound film *Shadow of Doubt* (Metro-Goldwyn-Mayer, 1935). Ricardo Cortez as her nephew and Virginia Bruce as his lady friend listen attentively as Collier tells them how they are going to beat a murder rap.

is given a new lease on life as an amateur lady detective devoted to saving young love at any cost. Her own isolation can be explained, it turns out, by a "lost love" in her past. So we also get the obligatory scene where the spinster gives the ingénue, however jaded in Trenna's case, the advice to "grab the man while you can" and to learn from Melissa's mistakes. All that's missing is her dragging out her old, unused wedding dress from a trunk in the attic. There is no time for that, as there's a murderer afoot and a mystery to be solved. I will remain silent about the film's resolution to avoid spoilers. Suffice it to say that Collier is in particularly fine fettle in a scene with the square-headed, twinkly-eyed Edward Brophy as Police Lieutenant Fred Wilcox. Nimble of wit and movement despite looking about twice his size, she keeps him off the scent with flirtatious byplay, while conveying an incriminating revolver secretly out of Trenna's apartment. Collier and Brophy's comic interaction is reminiscent of that between Edna May Oliver and James Gleason in the films of the "Hildegarde Withers" series.

As it happens, *Shadow of Doubt* is best understood on the background of such murder mystery comedies as *The Penguin Pool Murder* (1932) and *Murder on the Blackboard* (1934), both starring Oliver as spinster schoolteacher and amateur crime solver Hildegarde Withers, with Gleason as Police Inspector Oscar Piper, the more or less exasperated witness to her superior ratiocinative powers. While MGM was shooting *Shadow of Doubt* between December 22, 1934, and January 11, 1935, RKO was shooting the third in the Withers series, *Murder on a Honeymoon* (1935). Both films were released the same week.[21] In his *New York Times* review of *Shadow of Doubt* (March 11, 1935), Frank S. Nugent observed: "There was a time when cinema tales of murder could be solved only by trousered folk like Philo Vance, Charlie Chan, Perry Mason and a few other shrewd masculine criminologists.... [A] new school has developed specializing in female crime detectors, mostly amateurs," citing *Murder on a Honeymoon, While the Patient Slept* (starring Aline MacMahon as nurse-cum-detective), and *Shadow of Doubt* as examples.[22]

This popular subgenre of the murder mystery originated much earlier, though, in a 1907 serial novel called *The Circular Staircase* by Mary Roberts Rinehart. According to Denis Meikle, Rinehart wrote the novel to make fun of the self-important pulp mystery novels of her day. To her vast surprise, *The Circular Staircase* was taken seriously and met with great popular success, and its author was even credited with renewing the genre of the crime novel.[23] Central to Rinehart's original conception was the device of the amateur lady detective who proves a more able sleuth than the police. In this case, she was the wealthy Miss Cornelia Van Gorder. A play version called *The Bat*, co-authored with Avery Hopwood and starring Effie Ellsler, opened on Broadway on August 23, 1920, and stayed there for 867 performances. After this stunning success, *The Bat* was turned back into a novel. This in turn was sold to Hollywood and resulted in two excellent films: a silent version called *The Bat* from 1926 and an early sound version from 1930 called *The Bat Whispers*, both directed by Roland West. There is also a 1959 version starring Agnes Moorehead and Vincent Price.

Miss Van Gorder, then, was the first of a proud line of older woman amateur detectives that includes the aforementioned Hildegarde Withers in 18 novels by Stuart Palmer and six films; Mrs. Livingstone Baldwin Crane in Fred Ballard's 1929 play *Ladies of the Jury* and the 1932 and 1937 film versions starring Edna May Oliver and her successor at RKO, Helen Broderick; Agatha Christie's Miss Marple, who first appeared in the story "The Tuesday Night Club" in 1927 and in the novel *The Murder at the Vicarage* in 1930; and last but not least, Melissa Pilson. "While some of the mossbacks in the audience may sneer at the perspicacity, not to mention perspicuity, of these lady bloodhounds," Nugent continued in his review, "it is probable they will enjoy Constance Collier's two-fisted personification of the raw-boned and whale-boned Aunt Melissa.... For all the cerebrations she puts into the solution, Aunt Melissa never leaves much doubt in the audience's mind that, if it came to a showdown, she probably could get her man even if it depended on meeting him in a padded ring."[24]

The unique qualities Collier brings to her portrayal can perhaps best be appreciated if we allow ourselves to imagine other actresses who might have played the role, such as Edna May Oliver, Alison Skipworth, Lucile Watson, May Robson, or Marie Dressler. Oliver would have brought a Yankee spinster sensibility to her portrayal, making Aunt Melissa more straight-laced and severe, and the comic incongruity of her drunken nightclub scene would no doubt have been enhanced. Alison Skipworth's and Lucile Watson's considerable powers of realistic character portrayal and ability to exude both genuine warmth and the authority of experience would have been wasted in a film with no genuine emotions or psychological depth. It's hard to imagine either of these vigorous and preternaturally modern actresses (Skipworth was born in 1863!) as a self-pitying Miss Havisham–type cooped up for 20 years in an old house with only her servants for company. As for May Robson, keeping in mind her performances as autocratic old biddies in films such as *You Can't Buy*

Everything (1934), *Rainbow on the River* (1936), and *The Perfect Specimen* (1937), she would no doubt have hammed it up even more than Collier and made it seem highly unlikely that anyone would dare defy her wishes. Robson was a contract player at MGM at the time, but may have been otherwise engaged.

Marie Dressler would no doubt have been MGM's first choice had the film been considered prestigious enough for her, which is doubtful, though Dressler was unable to portray a patrician character with conviction, as opposed to a *nouveau riche* dowager or a dilapidated diva. Then there was the small problem that Dressler had been dead four months when shooting started. In the final reckoning, newcomer Constance Collier was a good choice, bringing a mixture of grandeur, perspicacity, and playfulness to the role.

Her efforts would largely go unrewarded. *Shadow of Doubt* remained her only starring role in a Hollywood movie, the only time in which her performance truly carries the film.

Déclassée: Jane Cowl
in *Payment on Demand* (1951)

She is theatre in the true sense of the word: she is beautiful and
she has magnetism and allure — and she can make you believe,
no matter how silly or tawdry it is, what she is saying.[1]

Liv Ullmann tells a story of how a woman once came up to her at an airport and said: "Didn't you use to be Liv Ullmann?" Jane Cowl might well have had similar experiences. By the time she moved to Los Angeles to work in film in the late 1940s, her glory days on Broadway were far behind her. Her last big hit on the Great White Way had been the Katharine Dayton–George S. Kaufman comedy *First Lady*, which ran for 246 performances at the Music Box Theatre during the 1935-36 season. In a youth-orientated film industry notorious for its short memory, she would have encountered uncertainty about who she was.

Yet Jane Cowl was a star of the American stage on par with Ethel Barrymore, Lynn Fontanne, and Katharine Cornell. Her career on Broadway spanned nearly 45 years, from her debut in the melodrama *Dorothy Vernon of Haddon Hall* (1903–04) till her final appearance as the title character in *The First Mrs. Fraser* (1947). She became a bona fide star as Mary Turner in Bayard Veiller's melodrama *Within the Law* (1912–13), which would be turned into several Hollywood movies, including *Paid* (1930) with Joan Crawford in the lead.[2] After Cowl's breakthrough, the author's wife, fellow actress Margaret Wycherly, said to her: "Don't fail to enjoy this achievement now, while it is happening. It can never be your *first* success again. From now on you'll have to prove that you can do it again, and better."[3]

Prove it she did, in a string of hit plays that included *Common Clay* (1915–16); *Lilac Time* (1917) and *Smilin' Through* (1919–20), which she co-wrote with Jane Murfin; Noël Coward's *Easy Virtue* (1925–26); Robert Sherwood's *The Road to Rome* (1927–29); S.N. Behrman's *Rain from Heaven* (1934–35); *First Lady* (1935–36); and John Van Druten's *Old Acquaintance* (1940–41). Max Reinhardt directed her in Thornton Wilder's *The Merchant of Yonkers* (1938–39), where she created the role of Dolly Levi. She was Tennessee Williams's first choice to play Amanda Wingfield in *The Glass Menagerie* (1945–46), but was unavailable and the part famously became a last hurrah for Laurette Taylor.[4]

Unlike *The Glass Menagerie*, most of Cowl's hit plays are forgotten now and even in her own day were often dismissed as "Jane's usual brew of smiles and tears."[5] But Cowl also took a stab at the classical repertoire, including *Romeo and Juliet* (1923), *Antony and Cleopatra* (1924), and *Twelfth Night* (1930). Her obituary in the *New York Times* noted that she had played Juliet 856 times.[6] Her interpretation of this role on Broadway and on tour is generally considered the high-water mark of her acting career and "one of the noteworthy achievements of the American theatre."[7] Cowl was 40 when she played Shakespeare's ill-fated young heroine and, according to Daniel Blum, "Her Juliet was acclaimed the greatest within memory."[8]

By the time she left for California in 1949, never to return, Cowl had racked up a string of 32 Broadway acting credits.[9] In comparison, Ethel Barrymore had 52, Lynn Fontanne 36, and Katharine Cornell 39. Unlike these other stars, though, Cowl was the author or co-author of nine plays, seven of which were successfully produced, according to her *New York Times* obituary.[10]

Jane Cowl was born Grace Bailey in Boston, Massachusetts, on December 14, 1883. Her year of birth is often mistakenly given as 1884 or 1890, the latter being a fiction she herself may have propagated, as 1890 appears in *Who's Who in the Theatre*, based one assumes on information she herself provided, and even on her gravestone.[11] Being born in the 1880s makes Cowl the contemporary of such actresses as Mary Boland, Billie Burke, Gladys Cooper, Lynne Fontanne, and Marjorie Rambeau, somewhat younger than Ethel Barrymore, born in 1879, and substantially older than Katharine Cornell, born in 1898.

The greatest influence on Cowl's life was her mother, Grace Avery Bailey, a singer and teacher of voice from Albany, New York. While Mrs. Bailey lived long enough to witness her daughter's Broadway debut in 1903, she did not live to see her name in lights, dying of uterine cancer on New Year's Eve 1905.[12] This led her daughter to spend every New Year's Eve thereafter alone communing with her mother's spirit.[13] Cowl's father Charles A. Bailey, a native of Lowell, Massachusetts,[14] appears to have played a minor role in his daughter's life.[15] Business reverses necessitated a move from Boston to Brooklyn, New York, while Cowl was still quite young.[16] Her formal education ended with two years at Brooklyn's Erasmus Hall.[17]

A year and a half after her mother's death, on June 18, 1906, Cowl married Adolph Klauber.[18] Klauber, born in Louisville, Kentucky, in 1879, was hired as the chief drama critic for the *New York Times* in the year of his marriage. He was later associated with the Provincetown Players, and would become his wife's manager and the producer of several of her plays, including *Romeo and Juliet*.[19]

Famous as much for her distinctive beauty as for her acting prowess, Cowl was known as "Crying Jane" for her emotional acting style in which she made effective use of her eyes, "immense and black as liquid tar."[20] Fellow actress and protégée Blanche Yurka recalled, "Because of her good taste, Jane always looked like a vision of loveliness." Cowl once told her younger admirer, "Remember, you are in the public eye until you shut the door of your bedroom at night. Never feel you can afford to look anything but your best, on or off stage."[21] In the words of another friend, she "didn't talk; she effervesced."[22]

As the epigraph to this chapter also indicates, Cowl was a charismatic and glamorous woman. As her sometime friend and former producer Joseph Verner Reed's "tell all" memoirs reveal, she could also be exasperatingly self-centered, difficult, and demanding. Reed's barbed portrait caused a scandal when it was published in 1935, because it made public Cowl's financial difficulties, but also because of the unmistakably satirical tone of his descriptions of the star, such as the following from their first meeting: "Imploringly her hands fluttered to her cheek. Those slender, olive-skinned hands, with their deep-tinted nails, and the wrists with a rustle of bracelets and lace, spoke of Cytheria. Her eyes were black, huge and moist; so black, so limpid, it was a wonder they didn't dissolve and run down her cheeks."[23]

Jane Cowl loved hats, which was fortunate considering her supporting role in *The Secret Fury* (Loring Theatre Corporation, 1950) was little more than a hat stand. Cowl played troubled heroine Claudette Colbert's aunt, determined to keep "smilin' through" all her niece's trials and tribulations on the way to a happy marriage. This was the only one of Cowl's four sound films to be released before her death in June 1950.

At the distance of several decades, we can be grateful to Reed for his pointed observations. As Cowl's modern-day biographer notes: "No one, as far as I can determine, has ever accused Mr. Reed of presenting false information."[24]

Perhaps to even the scales, other of Cowl's friends and colleagues came forward in later years to attest to her generosity and helpfulness. In her 1970 autobiography, Blanche Yurka

credited Cowl with giving her her first big break in the theater when she was cast in the
lead in Cowl's Broadway play *Daybreak* in the fall of 1917. Yurka describes her relationship
with Cowl as "a friendship which refutes the notion that generosity and good will cannot
exist among women of the theatre." The story takes on a more off-white tone, though,
when Yurka reveals that the part she was given originally belonged to Mary Boland and that
Cowl had Boland replaced ostensibly for forgetting her lines.[25] Replacing attractive, blond,
and bubbly Boland with somber, dark-haired, and brooding Yurka seems a bit like replacing
Reese Witherspoon with Patricia Clarkson, so Cowl's motives seem mixed to say the least.

───────

Jane Cowl, then, was one of the biggest and brightest stars on the American stage in
the teens and twenties, when the movie stars she would later support in Hollywood were
coming of age.[26] One of them was Bette Davis, who told biographer Charlotte Chandler,
"As a struggling young actress, I idolized Jane Cowl on the stage."[27] In later life, Davis also
told James McCourt, "Working with Gladys Cooper was one of the great privileges of all
time. Gladys Cooper and Jane Cowl both — I never got over it." She added that she "was
embarrassed at being the star in *Payment on Demand*" when Cowl was only in a supporting
role.[28] This was not just politeness on Davis's part. Never a woman to give an insincere
compliment, Davis wasn't threatened by the presence in her films of other talented actresses.
Rather the opposite. She understood that her star power would only be enhanced when
reflected and intermingled with the inner light of talented supporting players. *Now, Voyager*
and *Payment on Demand* are two of the best examples of this.

Payment on Demand (C. Bernhardt, Gwenaud, 1951) is significant in Davis's life and
career for several reasons that do not mainly have to do with its intrinsic qualities. It was
her first film to be produced after she left Warner Bros., though not the first of her freelance
films to be released. That honor went to *All About Eve*. Indeed, production on *Payment*,
which took place between January and April 1950, had been "expedited" to allow her to
take over the role intended for Claudette Colbert when the latter injured her back.[29] We
know, too, that the film was full of personal resonances for Davis. Not only did it mark the
film debut of her three-year-old daughter Barbara (B.D. Hyman), who appeared as Davis's
daughter Diana, but the storyline had some unhappy parallels with her own life. Entitled
Story of a Divorce until shortly before its release,[30] the movie's production had been marked
by increasing marital difficulties between Davis and her third husband, William Grant
Sherry. When Sherry knocked down Davis's co-star Barry Sullivan after a combined wrap
party and birthday celebration for Davis on April 3, 1950, Davis took their daughter and
moved out of the house.[31] The couple was divorced on July 3 of that same year.[32]

Though no claim can be made for *Payment on Demand* as one of the greatest of Davis's
films, it has been undeservedly neglected. About as obscure as its predecessor and companion
piece *All About Eve* is celebrated, *Payment* is a well-cast, well-made, and well-acted film
with interest both for Bette Davis fans and those favoring post-war domestic dramas. It was
directed by European emigré Curtis Bernhardt, who shared a writing credit for the film's
original screenplay with producer Bruce Manning. A Jewish escapee from Nazi Germany,
Bernhardt had been a director in Hollywood for a decade. By this point, he had worked
with Davis in *A Stolen Life* (1946); other dramas such as *My Reputation* with Barbara Stanwyck (1946), *Devotion* (1946) with Olivia de Havilland and Ida Lupino as the Brontë sisters,
and *Possessed* (1947) with Joan Crawford had given him a reputation as a woman's director.
Though both Robert Young and Wendell Corey were considered for the role of Davis's

hard-tried husband, it finally went to Barry Sullivan.[33] Sullivan had been in films since 1936 and was best known prior to *Payment* for his lead role in *The Gangster* (1947) and for playing Tom Buchanan in the first sound version of *The Great Gatsby* (1949), starring Alan Ladd and Betty Field.[34]

Payment on Demand is mainly set in San Francisco and details the "rise and fall" of the Ramseys' romantic and marital relationship. From humble beginnings, David Ramsey (Sullivan) makes a success of himself as a lawyer and businessman, driven on by his ambitious wife Joyce (Davis). The backstory is told in flashbacks, where a somewhat jarring note is introduced by Davis's use of her *Hush...Hush, Sweet Charlotte* "little girl" voice to suggest the character's younger self. At any rate, Joyce Ramsey is one of Davis's most unsympathetic characters, which is saying a lot, and which may explain why viewers have never identified with her and the film has vanished from view. Snobbish, manipulative, cold, and materialistic, Joyce needs to be taught a lesson. This is where Jane Cowl comes in.

Payment on Demand was the last of Cowl's four sound films to be produced and the last to be released.[35] Among the four, it is significant for being the one where she "finally left a creditable impression on movie audiences of what she was capable of doing."[36] Cowl's first film was *Once More, My Darling* (1949), starring Robert Montgomery and Ann Blyth and also directed by Montgomery. Cowl plays Montgomery's mother, a high-powered lawyer who disapproves of her son abandoning the law for an acting career. *The Secret Fury* (M. Ferrer, Loring, 1950) with Claudette Colbert and Robert Ryan saw Cowl in a classic aunt role, which only required her to make the usual sympathetic gestures as her troubled niece makes her tortuous way to a happy marriage. In the words of her biographer: "She was hardly more than a rook on a chessboard."[37] *No Man of Her Own* (M. Leisen, Paramount, 1950) with Barbara Stanwyck was somewhat more interesting, as Cowl plays an upper middle-class Illinois matron, who comes to suspect that the sympathetic young woman living in her house as her daughter-in-law is an impostor.

Cowl had more screen time in *The Secret Fury* and *No Man of Her Own* than in *Payment on Demand*, certainly, but their mother-in-law and aunt roles were strictly conventional. Emily Hedges in *Payment* was a worldly and cynical creature, who called forth Cowl's creative powers and enjoyment of acting. Her friend and biographer Richard Abe King observes: "If you have not seen Jane Cowl in *Payment on Demand*, you have not seen her at her best; or, moreover, the art of acting at its best." Cowl herself was "enthused" about the part.[38]

This is not to suggest that the appearance of a charming, worldly old harridan was something unprecedented in American films, however unusual it might have seemed by the start of the straight-laced 1950s. After all, the stupendous British character actress Alison Skipworth practically built a career on such portrayals in the early to mid–1930s; her Lady Catherine Champion-Chene in the film version of Somerset Maugham's famous play *The Circle, Strictly Unconventional* (1930), and Marches Bianca San Giovanni in Gloria Swanson's sound film debut *Tonight or Never* (1931) being two highpoints of delightful demimondaine decay. The 1930s was a decade that was franker about women's sexual desires than was possible in the post-war period, even in the case of "women of a certain age." In the pre-code era in particular, gigolos were not uncommon in American films, as well as their "protectors." Classic relationships of this kind are portrayed by Violet Kemble Cooper and Gilbert Roland in *Our Betters* (1933), again based on a Somerset Maugham play, and Mary Boland and Buck Winston (off screen) in *The Women* (1939). William Haines starred in a film entitled *Just a Gigolo* at MGM in 1931. In the 1930s it was even possible to imagine a younger man

Not the most flattering camera angle in the world, but with a little retouching both forty-three-year-old Barbara Stanwyck and sixty-something Jane Cowl come off well in this atmospheric still from Mitchell Leisen's *No Man of Her Own* (Paramount Pictures, 1950). Fast approaching death from cancer, Cowl had trouble retaining her lines on the set. Stanwyck, according to report, was endlessly patient with the fast fading star.

being genuinely in love with an older woman, at least if she was as svelte, stylish, and sophisticated as Billie Burke, who was wined and dined and ultimately wed by Reginald Denny in *Only Yesterday* (1933), Denny being seven years her junior even in real life. By the early 1950s, though, it seems an older woman with a younger lover could only be the object of pity and ridicule.

As Emily Hedges, Cowl has two scenes. We first encounter her as the socially prominent wife of a San Francisco bigwig, whom Davis wants to get in good with, to further her husband's career. Cowl recognizes her winning ways, saying only half in jest: "You are a ruthless climber, aren't you? You won't be a nobody." Davis reminds Cowl of herself and her modus operandi. "Recognize it?" Davis asks. Cowl responds: "I invented it." Cowl smokes and is hyper-elegant in a dark, conservative coat dress with simple but expensive jewelry. Davis, in comparison, looks like *Moby-Dick* in a white brocade halter-topped gown courtesy of Edith Head, a rare example of Head *not* giving good wardrobe. Cowl is mostly filmed seated from Davis's standing point of view, which is flattering. The two shots in profile are not so much so.

Cowl's most important scene as Mrs. Hedges comes somewhat later. Alone on a cruise after her divorce, Davis encounters the suave, debonair John Sutton. Prior to his revelation that he has a wife and two children at home in England, they pay a brief call on Cowl at her palmy Caribbean island home. Cowl, whom Davis describes as "a gay kind of old lady I knew years ago," has been divorced for 12 years. The villa, its appointments, and its mistress are all faded and jaded. Cowl has a buzz on, her formerly immaculate hair is limp, and she herself is gaudily dressed and much the worse for wear. She smokes her way through this scene, as she did her first. Mrs. Hedges is now living with her "protegé" Arthur (James Griffith), who spends his time writing a history of the island in iambic pentameter and painting murals. When the two men go off to look at the latter, Cowl has a chance to give Davis some advice, which is basically that loneliness is a terrible thing for a woman. She herself has gone from a dog to a widower to a woman companion to Arthur and, after him, who knows?

Emily Hedges's function in the film, then, is to serve as a foil to the heroine; a poignant lesson to Joyce Ramsey of the dangers lurking for any older, married woman who thinks she can "go it alone." In the words of the *New York Times*' astute critic Bosley Crowther: "Once again in her haughtiest fashion, [Davis] is making it evident to members of her sex how perilous it is for married women to aggravate their spouses."[39] However unfashionable this basically conservative and anti-feminist message may be today, it was no doubt a realistic reflection of the situation for many middle- and upper-class housewives who left their husbands in the mid–twentieth-century United States, a time when married women were referred to by their husband's name (e.g., Joyce would have been Mrs. David Anderson Ramsey). Emily Hedges shows Joyce Ramsey what she may become, as indeed Jane Cowl's fate may have been a poignant lesson to Bette Davis herself both on a personal and a professional level. When Davis reflected on aging, love, and sex in conversation with Charlotte Chandler many years later, when she was an old woman herself, she showed the impact *Payment on Demand* had made on her by quoting a line from her big scene with Jane Cowl: "When a woman grows old, loneliness is an island and time is an avalanche."[40]

By the time she sought refuge in Hollywood in the late 1940s, Cowl had been a woman alone, fighting an uphill battle for economic solvency and independence for nearly 20 years, ever since she and her husband were wiped out by the stock market crash of 1929. Adolph Klauber had not only been ruined financially, but his mental and physical health had given way and he died in late 1933 at the age of 54.[41] Cowl had to sell her house in Great Neck, Long Island, and her New York apartment at Sutton Place, auction off many of her belongings, and move into a hotel.[42] When she died, she was still in debt.[43] About two weeks prior to her death, Cowl underwent a major operation in a Santa Monica hospital. *The New York Times* reported on June 20, 1950, that her condition was good.[44] What they did not report

This scene from *Payment on Demand* (Gwenaud Productions, 1951) is worth all Cowl's other film scenes put together. Here she portrays a once powerful San Francisco society leader turned demi-mondaine divorcée in her overstuffed, moldering Caribbean villa. With her (from left) are Bette Davis as her frumpy, soon-to-be-divorced visitor, James Griffith as Cowl's sexually ambiguous companion, and John Sutton as Davis's dubious date.

was that she had cancer. Cowl died on the morning of June 22.[45] On her gravestone in Pierce Brothers Valhalla Memorial Park, North Hollywood, it is written: "Here lies Juliet."[46]

Payment on Demand was released on February 3, 1951, almost eight months after Cowl's death. After several different endings had been tested in previews, the producers decided on the most upbeat finale, where it is strongly suggested that the Ramseys will make a new start.[47] *Variety* noted that Bette Davis was in "top form" and that Cowl added "color and flavor to the drama ... as the aging, pathetic divorcee struggling for happiness in a Port-au-Prince villa."[48] Bosley Crowther, on the other hand, was unimpressed by the film. According to the *New York Times* critic, "The script ... includes everything but a simple and convincing demonstration of the reasons why a marriage hasn't clicked." While he found Barry Sullivan in the role of the husband "an incidental figure with neither color nor spine," he added, "In the way of color ... the late Jane Cowl throws in a bit in one scene as a cynical old lady, living in the West Indies with a gigolo."[49]

Mother Courage: Henrietta Crosman in *Pilgrimage* (1933)

She is probably the most unsympathetic mother
ever to appear in a John Ford picture.[1]

Once upon a time in Hollywood, no self-respecting studio could do without a resident old lady. Paramount had Alison Skipworth, Warner Bros.–First National Helen Lowell, RKO Edna May Oliver (who played old). MGM had May Robson, Jessie Ralph, and later May Whitty. And for a time in the mid–1930s, Twentieth Century–Fox had Henrietta Crosman.[2]

I will never cease to be impressed by the spirit, energy, technique, talent, and sheer guts with which these old women got down to work in a medium that hadn't existed for most of their adult lives. While younger stage stars like Ethel Barrymore, Jane Cowl, and Gladys Cooper hemmed and hawed about film and waited as long as possible before giving in to the inevitable in the 1940s, these women, most of them born before or during the Civil War, got down to business, got the job done and made an impression in American films that old women have never made before or since. I said *old* women, not older, for these women were unmistakably old. May Robson was born in 1858 and worked in Hollywood from 1927 till her death in 1942 at age 84. Alison Skipworth came west from New York in 1930, when she was 67, and retired at the age of 75. Jessie Ralph was almost 70 when she got a real start in the movies, Helen Lowell 68, and Dame May Whitty 71, though all had done a smattering of silent films.

Then there was Henrietta Foster Crosman, born in Wheeling, in what was then Virginia, on September 2, 1861,[3] the daughter of Major George H. Crosman and Mary B. Crosman (*née* Wick) and a grand-niece on her mother's side of the songwriter Stephen Foster. Crosman's grandfather was a general and she once said: "I should have been a man and a soldier."[4] She was educated at the Moravian Seminary in Bethlehem, Pennsylvania, and had originally intended to become a singer, but improper training made her lose her voice. Forced to provide for herself by her family's adverse finances, she decided to go on the stage, making her debut in 1883. Three years later, she married fellow actor J. Sedley Browne, but kept on working. The couple had a son, Sedley Browne, Jr., born in 1887, who later changed his name to George Crosman after his parents divorced in 1896. George predeceased his mother. The year of her divorce, Henrietta Crosman married newspaperman and future stage producer and silent film director Maurice Campbell, who was eight years her junior. Campbell would produce several of her plays, including two of her biggest successes: *As You Like It* (1902) and *Sweet Kitty Bellairs* (1903–04).[5] Crosman and Campbell had a son, Maurice Campbell, Jr.[6]

Daniel Blum's *Great Stars of the American Stage*, published eight years after Crosman's death, reports that she "liked roses, Julia Marlowe, the outdoors, and enjoyed sailing, playing golf, riding horseback, and hunting." She was also a "crack shot with a gun," though she "did not believe in the slaughter of animals and did not eat meat."[7] Crosman was "an ardent suffragist" and said in a speech in 1909, "I have worked since I was sixteen and have supported not only myself but four or five others as well, and I have not omitted to darn my husband's stockings or to rock the cradle. Some of those I took care of were men voters."[8]

Crosman wasn't the most productive or prolific of the many veteran actresses who made their way to Hollywood in the 1930s — she only spent four years in films at the tail end of her long acting career — but out of her 17 sound films there is one that will secure her place in American film history. To fully understand a film such as John Ford's *Pilgrimage* (1933), there are several contexts that need to be taken into consideration. It is worth asking, first of all, why a commercial studio such as Fox should find it a viable, maybe even potentially profitable option in the early 1930s to make a movie entirely about a bitter, snobbish, and domineering old farm woman from Three Cedars, Arkansas. It is worth inquiring, however briefly, into what other studios were doing at the time, with whom, and how it was going. And finally, it is worth considering what an actress such as Henrietta Crosman could bring to the film.

Taken as a whole, the 1930s was probably the single best decade to be an older actress in Hollywood. The movie colony may have been "lousy with old dames," as Columbia boss Harry Cohn so charmingly put it, but they were there for a reason.[9] The advent of sound had opened up a whole wealth of new storytelling possibilities, subtleties of plot and characterization and, not least of all, the need for actors who could talk. Who better suited than those who had been talking the longest? Not only were seasoned actresses needed to fill featured and supporting roles as mothers, grandmothers, aunts, and a wide range of domestic and professional roles, but a not inconsiderable number of the films being produced in the first decade of sound actually had older women in starring roles.

Thus, *Pilgrimage*, a film entirely focused upon the emotional life and psychological development of an old woman, was not unique, but exemplifies an interesting trend at this time. Films were being made about older women. Character actresses were being given top billing. Money was being made telling other stories than the perpetual youthful, heterosexual romance. Some of the most important examples of this trend are *Madame Racketeer* (1932) and *A Lady's Profession* (1933), both with Alison Skipworth in the lead; *Lady for a Day* (1933) starring May Robson, who garnered an Oscar nomination as Best Actress, as well as her *You Can't Buy Everything* (1934) and *Granny Get Your Gun* (1940); the Hildegard Withers murder mystery series (1932–37), starring in succession Edna May Oliver, Helen Broderick, and Zasu Pitts as a New England Miss Marple; *Ruggles of Red Gap* (1935) and *A Son Comes Home* (1936) with Mary Boland; and *Make Way for Tomorrow* (1937), *Of Human Hearts* (1938), and *The Captain Is a Lady* (1940) with Beulah Bondi. Other older actresses, such as Fay Bainter, Jane Darwell, and Billie Burke, were also being given their own films in the 1930s.

So how do we explain this unprecedented interest in the emotional lives of older American women? The stories being told in Hollywood films were, of course, an indirect reflection of stories and plots being created for the theater, as many of the earliest sound films were adaptations of stage plays. Broadway, which was the only theater that counted, was at this time also making full use of the dramatic potential of powerful, dynamic, and charismatic older women. Furthermore, there was a general perception in the period that wives and mothers "ruled the roost" in a way that was increasingly being seen as problematic. This was the stuff of drama. Finally, as we've already seen, there was an available pool of talented, experienced, and inexpensive actresses, who could be put directly into films and be expected to knuckle down and get the job done. No need to raise and train them, grow and groom them, as one had to do with budding stars.

Yet there may be a simpler explanation than all this for the prevalence of good parts for character actresses in the films of the 1930s. That explanation consists of only two words: *Marie Dressler*. The phenomenal success of this 60-something former vaudevillian and major has-been in a string of starring roles at MGM between 1930 and her untimely death from cancer in 1934, in films such as *Min and Bill* (1930), *Emma* (1932), and *Dinner at Eight* (1933), sent all the Hollywood studios into overdrive trying to create the next Dressler. They never succeeded, but it certainly made the 1930s, in the words of one film historian, "a glorious time to be weatherbeaten, dignified, and imperious on screen."[10]

Crosman brought to the role of Hannah Jessop half a century of acting experience. She made her stage debut in 1883 at the age of 22 and was seen frequently and continuously on the New York stage and in stock for the next 50 years under the management of such

When rural matriarch Hannah Jessop (Henrietta Crosman) is invited with other "Gold Star" mothers to visit the site of her soldier son's grave in France, she practically has to be carried kicking and screaming across the Atlantic. Her combative stance in *Pilgrimage* (Fox Film Corporation, 1933) is readily apparent in this still from her cabin with an unidentified woman in uniform.

important producers as Augustin Daly, Charles Frohman, and David Belasco. Her forté was "light, piquant comedy."[11] Crosman starred for the first time in *Mistress Nell* (1900–01), an historical play about King Charles II's mistress Nell Gwyn, that she also directed, and was, in the words of critic Lewis C. Strang, "decidedly the sensational feature of the theatrical season of 1900-01.

"Fame came to her," he added, "literally in a night."[12]

Some of the later highlights of her Broadway career were the 1902 revival of *As You Like It*; David Belasco's *Sweet Kitty Belairs* (1903–04), which ran for more than 200 performances and was deemed "one of the outstanding performances of Miss Crosman's career"[13]; two revivals of *The Merry Wives of Windsor* (1916 and 1928); the original Broadway production of Shaw's *Getting Married* (1916); and *Trelawny of the Wells* (1927), in support of Helen Gahagan (Douglas). Veteran drama critic John Ranken Towse thought her greatest artistic achievement was her Rosalind in *As You Like It*, which he deemed "one of the most satisfying expositions of the character I have seen."[14] When Crosman died, the *New York Times* wrote that she had been "acclaimed as the foremost Rosalind of her time": "She played in this role for 100 nights at the old Republic Theatre, the record in those days for a Shakespearean comedy."[15]

Though never a star of the first magnitude, Crosman was particularly appreciated for her beautiful voice ("A voice that interprets while it charms is the best of all gifts, and this Miss Crosman possesses"); her "glow of personality ... that made itself manifest in a smile of genuine happiness and pleasure"; and her "spontaneous vivacity," which John Ranken Towse observed was "one of the potent charms in her various embodiments."[16] Writing in 1916, Towse felt Crosman was "entitled to more general critical and popular appreciation than she has obtained." In his assessment, she was "an exceedingly bright and capable performer, of considerable range and much technical expertness."[17]

Scott Eyman observes that the performance John Ford got out of Crosman "reveals a skill with actresses that he preferred to keep submerged."[18] To call Ford a "woman's director" is probably still sacrilege in some quarters. Yet from *Pilgrimage* in 1933 to his final film *7 Women* more than 30 years later, he was able to elicit some excellent performances from the opposite sex. The roll call of character actresses that appeared frequently in his films includes Jane Darwell, Mae Marsh, Mary Gordon, Anna Lee, Tiny Jones, Mildred Natwick, and Una O'Connor.

Though she only did one film with Ford and never was part of his informal stock company, Crosman must take pride of place among Ford's actresses both because *Pilgrimage* was the only Ford film in which an older woman starred, but equally because it's a fine film held together by Crosman's sensitive performance in a role that could easily have ended up as a caricature. Nineteen thirties comedies and dramas alike are literally strewn with bossy older women, many of whom are "flat" characters to say the least. Hannah Jessop, both because of the film's main focus on her and because of Crosman's acting, emerges as a three-dimensional, rounded figure.

Pilgrimage represents an interesting departure from a classic plot pattern both in tragedy and comedy in which an older parental figure opposes the love match of a young man and woman. Rather than the romantic relationship between Jimmy Jessop (Norman Foster) and his childhood friend and neighbor Mary Saunders (Marian Nixon) being the main focus of the film, it is significant only for what it calls forth in Jimmy's mother Hannah. A strong-minded, wealthy, rural widow, she must come to terms with her own limitations and prejudices in the course of the film, where she indirectly is the cause of her son's death in the

First World War and rejects her own grandchild until she is offered a second chance. This chance comes on a "pilgrimage" to France, which she reluctantly embarks on with other "Gold Star" mothers of fallen soldiers to visit their sons' graves. Hannah saves the life of a young American would-be suicide in Paris. Through the parallel plot of his unhappy romance with a young woman whom *his* mother opposes, Hannah receives a kind of redemption, which allows her to return home and make peace with her son's lover and their love child.

As I've already indicated, the films of the 1930s are rife with domineering mothers and grandmothers, though most are not as rural and homespun as Hannah Jessop. What mainly distinguishes her from characters such as Helen Livingstone in *Shopworn* (1932), apart from a better script to work from, is undoubtedly Crosman's ability to inject realism even into the corny and melodramatic situations. If only read on the page, lines like "I'd rather see him dead than married to you" and "If you love her, you can't love me" sound just like Mrs. Livingstone in *Shopworn*, but there is a world of difference between Clara Blandick's more or less entirely unexplained change of heart and Crosman's slow realization throughout *Pilgrimage* of her own responsibility for the death of her son and her alienation from his girlfriend and child.

An expert on Ford's films writes: "Almost alone among Ford's characters, Hannah changes — from virulent raging intolerance to the sowing of tolerance." He claims further that "with this little old lady is born the first 'Fordian hero,' whom we will encounter in subsequent Ford pictures in the guise of Will Rogers, Henry Fonda, and John Wayne, among others, and whose judging, priesting, Christ-like interventions will momentarily but repeatedly redeem mankind from its myopic intolerance."[19] Veteran western film historian William K. Everson called Crosman's Hannah Jessop "the finest character actress performance in any Ford film, not even excepting Jane Darwell in *The Grapes of Wrath*."[20]

We can try and imagine a couple of Crosman's contemporaries in the role to see the difference she makes. Two obvious choices among actresses who were already in Hollywood, though at other studios, were May Robson and Jessie Ralph. They were both contemporaries of Crosman, born in 1858 and 1864 respectively. Both had extensive stage experience, including numerous Broadway credits, though unlike Crosman they had not been stars. Both played their share of domineering, matriarchal figures in 1930s movies. Robson was the more versatile, as evidenced by films as different as *Letty Lynton* (1932), *Lady for a Day* (1933), and *Reckless* (1935). Handsome rather than beautiful, she had a tendency to go overboard in the ranting and raving department when playing powerful, demanding dowagers. *It Happened in New Orleans* (1936) and *The Perfect Specimen* (1937) are two good bad examples of this. Jessie Ralph was a gloriously ugly and fairly limited actress, but was adept at portraying rich old biddies who had risen from humble beginnings, as in *San Francisco* (1936), *The Last of Mrs. Cheyney* (1937), and *They Met in Bombay* (1941). It is hard to imagine either of these women playing Hannah Jessop without resorting to their usual histrionic bag of tricks, which included waving their canes, shouting at the top of their lungs, gnashing their teeth, and assorted scrunched-up facial expressions. Strictly speaking, too, they looked too old to have a son the age of Jimmy Jessop.

Even in old age, Crosman was a beautiful woman, if we can still imagine beauty in an aged face that a scalpel or syringe has never touched. However tough and masculine her behavior and dress — and *Pilgrimage* is no fashion show — her face was so soft and feminine, that the combination lent her great variety of expression.[21] No one could look as fiery, even fanatical as Crosman, yet she could equally be sweet, demure, even coquettish (though not necessarily in the same film). In sum, Crosman was ideally suited to a role that required a broad range of emotional response and subtle character development.

It seems fortunate, then, that she got the lead in *Pilgrimage*, though we don't know exactly how it happened.[22] Her last show on Broadway had been the short-lived drama *Thunder in the Air* in November 1929. She had no particular position at Fox Films or in the film industry in general, nor much film experience beyond a handful of silent films made between 1914 and 1925. Ford apparently wanted to cast Mae Marsh, veteran of several films by his idol D.W. Griffith, but the studio vetoed that suggestion.[23]

Ford or one of the producers at Fox may have seen Crosman in a play she did in Los Angeles in August 1931 or, what seems more likely, in the only sound film she had to her credit at this point. *The Royal Family of Broadway* (G. Cukor and C. Gardner, Paramount, 1930) was based on a 1927 Broadway hit play by Edna Ferber and George S. Kaufman, which in turn was inspired by the Barrymore acting dynasty. An old trouper herself, Crosman is well cast in what was on the whole a tedious and overwrought film. She plays the family matriarch and veteran actress Fanny Cavendish, based on John, Lionel, and Ethel Barrymore's grandmother, Louisa Lane Drew, better known as Mrs. John Drew. In the film, Fanny symbolizes the "show must go on," fighting spirit of the Cavendishes and her death at the film's close gives it a finale more poignant than the histrionics building up to it would lead one to expect. Crosman is the best part of the film. She has one of her funniest moments on screen in an exchange with the Ethel Barrymore character, Julie Cavendish, played by Ina Claire. Julie has just read aloud from a letter indicating that her brother, Tony Cavendish (Fredric March), may have killed someone. Fanny responds with supreme insouciance: "Anyone we know?" She tells Julie at another point in the film, "Marriage isn't a career, dear, it's an instinct." Ironically, Fanny hates Hollywood and regrets that her son Tony (i.e., John Barrymore) has gone there.[24] Little did Crosman know that in two years time, she would be going there herself.

The Royal Family of Broadway was filmed at the Kaufman-Astoria studios in Queens, New York, while Crosman was still living on the East Coast and released on December 22, 1930. It seems likely she was brought to Hollywood more than two years later, in early 1933, expressly to do *Pilgrimage*. At any rate, she ended up staying there for four years, until her retirement in 1937 at the age of 76.

Pilgrimage was based on a story by I.A. Wylie that appeared in the *American Magazine* in November 1932. Fox had purchased the film rights a year before the story's publication.[25] Production on the film at Fox Studios took place in February, March, and April 1933. *Pilgrimage* was released in New York City on July 12, 1933, and generally on August 18. Crosman was present at the film's New York premiere at the Gaiety Theatre at Broadway and 46th St. It must have been a joyous homecoming for her to the city where she'd spent her entire adult life and the theatrical district that had seen all her triumphs. She gave a short speech, where she said: "My hair is growing white. If you like Hannah Jessop, you make me the happiest woman in New York." Quoting the speech in his review, the *Times* critic added: "This morning she has had her wish."[26]

Pilgrimage has been called Ford's "first great film."[27] Bret Wood finds that it "bears the traits that would come to characterize his later masterpieces: an examination of heroism and patriotism, a sense of melancholia and loss, a tendency toward rowdy comedy, and moments of breathtaking visual grace."[28] Naturally, the *mise-en-scène* of this studio-bound production seems stagey today and a far cry from the visual grandeur of the Monument Valley of some of Ford's later, more famous films.

On its release, the film in general and Crosman in particular received good notices. *Variety*'s critic found that Crosman "plays the Hannah character under wraps, leaving the impression of a reserve of power and vitality."[29] The reviewer for the *New York Times* wrote: "Miss Crosman, by some strange magic of her own, makes the old, commonplace virtues of motherhood not only dramatic, but fresh and clean and very touching.... From a technical standpoint the film is replete with expertly contrived bits.... Although it is Miss Crosman's film, the cast is uniformly good in support of her."[30]

Crosman never played another role on film to compare with Hannah Jessop. In addition to her six films at Fox, she worked briefly at Paramount, Warner Bros., MGM, and various other places. Her five best known films today are (according to a 2011 poll and in descending order of popularity) *Charlie Chan's Secret*, *The Dark Angel*, *Personal Property*, *Pilgrimage*, and *The Royal Family of Broadway*.[31] In *Charlie Chan's Secret* (G. Wiles, Twentieth Century–Fox, 1936), the fourteenth film in the popular detective series at this time starring Warner Oland, Crosman plays an entirely generic rich old lady role, though this old lady is intensely interested in spiritualism. The film has poor production values even for a B movie. *The Dark Angel* (S. Franklin, Samuel Goldwyn, 1935) starred Fredric March and Merle Oberon. As Oberon's grandmother, Crosman appears only in two brief scenes at the beginning of

Here Henrietta Crosman (left) is shown relaxing on the set of *Personal Property* (Metro-Goldwyn-Mayer, 1937) with the director W.S. Van Dyke's mother Laura Winston Van Dyke, who bears a striking resemblance to Jane Darwell. *Personal Property* was the last of Crosman's seventeen sound films.

the film and is bedridden to boot. In *Personal Property* (W.S. Van Dyke, MGM, 1937), Crosman's final film (and, incidentally, Jean Harlow's penultimate one), she had a fairly limited role as Robert Taylor's doting mother.

Personally, I get much more enjoyment out of *The Right to Live* (W. Keighley, Warner Bros., 1935) and *The Moon's Our Home* (W.A. Seiter, Paramount, 1936). In the first mentioned melodrama, Crosman's Millie Trent is witness to the wife of her invalid son falling for his brother and plays a pivotal role in proving at the film's conclusion that her sick son committed suicide rather than having been murdered by his adulterous wife. Josephine Hutchinson, George Brent, and Colin Clive starred. *The Moon's Our Home*, a classic screwball comedy based on a Faith Baldwin novel, stars Margaret Sullavan as a spoiled movie star and Crosman as her antediluvian tyrant grandmother. This was the kind of comic role May Robson and Jessie Ralph specialized in, but Crosman was able to infuse it with an uncommon naturalism.

Crosman retired from films and returned to the East Coast in 1937, where she made her home with her youngest son at 908 Edgewood Ave., Pelham Manor, New York. She died there at age 83 on October 31, 1944, after being ill for nearly a year. Her husband had died in 1942. She was buried next to him in Ferncliff Cemetery, Hartsdale, New York.[32]

Auntz: Cecil Cunningham
in *The Awful Truth* (1937)

"I want to go where there's life and I don't mean plant life."

Aunts! What would classic Hollywood films be without them? Aunts, often single, childless, "unproductive," yet how productive of the conflict, comedy, and companionship so essential to film narrative. How many of filmdom's great comic creations haven't been aunts? Aunt Pittypat in *Gone with the Wind*, Aunt Abby and Aunt Martha in *Arsenic and Old Lace*, Aunt Betsey Trotwood in *David Copperfield*. Not to mention Auntie Em in *The Wizard of Oz* and Aunt Fanny in *The Magnificent Ambersons*.

In the strict economy of the Hollywood feature film, with its temporal limitations and its usual focus on the story of one or two main characters, every other character is defined in relation to the protagonist and must justify his or her existence through what they can do to help or harm the protagonist and hence advance their story. So, why an aunt? What purpose do aunts serve in Hollywood films? What functions do they fulfill that would explain their ubiquity, particularly in the dramas and comedies of the Golden Age?

Well, an aunt is a significant type of supporting role, whether literally "supporting" the protagonist in doing what he or she wants to do, or the opposite, trying to harm or hinder the hero or heroine in achieving their goals. In film, as in real life, an aunt can be your friend, unlike your mother, who may say she wants to be your friend, but who will always primarily be your mother. An aunt can also be your foe, but unlike your mother she can't blackmail you emotionally and you don't have to listen to her. An aunt can be cool. She's not responsible for you, and your behavior is not a reflection on her character and reputation. An aunt can be cruel. She's not blinded by parental pride or a guilty conscience and can say it like it is. Film heroes and heroines are not infrequently orphans. It simpler that way, easier to wipe the slate clean and start fresh without too much parental encumbrance. Yet it would be a shame to send "love's young dream" into the world without so much as a relative on hand to witness their trials and triumphs. Hence the ubiquity of the aunt.[1]

Aunts come in all shapes and sizes. Because film often doesn't have time to elaborate much on the aunt's off-screen life, including the possibility of a family of her own and friends, she is frequently a spinster with all that dry, spare, lean and mean stereotype usually entails. Why are spinster aunts seldom buxom or heavy? Why are married aunts seldom thin or svelte? That would be creating an unnecessary confusion in the audience's mind. When time is of the essence, the first step in casting an aunt is to get the physical type right.

Thus, throughout American film history, there have been certain character actresses who have symbolized the very essence of the aunt by looking the part. Pride of place in this

43

Auntie Hall of Fame must go to Elizabeth Patterson, who would impersonate aunts on the big screen for decades, starting with Auntie Doe in *New Morals for Old*; one of Jeanette MacDonald's three eccentric aunts in *Love Me Tonight*; and Aunt Hester Fairfield in *A Bill of Divorcement* (all 1932). Keeping her company in the aunt pantheon are certainly Clara Blandick, Helen Broderick, and Laura Hope Crews. Younger than these fine actresses, but no less spinsterish, were the two Baltimore Mildreds: Mildred Dunnock and Mildred Natwick. Starting in the 1940s, their skillful aunt portrayals would crop up in everything from adaptations of Tennessee Williams to musicals. Further down the list come the occasional aunts, like Fay Bainter, Beulah Bondi, Alice Brady, Billie Burke, Alma Kruger, May Robson (when she wasn't someone's grandmother), and Helen Westley.

Ironically, despite the fact that she made her film debut as an aunt in *Their Own Desire* (E.M. Hopper, MGM, 1929) and is best remembered for playing an aunt, Cecil Cunningham wasn't really the aunt type. Toweringly tall—all of 5'8"—with a voice "the sound of an extra-dry martini spilled into a piece of parchment, a near–Wagnerian bass baritone,"[2] frequently wearing her hair quite mannishly cropped, her appearance was so butch as to make her too unconventional for most aunt roles. As one film historian describes her screen presence: "Rarely did a Cunningham performance carry a sexual overtone, yet volumes were conveyed by her voice, look, manner, and even the names of her characters.... Call it butchness or simply severity, with Cunningham you knew this was not merely someone's sweet old hetero aunt."[3] Even Cunningham, though, could be "tarted up" and she played her fair share of dowagers throughout her career.

Cecil Cunningham was born in St. Louis, Missouri, on August 2, 1888, the daughter of Patrick Cunningham, whom she described as a "professional baseball player and man-about-town."[4] She attended Humboldt School and Central High School, sang in a church choir, and worked as a switchboard operator before going to New York at 18 to become a model and chorus girl. By 1913, she had arrived on Broadway in a show called *Somewhere Else*, which ran for only eight performances. Several musical comedies followed with Cunningham in featured roles, including a revival of Gilbert and Sullivan's *Iolanthe* (1913); *Oh, I Say!* (1913) with music by Jerome Kern; and the hit *Dancing Around* (1914–15) with music by Sigmund Romberg. In 1915, she married the writer and lyricist Jean C. Havez, who was 16 years her senior. Havez was headed to Hollywood, where he would work for producer Hal Roach, write stories and gags for Harold Lloyd, and ultimately turn to writing the Buster Keaton films *The Three Ages* (1923), *The Navigator* (1924), and *Seven Chances* (1925). According to a fan, "his imagination gave American silent screen comedy what is considered some of its greatest moments," including the iconic moment in *Safety Last* (1923) where Lloyd hangs perilously from a clock atop a skyscraper.[5]

I can only assume that Cunningham accompanied her husband to California. That would explain her absence from the Broadway stage during the years of her marriage. At any rate, the Havez-Cunningham union did not last long. On August 17, 1917, the *New York Times* reported that Havez was suing for separation. Havez charged that his wife "abandoned him after he had assisted her to rise from a humble beginning to a place of prominence in her profession." He also alleged that "the case was aggravated by his wife's exhibition of temper before servants and by her disposition to brag about her earning capacity."[6]

Cunningham was back on Broadway on July 15, 1919, when she opened in her biggest hit to date: *The Greenwich Village Follies*. That was followed by the musical comedy *The Rose of China* (1919–20), which ran for 47 performances at the Lyric Theatre. She subsequently went into vaudeville as a headliner at the Palace Theatre in New York and worked

Swathed in dead furry creatures, Cecil Cunningham gives Barbara Stanwyck reason for concern about *My Reputation* in the 1946 Warner Bros. film by that name. With her in the doorway of his apartment is George Brent, who looks ready to take up battle with the dragon lady. Stanwyck, as the widowed mother of two young sons, is trying to look as innocent as possible during this unwelcome chance encounter with her mother's friend.

in radio. Increasing years, graying hairs, and possibly arrears may explain Cunningham's removal to Hollywood at the end of the 1920s. On arrival, she managed Ciro's nightclub before establishing herself as an actress in films.[7] Her ex-husband had died suddenly of a heart attack in Beverly Hills in 1925, so the way was clear for her.[8] Cunningham would remain in Los Angeles until her death from arteriosclerosis on April 17, 1959.[9] She was laid to rest in the Chapel of the Pines Crematory.[10]

Cunningham acted in approximately 75 feature films between 1929 and 1948 and worked for all the major studios, though mainly for Paramount (1930–42), MGM (1929–48), and RKO (1931–41). According to John Springer and Jack Hamilton, she "usually just played bits but enough of them so that she was never a stranger."[11] Though Cunningham was usually conspicuous even in her briefest appearances, more than a third of her roles were uncredited and some were even nameless. With such limited screen time, it was a good thing she "could do more with a look than most actresses could do with an armful of expertise dialogue."[12] In her final film, MGM's *The Bride Goes Wild* (N. Taurog, 1948), she even suffered the indignity of having her scenes deleted.

Apparently, Cunningham was in *Love Me Tonight*, *Mr. Deeds Goes to Town*, and *Saratoga Trunk* to mention just a few of her most humble parts. She played a laundress in the first, an unnamed bit part in the second, and who knows what in the third. A step up from this are the named parts in which she at least has one proper scene. I'm thinking of her role as Alison Skipworth's friend and former circus worker, Agnes, who heartily disapproves of W.C. Fields in the famous "road hog" sequence of *If I Had a Million* (N.Z. McLeod, Paramount, 1932); or the delightfully daffy murderess Mrs. Arlington in *Ladies They Talk About* (H. Bretherton and W. Keighley, Warner Bros., 1933), with her lorgnette and lapdog, who carries the "servant problem" into prison with her and gets into a fracas with her self-appointed African American maid, Mustard (Madame Sul-Te-Wan); or Madame "Feldy" de Lerchenfeld in *Marie Antoinette* (W.S. Van Dyke, MGM, 1938), the title character's governess and confidante, who reveals she is to marry the Dauphin of France.

A further step up the ladder are the named, credited characters who recur throughout the film and who have some sort of plot function. Can you recall Cunningham's roles in *Come and Get It, The Captain Is a Lady*, or *My Reputation*? Josie, Edward Arnold's quick-witted, sharp-tongued, watchful secretary in *Come and Get It* (H. Hawks, Samuel Goldwyn, 1936) is a typical Cunningham role. The same goes for Mrs. Jane Homans in *The Captain Is a Lady* (R.B. Sinclair, MGM, 1940). Mrs. Homans, togged out like an Edwardian grand-dame in pearls and lace, her hair piled atop her head, is a rich widow, who objects to the presence of a male resident at the old age home for ladies where Charles Coburn and Beulah Bondi seek refuge after they have lost their home. Mrs. Stella Thompson in *My Reputation* (C. Bernhardt, Warner Bros., 1946), Cunningham's final film role, is cut from the same mold. Weighed down with dead animal skins and other dowager appurtenances, Mrs. Thompson is usually seen in company with beleaguered heroine Barbara Stanwyck's imperious, widowed mother (Lucile Watson), except in the one pivotal scene when she discovers Barbara, a widow with two young sons, on her way unchaperoned into bachelor George Brent's apartment. *Quel horreur!*

Finally, at the pinnacle of Cunningham's role list we find Aunt Patsy in *The Awful Truth*. Directed by the legendary Leo McCarey, the film starring Irene Dunne and Cary Grant as "two of Park Avenue's finest,"[13] Lucy and Jerry Warriner, was shot at Columbia in a record-breaking six weeks from late June to mid–August 1937 and opened on October 21, 1937. Cunningham was billed fifth after the stars, Ralph Bellamy, and Alexander D'Arcy. As Dunne's modish, quick-witted, and worldly-wise aunt Patsy Adams, she is most prominent in the first half of the film.

To finally return to our central question then: Why an aunt? Specifically, why an aunt in *The Awful Truth* and what kind of aunt is she? First of all, Aunt Patsy is the ideal relative. She doesn't come encumbered with a raft of other relations, like aunts usually do. No cousins ever crop up, no mention is made of the existence of an uncle, unless it be in ever-optimistic Aunt Patsy's future. In the present, she is available to serve her niece's needs and, indeed, the needs of the film. Stanley Cavell, one of the few film scholars to reflect on the role of Aunt Patsy in *The Awful Truth*, writes: "Evidently [Lucy] needs not only encouragement and authority but instruction and preparation of a kind that a woman is fitter than a man to give. This would be why her 'Aunt' appears instead of her father — or rather why, when it is this woman, at her phase of the story we are unearthing, whose Aunt appears, it is Aunt Patsy (Cecil Cunningham) and not the woman's aunt of *Bringing Up Baby* (May Robson)...."[14]

Aunt Patsy's chief function, apart from being a sounding board for her niece Lucy Warriner (Dunne) and trying to get Lucy to loosen up, is to be what Henry James calls a *ficelle*. *Ficelle* means thread in French and James uses the term about a character who serves to link the other characters, a sort of facilitator between characters who for various reasons

do not often (or ever) have direct access to each other. As Aunt Patsy observes herself: "Every time I open the door, somebody walks in." Well, sometimes she has to bring them in. It is Aunt Patsy who corrals that big Oklahoman lug Dan Leeson (Bellamy) in the elevator and, for better or worse, introduces him to Lucy. It is Aunt Patsy who brings Lucy the news that her soon-to-be ex-husband Jerry (Grant) has been seen with the young heiress Barbara Vance (Molly Lamont).

A linking figure is particularly necessary in this film, because Lucy and Jerry are separated quite early on, and most of the film takes place during the 90 days they are waiting to be able to divorce. Their relationship must be repaired over time, at least in part through intermediaries and through the experience of being without the other.

Having made herself more or less redundant by guiding Lucy away from Dan and his domineering mother (Esther Dale) and back towards Jerry, whom Lucy admits she still loves, Aunt Patsy disappears from the film. As a parting gesture, she provides a locale for Jerry and Lucy's final, decisive tryst and a costume for Lucy as well[15]: a nightgown so voluminous and old-fashioned, we might well doubt it actually belongs to the fashion conscious Patsy Adams.

The Awful Truth (Columbia Pictures, 1937) was one of the few films in which Cecil Cunningham really got to strut her stuff. She plays Irene Dunne's live-in aunt, purveyor of advice and raiser of flagging spirits. Cunningham was a quintessential creature of the 1930s screen: sophisticated, worldly, chic, and just a bit butch. The mosquito netting she is wearing here, though, was clearly a misstep on the part of the Columbia wardrobe department.

We should notice that Aunt Patsy is less straight-laced and more "with it" than her niece. She chafes at being cooped up in their common apartment for several spinsterish months. "Nothing unusual ever happens around here," she sighs. "I want to go where there's life and I don't mean plant life." This free-spiritedness and unconventionality is the characteristic of a certain type of aunt we can call the cool aunt. Cool aunts are rare, much rarer than the stuffy, dowdy, and disapproving aunts or the sad, spinsterish, and sympathetic aunts (or a combination of the above), but they are some of the most entertaining aunts in Hollywood movies.

Aunt Patsy is one of the coolest aunts on record. The only aunt I can think of who goes her one better is Aunt Julia Warren in *Only Yesterday* (1933) and that is largely because she has a love life of her own. Aunt Julia is worth a brief discussion here, as a unique character in the annals of Hollywood filmmaking, even for the pre–Code Era which brought her to life. A former suffragette turned business owner, she gives a home and a job in her dress shop to her niece, unwed mother and film debutante Margaret Sullavan. Julia refers to Sullavan's illegitimate child as a "biological event" and "just something that happened" and has a younger, attractive boyfriend, Bob (Reginald Denny), with whom she enjoys an ideal romantic relationship. Bob wants to marry her, but she holds off, as she "has no patience with cradle-snatchers." She eventually gives in. And who plays her? Billie Burke, of course. Reginald Denny was eight years her junior even in real life, but then Mrs. Ziegfeld was ageless, wasn't she?

Other cool aunts who are worth a look are Aunt Kate Barnaby in *Go West Young Man* (1936), delightfully played by Elizabeth Patterson, who gives Mae West a run for her money and even sashays out of the film in parodic West fashion; most any of Edna May Oliver's aunts, such as Aunt Ben Wood in *Parnell* (1937), with the notable exception of Aunt March in *Little Women* (1933); 74-year-old May Robson as Aunt Jane in *Red-Headed Woman* (1932), who even drives a car, as opposed to her decidedly uncool Aunt Elizabeth in *Bringing Up Baby* (1938); and, last but not least, Mildred Natwick as colorful Aunt Amarilla in the Fred Astaire–Lucille Bremer musical *Yolanda and the Thief* (1945) ("Conchita, do my nails and bring them to my room!"). Who would have thought aunts could be so much fun?

Old Reliable: Esther Dale
in *My Reputation* (1946)

Esther Dale had no heart of gold beneath that gruff exterior.
Unpleasant to the end — that was Esther.[1]

To keep the complex machinery of a Hollywood film narrative running smoothly, there were a large number of small cogs in between the big wheels. Esther Dale was such a cog: Or, to use another metaphor, the types of roles she played were the almost invisible yet necessary glue that held parts of the story together.

Certainly, there was a legion of bit players, "under fives," and extras, who led a humbler existence in the movies than Esther Dale. Yet in the character actress hierarchy, Dale occupied a modest position. There was never any Ma Joad in Dale's life. There wasn't all of a sudden that one, brilliant, career-altering role, that would have elevated her to another level of recognition and might even have garnered her an Oscar nomination, as happened to a character actress of a similar type and in equally modest circumstances, namely Jane Darwell.

Far from the lofty heights of a May Robson, Fay Bainter, or Beulah Bondi, with their high-billed roles and Academy Award nominations, Dale spent a quarter of a century in movieland lending her iron-clad, mannish, and stony-faced presence to limited yet recognizable roles in more than 100 films between her 1934 debut as Claude Rains's secretary in *Crime Without Passion* (B. Hecht and C. MacArthur, Hecht-MacArthur) and a tiny part in *North to Alaska* (H. Hathaway, Twentieth Century–Fox) in 1960.[2] She worked for all the major studios, but most often at MGM, Paramount, and Universal. About a quarter of her appearances were uncredited and her highest billing seems to have been in *Wrecking Crew* (F. McDonald, Pine-Thomas, 1942), where she played the owner of a wrecking company and was billed fifth after Richard Arlen, Chester Morris, Jean Parker, and Joe Sawyer.

So, what is it possible to say about an actress like Esther Dale? Her film career would seem to lend itself well to one sentence summaries. David Ragan writes how she "played blunt-spoken, devoted housekeepers (Davis's indispensable Harriet in *Old Acquaintance*), dragonish mothers (Bellamy's in *The Awful Truth*), no-nonsense nurses (*Private Worlds*), prison matrons, and some of the screens most viperish gossips." John Springer and Jack Hamilton mention her "parade of domineering servants, brutal prison matrons and gossiping drabs." Alex Barris describes her as "a tall, grim-faced actress who alternated between scowling, disapproving neighbors and no-nonsense housekeepers and cooks." To James Robert Parish, writing in 1978, she was "a superior interpreter of no-nonsense domestics, commanding mothers, stern nurses, and prissy matrons." Finally and more recently, David Quinlan observes that Dale was "mostly seen as crusty types whose hearts of gold were well

In *Wrecking Crew* (Pine-Thomas Productions, 1942), Esther Dale (right) gets tough with Jean Parker as Mike O'Glendy, owner of a wrecking company. It was all in a day's work for Dale, who played her share of butch numbers both in and out of uniform. In private life, she was married to writer-producer-director Arthur Beckhard. The couple had no children.

hidden. She also played nosey neighbors, brisk housekeepers and nurses who would stand no intervention in their patients' care."[3]

In the limited space at their disposal in film encyclopedias and other reference works, these writers undoubtedly capture something true about who Dale was on screen.

None of them mention her role in *My Reputation* (C. Bernhardt, Warner Bros., 1946), where she was billed eighth, though they do mention a similar one in *Old Acquaintance* (V. Sherman, Warner Bros., 1943), where Dale was billed ninth as Bette Davis's loyal maid. Space allows me to go into greater detail about Dale's background, her acting experience, the types of roles she played, and why a character like the maid Anna in *My Reputation* is significant, not in spite of but because of her ordinariness.

Dale was 49 when she acted in her first film, though she looked older. She was born November 10, 1885, in Beaufort, South Carolina. Her father's family apparently came from Vermont, she studied at the Leland Gray Seminary in Townshend, Vermont, and would be buried in the Dale family grave in Townshend's Oakwood Cemetery. Dale also studied music in Berlin, before becoming a concert singer. She headed the vocal department at Smith College in Northampton, Massachusetts.[4]

Dale's most notable stage role was also her professional acting debut and her Broadway

There is plenty of static on the line between Bette Davis (left) and Miriam Hopkins (right) in *Old Acquaintance* (Warner Bros., 1943), based on a hit play by John Van Druten, who also wrote the screenplay with Lenore Coffee. Here Esther Dale is stuck between the combatants in a personal maid-companion role not unlike the one she would play in support of Barbara Stanwyck in *My Reputation* four years later.

debut, as the title character in *Carry Nation* by Frank McGrath. This biographical play about a legendary temperance advocate only lasted for 30 performances at the Biltmore Theatre, yet according to her director and friend, Blanche Yurka, it "succeeded in launching Esther as a dramatic actress."[5] The *New York Times* noted on Dale's death, "Though the play was studded with the names of young players destined for the theatrical heights — James Stewart, Mildred Natwick, Myron McCormick, and Joshua Logan — it had only a short run."[6] Barbara O'Neil and Karl Swenson were also in the cast.

Carry Nation was produced by Dale's husband Arthur J. Beckhard, who would produce all but one of her eight Broadway shows. Beckhard had become his wife's manager back when she was a "widely known lieder singer."[7] He continued to be so when she went into acting and he went into producing, first running a summer theater in Woodstock, New York, and later the University Players in West Falmouth, Massachusetts; "one of the most distinguished semi-professional groups ever assembled in this country," where future stars like Margaret Sullavan, Henry Fonda, and James Stewart learned their craft.[8]

Dale and her husband were the loved and respected mentors of several actors who would go on to have productive careers. One of their protégées, Blanche Yurka, remembered the couple fondly in her autobiography. After the 1929 crash and Blanche's brother Charlie's ensuing suicide, she writes, "One source of warm comfort to me was the growing friendship and devotion of producer Arthur Beckhard and his wife, the singer Esther Dale. These two sturdy, courageous human beings pulled me through many a trying time in the ensuing years. They had the gift of laughter and an abundance of patience and understanding."[9] Yurka staged *Carry Nation* and both co-wrote and acted with Dale, James Stewart, and Mildred Natwick in the Beckhard production that followed it, *Spring in Autumn* (1933), though it was hardly more successful. Beckhard only had two Broadway successes: *Another Language* (1932–33), Rose Franken's domestic drama in which Dale replaced Margaret Hamilton (in her Broadway debut); and *Goodbye Again* (1932–33), a comedy in which his wife did not take part.[10]

The couple's return to Broadway in two shows in 1945 and 1948 did not meet with an enthusiastic response. For the remainder of her career, Dale devoted herself to film work, where she became best known for her recurring role as Mrs. Birdie Hicks in the Ma and Pa Kettle series; and to work in several television shows between 1952 and 1961. Arthur Beckhard died in March 1961 and his wife passed away on July 23 that same year following surgery at Queen Angels Hospital in Los Angeles.[11]

∞

Dale specialized, as the quotations from film books above amply evidence, primarily in various types of working women: maids, cooks, housekeepers, as well as landladies, nurses, and prison matrons. As a cook, she served Norma Shearer in *The Women* (G. Cukor, MGM, 1939); Carole Lombard, as the first of three successively in her employ in *Made for Each Other* (J. Cromwell, Selznick International, 1939), who has a standard excuse for every mishap ("I'm only human"); and Abraham Lincoln (Raymond Massey) in *Abe Lincoln in Illinois* (J. Cromwell, Max Gordon Plays & Pictures, 1940), among others. Her maids included Madeleine Carroll's butch maid Matilda in suit and tie in *The Case Against Mrs. Ames* (W.A. Seiter, Paramount, 1936); the uncommonly genial Marta in *The Mortal Storm* (F. Borzage, MGM, 1940), who nevertheless turns out to be pro–Nazi and quits the Jewish family she is working for; Bette Davis's maid in *Old Acquaintance* (1943) and *A Stolen Life* (C. Bernhardt, Warner Bros., 1946); and the family factotum of the well-to-do Illinois family headed by Jane Cowl and Henry O'Neill in *No Man of Her Own* (M. Leisen, Paramount, 1950).

Her most significant nurse role was playing the "old school" matron in *Private Worlds* (G. La Cava, Paramount, 1935), who opposes psychiatrist Claudette Colbert and Charles Boyer's progressive treatment methods. Her forbidding face and solid physiognomy seemed particularly appropriate to a prison setting. Among many others, she lent her austere presence as a prison matron in *A Child Is Born* (L. Bacon, Warner Bros, 1939), a remake of *Life Begins* from 1932. Geraldine Fitzgerald starred in Loretta Young's old role as the pregnant accessory to murder, Grace Sutton, while Dale took over for Helena Phillips Evans in the considerably humbler, nameless, and uncredited role of "Prison Matron." In these types of working-class roles, Dale faced competition from actresses of a similar physical type, mainly Jane Darwell (1879–1967), with her in *Curly Top* (I. Cummings, Fox, 1935), *Untamed* (G. Archainbaud, Paramount, 1940), *Surrender* (A. Dwan, Republic, 1950), and television and always billed higher; and Marjorie Main (1890–1975), with her in *Crime Without Passion* (1934), *Dead End* (W. Wyler, Samuel Goldwyn, 1937), *Prison Farm* (L. King, Paramount, 1938), *The Women* (1939), *Women Without Names* (R. Florey, Paramount, 1940), and four Ma and Pa Kettle films (1947–52), starting with *The Egg and I* (C. Erskine, Universal, 1947), where Main rocketed to stardom, leaving Dale behind in the dust.

Dale also had a sideline in upper-class dowagers, most famously in *The Awful Truth* (L. McCarey, Columbia, 1937), where she played Ralph Bellamy's bossy mother, Mrs. Leeson; but also to good effect in her final role as Mrs. Maud Mansfield in *The Sound and the Fury* (M. Ritt, Twentieth Century–Fox, 1959). Mrs. Mansfield has one scene in the film, where Jason Compson (Yul Brynner) and his step-niece Quentin (Joanne Woodward) call on her and her maiden daughter Effie (Adrienne Marden). Quentin has been carefully coached in what not to say, but nevertheless makes a gaffe by asking about Mrs. Mansfield's persistent wheeze. Competition in the dowager department was less lethal in the 1950s than it had been during the 1930s and '40s, when Dale had to compete with the likes of Lucile Watson, May Robson, May Whitty, Helen Westley, and Laura Hope Crews.

So is *My Reputation* a forgotten classic in the Esther Dale canon? An unrecognized standout performance that will forever alter our perception of this stolid, solidly built, narrow-eyed, and steely-haired actress? Indeed not. The role of Barbara Stanwyck's trusty maid and companion Anna is not a great one by any means. It is better than most of Dale's film roles, but one can find more showy parts even for her, particularly as the stern matron in *Private Worlds* and the potential mother-in-law from hell in *The Awful Truth*.

So, why *My Reputation*? Well, for one thing it is a fine, though critically neglected, film from the hand of one of the most talented "woman's directors" of the 1940s, German immigrant Curtis Bernhardt, with a screenplay by Catherine Turney based on a 1942 novel by Clare Jaynes. Furthermore, Anna is an example of a classic type of role that you will find in the repertoire of almost any Hollywood character actress no matter how exalted, whether she is called a maid, mammy, dresser, or companion. Beulah Bondi, an A list supporting player if ever there was one, never played a maid, cook, or housekeeper, never played a servant, but she *did* play Anise, companion to Lucile Watson in *Watch on the Rhine* (1943) and Mrs. Boyce Medford, companion to Margaret Sullavan in *The Moon's Our Home* (W.A. Seiter, Paramount, 1937). A paid companion is just a lavender and old lace remove from what used to be called "domestic service." We even find Lucile Watson, another high-profile character actress with big parts, giving traditional support as a governess to Deanna Durbin and her sisters in *Three Smart Girls* (1936). Playing the heroine's paid helper was the meat and potatoes on the character actress's dinner table.

There is a necessary function, then, in many classic woman-centered Hollywood narratives, which requires that the female protagonist be accompanied on her life's journey, be it by a maid, mammy, chaperone, or companion. It is elemental to the whole concept "supporting player," that the actresses who play these roles are there to provide exactly that: support. While there will be characters in the film opposing the protagonist's goals and interests, the helper is there to smooth the way, give help and guidance, and serve her mistress with unswerving dedication. Support doesn't necessarily require uncritical, blind devotion or selfless adulation, though. Just think of Birdie Coonan in *All About Eve* (1950) with her ironic running commentary on Margo Channing's developing life story; Hattie McDaniel as Mammy in *Gone with the Wind* (1939), tsk-tsking at Scarlett's scandalous behavior; or any of the three talented actresses who interpreted the role of Cornelia Van Gorder's maid Lizzie Allen in *The Bat*, protesting vociferously at her endangering both their lives with her amateur sleuthing: Louise Fazenda in the silent version from 1926, Maude Eburne in the first sound version (called *The Bat Whispers*, 1930), and Lenita Lane in the 1959 remake starring Agnes Moorehead.

The maid is often a mirror of the mistress, however much distorted or inverted. Think of Hilda Vaughn as the lazy, slatternly, and ultimately blackmailing maid to Kitty Packard

(Jean Harlow) in *Dinner at Eight* (1933). Only vulgar, nouveau riche Kitty would think to hire someone so inappropriate. Sometimes it's enough that there is just someone there to lend an ear. I'm reminded of that hilarious scene in *Finishing School* (1934), where spoiled society woman and neglectful mother Helen Crawford Radcliff (Billie Burke) is "closeted" in her boudoir with her hapless maid Evelyn (Theresa Harris), who has to listen to her employer's endless complaints about her pseudo-difficult life. This being said, the vast majority of ladies' maids and other female domestics lead a far more anonymous existence on the big screen than those I've mentioned. Few of them got to be funny.

So let's get back to Esther Dale and Anna in *My Reputation*. Anna is a far cry from Birdie Coonan, Mammy, or Lizzie Allen. Yet she exemplifies what is the lowest common denominator for the function of the heroine's helper in the guise of a servant: unquestioned devotion, singularity of focus, and unlimited availability (i.e., "no family ties"). Her role and appearance are so modest as almost to make her fade into the woodwork, yet her presence provides part of the richness of the film's social fabric and serves as an ongoing reflection, however subtle and understated, on the protagonist's development throughout the film.

Anna's dogged devotion to her mistress, Jessica Drummond (Barbara Stanwyck), a recently widowed, upper middle-class woman in her early thirties with two teenage sons ("quite an adornment of Chicago's Lake Forest set"[12]), is signaled from the first moment we see her in the opening scene of *My Reputation*, the day after Paul Drummond's funeral. Anna has let Jessica sleep late and sent the boys off to swim. She pointedly interrupts the cook's reading Drummond's obituary aloud with a question about Jessica's breakfast, indicating that her chief concern is with her living employer rather than with the dead. In Jessica's subsequent meeting with her lawyer, Frank Everett (Warner Anderson), he recommends that she let most of her servants go, but assures her she can still afford to keep Anna. Jessica says she feels responsible for her and thus Anna's significance is made clear.

Overall, the character of Anna in the film is close to the novel on which it is based, *Instruct My Sorrows* (1942). In the novel, Jessica gets irritated at Anna for bringing up two black mourning dresses and Anna begins to cry: "This isn't just her job then, Jessica thought, feeling hysteria rising in herself again, it's her life. I am her home and her family and all the things she's never had. I am the child she's never had and the husband."[13]

Anna disappears from the film until after Jessica has returned from a four-day trip (with her friends Ginna and Cary Abbott [Eve Arden and John Ridgely]) to Lake Tahoe, where she encounters George Brent as the dashing military man Major Scott Landis, who is to be her love interest in the remainder of the film. We next encounter Anna in a brief scene encouraging her mistress to eat more. Jessica, dining alone in not-so-splendid isolation, asks her maid to bring in a plate and join her, but their scene is interrupted by the arrival of Frank Everett. Thus, we understand that Anna and Jessica's relationship is largely a given and will probably remain static. Time cannot be devoted to it, beyond what is required to further our understanding of the heroine's plight.

That is the function of the next scene, where Jessica and Anna are seen rolling bandages and knitting for the Red Cross, one of many reminders of the wartime setting of the film. Anna is concerned that Jessica should get out more. When Scott calls and it becomes apparent that Jessica is meeting him at his apartment, Anna smiles to think "what Mrs. Kimball would say." This is an example of Anna's choral function, as she is the audience's representative in the film, nudging us towards an appropriate response. Anna also functions as a contrast in the film, not to Jessica, but to Jessica's draconic mother Mrs. Kimball (Lucile Watson); "a wonderful museum piece," according to Scott; a stickler for etiquette and someone who has dedicated her life to social convention and made mourning a career ("Our kind of people wear black"). The scenes with Jessica alone at home with Anna in an otherwise empty house, the boys having gone off to boarding school, though they do not further the plot, are meant to indicate the mundane, uneventful, lonely life she is leading.

Anna has one last scene she when gets a little "high" on hot buttered rum on Christmas Eve ("There is no fool like an old fool," she mutters), after making a big dinner for the Abbotts and Frank Everett. Refusing to have Ginna help her in the kitchen with the washing up, Anna brings the boys in with her to get presents from their grandmother. While in the kitchen, she mentions *en passant* to Mrs. Kimball, "Major Landis is in there," arousing her curiosity. A scene of thinly veiled confrontation between Mrs. Kimball and Landis ensues. The brief scene in the kitchen with Mrs. Kimball and the boys is the only one in the film Anna has without Jessica. It is her last. She is said to be "out" during the dramatic New Year's Eve weekend that ends the film, indicating some kind of social life outside the Drummond household. Anna has served her purpose and we need no longer be concerned with her.

Could we imagine *My Reputation* without Anna? Surely, but it would have been a different film. Jessica might have had to come from a lower class to explain her lack of a maid, there would be no one at home to lend a sympathetic ear to her concerns, and there would be no self-effacing presence in the film to answer the door, tend to the mundane housekeeping duties, and take care of the boys when they are home from school. Jessica Drummond may have lost her husband, but she keeps her "wife."

The Dilapidated Diva: Marie Dressler in *Dinner at Eight* (1933)

She made age a beautiful thing on the screen.[1]

In MGM's film adaptation of Edna Ferber and George S. Kaufman's stinging satire on American high society, *Dinner at Eight* (1933), one of the greatest American actresses of the twentieth century played one of the greatest fictional actresses ever created by the human imagination. Top-billed in a talented ensemble cast the likes of which has seldom been seen in Hollywood or anywhere else, Marie Dressler played the aging actress and former femme fatale Carlotta Vance in what would prove her penultimate film role before cancer finally claimed her on July 28, 1934.

To Will Rogers, she was "queen of our movies." George Cukor called her "a law unto herself." To Molly Haskell, she was a gargoyle who became her own genre. Harold Lloyd said she was "the greatest comedienne of this generation." To her biographer Matthew Kennedy, she was "one of the movies' all-time great anomalies." A feminist film scholar has recently called her "the least effective representative of commercial desire ever to appear in American film."[2] Marie Dressler was all these things and more.

When filming started at MGM on March 13, 1933,[3] the Canadian actress who had been born Leila Marie Koerber in Cobourg, Ontario, on November 9, 1868, was 64 years old and had one year, four months, two weeks and one day left to live.[4] Dressler had been getting laughs on Broadway since 1892 and had her first personal success in *The Lady Slavey* four years later.[5] She worked steadily on Broadway and, from 1906, also in vaudeville, until the United States entered the war in 1917, when she devoted herself wholeheartedly to selling Liberty Bonds and other war work.[6] After World War I, Dressler found work in the theater increasingly hard to come by. By 1924, she was reduced to living in a small room usually reserved for servants at the Ritz-Carlton Hotel at Madison and 46th St.[7] Dressler only had two shows on Broadway in the 1920s and *The Dancing Girl* (1923) would be her last.

By the early 1930s, though, Dressler had made one of the most spectacular comebacks the world has ever seen. From being unemployed and unemployable, she rode the crest of the wave of theater-trained talent moving to Hollywood to contribute to the revolution engendered by the talkies. Dressler was no novice. Her film debut was in *Tillie's Punctured Romance* (M. Sennett, Keystone, 1914) with none other than Charlie Chaplin. It was the first feature-length comedy to be produced. It was based on "the greatest success of her stage career,"[8] *Tillie's Nightmare* (1910–11), where as the boardinghouse drudge Tillie Blobbs, Dressler opened with what would become one of her signature tunes: "Heaven Will Protect the Working Girl."

Dressler's close friend and the future screenwriter on *Dinner at Eight*, Frances Marion, convinced boy wonder MGM producer Irving Thalberg to test her for Garbo's sound film debut, *Anna Christie* (C. Brown, MGM, 1930).[9] Garbo talked all right, but she didn't talk to just anyone. She talked to Dressler's drink-sodden, pathetic and all too human Marthy Owens. From that moment, Dressler was a movie star.[10] Huge successes followed and everything she touched turned to gold. She won an Academy Award for Best Actress as Min in *Min and Bill* (G.W. Hill, MGM, 1930) with Wallace Beery and was nominated for *Emma* (C. Brown, MGM, 1932) the following year. She was the first movie actress ever to be on the cover of *Time* on Aug. 7, 1933.[11] She was Hollywood's most popular performer in 1932 and '33 in the annual exhibitors' poll.[12] According to one film historian, "Marie Dressler is the only woman in her sixties ever to achieve the status of top-grossing star in America."[13]

Dressler's personal life had always been stormy. As biographer Matthew Kennedy writes: "Nothing good in Marie's life lasted very long, except her friendships."[14] In imitation of her friend and 1890s co-star Lillian Russell, she had married a dashingly handsome ne'er-do-well in 1894.

The marriage only lasted two years.[15] Dressler may have thought she was married to

Fishnet realism, as Marie Dressler's Min gives an ambiguous embrace to Wallace Beery's Bill in *Min and Bill* (Metro-Goldwyn-Mayer, 1930). After Dressler's untimely death from cancer in 1934, Metro and several other studios spent the next decade or more trying to come up with a new Dressler, but the time when an aging, overweight, has-been vaudevillian could rocket to the top of the box office was over.

Dressler's last film to be released was the intelligent comedy *Christopher Bean* (Metro-Goldwyn-Mayer, 1933), based on a play by Sidney Howard that had been adapted from the French. Beulah Bondi reprised her stage role of the snobbish, grasping, petite bourgeois Mrs. Haggett, while Dressler took over for Pauline Lord as Abby, the cook and spiritual center of the dysfunctional Haggett family.

her long-time manager James H. Dalton, until she discovered not long before his death in 1921 that he already had a wife.[16] Between 1928 and 1932, Dressler had a "romantic friendship" with her sometime secretary-companion and fellow actress Claire DuBrey. DuBrey had moved on by the time *Dinner at Eight* dropped into Dressler's well-padded lap.[17] In the spring of 1933, she was living in style in a Colonial Revival house at 801 N. Alpine Dr. in Beverly Hills, that she had bought from the estate of razor tycoon King Camp Gillette and called "Loafhaven."[18] She also owned a second home in Santa Barbara, a nine-bedroom mansion called "Casa Lo Bello."[19]

As we have seen above, capsule descriptions of Dressler are easy to come by, but to understand what made her great we must delve deeper than cartoonish text bytes, conventional encomiums, and her curriculum vitae. We need to look at both the play and the film versions of *Dinner at Eight* to see the opportunities the role of Carlotta Vance offered Dressler and what she made of them. We need to examine the possible models for Carlotta Vance and how they can enrich our understanding of Dressler's performance. Finally, we need to understand the unique synergy between actress and role in this film, which was a capstone to a great career and a grand finale in a life devoted above all to the theater.

The structure of Ferber and Kaufman's *Dinner at Eight* was unusual in that it had no main plot, no clear protagonist, but rather chose to tell a congeries of interrelated stories from a cross-section of the rarefied, upper echelon of contemporary American society and the servants who made its carousel of pleasure and entertainment go round. George Cukor's biographer Emanuel Levy describes the film *Dinner at Eight* as a "straightforward, unobtrusive adaptation of a stage work with little attempt to go beyond a proscenium perspective" and points out that there are no exterior shots.[20] The choice to maintain the atmosphere of a sealed, private, and protected world of privilege and plenty was a canny one. The classic adaptation strategy of "opening up" the narrative in the form of added initial scenes from the "backstory" and location shooting would only have dissipated the claustrophobic tension of this high-wire world, where so many of its most prominent members are about to plummet.

Though the film hews closely to the original both in plot and dialogue, there are a few significant changes, particularly relating to Carlotta and her role in the denouement. With a star of the caliber of Dressler heading the cast list, it was inevitable that her part would be built up. In the play version, for example, the final curtain comes down on young daughter of privilege Paula Jordan (Madge Evans), alone on the stage, still blissfully ignorant about her lover Larry Renault's suicide, torn between the desire to find out why he has not shown up and the need to join the other guests at her mother Millicent Jordan's dinner party. In the film, screenwriters Frances Marion and Herman J. Mankiewicz decided to give a subtle twist to this storyline by having Carlotta staying at the same hotel as the faded former movie star and matinee idol Larry Renault (John Barrymore) and observing Paula leaving his room. Thus, Carlotta brings news of death and disaster to the dinner party, as Renault's suicide has just been discovered as she is coming away. We are given a beautiful scene between her and Paula in the library where, having interrupted a *tête-à-tête* between Paula and her fiancé Ernest DeGraff (Phillips Holmes), she tells Paula that Larry is dead.

In this scene in the film, more than any other, actress and role merge.[21] The worldly wise woman who has lived and loved full throttle all her life, who has been a tireless worker in the theatre for decades, who has provided for herself and others when there was neither kith nor kin to depend on, who has seen death and known despair, that woman is the shared quintessence of Marie Dressler and Carlotta Vance. When Dressler opens her heart and gives expression to a few fragments from her wide and varied experience, we cannot fail to be impressed. Dressler had loved both men and women, she had known success, fame, and accompanying wealth, but also many a dead end both personally and professionally. She had stayed on to care for a man who had never been free to marry her, even after she discovered his mendacity, because he was helplessly, terminally ill and he needed her. She had shared some of her most intimate feelings with other women and would will $50,000 to her African American maid, Mamie Cox, and Mamie's husband Jerry.[22] She had been ill almost to the point of death from typhoid fever in late 1902, an illness that had taken her mother's life while Dressler was still recovering.[23] Now she was ill yet again from a disease that would ultimately kill her, so weakened that she could only work at most three hours a day.[24] "In a scene filled ... with references to death and hard-learned lessons, Marie brings such knowing skill that it appears as a valedictory to her entire career."[25]

While the play's dialogue is sometimes condensed, Carlotta gains several wonderful lines. One of them occurs in the brief scene with ship owner Oliver Jordan's spinsterish secretary Miss Copeland (Elizabeth Patterson), who in the grip of excitement over meeting her idol blurts out that she had seen Carlotta on stage as a child. Clearly, Miss Copeland is not much younger than Carlotta herself, who sweeps out with the parting sally "We must have a nice talk about the Civil War sometime, just you and I." Mordaunt Hall singled out this exchange for praise in his *New York Times* review as "one of the lines that aroused gales of mirth from the first-night audience."[26]

More famously, Carlotta is given the final line of the film, which hardly needs repeating. As many will recall, she is going in to dinner with the bottle-blond bombshell Kitty Packard (Jean Harlow), when the latter remarks that she was reading a book the other day that said that "machinery was going to take the place of every profession." Dressler does one of her famous double-takes, looks Kitty up and down, and remarks with all the wisdom and experience of a woman of her many years: "My dear, that is something you need never worry about."[27] In the words of film historian Maria DiBattista: "The famous quip has all the zing of an unanswerable putdown, but it also comes as a compliment from a fellow professional."[28] *Variety* found it "a first-rate device, handing the curtain to the principal two comedy characters," whom they observed "have been shrewdly emphasized in the film version."[29] In both the brief scene with Patterson and the finale with Harlow, actress and role, Dressler and Vance, merge in a unique way. "While she looked you over, she told you off," Ethan Mordden once wrote of Dressler, "and there was simply no one else around who did it as well." Mordden considered Carlotta in *Dinner at Eight* Dressler's "one imperishable performance."[30]

So, where did Carlotta Vance come from? Obviously, she originated in Ferber and Kaufman's active imaginations, but was there any specific leading lady they might have had in mind in creating her? And whom might Dressler have had at the back of her head when she conjured her up for the film version?

Two stars of the late nineteenth- and early twentieth-century stage have been put forward as possible models for Carlotta Vance: Mrs. Patrick Campbell (1865–1940) and Maxine Elliott (1868–1940). Sheridan Morley claims in his book *Tales from the Hollywood Raj* that "the dowager played by Marie Dressler was closely modelled on Mrs. Pat."[31] Dressler biographer Matthew Kennedy suggests that Carlotta's "élan is modeled after one of Marie's contemporaries, British stage actress Mrs. Patrick Campbell."[32] After seeing his dear friend Constance Collier create Carlotta on Broadway, *Dinner at Eight* director George Cukor imagined someone like Maxine Elliott being the inspiration for Ferber and Kaufman's creation.[33]

Naturally, it doesn't need to be either-or. The available facts about Carlotta's life that appear in the play and film would seem to fit closely with what we know of Maxine Elliott's life and career. As much admired for her beauty as for her acting ability, Elliott had been a star from 1903 till her retirement in 1920. In addition to her star quality, Elliott was a shrewd businesswoman, who was advised by no less a figure than J.P. Morgan. In 1908 she built Maxine Elliott's Theater, which was not just named for her, but owned half-and-half by her and the Shuberts, making her one of the few female theater managers at the time. Elliott spent the 20 years of her retirement entertaining her rich and influential friends at her chateau near Cannes. These friends included both Edward VII and his grandson Edward VIII, later the Duke of Windsor (Carlotta refers to him as "Wales," i.e., the then Prince of Wales).[34]

Elliott seldom visited the United States after she moved to France, like Carlotta who hasn't been home in 10 years. When she was creating her characterization, Dressler would have had another model much closer at hand, namely the infamously acidulous British actress known as Mrs. Patrick Campbell, after her first and long dead husband. Stella Camp-

In Metro's ensemble extravaganza *Dinner at Eight* (Metro-Goldwyn-Mayer, 1933), veteran stage star Carlotta Vance (Marie Dressler) is forced to discipline her Pekingese "Tarzan" in the hallway of the Versailles Hotel. In the play version, the dog had been called "Benito," after the Italian dictator Mussolini.

bell spent time off-and-on in Hollywood between 1930 and 1935 and, according to Sheridan Morley, among her many compatriots in Tinseltown "few failed quite as spectacularly as Mrs. Patrick Campbell."[35] Campbell, who had been a striking, raven-haired beauty in her youth, had by this time settled into a fast-thickening and saggy old age, which made her and Dressler more similar in physical type than different. Not only that, Campbell had a fondness for Pekingese dogs, the most famous being the white Peke "Moonbeam."[36] There are several photographs of her with her lapdog that bear a striking resemblance to Carlotta Vance as Dressler portrayed her in all her dowager frippery and fustian, "under a heavy load of makeup, jewelry, pelts, and wounded pride."[37]

Coincidentally, on August 23, 1933, Mrs. Patrick Campbell opened in her last Broadway show, *A Party* by Ivor Novello, at the Playhouse Theatre at 137 W. 48th St., the very evening *Dinner at Eight* had its world premiere only a few blocks away at the Astor Theatre (Broadway and 45th St.) in New York City. In the torrential rain that evening, New York audiences thus had a choice between what Henry James referred to in a famous short story as "the real thing" and what may well have been a partial imitation.[38]

Director George Cukor, who according to Betty Lee was in agreement with most of producer David O. Selznick's casting for *Dinner at Eight*, recalled that Dressler was "not quite my idea for the part, not the way it was played on the stage by Constance Collier."[39] He felt that the *Dinner at Eight* role "was really written with someone like Maxine Elliott in mind, a great beauty, a leading lady.... Nevertheless, Marie was able to give the impression that she was a somebody. She had that quality, in spite of her looks; in the way she carried herself, the way she wore the clothes."[40] Louis B. Mayer also weighed in for Dressler and, indeed, there can never have been any doubt that the studio's biggest moneymaker would get this plum part. After the premiere, *Variety* noted that Dressler's role wasn't in "her popular vein," as it was "a dressed up part," but thought she handled "this politer assignment with poise and aplomb."[41] Mordaunt Hall, the noted *New York Times* film critic, also made a point of this being a new departure for the veteran actress: "It is a great pleasure to behold Marie Dressler away from her usual roles, dressed in the height of fashion..." Hall found her "splendid as the wise Carlotta."[42]

Marie Dressler as herself. After a life of hard knocks, Dressler signals both her ordinariness and aspirations to gentility through her quietly elegant pearl necklace and simple print dress.

Casting Dressler in such a sophisticated and glamorous role after she had spent most of her Hollywood years in simple cotton dresses and voluminous aprons, playing characters in lowly or middling socio-economic circumstances, was a calculated risk and might even be called casting against type. But Dressler wasn't playing herself in *Min and Bill* or *Emma* any more than she was in *Dinner at Eight*. Dressler was an actress. Her performance as Marthy in *Anna Christie* had proven that she could put mugging and other slapstick antics aside and give a naturalistic performance. Kennedy calls Marthy "one of the most accomplished characterizations she committed to film" and "the first sustained dramatic role of her career."[43] There were no limitations in Dressler's acting ability that would make it difficult for her to give a realistic portrait of a fellow actress and former stage star. Indeed, one could argue that the dilapidated diva Carlotta Vance was the film role closest to her own experience. Dressler had never been a great beauty, or owned her own theater, or retired to the French Riviera to play hostess to British royalty and other members of high society, but she had been a star of the American stage during roughly the same period as Carlotta Vance, had been the friend of every American president from Grover Cleveland to Franklin Delano Roosevelt, and she knew what it was like when the star began to fade.[44]

Dressler once said that "it is some comfort to know that mine is a face which once seen is rarely forgotten."[45] Maybe the most impressive aspect of Dressler's multi-faceted performance as Carlotta Vance is her ability to make us believe that she once was attractive to men; maybe not a classical beauty like Maxine Elliott, but attractive enough to amass their tribute in the form of the furs and jewels that bedeck her 5' 8" tall, 200-lb. person.[46] According to Victoria Sturtevant, Carlotta "wears the evidence of her history on her chest, like so many medals."[47] She tells Paula Jordan that men have been "my life's work." Even with "an ample figure like a rain barrel" and "a face that resembled a fallen cake," she makes us believe it.[48] Dressler's director, who initially "couldn't really picture her as a former beauty with scores of lovers," found that "she acquired a peculiar distinction, a magnificence.... [S]he knew how to make an entrance with great aplomb, great effect."[49]

In *Dinner at Eight* we are not just seeing a veteran actress and former star of the stage giving her final, great performance. We are witnessing a woman, her body wracked with terminal cancer, who nevertheless is able to turn on the full wattage of her star power, almost blinding us with her charisma, nobility, and courage. "The bulk of her body never deterred her," write John Springer and Jack Hamilton, adding, "[I]t was the bulk of her personality that gave her star quality all her life."[50]

No one who worked on *Dinner at Eight* is alive today. With the death of Karen Morley (Lucy Talbot) in 2003 at the age of 93 and assistant director Joseph M. Newman in 2006 at the age of 96, the living link with the film was broken. It took nearly three quarters of a century for the entire cast and crew to pass away. The first to go was Louise Closser Hale (Hattie Loomis) in the summer of 1933, a month before the film was released, followed by Dressler in the summer of 1934. Jean Harlow (Kitty Packard) died of kidney failure in 1937 and art director Fredric Hope that same year, following an appendectomy. Both were in their mid-thirties. John Barrymore (Larry Renault), Phillips Holmes (Paula Jordan's fiancé Ernest DeGraff), and May Robson (Mrs. Wendel, the Jordans' cook, who drops the aspic) all died in 1942, while Wallace Beery (Dan Packard) and assistant director Cullen Tate passed towards the end of the 1940s. Lionel Barrymore (Oliver Jordan), Jean Hersholt (stage producer Jo Stengel), Grant Mitchell (Ed Loomis), Hilda Vaughn (Harlow's insidious maid Tina), screenwriter Herman J. Mankiewicz, composer William Axt, and dress designer Adrian all died in the 1950s, while George S. Kaufman, producer David O. Selznick, Lee Tracy (Larry Renault's agent Max Kane), Elizabeth Patterson (Oliver Jordan's secretary Miss Copeland), and Edna Ferber passed away in the 1960s. Billie Burke (Millicent Jordan), cinematographer William H. Daniels, and film editor Ben Lewis all died in 1970, Edmund

Lowe (Dr. Wayne Talbot) and recording director Douglas Shearer in 1971, followed by screenwriter Frances Marion in 1973. Finally, Madge Evans (Paula Jordan), director George Cukor, Donald Ogden Stewart, who wrote additional dialogue, and sound mixer Charles E. Wallace all died in the early 1980s. By the late 1980s, all the minor cast members were also dead. Thus *Dinner at Eight* passed out of living memory.

The Last Dowager: Isobel Elsom in *Ladies in Retirement* (1941)

*Dowager: n. 1. The widow of a king, prince, or
person of rank. 2. A wealthy elderly woman.*

The spare dictionary definition above doesn't even begin to cover the persistent presence and symbolic significance of the dowager as she appeared in American films in the 1930s and '40s. If there was ever a time when older women wielded power in American society, it was in the first half of the twentieth century. This is reflected in the plays and films of the era, which show a preoccupation with the sayings and doings of powerful older women to a degree we are unlikely to see again.

As I write, I'm looking forward to the next episode of the lavishly produced British drama series *Downton Abbey* (ITV, 2010–), set in a country house in the Edwardian era. Maggie Smith, as the doddering, domineering, and delightful Dowager Countess of Grantham, is a living link to characters like Lady Beldon in *Mrs. Miniver* (1942), Mrs. Henry Vale in *Now, Voyager* (1942), and Fanny Farrelly in *Watch on the Rhine* (1943), but is also a reminder that dowagers are a thing of the past.

Dowagers were once thick on the ground in Hollywood, if they'll pardon the expression, starting with the advent of sound and well into the 1940s. They came in all sizes but tended towards "Large," as if significance must be accorded to their pronouncements at least partly because of their avoirdupois. Certainly, they gave a whole new meaning to the term "throwing your weight around." Dowagers were usually widows, leaving them unencumbered by husbands and with lots of spare time to stick their noses (be they patrician or potato) into other people's business. Dowagers were not necessarily aristocrats, but they definitely belonged to the upper-middle or upper class on either side of the Atlantic. Their power over other women could be acute, as they were social arbiters who gave or withheld their approval of younger and less powerful women's behavior. Their power over men also made itself felt, particularly hapless husbands (if they hadn't happily died), sons, nephews, and other male relatives. Dowagers could fulfill two of the basic functions of supporting cast members: They could either aid the protagonists in reaching their goals or hinder them, and sometimes, as in *Ladies in Retirement* (1941), they did both consecutively. Dowagers, in other words, were dramatic, which of course explains their presence in so many films of Hollywood's Golden Age, though we imagine they were a weighty presence in so-called "real life" as well.[1]

British character actresses often had the inside track as far as dowager roles were concerned. Maybe the greatest of them was Dame May Whitty, a relatively late arrival in Hol-

65

lywood, considering she was born in 1865 and didn't start in American films until 1937, when she was 71. The high points of Whitty's dowager role list were the wheelchair-bound battle-axe Mrs. Bramson in *Night Must Fall* (1937) and the bellicose, overbearing Lady Beldon in *Mrs. Miniver* (1942). She was Oscar-nominated for both roles.

Whitty belonged to the oldest generation of actresses to contribute to sound films, born in the 1860s or just before, as was the case with May Robson (1858–1942), who underwent the world's first recorded "extreme makeover" from apple seller to high society dame in *Lady for a Day* (1933) and got an Academy Award nomination for her efforts. Jessie Ralph (1864–1944) was more limited in ability, but amusing in comedies such as *The Last of Mrs. Cheyney* (1937) with Joan Crawford, as the plain-spoken Duchess of Beltravers; *The Bank Dick* (1940), as W.C. Fields's mother-in-law with the laughable moniker Mrs. Hermisilio Brunch; and *They Met in Bombay* (1941), starring Rosalind Russell and Clark Gable, as the folksy Duchess of Beltravers. Helen Lowell (1866–1937) lent her pinched, crabapple face to bossy old biddies in *Living on Velvet* and *Party Wire* (both 1935), among others, while Alison Skipworth was letter perfect in everything from *Strictly Unconventional* and *Raffles* to *Wide Open Faces* and *Ladies in Distress* during her all too brief tenure in Hollywood between 1930 and 1937.

Among screen dowagers born in the 1870s, we find maybe the greatest of them all, Canadian-born Lucile Watson (1879–1962), who ruled the roost in Hollywood from 1934 to 1951 and was particularly good in *Watch on the Rhine* (1943) as Bette Davis's blinkered mother, who must be "shaken out of the magnolias" and realize the threat posed by fascism even inside the sumptuous walls of her Washington, DC, residence. Others born in this decade who would get a stab at imperious older women roles were Alma Kruger (*These Three*, 1936), Helen Westley (*Splendor*, 1935), Constance Collier (*Rope*, 1948), Ethel Griffies (*Saratoga Trunk*, 1945), Ethel Barrymore (*Kind Lady*, 1951), and Laura Hope Crews (*The Silver Cord*, 1933). From the generation of the 1880s, I need to mention Edna May Oliver (*Pride and Prejudice*, 1940), Florence Bates (*A Letter to Three Wives*, 1949), and Beulah Bondi (*One Foot in Heaven*, 1941). Finally, a few actresses born in the 1890s, such as Cora Witherspoon (*The Mating Game*, 1959) and Evelyn Varden (*Hilda Crane*, 1956), would also be able to build a career on dowager portrayals, mainly because they looked older than their years and were suitably homely.

All this by way of introduction to my personal favorite among the classic British dowagers and one I regretted not having made room for in *Actresses of a Certain Character*: Isobel Elsom. Elsom was born Isobel Jeannette Reed in Cambridge, England, on March 16, 1893, the daughter of Joseph Reed, and was educated at Howard College in Bedford.[2] In her youth, Elsom was a great beauty of the blushing "English Rose" variety, though one suspects there may also have been a thorn or two. Early photographs show her with a mass of fair hair, melting eyes, and a firm chin that would only get firmer with age. With an aquiline profile even John Barrymore might envy her, Elsom remained handsome throughout her life. In her available films, from *Illegal* (1932) to *The Pleasure Seekers* (1964), from black-and-white to CinemaScope, she seems hardly to age at all.[3]

For more than half a century, Elsom interpreted dozens of roles in the theater, silent and sound films, radio, and television. She made her stage debut in the chorus of *The Quaker Girl* in London in 1911 at the age of 18 and worked steadily until she got a leading role in *After the Girl* in 1914. During the remainder of the teens and into the twenties, she worked on the London stage, on tour, and in silent films, culminating in two successive hit shows at the St. James's Theatre in 1923 (*The Outsider* and *The Green Goddess*) and her

Broadway debut in a play called *The Ghost Train* at the Eltinge Theatre in 1926 with the 23-year-old Claudette Colbert.

When the show ended in October, Elsom went directly into a new play by William Hurlbut called *Sin of Sins*, which opened at the Adelphi Theatre in Chicago on November 8, 1926. Theater historian Kaier Curtin writes that this was the first "lesbian love drama" written by an American playwright and "the first play with a lesbian character written in the English language."[4] Elsom played the role of the "predatory" lesbian and Gladys Lloyd, the soon-to-be Mrs. Edward G. Robinson, was her innocent victim. The play had only a short run after two out of three leading Chicago critics panned it.[5] It was never seen in New York. Elsom was commended by the critics, who found that she "carries off the hapless lady with thrilling effectiveness" and "acts the pathological lady for all the role's pathological power and none of its sensationalism."[6] Mathilde Len, writing for the *Chicago Daily News*, quipped: "Isobel Elsom, new to Chicago, is an actress of such unquestionable ability that admiration for her art overcomes revulsion for her part."[7] Who would have thought that this model of correct comportment and conventional ideas in so many films from the 1940s, '50s, and even into the '60s, once upon a time gave face and figure to one of the first lesbians on the American stage? Elsom herself remembered little about the production when Curtin interviewed her about it in 1978, but insisted, "I was not at all afraid of playing a lesbian. I thought it was a good role and right for me."[8]

In 1923 Elsom married pioneering British film director Maurice Elvey, who would direct nine of her silent films between the year of their marriage and 1927. Elvey was born in Stockton-on-Tees in England in 1887 and worked himself up from a pageboy at the Savoy Hotel in London to directing more than 300 films, according to his *New York Times* obituary.[9] He was active as a director between 1913 and 1957 and died 10 years later, by which time he and Elsom had long since divorced.

After *The Ghost Train* and *Sin of Sins*, Elsom was seen on Broadway in five consecutive failures from *The Mulberry Bush* (1927), a comedy by Edward Knoblock, again with Claudette Colbert; via *The Silver Box* (1928), a comedy by John Galsworthy with Halliwell Hobbes and Mary Forbes; to a revival of Dorothy Brandon's *The Outsider* (1928). Elsom didn't appear on Broadway again for a decade, until she returned to play Moll Flanders in Elmer Rice's history play *American Landscape*, which opened on December 3, 1938, at the Cort Theatre and closed in January 1939 after 43 performances.

American Landscape was followed by what was undoubtedly Elsom's biggest hit among her 17 Broadway shows between 1926 and 1957: *Ladies in Retirement* by Edward Percy and Reginald Denham. Her portrayal of the elderly yet still saucy ex–chorus girl Leonora Fiske was singled out in her *New York Times* obituary as her "best-known Broadway role."[10] Written for the 38-year-old British stage star Flora Robson, who played Miss Fiske's troubled housekeeper, the play opened at Henry Miller's Theatre on March 26, 1940, and ran for 151 performances followed by a seven-month tour.[11] Denham, who also co-wrote the screenplay for the Hollywood filmatization of *Ladies in Retirement*, had directed Elsom in her last British film, *The Primrose Path* (British and Dominions Film, 1934).[12] Through *Ladies in Retirement*, he provided her with an entree into the American film industry. When Columbia made a film version in 1941, Elsom was the only member of the Broadway cast to reprise her role. She moved to Los Angeles in early 1941 and would remain there till her death 40 years later.

When Elsom arrived in Hollywood at the age of 48, the first generation of actresses to interpret dowagers on the screen was on the wane. Helen Lowell was dead. Alison Skipworth had already retired from films. Nor need Elsom long fear competition from May Robson, Edna May Oliver, Jessie Ralph, Helen Westley, or Laura Hope Crews, who were all gone from the screen by 1942. Dame May Whitty was still going strong, though, as was Lucile Watson, who acted in films until 1951. They were joined in 1944 by the venerable Ethel Barrymore (1879–1959) in dowager roles, but these women were all substantially older than Elsom and had a grandmotherly look about them. Among her own contemporaries, Florence Bates (1888–1953), Beulah Bondi (1888–1891), Cora Witherspoon (1890–1957), and Evelyn Varden (1893–1958) would play their fair share of big screen battle-axes, but Elsom had the advantage over them in some cases in that she was matronly yet attractive, of "a certain age," but what age was hard to say. It might also be a comparative advantage to be English.

That being said, there were really only two character actresses in Hollywood who were in direct competition with Elsom for roles: Gladys Cooper (1888–1971) and Mary Forbes (1879–1974). All three were stage-trained actresses with extensive experience and appearances both in the West End of London and on Broadway; all had been beauties in their youth; and all were very, very British. Forbes had been in Hollywood since 1929 and Cooper arrived 10 years later, a year and a half before Elsom. In this competition, Cooper would ultimately place first, Elsom second, and Forbes third. While Elsom and Forbes played many more roles than Cooper, she got the showier, Oscar-caliber ones, such as playing Bette Davis's tyrannical mother in *Now, Voyager* (1942), the nun who gives Jennifer Jones a hard time in *The Song of Bernadette* (1943), and Mrs. Higgins in *My Fair Lady* (1964).

—⁂—

Elsom's debut role in Hollywood, Leonora Fiske in *Ladies in Retirement* (C. Vidor, Columbia, 1941), is a dowager with a difference. Outfitted in the period trappings of a rich, slightly flamboyant older woman of 1885, she is a lady with a past, whose "retirement" to a remote, pre–Tudor farmhouse in the Thames marshes is no doubt at least partly motivated by her desire not to encounter too much of that checkered past on a daily basis. Described by playwrights Percy and Denham as "a retired lady of easy virtue,"[13] her income has been earned not just on the stage, but through the patronage of rich men willing to support her in the style to which she has grown accustomed. This continues to the present day in the form of certain large checks that arrive regularly at her door. They allow Miss Fiske a comfortable, if not lavish, lifestyle in her reclining years, including a spacious house staffed with a housemaid, Lucy (Evelyn Keyes), and a housekeeper-companion, Ellen Creed (Ida Lupino).

Miss Fiske, then, is a distant cousin of such fictional courtesans as Aunt Alicia in *Gigi*, Madame Arnfeldt in *A Little Night Music*, and, of course, Marguerite Gautier (*Camille*). Like the two first mentioned dames, Leonora Fiske is a survivor, at least until she runs afoul of the spinsterish, self-effacing, yet determined Miss Creed. But unlike Alicia, who is still very much in the thick of things, Miss Fiske is a lady in retirement, a retirement she shares with her entirely female household. To emphasize their isolation and in ironic contrast to the less virtuous paths trodden by the ladies of "Estuary House," their nearest neighbor is a convent.

Elsom was perfect casting for a woman who is described in the play as "elderly — 60, perhaps," but who "emulates all the airs, graces, and gaiety of youth."[14] Character actresses, of course, frequently played roles older than their years, and at 48 Elsom had settled into her mature, padded, yet still striking beauty, which made her entirely credible as a former

Isobel Elsom's greatest role on stage and screen was playing the retired courtesan and murder victim Leonora Fiske in the psychological thriller *Ladies in Retirement*. Elsom created the role on Broadway and then went on to reprise it on film the following year. She was the only member of the stage cast to do so. Ida Lupino (right) plays the woman who murders her benefactress.

femme fatale. And Elsom was an ex–chorus girl to boot. Miss Fiske is described by her creators as "carefully rouged and enameled" and wearing "a somewhat obvious auburn wig, bright and curled and scented."[15] The wig was a wonderful piece of "business" that allowed Elsom to display the fussy primping of this still flirtatious old girl. She has a vividly, entertaining mock-seduction scene with a young man who suddenly materializes on her doorstep and turns out to be Ellen Creed's long lost, sticky-fingered nephew Albert Feather (Louis Hayward). With his appearance and the arrival of Ellen's two eccentric sisters (Elsa Lanchester and Edith Barrett), all the central pieces on the chess board are in place and the struggle can begin — a struggle to the death.

From Elsom's point of view, the role's major limitation was that Leonora Fiske only appears in the first act, which corresponds roughly to the first third of the film. There she portrays with perfect control the vain, pettish, but not unkind Miss Fiske, "a good-hearted woman with a shrewd sense of wit and a rather quick temper."[16] She gets involved in an escalating battle of wills with her housekeeper and companion Ellen Creed about whether or not the latter's two batty sisters should be allowed to remain in the house. Miss Fiske's insistence that they have overstayed their welcome and must leave, even though she knows they have nowhere to go, ultimately seals her fate. She spends the remainder of the film a corpse bricked up in an old oven in the middle of the living room. In a film that is all about playing and being played, Miss Fiske is ultimately defeated because she doesn't realize how much is at stake.

There were quite a few psychological thrillers about old ladies being presented on stage and screen in the 1930s and early '40s. These often unsympathetic older women didn't fare well in most of them, almost as if the culture was fantasizing about their extermination, exacting a form of symbolic punishment for their vanity, pride, and meddlesomeness. As an "old lady at risk" drama, *Ladies in Retirement* thus belongs to a subgenre of the thriller, which includes Edward Chodorov's *Kind Lady* (1935), Rodney Ackland's *The Old Ladies* (1935; entitled *Night in the House* in the U.S.), and Emlyn Williams's *Night Must Fall* (1936). *Kind Lady* was first filmed in 1935 with Aline MacMahon as wealthy art collector Mary Herries, the victimized yet ultimately surviving kind lady of the title; and remade in 1951 with Ethel Barrymore in the lead. The old ladies in Ackland's play faced no outside threat, but were at risk of being scared to death by one of their own kind. *Ladies in Retirement* most resembles *Night Must Fall* in which a stuffy, bossy, and invalid dowager, Mrs. Bramson, is brutally murdered by a disturbed young man who has inveigled himself into her affections. May Whitty played the role both on Broadway and when it was brought to the screen by MGM in 1937. On this background, *Arsenic and Old Lace* (play 1941; film 1944) emerges as an interesting twist on an established formula where the old ladies, for once, are not the victims.

Though she continued to work in films until 1964, Elsom's heyday on the big screen was the 1940s. She acted in 25 films during that decade and in some of her most visible roles, including *Ladies in Retirement, The War Against Mrs. Hadley, You Were Never Lovelier* and *Between Two Worlds. The War Against Mrs. Hadley* (H.S. Bucquet, MGM, 1942), a homefront film set among the political elite of Washington, DC, initially opposes two powerful rival hostesses who cannot abide each other: Laura Winters (Isobel Elsom) and Stella Hadley (Fay Bainter). The women are ultimately united in a common cause, though, after Mrs. Winters's son Tony is killed in action and it turns out that his bosom buddy was Mrs. Hadley's son Ted (Richard Ney). In this highly entertaining film, Elsom's part was smaller and considerably frumpier than Bainter's, but it was nevertheless a good, solid dramatic role in the wake of her success in *Ladies in Retirement*.

Maria Castro in *You Were Never Lovelier* (W.A. Seiter, Columbia, 1942) was also a showy role for Elsom and the kind she did well. Billed fourth, which was unusually high for her, she plays Rita Hayworth's classy godmother and Adolphe Menjou's cunning confidante in his attempt to help his second of four daughters fall in love, so the two younger ones can also marry. Elsom and Menjou's plotting and scheming ultimately leads Menjou's wife to suspect that they are having an affair, but Fred Astaire saves the day at the risk of imperiling his own relationship with Hayworth. Elsom looks particularly lovely in the final sequence at the celebration of Menjou and his wife's 25th wedding anniversary, where everything comes to a head and all is resolved in classic comedic fashion.

Between Two Worlds (E.A. Blatt, Warner Bros., 1944) was an ultimately tedious and unnecessary remake of the metaphysical fantasy film about what happens after we die, *Outward Bound* (1930). Here the action has been updated to a contemporary (World War II) setting with bombs dropping and death and destruction close at hand. Elsom takes up Alison Skipworth's marvelous role as the snobbish and otherwise unsympathetic Mrs. Cliveden-Banks. In this version, she is accompanied by her hard-done-by husband (Gilbert Emery). Just as in the original, she gets her comeuppance in the big "day of reckoning" scene with the "Examiner" (Sydney Greenstreet), who condemns her to live in a castle where

In the homefront drama *The War Against Mrs. Hadley* (Metro-Goldwyn-Mayer, 1942), Elsom (second from left, standing) is initially at daggers drawn with Fay Bainter (far left) as the eponymous heroine of the piece.

no one can visit her. Her cuckolded husband is rewarded by being allowed to play golf and see his old cronies in the next life. Elsom, elegantly turned out as always, with swept-up hair and all the customary airs and graces of the lady of fashion, tries to put a brave face on things, but can't help but hiss "You swine!" as she goes to her fate.

In addition to *My Fair Lady* (G. Cukor, Warner Bros., 1964), her penultimate feature film where she played Gladys Cooper's friend, Jeremy Brett's mother, and Audrey Hepburn's potential mother-in-law, Mrs. Eynsford-Hill, Elsom's most popular films today are *The Ghost and Mrs. Muir*, *Monsieur Verdoux*, *The Paradine Case*, *Lust for Life*, and *Love Is a Many-Splendored Thing*.[17] In *The Ghost and Mrs. Muir* (J.L. Mankiewicz, Twentieth Century–Fox, 1947), she has only a couple of scenes as Gene Tierney's teary-eyed, selfish mother-in-law.[18] In *Monsieur Verdoux* (C. Chaplin, Charles Chaplin Productions, 1947), she had a more substantial part as one of Chaplin's love interests, who gets left at the altar when the murderous monsieur played by Chaplin ducks out to avoid the wife he already has. As a gossipy Cumberland innkeeper who likes to say "okidoke," Elsom only had one scene in *The Paradine Case* (A. Hitchcock, Vanguard Films, 1947). In *Lust for Life* (V. Minnelli,

MGM, 1956), her single scene was as the mother of a woman who has rejected troubled painter Vincent Van Gogh (Kirk Douglas). Adeline Palmer-Jones in *Love Is a Many-Splendored Thing* (H. King, Twentieth Century–Fox, 1955) is another of Elsom's self-important, vain, and overdressed dowagers, who flirts with William Holden, makes life a misery for Jennifer Jones at the hospital where she works and ends up being admitted there after being bitten by a caterpillar.

By the late 1950s and early '60s, the traditional dowager's cultural authority had been so undermined as to make her mostly a figure of fun.[19] This development is clearly demonstrated by Elsom's career: She ended up as a Margaret Dumont–like straight woman to Jerry Lewis in four comedies: *Rock-a-Bye Baby* (F. Tashlin, Paramount, 1958), *The Bellboy* (J. Lewis, Paramount, 1960), *The Errand Boy* (J. Lewis, Paramount, 1961), and *Who's Minding the Store?* (F. Tashlin, Paramount, 1963). Elsom made up for the decline in film work with roles in television, racking up dozens of credits between 1950 and 1964. Overall, few actresses can have been busier than Isobel Elsom in the middle decades of the last century.

Elsom continued to do stage work, including Broadway shows, well into the 1950s. Her biggest success on the New York stage after *Ladies in Retirement* was a dramatization of Henry James's famous novella "The Turn of the Screw," in which she played the housekeeper Mrs. Grose and Beatrice Straight the governess Miss Giddens. Called *The Innocents*,

Her distinctively aquiline profile is still pristine, as Isobel Elsom (at age sixty-three) is seen here as a haughty, hyphenated dowager who makes trouble for Jennifer Jones (right) in *Love Is a Many-Splendored Thing* (Twentieth Century–Fox, 1955). At this late date, Elsom could do this kind of hoity-toity role with her head under her arm and her arm in a sling.

the play was directed by Peter Glenville and lasted for 141 performances at the Playhouse Theatre in the spring of 1950. Elsom was also in the cast of Glenville's next production, *The Curious Savage* (1950), a comedy with Lillian Gish, which only lasted 33 performances. By this time a favorite of Glenville's, Elsom was cast as Juliet's mother, Lady Capulet, in his 1951 revival of *Romeo and Juliet*, starring Olivia de Havilland in her Broadway debut and Douglas Watson. Evelyn Varden played Juliet's nurse. Elsom was also joined in the cast by her husband of four years, Carl Harbord, who played Friar John. A fellow expatriate born in Salcome, Devon in 1908, Harbord was 15 years younger than his wife. They married in 1947, when she was 54 and he was 39.[20] The couple may have met on the set of Universal's *Eagle Squadron*, a film about American fighter pilots in the RAF in the early days of World War II, which was produced in the spring of 1942. It was their only common film.

Harbord and Elsom also acted together in a play called *Hide and Seek* by Stanley Mann with Geraldine Fitzgerald and Basil Rathbone, which only ran for seven performances at the Ethel Barrymore Theatre in April 1957. It was Harbord's last Broadway show, while Elsom finished her more than 30-year career on the Great White Way that same spring in *The First Gentleman* (1957), a new comedy by Norman Ginsbury set in Regency England with Tony award–winning costumes by "Motley." Walter Slezak, Inga Swenson, and Peter Donat were also in the large cast, where Elsom played Caroline, Princess of Wales.

Harbord died in Los Angeles at the age of 50 on October 18, 1958. Isobel Elsom lived for another 22 years, dying of heart failure at the Motion Picture Country Home and Hospital in Woodland Hills, California on January 12, 1981.[21] Her ashes were scattered over the Pacific Ocean.[22]

Larger Than Life: Hope Emerson
in *Cry of the City* (1948)

Emerson couldn't possibly have known how adorable she was.[1]

The big hit Broadway show of the summer of 1930 was "a modern version of the one Greek classic that has lived most persistently through twenty-one hundred years," namely *Lysistrata* by Aristophanes from around 415 B.C. Norman Bel Geddes staged and designed the show and Gilbert Seldes adapted the text. "No great liberties were taken by either," writes Burns Mantle, "in the matter of cleaning up the lines and situations of the frankly rowdy Aristophanes." At the out-of-town opening in Philadelphia, Mantle adds, "the less elastically minded of the Quakers ... gasped quite audibly."[2]

The show about a group of ancient Greek women who occupy the Acropolis and "abstain from love until their men folk have made peace" and put an end to the Peloponnesian wars became "a social and theatrical event" and the success in Philadelphia "kept it out of New York for several weeks."[3] It finally opened at the 44th Street Theatre on June 5, 1930, and ran for 252 performances.

According to theater historian Mary C. Henderson, "modern dance made its conscious debut on Broadway" in this show, through the choreography of Charles Weidman and Doris Humphrey.[4] The enormous cast included Violet Kemble Cooper as Lysistrata, the instigator of the "wife strike," Miriam Hopkins, Hortense Alden, Sydney Greenstreet, and Ernest Truex. *New York Times* critic Brooks Atkinson called it "a memorable flow of color and motion."[5] Blanche Yurka, who replaced Kemble Cooper in the lead in early September, recalled in her memoirs, "It was really thrilling to realize that modern audiences on the island of Manhattan were laughing at the same humor which had 'mowed 'em down' in Athens over two thousand years before."[6]

In the midst of all this excitement, making her Broadway debut as Lampito, Lysistrata's deputy who rallies the Spartan women to the cause, was a 32-year-old woman, 6'2" tall in her stocking feet, weighing somewhere between 190 and 230 lbs., swarthy, dark-haired, with coal-black eyes.[7] That woman was Hope Emerson, who would go on to become a unique presence in American films of the late 1940s and '50s. On the eve of her first Broadway opening, her film career was still in the future. Yet she had already come far from her beginnings in the small Iowa town of Hawarden, where she was born on October 29, 1897. Hawarden (pronounced *Hay*-warden) is a community of about 2,500 on the Big Sioux River in northwest Iowa, almost at the exact center of the North American continent. On the cultural front, Hawarden can boast of being the birthplace of Emerson and writer Ruth Suckow (1892–1960), who died just three months before her.

Family tradition has it that Emerson's mother, Josephine Washburn Emerson, a performer in vaudeville in a troupe called "Angels Comedians," first tempted her daughter onto the stage to do a cakewalk when she was three.[8] One of the most valuable gifts her mother gave her was piano lessons. In future years, Emerson would be known for her "hot" piano act: "[H]er large figure huddled over a small piano was a popular act in supper clubs."[9] Playing in piano bars and clubs was her mainstay, especially when there was little other work to be had. In her youth, mother and daughter performed together, including a stint with a stage mystic and hypnotist known as "Caruthers the Psychic." Emerson would be given coded hand signals from her mother as to what to play when Caruthers had audience members whisper song suggestions in his ear, convincing them of his ability to convey this information supernaturally to Emerson.[10] Later, producer Billy House hired her and wrote her first vaudeville act, "June and Buckeye," which ran for three years.[11]

When she first arrived in New York, Emerson recalled, "she 'starved successfully' for several seasons before clicking as the leader of the Amazons [sic] in *Lysistrata*."[12] *Lysistrata* appears to have been Emerson's only stab at the classics, at least on Broadway. After the show ended in January 1931, she had to wait a year and a half for her next Broadway opening: a musical comedy at the Shubert Theatre called *Smiling Faces* (1932). As Amy Edwards, she "danced, sang, and played the piano."[13] That frothy failure was followed in 1936 by the "Wrestling Ring Rumpus" *Swing Your Lady*.[14] The lady in question was Emerson herself, in the role of the local blacksmith in Joplin, Missouri, Sadie Horn, "a gargantuan Amazon with a careless attitude toward life."[15] Sadie finds herself scheduled to wrestle the professional "Greek Hercules" Joe Skopapoulos (John Alexander). Ultimately, Joe falls in love with Sadie and "will not endanger her charms,"[16] so she has to forgo her moment of glory. But not only that: Sadie's replacement in the ring, the "man mountain" Noah Wulliver (Al Ochs), is the father of one of her illegitimate offspring! This "preposterous yarn" about a bunch of "riff-raff people" ran for 105 performances at the Booth Theatre,[17] a testament to Emerson's drawing power. "As that vigorous anvil woman of the hills," Brooks Atkinson wrote, "Hope Emerson is a monumental figure, though not very much of a comedienne."[18]

Her next Broadway show was a short-lived revival of the Oscar Hammerstein and Sigmund Romberg musical *The New Moon* (1942), followed by the comedy *Chicken Every Sunday* (1944–45), which ran for a respectable nine months. A kind of poor relation of *You Can't Take It with You* and *Life with Father*, the play was set in a boarding house where Emerson played a "former actress who yodels" in a "minor but noisy role."[19]

Emerson's next Broadway offering was a musical version of the Elmer Rice classic *Street Scene* (1947) with a book by Rice himself, music by Kurt Weill, and lyrics by Langston Hughes. It won two Tonys: for Weill's score and for Lucinda Ballard's costumes. Emerson was cast as the nasty neighborhood gossip of all time, Emma Jones, a role created by Beulah Bondi both in the original Broadway production at the Playhouse Theatre in 1929–30 and in the film version directed by King Vidor in 1931. Emerson had two songs, though no solos: "Get a Load of That" and "Ain't It Awful, the Heat?" Atkinson found her "vastly entertaining as the garrulous old crone" and raved about this "musical play of magnificence and glory," which "finds the song of humanity under the argot of the New York streets."[20]

The Magic Touch, a comedy by Charles Raddock and Charles Sherman, had the shortest run of any of Emerson's Broadway shows in September 1947. Emerson's final bow on a Broadway stage was also her only drama there. *The Cup of Trembling* (1948) was written and directed by Paul Czinner and starred his wife, Elisabeth Bergner, as a newspaper woman "sharing the torment of alcoholism with the audience." This "clinical study in a baffling

In her debut film *Cry of the City* (Twentieth Century–Fox, 1948), Hope Emerson was an absolute knockout as a murderous masseuse. Here she has a firm grasp on fellow player and bad boy Richard Conte, who for a brief time becomes her partner in crime. They also did *House of Strangers* and *Thieves' Highway* together at Fox.

disease" lasted only 31 performances at the Music Box Theatre. "After one of the longest plays Eugene O'Neill never wrote," quipped one reviewer, "It will be lucky if this painful spectacle does not drive most of the first-nighters to alcoholism." He found that Hope Emerson, as "a husky cook," was one of the several supporting cast members who "behave creditably" and "conspire to sober Miss Bergner up."[21]

By this time, Emerson had embarked on the last phase of her career, where new opportunities for work in film and television brought her to Hollywood for the final dozen years of her life. Her first film was shot between her last two Broadway shows, starting on December 26, 1947, and finishing in February 1948 with retakes and extra scenes in mid–March. Emerson's debut in *Cry of the City* (R. Siodmak, Twentieth Century–Fox, 1948) is so stunning it bears comparison with Judith Anderson in *Rebecca* (1940) and Agnes Moorehead in *The Magnificent Ambersons* (1942).[22] Unlike them, Emerson had to wait till her ninth film to be Oscar nominated, but she clearly knew what she was about on the screen from the start.

Unlike *Rebecca* and *The Magnificent Ambersons*, *Cry of the City* is no masterpiece. A "taut and grimly realistic melodrama ... of the documentary like school of film fiction,"[23] it is a well-crafted, well cast and finely acted urban crime drama with a dark, brooding, noirish atmosphere. Plot-wise it's a modern-day Cain and Abel story about two Italian American men, played by Victor Mature and Richard Conte, who chose different paths in life. Mature's character, Vittorio Candella, becomes a cop and Conte's Martin Rome a gang-ster.

Emerson doesn't appear until more than an hour into the movie and dominates it from there on out. In her first appearance in any film, Emerson is first seen coming down a long hallway, a huge, looming, white-clad figure, who turns on the lights as she comes. In the words of Boyd McDonald, it was "a prolonged star entrance unequaled by any I've seen since Mae West's dazzling entrance in *Catherine Was Great* on Broadway."[24] Emerson plays the murderous masseuse "Madame Rose," who runs her own massage institute, where she, in her own words, tries to make vain, rich, ugly old women look young again. Rose Givens, as is her proper name, has been in cahoots with a gangster, Whitey Leggett, to murder one of these ladies and steal her jewels, but a shady lawyer has got his hooks into them. When the lawyer is killed, the jewels come into the hands of Rome, the small time hood played by Conte. He tries to make a deal with Rose to help him get out of the country in exchange for the key to the locker in the 18th Street subway station, where he has stashed the loot. In their first meeting in the apartment at the back of her establishment, she almost strangles him to get the key, which he wisely hasn't brought with him.[25] The next morning, Rose enjoys a hearty breakfast and talks with her mouth full, while Martin will have nothing. Things start to go wrong when Rose pulls a gun and insists on Martin coming with her to get the jewels, before she gives him the money and boat ticket to South America ("What a thrill, to be riding in a cab and have Emerson pull her heater on you,"[26] one fan enthuses). You see, Martin has already tipped off the police. A desperate Miss Givens shoots Lieutenant Candella in the subway station, while struggling with her apprehenders, but is finally over-powered and placed under arrest.

Emerson is perfect casting for this grasping, vulgar, hulking urban creature, who wants the jewels in order to buy a place in the country where she can have fresh eggs and milk every day. She is simply enormous in her perfectly starched, clinically white uniform and speaks in a calm, dry, monotonous voice, that is effective and menacing. Even the deliberate way in which she says Martin's name is chilling. The *New York Times* singled her out for first mention after the male leads in their review, writing: "[A]mong fine supporting roles those of Hope Emerson, a thin-lipped, Amazon of a woman out of the Broadway stage."[27] In a vividly observed appreciation of Emerson in *Cry of the City*, Boyd McDonald writes: "To see her is not to see an actor acting but a person being, manipulating the audience by her mere existence rather than by technical effort.

"Emerson's main physical asset," he goes on, "apart from her large size" is "her depressed 'down' face with its fantastically cold eyes." He concludes, "She has her way with the audience as easily as she does with Conte."[28]

After *Cry of the City*, Emerson said half-humorously, "I got into the worst rut on the screen, killing, choking people, and playing jail matrons."[29] She was a highly gifted, but physically limited actress. What she could do with her voice, her bearing, and small, subtle gestures and expressions, no one could do better. On the other hand, her gargantuan phy-sique rendered her ridiculous in any role that required her to blend in or assume a conven-tional feminine demeanor. This contrast between the masculine and the feminine worked well in comedy, but not always in drama. I have in mind a particularly egregious example of miscasting in *House of Strangers* (J.L. Mankiewicz, Twentieth Century–Fox, 1949). Emer-son has a minor role as Debra Paget's widowed mother, Helena Domenico, in this saga of a maladjusted Italian American family, starring Edward G. Robinson, Susan Hayward, and Richard Conte. Covered head to toe in regulation widow's weeds, her hair done up in a

As the sympathetic warden in the "women behind bars" classic *Caged* (Warner Bros., 1950), Agnes Moorehead finds the dishonest and sadistic matron played by Hope Emerson (right) difficult to dislodge from her position. In this scene, they go head to head. While Emerson looks smugly at Moorehead, she for once has the star's privilege of looking inward.

thick twisted braid on the top of her head, Emerson looks and sounds about as Italian as Calamity Jane.

Twentieth Century–Fox had brought Emerson to Hollywood and put her under contract to do *Cry of the City*,[30] and then clearly was faced with the problem of what else to do with her. *House of Strangers* was one attempt, in addition to equally modest bits in *That Wonderful Urge* (R.B. Sinclair, 1948), *Thieves' Highway* (J. Dassin, 1949), and *Dancing in the Dark* (I. Reis, 1949). Emerson would make a total of 20 feature films and work for several other studios before her film career ended after a decade with a tiny part in the Jerry Lewis comedy *Rock-a-Bye Baby* (F. Tashlin, Paramount, 1958).

Her biggest opportunity during these years would come in 1949, when she was cast as the nastiest prison matron of all time, Evelyn Harper. *Caged* (J. Cromwell, Warner Bros., 1950) is a famous film and deservedly so. The huge, almost entirely female cast is brimming with talented actresses, including Eleanor Parker, Agnes Moorehead, Ellen Corby, Betty Garde, Lee Patrick, and Gertrude Michael. Yet standing literally and metaphorically head and shoulders above them all is Emerson. She was Oscar-nominated for her role, as were Parker and the writers of the original screenplay, Virginia Kellogg and Bernard C. Schoenfeld. It was an extremely competitive year, with multiple nominations for *All About Eve*, *Harvey*, *Sunset Blvd.*, and *Born Yesterday*. *Caged* lost on all three counts: Emerson to Josephine

Though she did her share of costume dramas, Hope Emerson had something quintessentially modern about her that made her best suited to stories of contemporary life. Here we see her (center left, under light) as Ma Tarbet in *Copper Canyon* (Paramount Pictures, 1950) with star Hedy Lamarr (center right). It is rare to see Emerson wearing so much makeup and the effect is about as cozy as putting red shutters on a Nissen hut.

Hull in *Harvey*; Parker to Judy Holliday in *Born Yesterday*, and the writers to *Sunset Blvd.* David Quinlan points out the ironic fact that Emerson lost to "one of the screen's smallest actresses."[31] Hull was an entire foot shorter than Emerson.

Emerson remained unmarried throughout her life and had no children. Her lesbian reputation seems to rest almost entirely on her performance in *Caged* and being bigger physically than most men. Neither of these factors can be used to understand her sexual orientation. Her cousin writes on a tribute page online, "Hope had her share of gentlemen trying for her affections and her hand in marriage, but she never married."[32] The only thing historian of gay and lesbian Hollywood William Mann comes up with relating to Emerson is that she attended parties hosted by Cole Porter and gay *Hollywood Reporter* columnist Mike Connolly.[33] This might only mean that she enjoyed socializing with gay men. Connolly, it turns out, considered Emerson "one of my closest friends in Hollywood." He may have been the last friend to speak to her before she died.[34]

Emerson's most important relationship throughout her life was with her mother Josie. Emerson's father Jack died in 1935 and at that point her mother's health began to decline.[35] Josie ended up in a wheelchair, but that did not prevent Emerson from taking her with her wherever she went, including film premieres. The story goes that at the premiere of *Caged*

Markedly older and thinner in this still from *Champ for a Day* (Republic Pictures, 1953), Hope Emerson is seen with her screen husband Charles Winninger behind the counter. As Ma and Pa Karlsen, owners of a motel, they befriend a young boxer played by Alex Nicol (left).

on June 10, 1950, Emerson and her wheelchair-bound mother were "surrounded by a deafening wall of boos and hisses" as they left the movie theater![36] When Josie died three years later, her daughter was devastated. Mike Connolly wrote, "I don't believe my friend Hope ever recovered from the death of her devoted mother, Josephine, who was also Hope's partner in the old days of vaudeville."[37]

After suffering from a liver ailment for some time, Emerson died in Hollywood Presbyterian Hospital on April 25, 1960, the seventh anniversary of her mother's death.[38] Her estate, valued at $75,000, was left to friends and family.[39] According to her *New York Times* obituary, "She maintained homes at Hawarden, Iowa, where she was born, and in New York and Hollywood."[40] After a private funeral service at Pierce Brothers Mortuary in Hollywood, Emerson came home to Hawarden for the last time and was buried next to her parents in Grace Hill Cemetery.[41]

Deep Freeze: Mary Forbes
in *You Can't Take It with You* (1938)

*"If you had any sense, young woman, you'd stay
where you belong and stop being ambitious."*

In her autobiography, Maureen Stapleton recalled the summer of 1948, which she spent in Westport, Connecticut, in a summer stock production of *The Beaux' Stratagem*, George Farquhar's early eighteenth-century comedy. Brian Aherne starred and directed. Stapleton played the modest part of Cherry, the landlord's daughter, and with no great success, as she recalled in the mid–1990s. Also in the cast of this classic Restoration comedy, playing Lady Bountiful, a wealthy widow and mother of the fair heroine, Dorinda, was an English actress called Mary Forbes. "Mary was a beautiful gray-haired lady, very distinguished and very, very dear," Stapleton writes. One morning at breakfast at the hotel in which they were staying, Stapleton declared to Forbes that she wanted to get married. "Oh *do*, ducky," Forbes responded. "It's wonderful. I've done it five times."[1]

When Stapleton worked with her in 1948, Mary Forbes was approximately 68 years old and had been living in the United States for 20 years. I say approximately, because the members of the Forbes family of actors seem to have liked to spread contradictory reports about their age, as is not uncommon among thespians. Usually, if there are several possible years of birth indicated for an actor, then the earliest one given by a reliable source is the one to go with. In that case, it would mean Mary Forbes was born in 1879, December 30, 1879, to be exact, in Hornsey, England, which lies north of Islington and is now part of Greater London.[2]

Forbes made her stage debut in England in 1907 and would work steadily, if not stellarly, in the theater for the next 40 years. In 1913, she made her American stage debut in an Edward Sheldon play called *Romance* at Maxine Elliott's Theatre. In the late 1920s, Forbes moved to California to pursue the new opportunities offered in the movie industry by the coming of sound. She would remain there until her death 45 years later, though stage work would take her elsewhere, including Broadway, up until the late 1940s.[3]

Forbes lent her stately presence to more than 130 feature films between 1929 and 1958. She worked the most and the longest at MGM, Universal, and Twentieth Century–Fox. In the 1950s, she was also seen in a few television programs, but during the last 30 years of her long acting career, she was first and foremost a movie actress. David Ragan calls her "perhaps Hollywood's queen of the dowagers."[4] It's a good thing he writes "perhaps," for there were many contenders for that title. Forbes's claim, despite her many films, is not as strong as, say, fellow Englishwoman Isobel Elsom. The majority of Forbes's film roles were

In several films, Mary Forbes (left) was little more than a dress extra, as here in ***Born to Love*** (RKO, 1931), starring Constance Bennett (center left), where Forbes played the uncredited role of a duchess. In this group photograph, we also recognize suave, dimpled Paul Cavanagh (standing) and Louise Closser Hale (far right) with something resembling a tea cozy on her head.

bit parts or "under fives" that is to say — she had less than five lines and usually only appeared in one scene. About half her roles were uncredited, so there may yet be new Forbes appearances in old films waiting to be discovered.

Today Forbes's five most recognizable films in order of popularity are *You Can't Take It with You*, *Ninotchka*, *The Awful Truth*, *Captain Blood*, and *The Picture of Dorian Gray*, though that doesn't necessarily mean she is recognizable in them. In *Ninotchka* (MGM, 1939), the Ernst Lubitsch comedy starring Greta Garbo and Melvyn Douglas, Forbes played an uncredited role as Lady Lavenham, who in the Internet Movie Database is described as "Indignant Woman in Doorway." I'm afraid this bravura performance has not fastened itself in my memory. In *The Awful Truth* (L. McCarey, Columbia, 1937), on the other hand, Forbes was considerably more visible in a credited role (albeit at the bottom of the list) as Mrs. Vance, one of Park Avenue's finest, mother to heiress Barbara Vance (Molly Lamont), and hostess at the party where newly separated Lucy Warriner creates a small scandal by pretending to be her soon-to-be-*ex*-husband Jerry Warriner's rather folksy sister. The Warriners were played by Irene Dunne and Cary Grant. In *Captain Blood* (M. Curtiz, Warner Bros., 1935), we find Forbes briefly appearing as Mrs. Steed, the wife of the governor of Port Royal. Her involvement in *The Picture of Dorian Gray* (A. Lewin, MGM, 1945) 10 years later was hardly more protracted. She played George Sanders's aunt, Lady Agatha, and was billed twelfth.

In many cases, Forbes was little more than a glorified dress extra. A dress extra was used to lend style and panache to party scenes and other scenes where sartorial elegance was called for. The reigning queen of the dress extras, Bess Flowers (1898–1984), lent her regal, perfectly outfitted, and quietly unassuming presence to more than 300 films from *Innocents of Paris* (1929) to *Good Neighbor Sam* (1964), yet most of us wouldn't be able to identify her if our lives depended on it. Next time you watch *Theodora Goes Wild* (R. Boleslawski, Columbia, 1936), *The Secret Life of Walter Mitty* (N.Z. McLeod, Samuel Goldwyn, 1947) or *Houseboat* (M. Shavelson, Paramount, 1958), see if you can't spot Bess Flowers. While you're at it, you can look for Mary Forbes, too.[5] She was uncredited as Mrs. Wyatt,

You Can't Buy Everything (Metro-Goldwyn-Mayer, 1934) was loosely based on the story of millionaire miser Hetty Green. May Robson (left) played the miser, while Mary Forbes put in an appearance as a well-heeled and well-meaning society woman trying to show Robson the error of her ways. As this still vividly demonstrates, Robson rather gets the better of her.

the governor's wife with a butch haircut at the ball in the first film; uncredited as Mrs. Pierce in the second; and uncredited as "British Society Woman" in the third, which was her final film.

Despite bit roles in a couple of films of the 1950s, by 1949 Forbes's film career was to all intents and purposes over and she went into semi-retirement. On July 24, 1974, the *New York Times* reported that she had died the preceding day in a nursing home in Beaumont, California, near Cherry Valley, where she'd lived for many years. She was survived by her husband, Wesley Wall, and daughter Brenda Forbes.[6]

As for Forbes's marriages, Stapleton may have exaggerated the number for effect, as I have only come across mention of three husbands in Mary Forbes's life. The first on record was E.J. Taylor, who was the father of Forbes's son Ralph Taylor, better known to the world as matinee idol and movie star Ralph Forbes (1896–1951).[7] Forbes also had a daughter who followed in her footsteps, Brenda Forbes (1909–1996), a Tony-nominated actress who worked on Broadway and in films until the end of her long life.[8] Mary Forbes's second husband was fellow actor Charles Quartermaine (1877–1958), born in Richmond, Surrey, and the brother of actor Leon Quartermaine, whose second wife was the actress Fay Compton. Quartermaine was seen with Forbes in her first important sound film *The Thirteenth Chair* (T. Browning, MGM, 1929). Finally, Forbes was married to house builder Wesley Wall, born in 1900 and thus more than 20 years her junior. Wall died in 1977.[9]

⁂

Playing Mrs. Anthony Kirby in *You Can't Take It with You* (1938) was no doubt Mary Forbes's best assignment during her years in Hollywood. Based on a Pulitzer Prize–winning, hit play by the fabled writing team of George S. Kaufman and Moss Hart, it was directed by the equally legendary Frank Capra, who saw this as "a golden opportunity to dramatize Love Thy Neighbor in living drama."[10] According to film historian Ed Sikov, *You Can't Take It with You* "captured the escapist spirit of the times better than almost any other play or musical for the simple reason that escapism was explicitly the play's theme."[11]

The film rights to *You Can't Take It with You* were bought by Capra's home studio Columbia Pictures for $200,000, which according to *Variety* made it "one of the higher priced plays to be bought in history."[12] On January 5, 1938, the *New York Times* wrote that "Columbia has begun testing for the principal parts in *You Can't Take It with You*."[13] Casting was complete by April 8.[14] Among the stellar ensemble cast brought together for the film, we find Jean Arthur and James Stewart as Alice Sycamore and Tony Kirby, the young couple who must overcome comic yet significant class differences to live happily ever after; Alice's unconventional parents, Penny and Paul Sycamore (Spring Byington and Samuel S. Hinds); Alice's equally quirky maternal grandfather, head of the clan and leader in a rebellion against materialism and blind conformity, Grandpa Martin Vanderhof (Lionel Barrymore); and Tony's parents, the millionaire businessman Anthony Kirby and his wife, Miriam.

Mr. Kirby was to be played by the outstanding character actor Edward Arnold. Capra later revealed that he had postponed the picture for two months to get Arnold, whom he had never worked with before. "Arnold had the power and presence of a J.P. Morgan," Capra writes in his autobiography. "He could be as unctuous as a funeral director, or as cold and ruthless as a Cosa Nostra chief." Capra also writes that Arnold "was anathema to directors": "In take after take he would blow his lines and shrug it off with that phony laugh. Other actors could wring his neck. They would have to give their all in take after take, just in case Arnold *didn't* blow his lines. The result: Arnold got all the attention. Distraught directors would okay *any* take that he finished, regardless of how the other tired-out actors fared.[15] In his autobiography, Capra runs through nearly the entire cast of the film, but does not mention Mary Forbes.

The screenplay was written by Robert Riskin, who was Oscar-nominated for his screenplays five times, including for *You Can't Take It with You*, and won for *It Happened One Night* (1934). As *Variety*'s reviewer pointed out, as much of the original Kaufman-Hart dialogue as possible had been retained.[16] The changes made were par for the course in adaptations of plays then and now. The setting shifts instead of being limited to the wacky Vanderhof family's home on the Upper West Side, near Columbia University. The story starts earlier in the sense that scenes are added to introduce Alice Sycamore, Tony Kirby, and their widely differing families, that chronologically fall prior to the opening scene of the play.

The "opening up" through depicting events from the backstory gives Forbes one of her best scenes in the film, which is also her first. Mrs. Kirby surprises her son Tony (James Stewart) kissing his secretary-stenographer Alice (Jean Arthur) at the office. Lest this risqué scenario sound like a throwback to the riotous pre–Code days, I hasten to add that Tony has already told his mother that he is in love with Alice and intends to marry her. At any rate, Mrs. Kirby gives Alice one of the most intimidating stares in film history and turns heel with the parting remark: "If you'll excuse me, I think I'll visit with your father for a while." In her next appearance, in a restaurant, Mrs. Kirby is gorgeously arrayed in full evening dress with roses in her hair and looks youthful and attractive. She and Mr. Kirby are giving a dinner for Lord and Lady Millbank, when Tony and Alice show up. Finally, Alice is properly introduced to her prospective mother-in-law.

Despite these added scenes, the main part of the action still takes place in the Vanderhof home. Mrs. Kirby's third scene, the only one she has in the play, is the big family get-together at the Vanderhofs' (which Mr. Kirby refers to as a "slumming tour"), where the Kirbys arrive a day early (Stewart's none too popular surprise) to find the family having "a quiet evening at home," i.e., total chaos reigns. Alice's plainspoken mother, Penny Sycamore, insults Mrs. Kirby by saying that occultism is a silly hobby (to Mr. Kirby's evident amusement). Mr. Kirby ends up wrestling with an eccentric, artsy, Russian friend of the family, Boris Kolenhov (Mischa Auer), and everyone is arrested and taken down to the police station for disturbing the peace. Mrs. Kirby faints for the first of two times. This contretemps leads to a wonderful scene in the cooler with some shady ladies giving Mrs. Kirby the once over and Alice trying to defend her by saying, "Can't you see she's a lady?" At the court hearing, they run the risk of being fined, because Mrs. Kirby forbids her husband from explaining what they were doing at the Vanderhof house, fearing for her social position. Ultimately, of course, all is well and order is restored.

When *You Can't Take It with You* premiered on August 23, 1938, the original play was still playing at the Booth Theatre in New York. According to Sikov, it was "one of the few instances in which a Broadway play ran concurrently with its own movie adaptation."[17] The show closed on December 3, 1938, after an almost two-year run and 838 performances.

Opinions have been divided on the success of this filmatization. Writing in *Variety*, Roy Chartier commented that fun was had "at the expense of Edward Arnold, the stuff-shirt banker, and his wife, played excellently by Mary Forbes."[18] Forbes was seldom singled out for praise, or even mentioned in reviews, so this must have been gratifying. Frank S. Nugent, writing in the *New York Times*, concluded, "*You Can't Take It with You* jumps smack into the list of the year's best."[19]

Mary Forbes (right) was just one member of the multi-talented ensemble cast of Frank Capra's *You Can't Take It with You* (Columbia Pictures, 1938). Here she is seen with screen husband and tycoon Edward Arnold and wannabe danseuse Ann Miller during a disastrous dinner party on the Upper West Side, which puts all Forbes's social graces to the test.

The film's posthumous reputation has not been as favorable with film scholars and historians, though it remains a popular favorite. Capra expert Donald C. Willis takes the most critical stance, writing in his book *The Films of Frank Capra*, "The movie goes wrong in so many ways that it's a wonder it's any good at all." To Willis's way of thinking, Capra's expansion of Mr. Kirby's role into what the director calls a "villain-hero" in his autobiography was a mistake: "Ironically, it's when the stage is all Arnold's that the movie is at its worst. Far from eliminating what Capra calls the 'cardboard bad guy' of the play, he and Riskin play right into that tired variation, the cardboard-bad-guy redeemed. You can see the redemption coming a mile down the track, and it's a slow freight." Willis also find fault with the expansion of the storyline to include actions and settings that are only mentioned in the play. The original is restricted to the Vanderhof home, as mentioned, while the film knows no such limitations; the sets range from the business headquarters of the Kirby empire to the local jail and the courtroom. "It's wildly different locations are like the sets for three or four different movies," writes Willis. "It has no mobility, no continuity between sequences."[20]

Ed Sikov points out that the Vanderhofs' wealth, modest as it is, is a key element of the comic fantasy. He adds: "It's much easier to embrace a philosophy of personal fulfillment when you're assured of being fed, housed, and clothed without having to lift a finger."[21] Joseph McBride also remains unconvinced that there is any deep ideological critique or genuine spirit of revolt in *You Can't Take It with You*: "It is, by and large, a safe nonconformity, without risk of adverse economic or social consequences and therefore a meaningless form of pseudo-revolt."[22] Willis observed in 1974, "The philosophic import of these scenes [at the Vanderhofs'] is appalling: these free spirits are silly buffoons obsessed with inconsequential matters, the implicit point being that to be free is to be a jerk." Willis suggests that in a film where even the tycoon Kirby is converted to Grandpa Vanderhof's dubious philosophy, Mrs. Kirby has a special function as a "last holdout," who "remains skeptical of the joys of lunacy at fadeout, though it looks as though she's succumbing."[23] McBride concludes on a more positive note: "Simplistic and rough and uneven though it may be, it is an infectious, all but irresistible film whose virtues are in the broad but delightful playing of its ensemble cast and in the director's often masterful orchestration of comic business."[24]

Clothes Horse: Marjorie Gateson
in *Cocktail Hour* (1933)

The 1930s seemed to spawn a whole school of Classic Bitches.[1]

Where do character actresses in the movies come from? Well, the short and simple answer is that they come from the theater. Every single female supporting player I can think of was stage trained, with the exception of the African American actresses. In their careers, it was not unusual that playing maids on the big screen followed, or even accompanied, being a maid in real life. But for the rest, a solid background in live acting was a common denominator and a career stepping stone for several generations of Hollywood character actresses, whether they once had been stage stars, like Ethel Barrymore, Billie Burke, and Alice Brady, or had been character players from the start, like Beulah Bondi, Elizabeth Patterson, and Helen Westley. Some had Broadway careers, others worked mostly in stock and touring companies, but roles in so called "straight" plays (that is to say, comedy and drama) predominated. Marjorie Gateson was different in that she was "strictly a product of musical comedy,"[2] rather than what was known as the "legitimate" theater. The woman who came to be recognized on the big screen as "one of our most stately and sophisticated matrons"[3] started her near-six-decade-long career in the chorus.

Marjorie Augusta Gateson was born in Brooklyn, New York, on January 17, 1891. Her father, Daniel T. Gateson, was a Brooklyn contractor; her mother, Augusta Virginia Gateson, was a "teacher of speech art"; and her maternal grandfather was the Rev. John D. Kennedy, rector of St. Mark's Episcopal Church in Brooklyn.[4] Gateson grew up with three siblings: a brother who became an Episcopal rector; a brother who became a mining engineer; and a sister, who was living with her mother at 68 Beverly Road, Kew Garden, Queens, at the time of Mrs. Gateson's death from a heart attack in 1934.[5]

Augusta Gateson was without a doubt the biggest influence on her daughter's life. There are many examples of strong bonds between mothers and their actress daughters. In this book alone, you can read about Jane Cowl and her mother Grace Avery Bailey, Josephine Hull and Mary Elizabeth Tewksbury Sherwood, and Hope Emerson and Josie Washburn Emerson. Beyond maternal support and encouragement, Gateson had the added benefit of her mother's professional guidance and instruction. Augusta Gateson taught speech at the Brooklyn Conservatory of Music, where her daughter would be a student, gave dramatic readings, and according to her obituary "had a studio in Carnegie Hall until a year before her death."[6] Gateson said herself that her "diction, poise and love of the theater stemmed from her mother's teaching and were responsible for her generally portraying women of elegance and social standing."[7]

On the back of this press photograph, issued in connection with the release of *Private Number* (Twentieth Century–Fox, 1936), we can read: "Showing the clever use of wide beige ribbon draped into a becoming off-the-face hat, this model is designed for Marjorie Gateson, who plays the role of a smart Park Avenue matron." The aforesaid matron was Paul Harvey's dutiful wife, Robert Taylor's doting mother, and Loretta Young's reluctant mother-in-law in the film.

Marjorie Gateson made her Broadway debut in a new musical called *The Dove of Peace*, which opened at the Broadway Theatre on November 4, 1912, and ran for 12 performances. She was 21 years old and part of the chorus. The *New York Times* reviewer thought the show needed more comedy and tunes, but mentioned especially that the chorus was "exceptional" and that it "sang some exceedingly difficult music extremely well."[8] Gateson had better luck with her next Broadway outing, *The Little Café*, where she played two named roles. The show was a hit and ran for 144 performances at the New Amsterdam Theatre from November 1913 till March 1914. *Around the Map* (1915–16) was another step up the ladder, though she didn't yet have any songs of her own, nor rate a mention in the *New York Times* review. As Lizzie O'Brien in the Jerome Kern–P.G. Wodehouse–Guy Bolton musical *Have a Heart*, which played at the Liberty Theatre in early 1917, she had a couple of songs. She was mentioned in the *New York Times* review, too, though only in a list of "the principals less well known."[9] As Pinkie Pestlewaite in *Fancy Free* (1918), she could read that she and a couple of her co-stars were "pleasant all, if not particularly distinguished," while a young dancer called Marilyn Miller ("very young and most charming") and leading man Clifton Crawford got all the praise.[10]

Gateson continued to work steadily on Broadway until 1930. Despite being described in her mother's 1934 obituary as "the former prima donna of Broadway musical shows," she was never a star with her name in lights, but played good, solid, principal roles in a variety of musical comedies with mostly decent runs. She was in the *Shubert Gaieties of 1919*, which was suspended for a month due to the Actors' Equity Strike. She was seen as Amy Shirley in *Little Miss Charity*, a musical remake of a failed farce from 1918 called *Not with My Money*, which rose from the ashes at the Belmont Theatre in the fall of 1920 and was reviewed by Alexander Woollcott, no less. He found "the choice of such a piece for such a purpose ... quite puzzling, for it has few of the ingredients that have come to be accepted as making the basis for an evening of merriment, innocent or otherwise." Woollcott thought that Gateson gave "some agreeable aid" to Frank Moulan, the only "old standby" in a cast that "numbers a good many people that have yet to make their fame on Broadway."[11]

Gateson worked steadily in Broadway musical comedies until 1927. *The Love Letter* (1921) with Alice Brady and Fred and Adele Astaire saw only 31 performances. *For Goodness Sake* (1922), with the Astaires once more, was more successful. They were "ingratiating" and "delightful comedians"; she was "the personable if oversure Marjorie Gateson."[12] *Lady Butterfly* (1923), no relation of "Madame," lasted three and a half months. In *Sweet Little Devil* (1924), starring Constance Binney, "Miss Marjorie Gateson was a charming girl of the merry-merry, intent upon saving the hero from the perils of the possession of property."[13] Her last musical comedy, *Oh, Ernest!* (1927), a musical version of *The Importance of Being Earnest*, did not please Brooks Atkinson, who wrote, "From almost any point of view it seems to be below the average of musical comedies" and likened it to "a dance of death on the coffin lid."[14]

Gateson had her first role in a straight play, and a leading role to boot, as Nina Buck-master, "a woman candidate for the Mayoralty of a small town,"[15] in the comedy *So This Is Politics*, which opened at Henry Miller's Theatre on June 16, 1924, and ran until October. *Hidden* (1927) was her first drama, written by William J. Hurlbut and directed and produced by David Belasco at the Lyceum Theatre. Atkinson found this psychoanalytically inspired play about a woman falling in love with her sister's husband "tedious."[16] Gateson was in a supporting role and escaped injury from Atkinson's razor-sharp pen; in fact, she wasn't mentioned at all. *Hidden* was followed by its diametric opposite, a helium balloon of a French-inspired farce, *The Great Necker*, about a Don Juan who finally settles down. Gateson played "the somewhat superfluous part of the bridegroom's friend, [who] has little to do beyond arranging flowers in vases and looking interested when he speaks of his profligate past."[17]

All in all, Gateson seems to have been more fortunate in her choice of musicals than straight plays. *Security* (1929) landed her again in a rarified atmosphere of marital infidelity and upper-class decadence, which would prove her fictional "slice of life" for the remainder of her career, though she had not yet been promoted to the leading role of the wronged wife.

That happened in a comedy called *As Good as New* in late 1930; it was her last Broadway show before she went to Hollywood.[18] Her role there as Mrs. Eleanor Banning, a married woman of the moneyed class with certain marital complications, who cares more about appearances than realities, was prophetic casting.

For nearly three decades and in dozens of films at all the major studios, Gateson would be identified with one basic role: the elegant, upper-class married lady.[19] I can't think of any character actress who, through nearly 100 feature films, so consistently portrayed the same type as did Marjorie Gateson. By the time she arrived in Hollywood in 1931, she was 40 years old, had settled into a sort of timeless, classical beauty and maintained a slim and trim body that was neither too thick nor too thin. She was also of average height and thus in every way physically disposed to become a living, breathing, and talking dressmaker's dummy.[20] But Gateson was, of course, more than that. With Gateson in your film, you were not just getting someone who could wear clothes, but an actress who could create an entire atmosphere of breeding and gentility through her mere presence. Anyone wanting to study the development of ladies' fashion in the 1930s and '40s, should spend a week with Marjorie Gateson's films.

Considering the type of woman she was always called upon to portray, it is no criticism when I observe that with Gateson it was all about the surface, the front. Her talent was in the effortless projection of good manners, poise, and flawless diction that, however natural they appear, it takes years to perfect. Gateson may have been just as perfect in real life, no doubt decades of playing these roles would have left their mark, but we must not undervalue the work involved in becoming such a thoroughly artificial creature, in the same way as we

In the 1930s and beyond, Marjorie Gateson was the high-water mark of sartorial elegance in dozens of films, such as here in *The Man I Marry* (Universal Pictures, 1936). She was a well-preserved forty-five when this picture was taken and had already been in over forty films since 1931. Her film career lasted until 1953, when she switched her allegiance to television before retiring in 1968.

might admire a traditional Japanese Geisha or a Kabuki actor. The meticulous attention to social forms, manners, and rituals that has always distinguished the upper classes on either side of the Atlantic, found its classical expression in the characters Gateson portrayed. The stunningly elegant and polished women she impersonated were from a socially conservative, mid–twentieth century point of view a high-water mark of American culture and civilization. These women were social arbiters and leaders; whether in reality or fiction, boy, did they make the social carousel go round!

Marjorie Gateson, then, was an absolute triumph of typecasting, but the type was one she herself had largely created. According to John Springer and Jack Hamilton, writing in 1974: "It's easy to remember Miss Gateson. She had a distinctiveness which set her apart from the Nella Walkers and Nana Bryants and others who played similar roles. It isn't so easy to remember most of the roles."[21] As her body of work is so remarkably unified, any part could be taken to stand for the whole. Her portrayal of Ada Stanhope in *Coming-Out Party* (J.G. Blystone, Fox, 1934), for example, is representative of the many society women she played who were also mothers (and usually bad ones). As Frances Dee's regal Park Avenue mama, Gateson resents her husband being more fond of his yacht than he is of her; says "my dear" a lot; and is primarily concerned with her daughter making an advantageous marriage: "Tradition is a wonderful thing. The women in our family have always upheld it." She accuses her daughter of "talking like a shop girl" when Dee says she wants to feel passion for the man she marries. Gateson assures her that if she marries a man from her own set with her own standards, he will never let her down and tries to push her into the arms of an eligible bachelor. This scion of a suitably posh family tries to get intimate with Dee on an unchaperoned trip and nearly gets them killed by drinking and driving. Band leader Harry Green sums it up at the party: "Her mother's drunk with class consciousness and her father's demented over a yacht."

Coming-Out Party is a drama, but Gateson also played her share of comedies. In *Goin' to Town* (A. Hall, Emanuel Cohen Productions, 1935), starring Mae West, she was billed fourth as Mrs. Crane Brittany, a scheming society woman with a penchant for betting on the horses. She gets her gigolo (Ivan Lebedeff) to try and prevent West's horse from running after she has made an outside bet with West for $20,000. Lebedeff fails and Cactus wins big. In an effort to make herself good enough for snooty Paul Cavanagh, West later marries Gateson's nephew (Monroe Owsley) in a marriage of convenience that bolsters his sagging fortunes. Gateson engineers a plan involving Lebedeff to entrap West and disgrace her, obtaining a divorce for her nephew, but the hapless Lebedeff ends up killing him instead. This was a substantial part for Gateson and of the kind she did best. Critic André Sennwald considered *Goin' to Town* a sign that Mae West was in decline and "as daring an adventure in gutter vulgarity as anything the lady has yet attempted on the screen."[22]

I have chosen to discuss more in detail a role that nevertheless represents a variation on the theme of the sophisticated, snobbish, and cosmopolitan older married woman. By the time she came to do *Cocktail Hour* in 1933, Gateson had quite the track record as "the quintessence of the aristocratic blue blood, generally the mercenary wife who deserved to be wronged."[23] What is interesting about her role in this Columbia melodrama directed by journeyman director Victor Schertzinger is that her character, Mrs. Pat Lawton, has a "modern" and sophisticated attitude about her husband's philandering. She accepts his dalliances with equanimity and, the film suggests, possibly has some of her own.

Cocktail Hour is primarily the story of "the Escapades of an Unconventional Woman Artist,"[24] Cynthia Warren, played by Bebe Daniels. Cynthia, a commercial artist, is being pursued by several more or less suitable men, including the married philanderer William Lawton (Sidney Blackmer), who only reveals he has a wife after their affair is well underway; a callow French prince, Philippe (Barry Norton), with his mother, the folksy Princess de Longeville (Jessie Ralph), in tow; and the sensible choice, the wholesome American millionaire publisher and Cynthia's employer, Randolph Morgan (Randolph Scott).

Gateson's major scene is at the Parisian party hosted by the Princess de Longville, where Mrs. Lawton makes a big entrance. She says she is in Paris for the races and her husband is "on the trail of his latest charmer." Thus, it is clear that Lawton has told her about the affair and she speaks of it quite openly to other women at the party, saying she is glad this one has money of her own, so it won't cost them so much. When Pat Lawton and Cynthia Warren first meet, with William Lawton and another woman listening in, Pat thanks Cynthia for amusing her husband on the trip over from New York and invites her down to their house in the English countryside. Gateson later says to her husband: "Your taste is improving, William." Mrs. Lawton is very calm, cool, and collected about it all and it doesn't seem as if she is just "trying to be brave." *Cocktail Hour* is a classic 1930s exploration

Playing attractive, sophisticated society matrons of a certain age, Marjorie Gateson was in a league of her own. Her grace under pressure was often on display in trying social circumstances, such as here with the upper-crust, stuffed-shirted groom in *The Man I Marry* (Universal Pictures, 1936). Gerald Oliver Smith (right) is not able to hide his dismay at the bride's late arrival at their wedding rehearsal. Needless to say, Smith did not end up as the man of the title.

of the limits on a woman's freedom. Cynthia likes to think herself a modern, liberated woman of the world, despite her simple Kansas farm origins, but she gets burned by Lawton and is all set to marry her boss at the end. For those of you wondering about when the "cocktail hour" actually was: four o'clock.

Gateson was given one starring role during her 22 years in Hollywood. *The King's Vacation* (J. G. Adolfi, Warner Bros., 1933) was the unlikely story of a king who wanted to abdicate and return to a simpler life and the morganatic wife he gave up to ascend the throne. The king was played by the most unlikely male movie star who ever lived, corpse-like George Arliss, and his scorned ex-wife was portrayed by Gateson. Despite the royal trappings and the outlandish plot, Gateson's role as Mrs. Helen Everon was more or less exactly the type she was always portraying. This time outfitted with a palace in Paris and an ardent boyfriend played by Vernon Steele, she ultimately ends up sending her husband back to his queen (Florence Arliss).

Gateson acted in her last film in 1953, when she, like Agnes Moorehead and Isobel Elsom after her, lent elegant dowager support to Jerry Lewis in one of his characteristically zany comedies: *The Caddy*. Gateson played Donna Reed's elegant mother and the hostess at a weekend for professional golfers at her home, where Dean Martin is an invited guest and Lewis a gate crasher. As Mrs. Grace Taylor, Gateson is first seen urging the guests to have more food from the breakfast buffet. Later she makes the fatal suggestion that, as Martin's caddy, Lewis can do double duty as a server during the evening party. Lewis drives butler Clinton Sundberg to distraction by having animated conversations with his girlfriend on a living room phone and pushing him so he upsets a whole tray of food over portly Grace Hayle.

Nineteen fifty-four marked the final turning point in Gateson's professional life, when she moved back to her native New York and took up the role of Grace Harris Tyrell in the original cast of the CBS soap opera *The Secret Storm*. This was her ultimate dowager role and one she would play for no less than 14 years. *The Secret Storm* lasted until 1974.

Some years prior to her death, Gateson suffered a stroke, which (as David Ragan wrote while she was still alive) "rules out all possibility of her acting again."[25] She spent her declining years at the Mary Manning Walsh Nursing Home at 1339 York Ave. on Manhattan's East Side and died there from pneumonia on April 17, 1977, at the age of 86.[26] She was laid to rest in Mount Olivet Cemetery in Maspeth, Queens, New York.[27]

Monster Mom: Louise Closser Hale in *Another Language* (1933)

Another Language *is perhaps the classic indictment of matriarchy.*[1]

She attended that famous dinner at eight (albeit as a last-minute replacement), danced with Harold Lloyd, and fired Al Jolson in black face. She got chewed out by Lionel Barrymore as Rasputin, climbed the pyramids with Myrna Loy, and was one of the most manipulative moms on record. She had a yen for Ramon Novarro, flirted with Eugene Pallette, and gave Joan Crawford an alibi. Louise Closser Hale did all these things with flair and panache, with perfect comic timing or riveting realism as the situation called for. For this and so many other reasons, she is right up there with Alison Skipworth, Beulah Bondi, Florence Bates, and Lucile Watson in my personal pantheon of Hollywood's greatest character actresses.

Before she was preserved forever on celluloid, though, Hale gave number of performances that are forever lost to us. Let's turn to the beginnings of her life and extensive stage experience to see who she was, where she came from, and how her first 57 years were spent. Louise Closser was born in Chicago on October 13, 1872, and raised in Indianapolis with her two sisters Belle and Myla Jo. Her parents were Joseph A. Closser (1844–1897), a grain dealer who died when Hale was 15, and Louise M. Closser (1847–1932), who lived to be 84 and died in Indianapolis just a little over a year before her daughter.[2] Louise's family had no connection with the theater. She would recall in an interview in 1914 that "the first woman she ever knew who had been associated with the stage was a retired actress, with a happy family in a Summer hotel." Twelve-year-old Louise felt that "in some way or other she must make known her passion for the theatre to this wondrous being." She knocked on the actress's door wearing an old pair of blue tights and "struck an attitude that she felt would force any one into the belief that she was of the talented," only to have the door closed in her face with peals of laughter.[3] Apparently Louise's decision to go on the stage was "greatly to the scandal of her family."[4]

After having attended public schools in Indianapolis and studied at the American Academy of Dramatic Art in New York and the Boston School of Oratory, Closser made her stage debut in Detroit in 1894 in a play called *In Old Kentucky*. She was 22, but for the next 40 years was destined to play "elderly and middle-aged women, kindly ones, gentle ones, cantankerous ones, grandmothers, mothers, old maids."[5]

Closser met and married fellow actor Walter Hale in 1899 and would be known professionally as Louise Closser Hale from 1906, the year she embarked on a parallel career as a writer. Born in Chicago in 1869, Walter Hale was a successful actor with several shows on Broadway between the late 1890s and his retirement from acting in 1914.[6] He and his wife both had supporting roles in the "drama of Western life" *Arizona* by Augustus Thomas in 1900–01.[7] It was their only Broadway show together and Hale's Broadway debut. With the exception of a lengthy run as Miss Hazy in *Mrs. Wiggs of the Cabbage Patch* in London (1907–09) and the years 1916 to 1919, Hale would be seen continuously on Broadway for three decades.[8] Some of the highlights of those years were the original productions of Shaw's *Candida* (1903–04), O'Neill's *Beyond the Horizon* (1920), Zona Gale's *Miss Lulu Bett* (1920–21), Rachel Crothers's *Expressing Willie* (1924) and the first revival of Ibsen's *Peer Gynt* (1923). Hale also lent her manifold talents to *The Blue Bird* (1910–11), where she played "an amusing if somewhat matter of fact fairy"[9]; *Ruggles of Red Gap* (1922), where she created the role of the socially ambitious Mrs. Floud, that would be incarnated by Mary Boland on film; and *Malveloca* (1922), the translation of a Spanish play with Jane Cowl in the lead, where Hale and Jessie Ralph were among "the props and pillars to a somewhat heavy enterprise."[10]

In *Candida*, described by one reviewer as "a literary and dramatic event of the highest delight," Hale played the spinsterish secretary Proserpine "Prossy" Garnett, "a neat and finished character study deserving the highest praise,"[11] which became one of her signature roles. *Beyond the Horizon* was Eugene O'Neill's first full-length play and won the Pulitzer Prize in 1920. Alexander Woollcott called it "an absorbing, significant, and memorable tragedy," found the cast headed by Richard Bennett and Edward Arnold as the ill-fated Mayo brothers to be "uncommonly fine," and wrote of Hale in the role of the embittered mother-in-law Mrs. Atkins: "[She] darts (like a trout for a fly) at the best part that has come to her since Prossy bridled in *Candida*."[12] *Beyond the Horizon* ran for a respectable 111 performances at the Morosco Theatre.

Hale hit another high note in yet another Pulitzer Prize winner at the close of 1920: *Miss Lulu Bett*. The titular heroine's decrepit grandmother was "acted, inevitably and perfectly, by Louise Closser Hale," but Woollcott remained unimpressed by the "rather dull and flabby play ... somewhat sleazily put together by a playwright who has but slight sense of dramatic values and no instinct at all for the idiom of the theatre."[13] Comparing the two old women she had played in the previous year, the 49-year-old Hale wrote in the *New York Times* on February 6, 1921: "I believe I enjoy playing Grandma Bett because she is frail and does not require a tremendous attack of vital force the minute the curtain goes up. The Lord knows she is on the stage all the time, and I generally judge a good part by the length of time I am permitted to sit in the wings and work on my next Summer's underwear.... Last year, in *Beyond the Horizon*, I had one of those well-placed roles: two good scenes only and time for lots of underwear."[14]

The Theatre Guild and legendary director Theodore Komisarjevsky's *Peer Gynt* was the first revival on Broadway since the original production in 1907. This time Joseph Schildkraut played Peer and Hale his mother Aase, while an 18-year-old Selena Royle was his ever-faithful Solveig. Hale's Aase was "spirited in the minor moods of the character, but it somehow missed the exultation and the pathos of the death scene," John Corbin writes.[15] The satire on psychoanalysis, *Expressing Willie*, was only a moderate commercial success at the 48th Street Theatre, but got a rave review from Corbin. He concluded with an encomium to Hale, who played *nouveau riche* Willie's down-to-earth mother, Mrs. Smith: "As to Louise Closser Hale, anything said would be too little. Miss Crothers has given her a character of the first water and she renders it with the pristine humor of her Prossy in Shaw's *Candida*, enhanced by the broader technique and the ripened feeling for life that have come in the intervening years."[16]

Part of this "ripened feeling for life" had been caused by the one tragedy of Hale's existence: her husband's death from cancer on December 4, 1917, at the age of 48. After quitting the stage, Walter Hale had concentrated on his art work and even had his etchings exhibited at the Paris Salon. The couple made their home in an apartment at 27 Washington Square North, a seven-story Renaissance palazzo-style building which is still standing on the corner of MacDougal Street.[17] By all accounts, the Hales' marriage was a singularly happy one; it included extensive travels and collaboration on several books, which she wrote and he illustrated.[18] It had started back in 1906 with a novelized travel book called *A Motor Car Divorce*. "She wrote it from experiences she had on a motor trip with her husband," noted the *New York Times*, before hastening to add: "with whom incidentally she was always very happy."[19] Several other travel books followed, such as *We Discover New England* (1915) and *We Discover Old Dominion* (1916), and novels such as *The Actress* (1909) and *Her Soul and Her Body* (1912). In summer of 1916, the couple traveled to war-torn France. Walter Hale spent time "sketching and writing behind the lines with the British forces," which resulted in an illness requiring an operation in May 1917.[20] He was buried at Graceland Cemetery in his native Chicago.[21]

Louise Closser Hale's unique brand of dry, understated humor was used to excellent effect in *Dinner at Eight* (Metro-Goldwyn-Mayer, 1933). Hale plays Park Avenue socialite Billie Burke's more modestly well-off cousin with a subtle yet barbed running commentary on her fluttery relation's ridiculous sayings and doings. From left: Grant Mitchell, George Baxter, Hale, Jean Harlow, Wallace Beery, Edmund Lowe, Karen Morley, and Billie Burke.

Louise made her film debut at Paramount a dozen years after her husband's death in a crime drama called *The Hole in the Wall* (R. Florey, 1929), starring Claudette Colbert and Edward G. Robinson. It seems likely, though, that she was brought to Hollywood to reprise her role in the film version of what would prove her final Broadway show, *Paris*, which closed at the Music Box Theatre in March 1929. There Hale played Cora Sabbot, a meddling mother who tries to break up her son Andrew's Parisian romance with an actress, while herself being drawn into a pseudo-romance with a younger man. With her reprise of the role in *Paris* (C.G. Badger, Fox, 1929) and her similarly matriarchal efforts in *The Hole in the Wall*, Hale was well on her way to becoming "the movies' domineering *grande dame* of all time."[22]

Considering that she only spent four years in Hollywood, Hale's film output is remarkable, not just in quantity (30 films), but primarily in quality and variety. She worked for most all the major studios — Paramount, Warner Bros., Fox, Columbia, and RKO — and finally found a home at MGM in February 1932, where she acted in 11 films. Hale supported many of the biggest stars of the early 1930s: Constance Bennett in *Born to Love* (P.L. Stein, RKO, 1931), Janet Gaynor in *Daddy Long Legs* (A. Santell, Fox, 1931), Myrna Loy in *Rebound* (E.H. Griffith, RKO, 1931) and *The Barbarian* (S. Wood, MGM, 1933), Ann Harding in *Devotion* (R. Milton, RKO, 1931), Jean Harlow in *Platinum Blonde* (F. Capra, Columbia, 1931), Marlene Dietrich in *Shanghai Express* (J. von Sternberg, Paramount, 1932), Bette Davis in *The Man Who Played God* (J.G. Adolfi, Warner Bros., 1932), Joan Crawford in *Letty Lynton* (C. Brown, MGM, 1932) and *Today We Live* (H. Hawks, MGM, 1933), Tallulah Bankhead in *Faithless* (H. Beaumont, MGM, 1932), Carole Lombard in *No More Orchids* (W. Lang, Columbia, 1932), Kay Francis in *Storm at Daybreak* (R. Boleslawski, MGM, 1933), and last but not least, Helen Hayes in three films: *The Son-Daughter* (C. Brown, MGM, 1932), *The White Sister* (V. Fleming, MGM, 1933), and *Another Language* (E.H. Griffith, MGM, 1933).

Whatever Hale lacked in natural beauty, her face more than made up for in its comic and dramatic possibilities. With characteristically dark-ringed, raccoon eyes, lips made for pursing, and a button nose, Hale's face could express any mood from stony impassiveness to goggle-eyed surprise. A subtle and sophisticated comedienne, she could deliver a cutting line with the precision of an expert fencer. Often the comic effect in her scenes was created by the juxtaposition of Hale's homely, prim face and formless figure with some entirely unsuitable situation or line of dialogue. One of her best roles, however limited, was as Billie Burke's less privileged cousin Hattie Loomis in *Dinner at Eight* (G. Cukor, MGM, 1933), who only gets invited to the dinner when the aristocratic guests of honor decide to go to Florida instead. At one point, before they go in to eat, Hattie is listening to the bottle-blonde bombshell Kitty Packard (Jean Harlow) say how much fun she is having at New York penthouse parties. When Kitty is done, Hattie sighs: "All my life I've wanted to be a penthouse girl." She is well mated with an equally down-to-earth husband, Ed (Grant Mitchell), who chimes in loyally: "You'd be good at that."

Other equally fine comic moments are to be found in *Shanghai Express, Faithless, The Son-Daughter, The Barbarian*, and *Storm at Daybreak*, to name but a few. In the first film, Hale plays Mrs. Haggerty, a first-class passenger with a remarkable curly wig, who tries unsuccessfully to smuggle her dog, Waffles, aboard the Shanghai Express. Hale also has a small but terrific part in *Faithless*, as a grasping, earthy old bag of a landlady with whom Bankhead stays when she's down on her luck. Hale gets the heroine's shoes in lieu of rent and later celebrates her wedding with a drink, exclaiming characteristically, "Down the rathole!" *The Son-Daughter* gives us Hale as the dutiful maidservant to Helen Hayes; she sticks with her mistress till the bitter end. In hilarious Chinese drag as Toy Yah, Hale outdoes anything in the subsequent *The Good Earth* (1937) or *Dragon Seed* (1944), though Maria Ouspenskaya in *The Shanghai Gesture* (1941) could give her a run for her money in the "Most Outrageous Looking Caucasian Woman Pretending to be Chinese" category.

In *The Barbarian*, Hale is in fine fettle as Myrna Loy's trusty sidekick in Egypt, who admires Loy's love interest "The Barbarian" Ramon Novarro from a safe distance. Powers, as she's called, wears pince-nez and goes on a particularly comical camel ride in the desert, saying of the pyramids that they "look like a camel's gymnasium" and about the camel himself, "Nobody on earth knows me that well!" In real life, Hale had actually "toured Algiers and a portion of the Sahara Desert by automobile" 22 years before she made this film.[23] Finally, *Storm at Daybreak* gave Hale yet another prime comic role as Walter Huston's sister and Kay Francis's sister-in-law, who shares their big house on a Serbian estate. Hale for once gets a love interest of her own, when portly Hungarian officer Eugene Pallette invades the household. She and Pallette perform a hilarious dance and have a tryst eating chicken in the kitchen. "How dare you? How dare you?" Hale exclaims when Pallette makes his move, adding, "Come into the kitchen."

In December 1932, the *New York Times* reported that Hale was "seriously ill at her home with bronchial pneumonia."[24] She rallied sufficiently to have six more of her sterling performances preserved on celluloid at MGM in the space of only six months: Mina in *The White Sister* (production started mid–December 1932), Applegate in *Today We Live* (production started late December 1932), Powers in *The Barbarian* (production started early February 1933), Hattie Loomis in *Dinner at Eight* (produced from late March to mid–May 1933), Militza Brooska in *Storm at Daybreak* (production started late April 1933), and Mother Hallam in *Another Language* (produced in May and June 1933). It was almost as if Louis B. Mayer knew he was going to lose her and rushed her into as many films as possible, as he was doing at this very moment with cancer-ridden Marie Dressler. More likely, the MGM mogul was hoping Hale might become a new Dressler.

That was not to be. On July 25, 1933, Hale was out shopping when she was overcome by the heat. "Her collapse was followed by a heart attack," the *New York Times* reported, and she died at noon on July 26 at the Monte Sano Hospital in Glendale.[25] Two days later, *Another Language* was released.

On her death, Hale's estate was valued at $63,627.[26] She left $1,000 bequests to several charities, including the Authors League of America, the Actors Fund of America, and the Motion Picture Relief Fund of Hollywood. Apart from willing Walter Hale's artworks to his niece, the residual estate was divided equally between Hale's two sisters, Myla Jo Closser of New York City and Belle Closser Wilson of Indianapolis. In her will, Hale requested an Episcopal funeral service "as simple and as inexpensive as possible." She wished to be cremated and asked that "no friend or kin accompany the body further than the church door." "If I live in the memory of my friends," she wrote, "I shall have lived long enough."[27]

On April 22, 1934, a memorial service was held for Louise Closser Hale at the Little Church Around the Corner in New York, under the auspices of the Episcopal Actors Guild with Hale's sister Myla Jo present. In his eulogy, Otis Skinner said that "no person had ever been more sincerely loved in Hollywood than Mrs. Hale."[28]

Another Language was Louise Closser Hale's final film and she went out with a bang. Production began at MGM on May 24, 1933, and the film premiered only two months

Robert Montgomery is stuck between a rock and a hard place in *Another Language* (Metro-Gold-wyn-Mayer, 1933) in the form of his mother (left), played by Louise Closser Hale, and his wife (right), played by Helen Hayes. Some consider this Hayes's best 1930s film, which is perhaps not saying a lot. She herself would have been the first to admit that her early sojourn in Hollywood was not terribly productive.

later. It was based on a Broadway hit play by Rose Franken, produced and staged by Esther Dale's husband, Arthur J. Beckhard. The play ran for an impressive 344 performances at the Booth Theatre from April 1932 till February 1933, before a return engagement with a few changes of cast at the Waldorf Theatre. The play closed just days before the film version opened. Chosen to helm the film was veteran director Edward H. Griffith, who directed 61 films between 1917 and 1946, including *Holiday* (the original version from 1930), *The Animal Kingdom, Biography of a Bachelor Girl, No More Ladies*, and *Café Society*. Griffith is known for his silent films, but also had success as the director of high society comedies and films based on Broadway plays. He had previously directed Hale in *Rebound* (1931), based on a play by Donald Ogden Stewart. Rose Franken was not involved in the screenplay, which was written by Herman Mankiewicz and Stewart, based on an adaptation by Gertrude Purcell.

As the young married couple Stella and Victor Hallam, Helen Hayes and Robert Montgomery were chosen to head the talented ensemble cast that would bring this story of divided loyalties, marital woes, and domestic dysfunction in a lower middle-class New York family to life on the screen. Hale was selected to play the role created by Margaret Wycherly on Broadway, as the mean-spirited, narrow-minded matriarch Mrs. Hallam, mother of four married sons, who deeply resents her youngest and favorite son, Victor (Montgomery), having eloped with the artistic, free-spirited, and unconventional sculptor, Stella (Hayes). Henry Travers was cast as the downtrodden father figure, Pop Hallam. John Beal (grandson Jerry), Hal K. Dawson (son Walter), Irene Cattell (daughter-in-law Grace), and Margaret Hamilton (daughter-in-law Helen) reprised their stage roles as younger members of the Hallam clan, together with Maidel Turner (daughter-in-law Etta), Minor Watson (son Paul), and Willard Robertson (son Harry).[29]

Another Language was Helen Hayes's sixth film at MGM in the early 1930s. In her recollection, head of production at the studio, Irving Thalberg, had needed the writing skills of Hayes's husband, Charles MacArthur. "To keep him happy," Thalberg brought Hayes out to Hollywood, too. She signed a contract stipulating that she would spend six months in Hollywood and six months in New York. Hayes's succinct summary of the years she and her husband spent in Tinseltown was that "Charlie had a better time than I did." Hayes felt she was "relegated to weepy melodramas in which I would die more deaths than Sarah Bernhardt or a Wagnerian soprano."[30]

Playing Stella Hallam in *Another Language* was the exception to the rule. Reviewer Mordaunt Hall felt that this was "the best role allotted to her since she has been in Hollywood."[31] Ironically, Thalberg was also indirectly the reason why Hayes got to play Stella. According to Hayes's biographer Kenneth Barrow, she was "rushed in" as Norma Shearer's replacement when Thalberg had a severe heart attack in late 1932 and Shearer chose to stay at home and nurse him.[32]

This was Hayes and Hale's third and final collaboration. During breaks in filming, they would play cards. Hale wrote in an article published during these years that Hayes "wrote me a little note once and said she would like to be like me when she grows to be my age, and my note was crossing hers at that time in which I admitted, if I could ever be a young woman again, I would like to be like her!

"And this is very generous of me," Hale added, "for she still owes me two cents from the last game of Russian bank."[33]

After the opening credits, the film shows a photo album of the various family members, starting with Hale as Ma Hallam and ending with Hayes as Stella. From the beginning, their polarity is suggested. Hall is correct in pointing out that the film "does not materially differ from the original, except for a permissible introductory episode."[34] The play has been opened up by starting with a scene between Victor and Stella on the boat from Europe in which they discuss where they are to stay when they arrive in New York: *chez* the Hallams or, as Stella would prefer, at a hotel. Victor insists they go straight to the family, as Tuesday night is always spent visiting his mother.

From the scene on the boat, we cut to their arrival in New York City. Mother Hallam is not at the dock to meet them, but Victor's three brothers and their wives are. Stella has not met any of the family before, as she and Victor eloped. There is then a brief scene at the family home, where Stella meets her mother-in-law for the first time and their power struggle begins in a discussion about where to put the long-stemmed anemones Stella has brought as a gift. Mrs. Hallam has no vase large enough for them and Stella creatively suggests they use the umbrella stand. Rather than appreciate the beauty of the flowers, Mrs. Hallam seems to blame Stella for getting her husband to spend so much money on something unnecessary. This small incident beautifully and efficiently brings out their differing value systems: Mrs. Hallam's practical, penny-pinching materialism and conventionality vs. Stella's love of beauty and keen aesthetic sense.

The film then cuts to the young marrieds' apartment in a fifth-floor walk-up, small but artistically and tastefully decorated. It is breakfast time and it turns out three years have passed. Stella wants them to go off on a trip. Their planned visit with the family that Tuesday evening is delayed by Victor working late and Stella wanting to finish a bust of her husband in her art class. In a brief scene from the classroom that is not in the play, her teacher suggests Victor may have a weak mouth. The play proper begins at this point, with their late arrival at the Hallam house, which brings about a confrontation between Stella and her in-laws. We then have the riveting first meeting between Stella and Victor's nephew, the handsome and artistically inclined Jerry. As Hall points out, it is Stella and Jerry who "speak another language."[35] In a bid to make some small change in the family routine, Stella suggests they meet at their place next week, to Mrs. Hallam's evident dismay.

Cut to the following week. Jerry shows up early, as Stella invited him to, and they go for a walk in the rain that Victor had earlier refused. Increasingly, the plot revolves around Jerry's developing love for Stella, of the "tea and sympathy variety," that the rest of the family is unaware of. They practically throw him into Stella's arms at the next get-together. Jerry rushes out after having danced with and kissed Stella on the family's encouragement and broken the bust of Victor in a rage. Stella finally gives Mrs. Hallam a piece of her mind, and she promptly responds by having an "attack." This doesn't prevent her from leaving with all the others, though, including Victor, who spends the night at his parents' house.

The final segment shows Stella coming over to apologize to Mrs. Hallam and telling her husband she needs time to figure things out. Jerry's parents come over and are worried because he has not slept at home and the truth comes out. Victor pretends to have known all along about Jerry's "puppy love" and says that he and Stella had a good laugh over it. Stella shows him up for lying and, somewhat incredibly, he saves his marriage by leaving with her in the rain to confront their future together. Mrs. Hallam only plays a subsidiary role in this part, making her entrance just before her son and Stella leave. She is now, finally, powerless to hold him back.

In his *New York Times* review, Mordaunt Hall thought this "an excellent pictorial adaptation of the stage work." He calls Mother Hallam a "selfish shammer" and writes that she is "acted by the late Louise Closser Hale whose performance is wonderfully real."[36] More recently, John Springer and Jack Hamilton give Hale even higher praise, reminding us in *They Had Faces Then* that she was "that smothering mother in *Another Language*—the one who always had a convenient heart seizure to end any family crisis, usually caused by her in the first place. In a time when terrible moms abounded, Mrs. Hale's was one of the most realistic in one of the best character performances of the time."[37]

As these authors indicate, *Another Language* is only the tip of an iceberg of "domineering mothers" films produced from the 1930s on. Not as famous as the film that gave a name to what was increasingly being perceived as an unhealthy relationship between mothers and their children, *Another Language* is nevertheless of such quality in its script, casting, and acting, that it bears comparison with the absolute classic of the genre: *The Silver Cord* (1933). Like *Another Language*, *The Silver Cord* was based on a hit Broadway play, in this case by Sidney Howard, who would go on to more lasting fame for writing most of the screenplay to *Gone with the Wind*. Up until 1939, at any rate, he was best known for *The Silver Cord*, which opened at the John Golden Theatre on December 20, 1926, and ran for 112 performances, before being respectfully and effectively adapted into a film of the same title, starring Laura Hope Crews, Irene Dunne, and Joel McCrea. Crews was reprising her stage role as the widow Mrs. Phelps, an absolute masterpiece, if you will, of monstrous

As a frustrated artist and wife, Helen Hayes (right) feels drawn towards her husband's sensitive young nephew (center), played by John Beal, another outsider in the crass, materialistic, and relentlessly middle-class Hallam family. Things come to a head with mother-in-law Louise Closser Hale (left) at a boisterous family gathering in Hayes and Robert Montgomery's cozy fifth floor walk-up. MGM produced an excellent filmatization of *Another Language* (1933) in which Beal, Irene Cattell, Hal K. Dawson, and Margaret Hamilton reprised their stage roles.

manipulation and smothering motherhood. *Another Language* is different from *The Silver Cord* in that it has a greater complexity of family relationships between both parents, their four sons, ditto daughters-in-law, and even a grandson. Franken's play also shows a lower middle-class family (apron strings rather than silver cords) and covers a longer time span than the upper-crust setting and intensive plot of *The Silver Cord*.

By the early 1940s, concern about "momism" had reached such heights that entire books were being written about this phenomenon and its potentially disastrous consequences for American manhood and hence American society. The most famous (and, one might add, vitriolic) book was Philip Wylie's *Generation of Vipers* from 1942. You can get some idea of the tone and general level of his argument from his description of the object of his disaffection, the bad mother, whom he refers to throughout as "mom": "She is a middle-aged puffin with an eye like a hawk that has just seen a rabbit twitch far below. She is about 25 pounds overweight, with no sprint, but sharp heels and a hard backhand which she does not regard as foul but a womanly defense. In a thousand of her there is not sex appeal enough to budge a hermit ten paces off a rock ledge." This undeniably sounds a lot like

Hale's Mother Hallam. It was Wylie's claim that "megaloid momworship has got completely out of hand."

"Our land," he continues, "subjectively mapped, would have more silver cords and apron strings crisscrossing it than railroads and telephone wires. Mom is everywhere and everything and damned near everybody, and from her depends all the rest of the U.S."[38]

A more level-headed, "scientific," and objective approach to this troubling topic was attempted by the psychiatrist Edward A. Strecker in 1946. The question is if his book *Their Mothers' Sons* isn't at least as misogynistic and homophobic as Wylie's, despite Strecker trying to distance himself from the author of *Generation of Vipers* by opening statements like "Mr. Wylie's mom is described in too vindictive terms to satisfy a trained psychiatrist." Like Wylie, though, Strecker tries to distinguish between the mother and the "mom." "What constitutes a mom?" he asks. "How does she differ from a mother? Fundamentally, a mom is not a mother. Mom is a maternal parent who fails to prepare her offspring emotionally for living a productive adult life on an adult social plane." According to Strecker, moms are not "distinctively marked" outwardly and silver cords come in different lengths, but "in every mother, no matter how mature she may be, there are traces of mom." He even includes fathers in some instances: "Yes, sometimes pop is a mom." In the final analysis, "momism is the product of a social system veering toward a matriarchy in which each individual mom plays only a small part."[39]

Wylie and Strecker are writing about American society in general and do not specifically analyze "mom" on stage or screen. That task was left to W. David Sievers in his magisterial tome *Freud on Broadway: A History of Psychoanalysis and the American Drama* (1955). However misguided we may find Sievers's rudimentary, "old school" psychoanalysis and his equally outmoded views on gender and sexuality, there is no denying that he has amassed an impressive and useful store of information on American drama in the first half of the twentieth century. Sievers claims that "one of the most striking changes in American *mores* brought about by psychoanalytic concepts has been the desentimentalization of the role of mother. [Wylie] ... gave her the final *coup de grace* in his *Generation of Vipers*." Sievers claims, "Of all the psychoanalytic themes that appeared in the drama of the twenties, the Oedipus complex was the most frequent one, appearing in at least 50 plays between 1923 and 1934. Its most characteristic form was that of the dominating mother and fixated son whose life was warped by her jealousy of his sexual partner. *The Silver Cord* best illustrates the category." Sievers also discusses Clifford Odets's *Awake and Sing!* as the "classic picture of the matriarchal American family and its passive-dependent males" and writes that it "was equaled only once during the drama of the thirties — in Rose Franken's *Another Language*":

> Here the family is free of the economic pressures that aggravates the neurosis of Odets' people, and the picture is, therefore, all the more insidious.... [Franken] exposes the Freudian pattern of the Hallam family in terms that are psychologically perceptive without resorting to obvious analytic terminology.... All of the Hallam wives are sexless, emotionally sterile creatures ... none in love with their husbands because the Hallam males are incapable of love except for their mother.[40]

Sievers also contends, "So familiar had the pattern of matriarchal dominance become by 1929 that in reviewing *Your Uncle Dudley*, Robert Littell felt constrained to cry out, 'There ought to be a closed season during which playwrights are not allowed to paint mothers black and then shoot them. It's too easy.'"[41] While this theme may have been played out in the theater, in American films moms were just getting started. *The Silver Cord* was the first notable example of "momism" on film, but dozens of titles can potentially come under this rubric once we have a frame of reference to identify them with. Neglectful mothers, domineering mothers, immature mothers, selfish mothers, manipulative mothers, and downright cruel mothers make for compelling drama, as we can see in films such as *After Tomorrow* (1931), *The War Against Mrs. Hadley* (1942), *This Land Is Mine* (1943), *My Reputation* (1946), and *The Story on Page One* (1959). These films also demonstrate that playing powerful mothers gave many talented character actresses the best acting opportunity on film they would ever have, as my chapters on Clara Blandick in *Shopworn* (1932), Helen Westley in *Splendor* (1935), Evelyn Varden in *Hilda Crane* (1956), and Marjorie Rambeau in *Slander* (1957) demonstrate.

Madame Noir: Esther Howard
in *Born to Kill* (1947)

*"She was a charming, middle-aged lady
with a face like a bucket of mud."*

It sounded like a scene from one of her more sordid films. In the early evening of October 20, 1926, a handsome, 33-year-old man had been found unconscious in his room at the Times Square Hotel in New York by a hotel attendant. The house physician had been called and pronounced him dead. It was suicide. The dead man had swallowed Lysol. He had registered early in the afternoon that same day, giving his place of residence as Chicago. He had been visited by several friends in his room during the afternoon. A detective from the West 47th Street Station arrived at the hotel at the same time as the dead man's wife. As the *New York Times* would report the next day: "She was unable to ascribe a cause for her husband's act, but said that up to last Saturday he had been a member of the cast of *Black Belt*, which had been playing in Chicago." The play was a failure and closed. The actor had come to New York seeking new employment.[1]

The actor's name was Arthur Albertson. His wife, as the article made clear, was also on the stage and currently "a member of the cast of *Sunny*, now playing at the New Amsterdam Theatre."[2] The New Amsterdam Theatre at 214 West 42nd Street, where *Mary Poppins* is playing as I write, is only a block and half from where the vast brown bulk of the Times Square Hotel still looms on the corner of 43rd Street and 8th Avenue. Esther Howard, for that was the actress's name, would have been at her dead husband's side in five minutes, but the walk from the theatre to the hotel must have seemed the longest of her life.

Or maybe not. We can't be certain how she reacted to this shocking piece of news. If a married man comes back to town, checks into a hotel rather than his conjugal home, and asks a friend to seek out his wife, as the newspaper reported, it seems an estrangement of some kind has taken place. If Howard knew why a still young, successful, and good-looking man would suddenly commit suicide in such a gruesome fashion, without leaving a note or a message of any kind, she wasn't telling. Maybe she carried the secret to her grave nearly 40 years later.

In late October 1926, Esther Howard was 34 years old and nearing the end of the longest running show of her career. *Sunny*, a musical comedy by Jerome Kern, Otto Harbach, and Oscar Hammerstein, starring Marilyn Miller in the title role, had opened on September 22, 1925, and ran for a record-breaking 517 performances. This was Howard's ninth show on Broadway, where she had been seen regularly since her debut in 1917 and would keep working steadily until 1929. Albertson, a Southerner born in Waycross, Georgia, in 1891, had also had his share of success.[3] He made his Broadway debut in 1919. Before his untimely death he was seen in five shows in New York, the last being *The Virgin*, which ended in April 1926. Albertson had also acted in a number of short films and a few silent features between 1914 and 1917, before committing himself entirely to a stage career.

Esther Howard came from an artistic family. Her father, William Howard, had moved from Boston to Montana to become musical conductor of the Butte Opera House. He brought with him his wife, formerly Martha Boggs, a dramatic soprano who had toured the country with John Philip Sousa. Esther was born while they lived in Montana, on April 4, 1892. When their daughter was five, the time had come to return to Boston. Esther was sent to school, where she "struggled bravely." She told the *New York Times* in 1927 that "she hated school, loathed education and everything even remotely associated with learning." Nearly 20 years after she graduated from the Girls' Latin School in Boston, "she still cherishes a horror of it all." Her parents had to give up their plans for their daughter to become a schoolteacher. While still a senior in high school, Esther read in the newspaper that "supers" were wanted at the Tremont Theatre for the mob scene in *Madame X*, starring none other than Sarah Bernhardt. "The call was for 10 o'clock that same morning. The girl went to school as usual, but during the Greek recitation she staged a fainting spell and fell down so realistically in the midst of the reading of Sophocles's *Electra* that she was excused and sent home. Fifteen minutes later she turned up at the stage door of the Tremont and landed her first job."[4] Howard thus auditioned two times that day. It was gutsiness like this that would carry her through more than four decades on stage and screen.

About two years after this "coup" in her hometown, Howard got into a stock company at Lynn, Massachusetts, 15 miles north of Boston. After a season there playing small bits, she felt she was ready for New York and Broadway.[5] By yet another stroke of luck, she got into Grace George's company, which was going into a season of repertory at the Playhouse Theatre at 147 W. 47th St. There Howard made her Broadway debut on October 11, 1917, in a play called *Eve's Daughter* by Alicia Ramsey. Apart from the leading lady, Grace George, the company included such familiar faces as British character actresses Alison Skipworth and Florence Edney, young leading man and future horror film regular Lionel Atwill, and soon-to-be silent screen star Rockcliffe Fellowes. It must have been the best acting school in the world for Howard, who was 25 years old. She performed in three more plays with Grace George: *L'Elevation* (1917, 38 performances), *The Indestructible Wife* (1918, 22 performances) and *She Would and She Did* (1919, 36 performances).[6] Her parts weren't large or important, but it was good experience and paid the bills.

On September 12, 1919, the day after Howard opened in *She Would and She Did* at the Vanderbilt Theatre at 148 W. 48th St., Arthur Albertson made his Broadway debut only three blocks away in a play called *Civilian Clothes* at the Morosco Theatre. Unlike Howard in her debut performance, Albertson was "noticed" by the *New York Times*. The legendary critic Alexander Woollcott mentioned him among the cast members who gave "good performances" and who "all played with vim" in this comedy "on the pangs of demobilization."[7] Once the play closed in January 1920, it would be nearly three years till Albertson's next Broadway opening.

She Would and She Did ended in October 1919. Sometime between then and the summer of 1920, Howard met producer Edgar MacGregor "over an ice cream soda in Gray's drug store."[8] He was casting a musical comedy to be tried out in Atlantic City. Without Howard having any previous experience with musicals, he gave her a role. The show was *The Sweetheart Shop* with songs by George and Ira Gershwin. After a lengthy trial run in Chicago, it opened at the Knickerbocker Theatre on August 31, 1920. As Minerva Butts, "a country girl who becomes a vampire," Howard even had three songs with the boys of the chorus: "I Want to Be a Blooming, Blushing Bride," "She's Artistic," and "My Caravan." The *New York Times* found the musical "breezy and highly melodious" and "patently a good, popular entertainment, despite or haply because of a highly conventionalized book..., although a few more jokes would not retard it any." Lead comedian Harry K. Morton received most praise, but "[n]ext to Mr. Morton the honors of the evening went to Esther Howard."[9] The show lasted eight weeks.

With one exception, Howard would stick to musical comedy for the remainder of her Broadway career. Among the stars she would support "out of town" in the early 1920s were female impersonator Julian Eltinge and song and dance man Bert Williams. She was performing with Williams the night he died.[10] Back on Broadway, she came in as a last-minute replacement in *Sonny*, a "play with music" at the Cort Theatre, which had only a brief run in August and September 1921.[11] Howard hadn't been seen on Broadway for another year and a half, when she returned in a show that would prove the first of three huge hits. *Wildflower*, a vehicle for the star of *Orange Blossoms* Edith Day, with music by Herbert P. Stothart and Vincent Youmans and book and lyrics by Otto Harbach and Oscar Hammerstein, opened at the Casino Theatre on February 7, 1923, and ran for 477 performances. As "siren" Lucrezia La Roche, Howard was "mildly entertaining" and had two songs with Olin Howland: "I'll Collaborate with You" and "The World's Worst Women."[12]

After *Wildflower* closed on March 29, 1924, Howard was not seen on Broadway for more than a year. *Tell Me More*, another musical comedy with music and lyrics by the Gershwin brothers, ran for 100 performances at the Gaiety Theatre from April to July 1925. As Jane Wallace she had four songs, including the audience favorites "Kickin' the Clouds Away" and "My Fair Lady." The *New York Times* reviewer found that Howard "has her moments of comedy," but "seems rather at a loss in the serious moments."[13]

Meanwhile, Arthur Albertson had been receiving good notices on Broadway as an "upstanding mine expert" in Sophie Treadwell's "play of American life in Mexico," *Gringo* (1922–23); and as a reporter in the thriller *In the Next Room* (1923–24). The *New York Times* wrote: "Newspaperdom will be grateful to see at last one reporter, acted by Arthur Albertson, who is not only sagacious but well mannered."[14]

Both *Gringo* and *In the Next Room* were produced and staged by Guthrie McClintic, who had married Katharine Cornell in 1921. "Kit" Cornell and "Guth" McClintic first met in January 1919, just as she was setting off with the third touring company of the hit play *The Man Who Came Back*. Playing a supporting role as Olive, confidante to Cornell's heroine Marcelle in a San Francisco cabaret scene, was none other than Esther Howard. Cornell biographer Tad Mosel relates that

> in spite of good and competitive reviews that would have alienated her from any leading lady, Esther Howard ... became Kit's sidekick offstage as well.... Together they braved the rigors of touring. The junk towns and drafty dressing rooms in firetrap theatres; sitting up all night in stifling day coaches or putting up at bad hotels with inedible food; three-thirty calls to catch four o'clock trains on zero mornings in towns without taxis; battling blizzards with suitcases to make the railroad station on time.... Esther Howard's competence on the stage was one of the reasons why she and Kit were able to become good friends; her good reviews, rather than being a threat were an attraction.[15]

No doubt Albertson met McClintic and Cornell through his wife and their good friend Esther Howard, whom McClintic "came to love as much as Kit did."[16] One can only wonder if there was anything more to the Albertson-McClintic connection on the one hand and the Howard-Cornell friendship on the other.[17] Cornell was six years younger than Howard and McClintic was two years younger than Albertson. Mosel mentions that Clifton Webb was also a mutual friend at this time. On September 22, 1925, he and Howard opened in a new show at the New Amsterdam Theatre called *Sunny*, starring Marilyn Miller. It was a huge hit and was still running on October 20, 1926, the day Howard became a widow.

But the show must go on. Fortunately, in Howard's recollection her part in *Sunny* gave her "nothing to do but change clothes seven times."[18] It's true, she didn't have any songs. When the show finally ended, Howard went into a "fair-to-middling" summer revue at the Earl Carroll Theatre called *Allez-oop* (1927); according to the *New York Times*, "The capable Esther Howard is not treated as well as she deserves, but, with Bobby Watson, she sings one highly amusing song."[19] In the comedy *A Lady for a Night* (1928), Howard took over the leading role on only 10 days notice, when the actress Georgia O'Ramey suddenly died.[20] Howard's final show on Broadway was the Sigmund Romberg–Oscar Hammerstein sensation *The New Moon* (1928–29), where she played Clotilde Lombaste and sang "Ladies of the Jury" and "Funny Little Sailor Man" for 509 performances, first at the Imperial Theatre and later back at the Casino, where she had played in *Wildflower*.[21]

In the early 1930s, Howard joined the great migration from Broadway to Hollywood. She made her feature film debut in *The Vice Squad* (1931), starring Paul Lukas and Kay Francis, with her old Broadway co-star Rockcliffe Fellowes in a supporting role as a corrupt police detective. It was a Paramount film directed by John Cromwell, which pretty much explains how Howard got her start in the movie business. Cromwell had been directing films since 1929, but had been an actor much longer. In the late teens, he was part of Grace George's repertory company and did two shows with Howard. Cromwell would also give her a small, uncredited part in *Sweepings* (RKO, 1933) and, many years later, a walk-on in *Caged* (Warner Bros., 1950), which was one of her last films.

Howard was in several familiar films in the 1930s, but not so you'd notice: *Life Begins* (J. Flood and E. Nugent, First National, 1932), as a friend of Elizabeth Patterson; *Dead End* (W. Wyler, Samuel Goldwyn, 1937), as a loud-voiced neighbor; *Rebecca of Sunnybrook Farm* (A. Dwan, Twentieth Century–Fox, 1938), as a mother; *Marie Antoinette* (W.S. Van Dyke, MGM, 1938), in an uncredited bit part as a streetwalker. Out of her 60 feature films, more than two thirds of her roles were uncredited, but it's the remaining third that counts.

Howard's first significant dramatic role was as Vi in *Merrily We Go to Hell* (D. Arzner, Paramount, 1932). Vi is a fast-living, hard-drinking part of the barroom set around newspaperman and aspiring playwright Jerry Corbett (Fredric March). Divorced, but still in love with her ex, she encourages heroine Joan Prentice (Sylvia Sidney) to fight for her marriage, but also to "get out in time," if the trouble gets too serious. Maybe Howard was speaking from experience. She and Skeets Gallagher have a choral role in relation to Sidney and March, before, during, and after their rocky marriage. Forty years of age when the film was produced, Howard looks handsome and markedly younger than in the films of her "major phase." She is stylishly dressed throughout the film and wears a lot of jewelry.

Like her Josie in *The Vice Squad*, Vi was a harbinger of things to come, all those hard living, hardbitten women on the seamy side of life Howard would portray in the coming decade. Unlike some character actresses who got their best opportunities during their early years in Hollywood, Howard's roles only got better. The 1940s were her heyday, when the grim, gritty texture, urban underworld settings, and world-weary outlook of film noir suited her to a tee. Like the other character ladies of noir — Judith Anderson, Agnes Moore-

Esther Howard played straight woman and wife to Andy Clyde in a dozen comedy shorts at Columbia between 1935 and 1952. Howard showed an equal adeptness for comic and dramatic roles during her twenty-plus year film career.

head, Rosalind Ivan, Florence Bates — she was the right actress in the right place at the right time.

Howard had a quality that none of these other actresses had: a folksy, earthy, time-battered and "lived-in" look to her face and body, that made her truly a woman of the people compared to these other, more regal and refined actresses. Not that Howard didn't play her share of dowagers. They were often of the overstuffed and overdressed kind, not least of all in a stunning series of films at Paramount throughout the 1940s for celebrated writer-producer-director Preston Sturges. In order of release, they were: *The Great McGinty* (1940), *Sullivan's Travels* (1941), *The Palm Beach Story* (1942), *The Miracle of Morgan's Creek* (1944), *Hail the Conquering Hero* (1944), *The Great Moment* (1944), and *The Beautiful Blonde from Bashful Bend* (Twentieth Century–Fox, 1949).

Sullivan's Travels, starring Joel McCrea and Veronica Lake, was arguably the best of a brilliant lot. Howard plays Zeffie Kornheiser, a predatory widow who lives with her spinster sister-in-law Ursula (Almira Sessions). Mrs. Kornheiser takes on McCrea's John Lloyd Sullivan as a hired hand and potential lover boy, outfitting him in her dead husband's suit and trying to hold his hand at the movies. Overdressed and elaborately coiffed, she clucks around him like a brood hen and has a wonderful scene with Sessions where she admires McCrea's "torso," suggesting that some people are more sensitive to these things than others. Sessions is very much the wet blanket she was physically so well-endowed to portray, looking on with a disapproving, beady eye. After being locked in a bedroom with a picture of the late Mr. Kornheiser over the mantle, McCrea finally makes his escape on a sheet down from the window, tearing his pants and ending up in a water barrel. This is his first adventure on his solo trek as an undercover reporter seeking to discover "how the other half lives." Today *Sullivan's Travels* is Howard's most popular and highly rated film.[22] She was to Sturges what Jane Darwell was to John Ford.[23]

By the early 1940s, Howard was in her early fifties and showing signs of wear that only made the "local color" element she could lend any film all the more effective. What had once been a brassy, blonde, in-your-face kind of prettiness was now an asymmetrical, sagging, goggle-eyed, and sunken-chinned visage with every drink, cigarette and tear engraved on its surface. But Howard was still feisty and full of hell, qualities her characters also often manifested.

Apart from the Sturges comedies, Howard's best opportunities in her second decade in film were all set in the dark, dusty, smoky, liquor-sodden underbelly of the big city. In

Esther Howard (left) made only the briefest of appearances in *My Favorite Blonde* (Paramount Pictures, 1942), starring Bob Hope (center) and Madeleine Carroll (right). Like Cora Witherspoon and Florence Bates, Howard was effective playing overdressed dowagers with a streak of vulgarity and repressed desires.

Tales of Manhattan (J. Duvivier, Twentieth Century–Fox, 1942), *Murder, My Sweet* (E. Dmytryk, RKO, 1944), *The Great Flamarion* (A. Mann, Republic, 1945), *Detour* (E.G., Ulmer, Producers Releasing Corp., 1945), *The Falcon's Alibi* (R. McCarey, RKO, 1946), *Dick Tracy vs. Cueball* (G. Douglas, RKO, 1946), and *The Velvet Touch* (J. Gage, RKO, 1948), Howard portrayed a gallery of uniquely real characters that are her true artistic legacy. These characters were waitresses, con women, landladies, alcoholics, vagrants, and demimondaines. They were women alone, at the end of their rope and the end of their lives. They were a nightmare vision of what life could do to you.

In *Murder, My Sweet*, Dick Powell as Philip Marlowe describes one of these women, played by Howard, tellingly: "She was a charming, middle-aged lady with a face like a bucket of mud." He goes on: "She was a gal who would take a drink, if she had to knock you down to get the bottle." Never at a loss for words herself, Howard's character Jessie Florian goes Margo Channing one better when she tells Marlowe to "Hold on to your chair and don't step on no snakes." As she tightens her robe around her disheveled figure, she says coyly: "No peeking."

This brings us to Howard's single greatest performance, as the beer-guzzling, card-playing, vulgar and vengeful landlady Mrs. Kraft in Robert Wise's noir classic *Born to Kill* (1947), starring Claire Trevor and Lawrence Tierney. Wise was a four-time Oscar-nominated director, who won for *West Side Story* in 1961. He was active as a director from the time he shot the additional sequences for *The Magnificent Ambersons* (1942), that through no fault of his own so infamously mar the ending of that butchered masterpiece, until five years before his death at age 91. *Born to Kill* was his sixth film. Production started at RKO in early May 1946, with some location shooting in San Francisco and at El Segundo beach in Southern California, and was completed by June 21, though the film was not released till May 3, 1947.[24] Based on a 1942 novel by 19-year-old, first-time author James Gunn called *Deadlier than the Male*, the screenplay was written by Eve Greene and Richard Macauley.[25]

At the beginning of the film, Sam Wild (Lawrence Tierney), a big hunk of a man with anger management issues, kills his on-again, off-again girlfriend Laury Palmer (Isabel Jewell) in a fit of jealous rage when he finds her with another man. By chance, San Francisco socialite and recent divorcee Helen Brent (Claire Trevor) discovers the body. Laury is the neighbor and good friend of Helen's Reno landlady, Mrs. Kraft (Esther Howard), who, beyond a blind loyalty to her friends, is chiefly characterized by her tendency to live vicariously through others and to drink beer to excess. As the dead Laury's friend and the beneficiary of her will, it is Mrs. Kraft who drives the action forward through hiring shady private detective Matthew Arnett (Walter Slezak) to investigate the brutal murder. Her motivation is her deep devotion to Laury, though she ultimately fails her and somewhat inexplicably gives in to Helen's threats that she will be killed if she doesn't call off the investigation.[26] Sam Wild is ultimately "hoist by his own petard," when his lover Helen, realizing her own and her sister Georgia's danger, betrays Sam by refusing to pay blackmail to Arnett, knowing he will go to the police.

Howard really lets it all hang out in this role. With one glassy eye grotesquely larger than the other, hair awry, and simian, collapsed facial features, she looks like a dyspeptic Pekingese and much older than her 55 years. One of her best scenes is set in the deserted dunes, where Mrs. Kraft successfully escapes from the clutches of Sam Wild's sidekick and henchman Mart (Elisha Cook, Jr.), her would-be murderer, by sticking him in the leg with a hat pin. The effectiveness of this scene is largely due to the fact that one can't possibly imagine how the "glamor girl," as Mart mock ingratiatingly calls her, is going to get out of

One of Esther Howard's most riveting roles was as the vengeful, beer-guzzling, and remarkably resilient Reno boardinghouse keeper Mrs. Kraft in the thriller noir *Born to Kill* (RKO, 1947). In the film (based on the novel *Deadlier Than the Male* by James Gunn), a social register divorcee (Claire Trevor) gets mixed up with a brawny screwball (Lawrence Tierney). After her friend and neighbor is brutally murdered by Tierney, Howard is determined to track down her killer and hires Walter Slezak (left) to help her.

this alive. She's as much out of place in the sand dunes of San Francisco as a camel would be in the red light district. Mrs. Kraft's final big scene is a no-holds-barred showdown with Helen in the older woman's seedy San Francisco hotel room (Kraft to Brent: "You're the coldest iceberg of a woman I ever saw with the rottenest inside"). Despite the "fatal attraction" between Helen Brent and Sam Wild, this is a story where women ultimately place their relationships with other women above their relationships with men. It is equally original to have a storyline with an elderly, overweight lush as the antagonist. Mrs. Kraft is just about the most unlikely avenging angel you ever saw.

Though Howard played Kirk Douglas's dying Irish mother in the boxing film *Champion* (M. Robson, Stanley Kramer Productions, 1949), Mrs. Krantz was Howard's last major film role. She hung on till 1952, mostly in bit parts and shorts. She died of a heart attack in Hollywood on March 8, 1965. She was almost 73 years old and hadn't been seen on the screen in 13 years. She was interred at Forest Lawn Memorial Park in Glendale. Her simple gravestone gives her name and dates and between them is engraved the word "Daughter."[27]

Asylums and Old Lace:
Josephine Hull in *Harvey* (1950)

*"Myrtle Mae, you have a lot to learn,
and I hope you never learn it."*

How many actresses have become stars in their sixties? I can think of two: Marie Dressler in the movies and Agnes Moorehead on television. And then there's Josephine Hull, who was not "officially listed as a star" until her third to last Broadway show, *The Golden State*, in 1950.[1] Hull was an actress for half a century, but she only made five films. Two of them were *Arsenic and Old Lace* and *Harvey*. It is a bit as if Meryl Streep had only made five films and two of them were *Kramer vs. Kramer* and *Sophie's Choice*.[2] All told, Hull had a fabulous career. Thirty-seven shows on Broadway, including three that she "helped to Pulitzer Prizes."[3] An Oscar for what was only her fourth film. A star on the Walk of Fame for only five films. Add to that being married to the man of her dreams. Not bad for a little girl from Newtonville, Massachusetts.

Newtonville is 8.5 miles straight west of Boston. The Massachusetts Turnpike cuts right through it. That's where it all started for Mary Josephine Sherwood on January 3, 18??. Yes, well, sometime in the late 1870s. Hull's birth year, if not birth day, is a mystery and she preferred it that way. It was her secret, "jealously guarded all her life." She even stipulated that no date of birth was to be carved on her gravestone.[4] The year that is usually given, 1886, is a blatant absurdity, as Hull graduated from Radcliffe College in 1899 and was unlikely to have done that at age 13.[5] Eighteen eighty-six was the year her father died. He was William H. Sherwood, an importer of perfumes; her mother was Mary Elizabeth Tewksbury, who would be the greatest influence on her daughter's life until Mrs. Sherwood's death in 1909.[6]

The *New York Times* noted on Josephine Hull's death that she "seemed hardly the type for the theatre."[7] She was only 5' 2½" tall and had a bit of a Gloria Swanson thing going on with a large head on a small body.[8] In youth, she had been described as "a very delectable little person."[9] Hull put on weight quite early in life and soon settled, however reluctantly, into a comfortable, pleasantly plump body. That, in addition to her not exactly classical facial features, would consign her to supporting roles for most of her career. Critics would sometimes be unkind about her looks. One wrote in his review of *The Solid Gold Cadillac* (1950) that she had "the body of an old coal barge and the face of an ugly English pug." Hull was deeply hurt.[10] Another was not quite so lacerating, writing, "Josephine Hull is the nearest thing to a human plum pudding there is."[11]

As a child in Newtonville, Josephine wanted to be a nurse or a doctor.[12] Later, "the choice lay between the stage and music."[13] The young lady got a college education at Radcliffe, and went on to study music at the New England Conservatory in Boston, before making her first professional stage appearance with the Castle Square Stock Company in 1905, when she must have been in her mid-to late twenties.[14] Josephine Sherwood's Broadway debut took place on December 20, 1906, when she played Fantine in a dramatization of *Les Miserables* called *Law and the Man* at the Manhattan Theatre at 102 W. 33rd St. It was in connection with her second Broadway show, *The Bridge*, in April 1909, that she met the love of her life and her future husband, fellow cast member Shelley Hull. Her mother died the following month: "Now this radiant spirit, charged with life and gaiety, had come to restore her to the light."[15] The couple was married in 1910, a year after their first meeting. Josephine stopped working when they found it hard to juggle two careers. They were unable to have children.[16]

Shelley Vaughan Hull was born circa 1884 in Louisville, Kentucky, had a successful career on Broadway starting in 1903, and was declared a star in the papers for the first time on October 13, 1918, as his proud wife noted in her diary.[17] Just three months later, Shelley Hull would be dead, his life brutally cut short by pneumonia on January 14, 1919. His widow returned to Broadway on Christmas Day 1922, not as an actress, not as Josephine Sherwood, but as the director "Mrs. Shelley Hull" (with O.P. Heggie) of a play by Jesse Lynch Williams called *Why Not?* It was at this time, in early 1923, that she also took over the staging of a shocking new play by John Henry Lawson called *Roger Bloomer*, starring her brother-in-law Henry Hull as the troubled adolescent hero of the title. Try to imagine Josephine Hull, who had once balked at playing a pageboy because the costume would show her legs, directing a play in which "nothing had been omitted," including "a mocking orgy of Sex and Obscenity."[18] Her biographer remarks that "it is clear from mutterings in the diary that she did not welcome her assignment with glee."[19]

The comedy *Neighbors*, which ran briefly in late 1923 and early 1924, marked Hull's return to the Broadway stage as an actress. She would be seen regularly, if not always successfully, on the Great White Way for the next 30 years, racking up an impressive 37 Broadway shows. Many of these shows had short runs, but this was more than made up for by the enormity of her successes. During her "major phase" on Broadway, Hull had four defining roles: Penny Sycamore in *You Can't Take It with You* (1936–38), Aunt Abby in *Arsenic and Old Lace* (1941–44), Veta Louise Simmons in *Harvey* (1944–49), and Laura Partridge in *The Solid Gold Cadillac* (1953–55). These four shows ran for a total of 4,583 performances and 10 years. Two of these roles she reprised on film.

Craig's Wife (1925–26) by George Kelly marked the first turning point in her career, as it was her first hit on Broadway with 360 performances (at the Morosco Theatre) and the first of her plays to win the Pulitzer Prize.[20] Hull created the role of the Craigs' sympathetic neighbor, Mrs. Frazier, who acts as a foil to the obsessively house-proud Mrs. Craig. Billie Burke played the role in the original film version, starring Rosalind Russell and John Boles. What followed for Hull during her next 10 years on Broadway, though, was a long chain of no less than 15 flops, which was broken only by a moderate success in a new play by John Golden and Hugh Stange called *After Tomorrow* in 1931. *After Tomorrow* is doubly significant, because it brought Hull before the movie cameras for the first time.

Hull's five films were made over a period of nearly 20 years. In the early thirties, she made *After Tomorrow* and *Careless Lady*, in the early forties *Arsenic and Old Lace*, and finally in the early 1950s *Harvey* and *The Lady from Texas*. *After Tomorrow* (F. Borzage, Fox, 1932) is the lost gem in the Hull crown. It isn't entirely lost, fortunately — in fact it was released on DVD in 2008 — but compared to the vast renown of *Arsenic and Old Lace* and *Harvey* it might as well have been made in Uzbekistan. Hull plays Mrs. Piper, a "monster mom" and "one of the deadliest of the species."[21] Unlike the prototypical Mrs. Phelps in Sidney Howard's 1926 play and the 1933 film *The Silver Cord*, Mrs. Piper is a working class woman who has devoted herself entirely to her son, Peter (Charles Farrell). Though a grown man, he still refers to himself as "Mrs. Piper's boy." Peter has been engaged for three years to a girl down the street, Sidney Taylor (Marian Nixon), but because they both have their parents to support, they find it hard to save enough money to get married. Farrell is a salesman and only earns 20 dollars a week and Sidney works as a secretary in the Empire State Building. Things start looking up when Peter gets a raise, but Sidney's sexually frustrated mother, Else Taylor (Minna Gombell), runs off with their lodger, giving her husband Willie (William Collier) a heart attack. The wedding money has to be used to pay his medical bills.

In her expert characterization, Hull is manipulative, coquettish, and childish. She easily takes offense, but is not as cunning and insidious as Mrs. Phelps. Mrs. Piper is armed with an arsenal of clichés, such as "A man's best friend is his mother," "A sharp tongue is the penalty of a keen brain," and "There's no love like a mother's." Mrs. Piper also has some more unconventional opinions, believing "it's best for a man's sex education to come from his mother." She refers to herself as a "mother bird" and surprisingly makes daughter-in-law Sidney a brassiere as a wedding present. Willie calls her an "old sea cow." Hull said of her that she was "a dreadful old cat, but I loved her."[22] Mrs. Piper is romantically interested in her widowed neighbor, a chewing gum salesman, who beat his late wife. Go figure. The possibility is mooted that they may marry at the end of the film, when Peter surprises them in an embrace on the sofa and demands to know the older man's intentions. The salesman then informs him that Peter's $100 investment in clove chewing gum ("It takes your breath away!") is now worth $740, which he can have at any time. This is the *deus ex machina* that allows the young couple finally to get married.

After Tomorrow was released on March 13, 1932. Despite being described as "a tiresome little item," the film is really quite witty, especially William Collier's wisecracks, which he apparently came up with himself, though he was denied screen credit.[23] Mordaunt Hall found Mrs. Piper a "boring bromide" and thought Hull gave "a good performance in the uninteresting rôle."[24] Springer and Hamilton found her to be "priceless in the part but the film was hardly worth it."[25]

Hull finished her scenes from *After Tomorrow* on January 11, 1932, and went almost immediately into a new project, which had the working title *Widow's Might*.[26] *Careless Lady* (K. McKenna, 1932), as it would ultimately be called, was also made for Fox Film Corporation and starred Joan Bennett as Sally Brown and John Boles as Stephen Illington. It featured Minna Gombell, Hull's *After Tomorrow* co-star, as Yvette Logan, an assistant in a dress shop and the heroine's confidante. Hull had a small role as Cora, one of two family aunts. A romantic comedy with a mass of mishaps and complications, the plot focuses upon frumpy Sally Brown's attempt to get enough experience "in a nice way" to attract men; Stephen Illington being the one she both uses to attract others and ultimately marries. The film was produced with lightning speed starting January 14 and ending in early February and was released on April 3, 1932.

Hull's experience in Hollywood "terrified her at first": "There were times when I sat in a corner of the stage on the verge of tears because I was sure I had done everything wrong."[27] Overall though, making both films was a pleasant experience, and her friends

Louise Closser Hale and Grant Mitchell made sure she had a good time during her off hours as well.[28] Hull went happily home to New York on February 8, 1932, and probably never gave another thought to acting in movies until the chance arose to reprise her standout performance in *Arsenic and Old Lace* almost 10 years later.

Enough has been said and written about Joseph Kesselring's modern classic. Readers may be interested to learn, though, that W. David Sievers claims that Kesselring took "the old hereditary view of insanity" and was "said to have intended the play seriously and to have been excluded from rehearsals while the [stage] producers, Crouse and Lindsay, proceeded to burlesque it."[29] We can be glad they did. Both the play and Frank Capra's brilliant filmatization are a perennial delight and one of the absolute highpoints of American popular comedy. It is impossible to imagine anyone else as Aunt Martha Brewster than her creator on Broadway and in "glorious black and white" on the big screen, Josephine Hull: "for those who saw Josephine, she was *she*."[30] Hull and Jean Adair were, in Capra's recollection, each paid $25,000 for their work on the film, which seems a paltry sum given the millions the film has earned the producers down through the years.[31] William Carson writes that Hull and Adair "had to be content with less than they had at first stipulated."[32] At any rate, *Arsenic and Old Lace* "established Josephine among the immortals in Broadway's Hall of

Here are two pious old ladies you don't want to get mixed up with, at least not if you're a lonely old bachelor. Josephine Hull (left) and Jean Adair (right) originated the roles of Abby and Martha Brewster in Joseph Kesselring's madcap stage comedy *Arsenic and Old Lace* and went on to reprise their roles in the film version (Warner Bros., 1944).

Fame."[33] For someone who "had an overmastering desire for popularity," that would have been payment enough.[34]

⸺∞⸺

Despite her success as Aunt Martha in *Arsenic and Old Lace*, Josephine Hull's greatest film role was Veta Louise Simmons in *Harvey* (H. Koster, Universal, 1950). An upper-middle class widow, Veta is trying to marry off her soon-to-be spinster daughter, Myrtle Mae (Victoria Horne), while trying to avoid social ostracism because of her brother Elwood P. Dowd's (James Stewart) eccentric behavior. Veta and Myrtle Mae are living with bachelor Elwood, who has inherited everything from his and Veta's mother, including the family home at 348 Temple Drive. After Elwood crashes a ladies' "musicale" hosted by Veta and scares off all the guests with his 6' 3½" invisible rabbit friend Harvey, Veta makes the momentous decision to have him committed to "Chumley's Rest." This kicks off a series of misunderstandings, whereby Veta herself is committed to the insane asylum and they all go chasing after Elwood on what may best be described as a wild rabbit chase.

Whether trying to get her daughter married, her brother committed, herself released, or ultimately deciding that Elwood must remain as he is at any cost, Veta Louise is front and center in *Harvey*. The romantic pair, Nurse Kelly (Peggy Dow) and Dr. Sanderson (Charles Drake), the comic version of the romantic pair, Myrtle Mae and Wilson (Jesse White), and even Elwood and his invisible rabbit have to step aside when the doughty dowager dynamo throws herself into the fray. When you think about it, Elwood is nearly entirely passive throughout the film. It is Veta who is the driving force in the plot and it is in her changing goals and motivations that much of the suspense and interest of the film lies. Will she sacrifice her brother's freedom and well-being to increase her daughter's marital opportunities?

As Veta Louise Simmons, Hull starts out in an elaborate lace and brocade dress and later appears in a series of hats festooned with flowers or huge ostrich feathers. She is very short indeed, particularly compared with long and lanky daughter Victoria Horne, and looks markedly older and thinner than in *Arsenic and Old Lace*. Even her dowager bosom is shrunken. Hull's performance is full of nice touches. When speaking to her friend and ally Judge Gaffney (William H. Lynn) on the phone in the opening scene, she puts the receiver down and pulls down her corset before addressing him, just as the first guests at the "program tea and reception" of the "Wednesday Forum" arrive.

One of Hull's best moments is when she is being bodily carried into the asylum "Chumley's Rest" by male nurse Jesse White. Her calves and ankles are surprisingly slender, making it likely a body double was used. We never see her face. In real life, "the quickest way to her heart was to comment on her tiny and beautifully shaped feet."[35] Hull's facial expressions when we do see them are often priceless, as when she observes with trepidation the bouncing bosoms of the singer at her party, Mrs. Tewksbury (Aileen Carlyle), as the latter trills "Hop, hop, hop, hop, hippity, hop!" In another of Veta's big scenes, she meets her daughter and Judge Gaffney on her return from being manhandled at "Chumley's Rest." She is appalled that all the doctors there think of is sex. To have a woman of her age and station even say the word "sex" is almost shocking. It is a sign that times are changing, changes that would sweep Veta Louise Simmons and all her kind right out of the American cultural imagination.

It's important to recognize that Veta belongs to the proud American stage and screen tradition of the dizzy dame. The dizzy dame or flibbertigibbet could theoretically be of any age, but was usually of a "certain age," meaning somewhere in mid-life, with grown children and a resigned or deceased husband. The great era of the dizzy dame in drama and film was the years between the great wars. Mrs. Wheeler in Booth Tarkington's play *Clarence* (1919) is the first important occurrence of this character type, enacted by Mary Boland on Broadway and Spring Byington in the 1937 film version. Boland and Byington were just two members of this zany sisterhood, whose surnames seem all to start with "B," Billie Burke and Alice Brady being two other important players of this type of role.

Examples of the species are legion in early talkies and later 1930s comedies, particularly of the screwball variety. I'm thinking of Bridget Drake in Rachel Crothers's *When Ladies Meet* (1932), created on Broadway by Spring Byington, on film in 1933 by Alice Brady and by Byington again in the 1941 remake. I'm thinking of practically any character portrayed by Billie Burke in the 1930s, with the notable exception of her first two films *A Bill of Divorcement* (1932) and *Christopher Strong* (1933). All Burke had to do was open her mouth and let out that helium voice and the character was there. Her Millicent Jordan in *Dinner at Eight* (1933) is the apotheosis of the dizzy dame; her monologue about the frustrations of the hostess is the dizzy dame declaration of independence. Even Glinda in *The Wizard of Oz* (1939) is a member of this light-headed sorority. Alice Brady as Aunt Hortense in *The Gay Divorcee* (1934) and, of course, Angelica Bullock in *My Man Godfrey* (1936) are two other classic examples. Not to mention Mary Boland as the exuberant social climber Effie Floud in *Ruggles of Red Gap* (1935) and the Countess de Lave in *The Women* (1939). "L'amour, l'amour, how it lets you down."

What all these characters have in common is that they are self-centered, seemingly addle-brained women, who make sure everyone's eyes and ears are focused on them. They are what it's all about, along the lines of "But enough about me, what do you think of me?" This is terribly refreshing in a period when so many older women are stuck in the self-sacrificing mother routine, whether their offspring are gangsters, ill-fated lovers, or just plain selfish; not to mention the legion of lovelorn spinsters, life's eternal bystanders, who can at most throw some acid into the mix or a spanner into the works. Give me a dizzy dame any day. With style and aplomb they sashay through life's trials and tribulations with enough blinkers on for an entire horse brigade. Still, they surprisingly often get what they want and they are never bored or — worse yet — boring.

It's worth asking how the dizzy dame came to be such a significant presence in American plays and films. Well, for one thing, she was entertaining. As an alternative to playing the straight woman of a Margaret Dumont kind to some type of male comedian, this was a way for women to take center stage and be the funny ones. Husbands, lovers, sons, brothers, all they could do was stand back and hope it would all blow over. Just think: Who is the funniest in *Harvey*? Is it James Stewart? Is it Jesse White? Is it Cecil Kellaway as Dr. Chumley? Of course not. It's Josephine Hull.

In his paragraph-long encomium to Hull in the *New York Times*, Bosley Crowther wrote that she "plays Elwood's sister with such hilarious confusion and daft concern that she brings quite as much to the picture as does Mr. Stewart ... It would be an unhappy screen version that did not contain her rotund frame, her scatter-brained fussing and fluttering and her angelic gentleness of soul."[36] Springer and Hamilton also reflect on why Hull was so ideally suited to playing dizzy dames: "She might have looked dear and dumpy, but she was filled with surprises. She had a feminine balkiness and a fey, almost evil mischief about her that enabled her to stand up to the world of men and win her points."[37] And that's exactly what a dizzy dame does.

Josephine Hull was seldom seen on the big screen, as she acted in only five feature films between 1932 and 1951. One of the absolute high points was her reprise of her stage role as Veta Louise Simmons in Mary Chase's Pulitzer Prize–winning comedy *Harvey*, when it was made into a film in 1950. In this picture, Veta and her spinster daughter Myrtle Mae (Victoria Horne, left) are throwing a party for their imperious cousin Mrs. Ethel Chauvenet (Grayce Mills, center).

Unlike Veta Louise, created by Mary Chase, most of these dames were figments of the male imagination. It's likely that many of them are a manifestation of frustration with perceived feminine illogic and emotionality and the extent to which women were ruling the roost, at least in the moneyed and educated classes. The authors' motivations don't really matter, though, when the results are so enjoyable. The Veta Louise Simmonses and Millicent Jordans and Effie Flouds may not be feminist icons exactly, but neither are they victims, sex symbols, or shrews. Back in 1963, Carson explained the appeal of a character like Veta: "Men laugh at her because they find her uproariously funny in her perplexities, but they see her only from the outside. Women have an altogether different point of view, and she gives them a splurge of empathy. It is easy for them to imagine themselves in her place."[38] Though we might want to respond that surely reactions to Veta aren't necessarily so clearly divided by sex, there is much truth to what Carson writes, especially for the original audience living in a more gender-segregated world.

Normally, Hull would not have been on hand to personally receive her Academy Award for *Harvey* at the Pantages Theatre in Los Angeles on March 29, 1951. She had gone home to New York after the film was in the can in early June 1950 and spent the remainder of the year nursing ailing relatives and in a short-lived Sam Spewack comedy, *The Golden State*, when she received word early in 1951 that she was wanted for another film at Universal.[39] Production had just started on the film in late March 1951 and thus she was able to attend the Academy Awards "tightly curled and decked out in a mink stole borrowed from the costume department."[40]

The Lady from Texas (J. Pevney, Universal, 1951) was Hull's only period costume drama, her only western, and her only film in glorious Technicolor. Clearly made to exploit Hull's wacky screen persona, the film tells the story of a beleaguered, eccentric Civil War widow, Miss Birdie Wheeler, who needs a little help from her friends to get back in touch with reality and keep her ranch out of the hands of rapacious neighbors. Hull's good friend Gene Lockhart played the judge who presides at Miss Birdie's sanity hearing. A love story between a ranch hand and a cook was thrown in for the price of the ticket. The shoot was over in late April 1951 and Hull left Hollywood never to return.

Apparently, "the fluttery, bewildered little person the public came in later years to identify with Josephine Hull was just about as far as anything could be from the real article."[41] Daniel Blum averred in 1952 that "the scatter-brained ladies she creates so brilliantly are the antithesis of the lady herself who has an even disposition and a well-balanced mind."[42] Jessie Royce Landis, who helped form the Theatre Wing of British War Relief with Hull during World War II, writes in her autobiography: "Josephine generally plays lovable, pixy, vague, somewhat dizzy women on the stage, but she is anything but a dizzy personality. She was appointed secretary of our organization, and worked like a little beaver."[43] Hull's stage director in *Arsenic and Old Lace*, Bretaigne Windust, said: "Everything about her suggested warmth and pleasantry, and softness. But actually she was a woman of very decided opinions about many things. And when she had understood and digested a point of view in any direction, it was almost impossible to shake."[44] Yet she had one characteristic that might well remind us of Aunt Abby, Penny Sycamore, or Veta Louise Simmons: "[W]hat Josephine did not like, Josephine did not see. She was mistress of the art of ignoring."[45]

An episode from the end of her life illustrates three salient aspects of Hull's character: her "whim of iron," her fine manners, and her wit. Early one morning in August 1954, she fell over a table in her room at the Essex House and found she could not get up. She was able to crawl over to the telephone, which stood on a small table, and call the office downstairs. "Would the clerk please be so kind as to send a bellboy up to 607?" she asked. Wearing just a nightgown and ever aware of the proprieties, she added: "Be sure to send a *married* bellboy." Always the trooper, she gave what would prove the final stage performance of her long career that evening with a broken rib and a solid dose of codeine.[46]

As if *You Can't Take It with You*, *Arsenic and Old Lace*, and *Harvey* were not enough, Hull was to be vouchsafed yet another hit before her days on Broadway were spent. *The Solid Gold Cadillac*, co-authored by George S. Kaufman and Harold Teichmann, was Kaufman's final play on Broadway. Alas, Hull suffered a series of paralytic strokes during the last three years of her life. The first struck in May 1954, forcing her to withdraw from the show. She returned, briefly, three months later, playing her final performance on August 24, 1954.[47] She died "very quietly" at the St. Barnabas Hospital in the Bronx on March 12, 1957. There were no survivors, all her family having preceded her in death. Her funeral was held in the Little Church Around the Corner at Fifth Avenue and 29th Street two days later.[48] Josephine Shrewsbury Hull returned to her native ground when she was buried with her husband in Newton Cemetery.[49]

Maid in America: Patsy Kelly
in *Private Number* (1936)

*Blessings on you, Patsy Kelly. How many nights at the
movies have you rescued, at least for a moment
or two, just because you were there.*

No very convincing case can be made for the innate greatness of *Private Number* as an artistic creation. The film is a generic drama of a kind the studios churned out in great numbers in the 1930s and '40s, though the production values here are good, the casting is excellent, and the performances, despite the basic triteness of the material, are outstanding. Even the dismissive reviewer for the *New York Times* had to admit that "the picture is well acted throughout."[1] In their encomium to Patsy Kelly in *They Had Faces Then*, John Springer and Jack Hamilton single out *Private Number* as one of her worst films. "Blessings on you, Patsy Kelly," they write. "How many nights at the movies have you rescued, at least for a moment or two, just because you were there. Of course, even you couldn't do anything for *Ever Since Eve* or *Private Number* or a picture or two like that. But it wasn't because you weren't trying."[2] James Parish and William Leonard refer to the film as a "wilted Loretta Young–Robert Taylor" feature.[3]

I've nevertheless chosen to discuss *Private Number* out of Kelly's nearly 40 feature films, because it's a good example, in general, of the role and function of the "comic second" and, in particular, of what Kelly could bring to a film in this type of role. In summing up her screen career in 1975, Alex Barris wrote: "When she wasn't being the heroine's buddy, she was somebody's irreverent maid."[4] In *Private Number*, she was actually the heroine's buddy *and* somebody's irreverent maid. To my mind, too, there is a limit to how bad a film can be that has bedroom-eyed and aquiline-nosed Basil Rathbone as a horny butler, stately Marjorie Gateson as a ultra-chic society dame, and homely Jane Darwell as a fractious cook, not to mention Patsy Kelly.

A "comic second," short for comic secondary leading actor, was a featured player who typically played the hero or heroine's best friend, a sidekick with specific and important functions in the film narrative. Judith Roof has written an entire book about female comic seconds called *All About Thelma and Eve: Sidekicks and Third Wheels*. Though the book chiefly deals with Eve Arden and Thelma Ritter (Patsy Kelly is relegated to a footnote,[5]) much of what Roof writes is relevant to Kelly's typical roles in Hollywood films. According to Roof, comic seconds are "modernized versions of the Shakespearean fool"[6] and have several essential functions in a film. First of all, they serve as mediators between the characters in the film and between the film and the audience.[7] Speaking specifically of Ida Corwin in

Veteran funny girl Patsy Kelly, who we can imagine spent more time in the kitchen on film than she did in real life, is here shown as the wisecracking maid Etta in the screwball comedy *Merrily We Live* (Hal Roach Studios, 1938). The caption to this press photograph informs us that in addition to playing "a very important role" in the film, Kelly "knows that kitchen work is made easier by scientific assistance" and is here demonstrating a "Kitchen Aid mixer." Product tie-ins are nothing new.

Mildred Pierce, Roof writes: "Ida is the character who lets us in; if she is the protagonist's best buddy, she is ours as well."[8] Roof adds that comic seconds "provide humor, wisdom, a point of identification, and the possibility of narrative alternatives until they disappear at the end."[9] "Female comic seconds," she observes, "seem to have a magical insight their male counterparts often lack or exercise sparingly."[10] Roof points out, "They can do 'unfeminine' things in unfeminine ways because they aren't represented as sufficiently womanly. At the same time, their freedom actually presents a broader vision of what women can do and how they can do it."[11] Comic seconds also "enable the enunciation of scandalous material in the form of wisecracks and sarcastic remarks."[12] All this makes good sense when we consider the wisecracking, loud-mouthed, and brassy characters commonly portrayed by Patsy Kelly.

Comic seconds were not restricted to comedies. One might say, they were all the more necessary to lighten the tone in dramas, such as *Private Number*. The film was shot in a month starting March 26, 1936, under the direction of Roy Del Ruth, and starred Loretta Young and Robert Taylor. The *New York Times* wrote: "Worthy of special notice are Patsy Kelly, as another maid, and her steady fellow, Joe Lewis, who supply much needed comic interludes." The same reviewer suggested that by the mid–1930s, the storyline was dated, calling the film "a sermon on a social problem that may conceivably have disturbed some of the upper 5 per cent of our population and a few amorous members of the lower classes before the advent of that great leveler, the depression." The "social problem," as he put it, was "whether or not the marriage may properly proceed between the parlor maid and the scion of the house."[13]

If "the plot creaks," as the *Times* critic also wrote, there was good reason. The story that found its final form in the film *Private Number* was hardly in its first youth. It had a 20-year history by the time Twentieth Century–Fox released its remake on June 5, 1936. It originated as a hit Broadway play by Cleves Kinkead called *Common Clay*, which opened at the Republic Theatre on August 26, 1915, and gave Jane Cowl one of her first starring roles as the hard-done-by, genteelly poor, struggling-to-stay-respectable heroine Ellen Neal. In the wake of the Broadway success, *Common Clay* was "novelized" under the same title in 1916. The first film version appeared in 1919, starring Fannie Ward. Fox Film Corporation produced the first sound film based on *Common Clay*, which was released in 1930 and starred Constance Bennett and Lew Ayres. Bennett had cornered the market on "women at risk" films during this period. Both these film versions stuck close to the original story of an underprivileged, attractive young girl, Ellen, trying to survive in a man's world, who takes a job as a maid in a fine family and falls in love with her employers' son. Pregnant and unwed, she is arrested in a raid on a speakeasy and, as fate and melodrama would have it, the judge presiding at the trial is actually her father. He had seduced and impregnated an actress in his youth, who promptly and obligingly committed suicide rather than bring shame on his proud family name. Father and daughter are reconciled and with this sudden social advancement, Ellen becomes wife material after all.

The various forms of this story between its inception in 1915 and *Private Number* in 1936 tell an interesting tale of changing priorities, interests, and ideological pressures from early World War I era till the Great Depression. Dealing with such touchy topics as premarital sex, illegitimacy, and sexual harassment, we can learn a lot from the various versions about where the limitations on public entertainment ran during the two decades when *Common Clay* was central to American culture. Maybe somewhat surprisingly, these limits seemed to become narrower as time progressed. The portrayal of men's aggressive sexual advances towards the heroine, for example, is much more explicit in the original play. Not primarily a love story, *Common Clay* is a powerful indictment of the sexual double standard, which focuses more on the reaction of the older men in the community to Ellen and her lover's relationship, than the development of the love affair itself.

By the time *Private Number* came along in the post–Code era, the entire illegitimacy storyline has been jettisoned and with it Ellen's biological father, Judge Filson. The producers this time found it necessary to appease the Production Code Administration by inventing a secret marriage between Ellen and the hero, Richard Winfield, as he was now called, which makes their child legitimate. Predictably, the film version spends more time on the development of the young lovers' romantic relationship than the original play.

The *Private Number* screenplay by Gene Markey and William M. Conselman is thus the furthest from the original of the three film versions. Beyond the exclusion of characters from the play, such as Ellen's real father and adopted mother Mrs. Neal, it introduces characters and storylines that are completely new. One of these is the comic subplot of Ellen's fellow maid and confidante Gracie, played by Patsy Kelly, and her boyfriend Smiley Watson (Joe E. Lewis).[14] The role of the sexually simmering butler, now called Thomas Wroxton (Basil Rathbone), has also been enlarged to the extent that he, rather than Ellen's father-in-law, becomes her chief antagonist. After his plans to marry Ellen himself fall through, Thomas reveals to her in-laws, Perry and Maggie Winfield (Paul Harvey and Marjorie Gateson), both that she is pregnant and that she has been arrested in a raid on a house of ill repute. Ellen's complete innocence in connection with her arrest is revealed in a big concluding trial scene, as in the original play. *Private Number*, too, ends happily "when young Winfield reaches great heights in lovey-dovey palaver, hands the butler a beautiful sock and gathers his little family to his manly brisket."[15]

Though Roof points out that the characters commonly portrayed by Eve Arden and Thelma Ritter are "definitely out of the mating game,"[16] Kelly's comic maids and best friends sometimes get paired up with some "Joe," as indeed happens in *Private Number*. Here the guy in question is fellow comedian Joe E. Lewis in his film debut. Despite this ostensibly romantic relationship, a kind of comic contrast to that of the more attractive, genteel, and ideal Ellen and Hugh, Gracie is primarily focused on Ellen throughout the film. As a supporting player, she is not in the film, after all, to have fun on her own, but rather to aid and abet the heroine in reaching her goals. Gracie is the first person Ellen meets when she knocks at the back door of Winfield Manor seeking work. Gracie is the one who gets her a job as a maid. Gracie runs interference whenever the butler, jokingly referred to as "His Nibs," tries to talk to Ellen alone. Gracie enacts one of her most important plot functions, when she tells the Winfields that Ellen is married to their son and carrying their grandchild. Gracie is there throughout the film to lend a sympathetic ear and a helping hand. It is when Gracie is not present to protect her, that Ellen lands herself in a pickle and gets arrested. Finally, Gracie helps get Ellen a lawyer, so she can fight for her child and her marriage. In keeping with her function as comic relief, Gracie also has interludes of pure comedy with little plot function, as when she borrows the cook's oversize bathing suit, dives in feet first, manages to lose her suit in the water, and can't get out till Ellen and Hugh are finished talking.

"There is no doubt," Roof writes of films that show a strong bond between the female star and a female sidekick, "that the lesbian tone is often present."[17] Nice choice of words. Actual woman-on-woman action would, of course, be *ganz verboten*, so what we get is a lesbian *tone*. What does that mean, exactly? How do we account for it? Ironically, the very studio system that after the introduction of the stricter production code in 1934 was more dedicated than ever to keeping dyed-in-the-wool lesbian characters and situations off the screen, was the same system that was manufacturing quasi-lesbian characters and storylines. Classical Hollywood films paradoxically put a number of female supporting players in what I would call a lesbian *position*, that is to say it put actresses like Agnes Moorehead and Cecil Cunningham in a position where their attention, their focus, their emotional life was primarily directed toward another woman, i.e., the female star and lead character of the film.

When these actresses in addition had certain physical characteristics that rendered them less than conventionally feminine, presto! a lesbian is born.

I think gay and lesbian film historians do a disservice both to our communities and to the actresses involved, if we insist too stridently on the lesbian sexual orientation of certain character actresses on the basis of only the thinnest veneer of what one can call historical evidence. I'm not in a position to say categorically that Judith Anderson, Agnes Moorehead, Spring Byington, Cecil Cunningham, Hope Emerson, and Marjorie Main were *not* lesbians, but they certainly didn't identify as lesbians (unlike Patsy Kelly). As gay historian William Mann admits in his magisterial book *Behind the Screen: How Gays and Lesbians Shaped Hollywood*: "[D]espite the claims of some spurious but oft-repeated quotes that label Anderson, Main, Moorehead, and others as 'dykes,' in truth none of the gay survivors interviewed for this study recalled ever having met them or hearing any stories about them."[18]

Clearly, in the case of all these women, their lesbian reputation rests largely on the types of roles they played. In all fairness and honesty, no interpretation of or argument about an individual's sexual orientation can be taken seriously when it is solely based on her having played one or more roles that are open to a lesbian reading. We owe these character actresses, I think, the same scholarly consideration as to standards of evidence that we would apply to biographical writing about stars like Tallulah Bankhead, Greta Garbo, or Marlene Dietrich, figures whose lives are better illuminated in the form of primary sources. Ultimately, too, I think it matters little to these character actresses' legacy and significance whether or not they had one or the other sexual orientation. They lived their lives largely out of the limelight, they dedicated themselves to the serious work of acting, and that is their gift to us no matter what sexual road we ourselves are traveling down.

In the case of Patsy Kelly, things are much simpler and less caution is required. Out of all the supporting actresses that have been thought to have had a sexual and romantic interest in their own sex, Kelly is the one undeniable, self-declared, card-carrying lesbian. During her heyday in Hollywood, she lived openly with her lover, the actress Wilma Cox.[19] Boze Hadleigh, who interviewed her twice at the home of a mutual friend in 1979, describes her as "blithely lesbian." "I knew how I was, I knew that was that, and I didn't think it was so bad," she told Hadleigh, especially compared with her mother's fate as the wife of a violent drunk. When asked if she had ever considered getting married, she responded in the negative: "I'm a dyke. So what? Big deal!" Hadleigh congratulated her on her honesty. "Let's have a toast," she suggested. "To honesty. It's not the best policy, but it's the only way to fly!"[20]

Patsy Kelly was born Sarah Veronica Rose Kelly in Brooklyn on January 12, 1910, as the sixth child in the Kelly brood. Her father was New York City policeman John Kelly. He and Patsy's mother, Delia Kelly, had migrated to the United States from Ballinrobe in County Mayo, Ireland. "Patsy" was a nickname her brother gave her.[21] She was a tough kid, who grew up on 62nd St. between 9th and 10th Ave., which forms the southern perimeter of the Lincoln Center today and runs into the large apartment blocks of Amsterdam Ave. Patsy wanted to be a fireman and hung around the local fire station in her spare time.[22] She was soon packed off to Jack Blue's dancing school, probably in an attempt to encourage more conventionally feminine behavior and to channel her energies into something constructive and socially acceptable. She was willing to go, as long as it wasn't "that ballet crap."[23] Patsy became a tap dancer. There was another 10-year-old girl of Irish extraction at the school, Ethel Hilda Keeler, originally from Nova Scotia. She would be known to the world as Ruby Keeler. Fifteen years later they would be in a film together at Warner Bros., *Go Into Your Dance* (A. Mayo, 1935) and more than half a century later they would be in a smash hit Broadway revival of the musical *No, No, Nanette* at the 46th Street Theatre. So the paths of life and career cross and recross.

Back in 1923, at any rate, 13-year-old Patsy had been getting on so well at the school, she'd advanced from pupil to instructor at $18 a week. One day she went with her brother Willie, who was auditioning for Frank Fay at the Palace Theatre on Times Square. Fay ended up hiring Patsy instead.[24] According to her *New York Times* obituary, she spent three years "trouping with Frank Fay across the country."[25] On November 28, 1927, at the tender age of 17, she found herself making her Broadway debut, when she joined Fay and the rest of the cast for the premiere of the new musical revue *Harry Delmar's Revels* at the Shubert Theatre. The show lasted 112 performances.

Kelly used to say: "I started at the top and worked my way down."[26] She was in demand and was almost continually employed on Broadway for the next five years. *Harry Delmar's Revels* was followed by *Three Cheers* (1928–29), *Earl Carroll's Sketch Book* (1929–30), and *Earl Carroll's Vanities* (1930–31). *Three Cheers* was Will Rogers's last Broadway musical. After 210 performances at the Globe Theatre, they went on a two and a half month tour.[27] A month later, the curtain went up at the Earl Carroll Theatre on what would prove the tremendously successful two-act musical revue *Earl Carroll's Sketch Book* with music and lyrics by Yip Harburg and Jay Gorney. From this show, Kelly went directly into Earl Carroll's next offering *Earl Carroll's Vanities*, which opened at the New Amsterdam Theatre on July 1, 1930. The huge ensemble cast included Jack Benny in his Broadway debut and Thelma White.

Kelly's longest break between shows was between *The Wonder Bar* and *Flying Colors*, which was her last show before she pulled up stakes and moved to California. *The Wonder Bar* (1931) was a "continental cabaret drama" adapted from the German and starred Al Jolson. As Electra Pivonka, Kelly sang "The Dying Flamingo" and "Elizabeth (My Queen!)." The show was made into a film in 1934, though not with Kelly. She was given star billing for the first time in *Flying Colors* (1932–33). With her on the marquee of the Imperial Theatre were Clifton Webb and Charles Butterworth. According to Parish and Leonard, the show didn't find favor with the critics, but it ran for four and a half months nevertheless.[28] Once it ended in late January 1933, it would be 38 years nearly to the day until Patsy Kelly appeared on Broadway again.

All of Kelly's Broadway shows were successful, save *The Wonder Bar*; the *Sketch Book* most of all with 392 performances. But it was time to move on. Producer Hal Roach had offered her a movie contract. Kelly's first assignment was to replace Zasu Pitts as Thelma Todd's partner in a series of Roach's popular comedy shorts. There would be 25 of them before Kelly was done, though not all with Todd, who died under mysterious circumstances in 1935. Roach also produced six of Kelly's feature films, including *Pick a Star* (E. Sedgwick, 1937), *Merrily We Live* (N.Z. McLeod, 1938), and *Topper Returns* (R. Del Ruth, 1941).

In the 1930s and into the early '40s, Kelly was both a star and a supporting player in Hollywood. She starred in her short films and a few features, such as *Pigskin Parade* (D. Butler, Twentieth Century–Fox, 1936), Judy Garland's first film; and *My Son the Hero* (E.G. Ulmer, Atlantis Picture, 1943), a sad mess from start to finish. More importantly, she was one of the sassiest, funniest "comic seconds" in Hollywood in several high-profile features. Among my favorites are *The Girl from Missouri*, hilarious as Jean Harlow's man-loving champion and bosom buddy, Kitty Linnehan who tries valiantly to save Harlow from the wages of sin; *Pick a Star* (Mischa Auer: "Do you mind if I smoke?"/Kelly: "I don't care if you burn"); *Merrily We Live*, stuck in the kitchen as Billie Burke's maid and a sardonic witness to this classic screwball comedy's mayhem (to the butler who's quitting: "You can't desert before dessert!"); and *Topper Returns*, helium-voice Billie Burke's maid yet again. In 1938, the *New York Post* called her "the most sought after feminine funster in Hollywood."[29]

In her *New York Times* obituary, Peter Flint tried to sum up this phase of her career: "With her gamine features, bobbed hair and sassy growl, the comedian was an ideal foil as the plain–Jane confidante of a generation of Hollywood actresses, breezily making light of the romantic burdens of such stars as Jean Harlow, Alice Faye, Loretta Young, Judy Garland, Virginia Bruce and Joan Blondell."[30] In an interview late in life, Kelly deftly described her niche in Hollywood films: "I was a domestic, an uppity, loud, butch maid.... I was there to liven up the proceedings and give 'em a little low humor. That's why my roles were pocket-sized; a lot of me would have been like a tidal wave; the males wouldn't have known what hit 'em. That's why when I did bigger roles, they had to pair me with another actress. Somebody more ... all that Hollywood stuff."[31] One might also say, then, that Patsy Kelly was more a character than a character actress.

After 10 years and more than 30 feature films, Kelly's heyday in Hollywood was suddenly over. Boze Hadleigh ascribes the abrupt demise of her acting career to three factors: her alcoholism, her uncustomary frankness about her lack of sexual interest in men, and rumors that she was jinxed.[32] William Mann thinks it was mostly the drinking, "which eventually discouraged producers from hiring her."[33] As for the jinx, Thelma Todd was only the first of a series of Kelly's bodacious blonde co-stars who died young. Lyda Roberti, who was with her in *Pick a Star* and *Nobody's Baby* (G. Meins, Hal Roach, 1937) and two shorts, died of a heart attack in 1938 at age 31. Carole Landis, who starred in *Topper Returns* and *Road Show* (H. Roach, Hal Roach, 1941), committed suicide, though not until 1948. Not to mention Jean Harlow. As if all that wasn't bad enough, Kelly was in the car with entertainer Jean Malin in August 1933, just months after her arrival in Hollywood, when he accidentally drove off the Venice Pier and drowned. Kelly survived, but was in a coma for several days.[34]

According to William J. Mann, Kelly was "on the skids for much of the 1950s."[35] Her professional opportunities had dried up to such an extent that she sought refuge with her best friend Tallulah Bankhead. She went with Bankhead when she did her $20,000-a-week cabaret act in Las Vegas in 1952, and in 1955 toured with her in *Dear Charles* (in Kelly's own opinion "No masterpiece!"), though Alice Pearce replaced her on Broadway.[36] Beyond that, according to Bankhead biographer Lee Israel, "She answered phones, helped Tallulah dress and undress, ran tubs, made drinks, drank along, and listened attentively."[37] Bankhead was infamous for her helplessness and impracticality. Kelly coined a classic phrase to describe her friend and erstwhile employer: "She dropped an egg and stood aside."[38] Hadleigh points out the irony of Kelly actually becoming the star's maid that she so often portrayed in film.[39]

Things began to look up workwise for Kelly in the 1960s. She returned to the big screen for the first time in 17 years in *Please Don't Eat the Daisies* (C. Walters, MGM, 1960). Picking up where she'd left off, she played Doris Day and David Niven's New York maid. Her role in the cult classic *Rosemary's Baby* (R. Polanski, William Castle Productions, 1968) was somewhat larger and certainly more interesting, as Ruth Gordon's plump friend and Mia Farrow and John Cassavetes' increasingly creepy neighbor, Laura-Louise McBirney. Kelly also made appearances on television in series such as *The Untouchables* (1960), *Burke's Law* (1964), *The Man from U.N.C.L.E.* (1967), and *Bonanza* (1968). In 1963, Kelly was arrested with two female companions after a drunken brawl in La Jolla. "In the New Hollywood," writes Mann, "such misbehavior was no longer career suicide; in fact, the resulting publicity reminded producers Patsy was still around."[40]

More than the moderate resurgence of Kelly's film career, though, her most remarkable comeback took place on January 19, 1971, when she returned to the Broadway stage for the first time in almost 40 years. The show was a revival of *No, No, Nanette*, which also marked

After several decades of not having a career at all, just jobs, Patsy Kelly made an honest-to-goodness comeback in the early 1970s with featured roles in two hit musicals and work in film and television. Here nearly seventy years old, jowly and still pugnacious, Kelly (left) is seen in her final feature film *North Avenue Irregulars* (1979) with an equally incognito Virginia Capers (back) and Barbara Harris (right).

the return of Ruby Keeler to Broadway after a 40-plus year absence. Kelly played the servant Pauline to thundering applause. Alex Barris describes the audience's reaction: "Predictably she stopped the show at most performances. Not only because she was so funny (which she was) but because the audience recognized one of its favorite Hollywood memories — Patsy Kelly as the funny maid."[41] On March 28, 1971, she received a Tony for Best Featured Actress in a Musical on the stage of the Palace Theatre, where she'd started out as a child stooging for Frank Fay all those years ago.[42]

According to Barris, *No, No, Nanette* marked the beginning of "the nostalgia craze of the early 1970s."[43] It lasted a stunning 861 performances. Martha Raye ultimately took over Kelly's role. Just a little over a month after *Nanette* closed, Kelly was back on Broadway for the opening of *Irene* at the Minskoff Theatre with Debbie Reynolds in the title role and Kelly as her folksy Irish mother, Mrs. O'Dare. Jane Powell later took over the lead. Kelly stuck with the show and also did the "long and arduous road tour," which ended in Southern California.[44] Despite the fact that her two songs had been cut (maybe because of it; Kelly was no natural singer), her performance as Mrs. O'Dare garnered her a second Tony nomination. This time she lost to Patricia Elliott for *A Little Night Music*.

It was ironic that an actress who had been considered "a scandal just waiting to happen" and had a "then-shocking openness about her lack of sexual interest in men" should end her film career in two films by squeaky clean Walt Disney Productions.[45] *North Avenue Irregulars* (B. Bilson, 1979) was the last of them, where she played Rose, a member of an undercover group of lady pensioners and local parishioners fighting organized crime in their home town. Jowly like a bulldog, wearing a huge pair of dark glasses and a trenchcoat, her brown hair still brown and characteristically bobbed, Kelly looked delightfully comical. In 1979, she made two appearances on TV's *The Love Boat* that would prove her final performances.

After a lengthy battle with cancer, Patsy Kelly died at the Motion Picture and Television Country Home and Hospital in Woodland Hills on September 24, 1981. She came home to Broadway, though, as her funeral mass was held right in the heart of the Theater District, at St. Malachy's, the Actors' Chapel, at 239 W. 49th St.[46] Kelly was laid to rest with her parents in the sprawling Calvary Cemetery in Woodside, Queens, with the Brooklyn-Queens Expressway as a none too scenic backdrop.[47]

Grandmommie Dearest:
Alma Kruger in *These Three* (1936)

It was said that Miss Kruger had
four distinct careers in show business.[1]

On April 17, 1898, readers of the *New York Times* found the following item in Charles Plunkett's column "The Drama":

Alma Kruger is a young American actress, a graduate of Mr. Sargent's school who has lately been serving her novitiate in the "legitimate." As "leading lady" in the support of Louis James she has acted Juliet and Lady Macbeth. This sort of experience has its value in the beginning, but a young actor of promising gifts needs the tempering and chastening influence of critical audiences to help in the proper development of those gifts. The applause of Haverstraw is agreeable, doubtless, but it is not heard far away.[2]

Accompanying the text was a picture of an attractive, though not conventionally beautiful, young woman with dark, soulful eyes, heavy eyebrows, and a mass of equally dark, curly hair loosely framing a strong face with a slightly retroussé nose and a prim mouth.

Alma Kruger was 26 when this photo was taken. She was born on September 13, 1871, in Pittsburgh, received her schooling there, and graduated from the King's School of Oratory.[3] She next appears in the columns of the *New York Times* on May 17, 1903. The item from the arts page tells us that David Belasco's *The Heart of Maryland* will play a week's engagement at the West End Theatre, starting the following evening: "The leading character, Maryland Calvert, will be portrayed by Alma Kruger, who was the original successor to Carter in the part."[4] *The Heart of Maryland* had originally opened on Broadway in 1895 with Mrs. Leslie Carter, nine years Kruger's senior, in the starring role and Maurice Barrymore as her leading man. Kruger had taken the show on a successful tour, of which this week in New York was no doubt a part.[5]

As her *New York Times* obituary noted, Kruger had "four distinct careers": "the first as a leading lady, the second as a character actress, the third as a radio actress, and the fourth in motion pictures."[6] Kruger was a member of a number of repertory companies during her early years in the theater, the most famous being the company of renowned Shakespearean actors E.H. Sothern and his wife Julia Marlowe. With them she had the opportunity to play a number of important roles from the classical repertoire, including Gertrude in *Hamlet*, Nerissa in *The Merchant of Venice*, and Olivia in *Twelfth Night*. Her Gertrude was described as "a dignified performance of the part ... [I]n the closet scene between Hamlet and herself her acting was worthy of the company she appeared in."[7] Kruger made her Broadway debut with the Sothern-Marlowe company at the Lyric Theatre on January 21, 1907, as Herodias in the play *John the Baptist*. That spring she travelled with the company to England, where she made her London debut in Gerhart Hauptmann's *The Sunken Bell* at the Waldorf Theatre on April 22, 1907. She played Magda, a role she had also played on Broadway.[8] She was 35 years old.

Kruger also performed in new plays throughout her career, such as Clyde Fitch's melodrama *The Straight Road* (1907) and John Valentine's comedy *The Stronger Sex* (1908–09). In the former, she supported "the emotional actress" Blanche Walsh in the leading role as Moll O'Hara, a girl of the slums, who is saved from despair and degradation by a vision of the Virgin Mary in a moonbeam; it was "a remarkable piece of stage realism" according to the *New York Times*.[9] In the latter, the leading lady was British-born Annie Russell, returning to "the field of 'polite society' comedy" that Broadway generally associated her with.[10] *The Stronger Sex* was a light play about a woman discovering that her husband has married her for her money and determining to win his heart.

Fast forward to September 17, 1935, and the opening of a new drama at Cort's 58th Street Theatre. *Few Are Chosen* by Nora Lawlor deals with "a class of seven novitiates entering a convent for preliminary study preparatory to becoming nuns."[11] In the role of Mother Mercy, the mother superior of the convent, we find 64-year-old Alma Kruger. Brooks Atkinson wrote that "the theme is not sturdy enough for discussion in the theatre," but the play was "acted lovingly" and "when the acting is as keen as it is ... in the Mother Mercy of Alma Kruger ... *Few Are Chosen* has its moments of quiet exultation."[12] This play, which was a failure and closed after only 15 performances, would not be worth mentioning if it were not for the fact that her performance here brought Kruger to the attention of director William Wyler.[13] Wyler would be responsible for launching Kruger on the fourth and final phase of her long and varied acting career, when he brought her to Hollywood only a month and a half later to take a leading role in his filmatization of Lillian Hellman's celebrated play *The Children's Hour*.

By this time, Kruger was one of the most experienced actresses on Broadway. Unlike those who featured mainly in comedies and dramas of recent vintage, Kruger had honed her craft in a series of Shakespeare productions, as we have seen, in Ibsen, and playing the leader of the chorus in no less than three different Greek tragedies: Euripides' *Iphigenia in Tauris* (1915), Euripides' *The Trojan Women* (1918), and Sophocles' *Electra* (1932), with Blanche Yurka in the title role and Mrs. Patrick Campbell as Clytemnestra. In Ibsen's *John Gabriel Borkman* (1915), Kruger had played Ella Rentheim, a woman who must come to terms with a life spent loving her twin sister's husband. In 1928 she played the heroine's fussy aunt-in-law in *Hedda Gabler* with Eva Le Gallienne in the title role.

By the time *Hedda Gabler* came along, Kruger had long since entered the second phase of her career, as a character actress. She had joined the Civic Repertory Company and acted in 11 of their productions between January 1927 and March 1931, including playing Fernandita in *The Lady from Alfaqueque* (1929); Lady Capulet in *Romeo and Juliet* (1930) with Donald Cameron and Eva Le Gallienne in the leads; Nanine in *Camille* (1931), again in support of Le Gallienne; and Miss Agatha in Susan Glaspell's Pulitzer Prize–winning *Alison's House* (1931). The Civic Repertory Company operated out of the Civic Repertory Theatre at 107 W. 14th St., just off Union Square. The company's leading lady, manager, and guiding spirit was Eva Le Gallienne.

Thus, though she was unknown and untried in Hollywood, it was an actress with impressive acting credentials whom Wyler was bringing to his producer Samuel Goldwyn and into the cast of the film that would be known as *These Three*. Kruger had one last hurrah on Broadway, though, before boarding the train for the coast and that was as Lady Catherine de Bourgh in a new dramatization of Jane Austen's *Pride and Prejudice* by Helen Jerome. Lucile Watson was also in the cast, as the daffy Mrs. Bennett. Watson was described by the *New York Times* as "incorrigibly comic," while Kruger "sweeps pomposity before her" in her sterner role. Brooks Atkinson found the play "full of salty lines and charmingly populated with spirited performers who know how to lard conversation with gleaming malice."[14] *Pride and Prejudice* was Kruger's biggest commercial success on Broadway and ran for 219 performances at the Plymouth Theatre starting November 5, 1935, and ending in May 1936. By then, she was long gone. Production on *These Three* had begun on November 20, 1935. Kruger was let out of her contract, or more likely bought out, and left the cast on December 1, being replaced by Beatrice Terry.[15] She would never return to Broadway.

⚬⚬⚬

It has seldom, if ever, been pointed out that Lillian Hellman's *The Children's Hour* (1934) is played out in a world entirely dominated by women. Both play and film explore the mores and rules of engagement in what, in a more gender-segregated society, would have been considered the woman's sphere, specifically the part of it dedicated to the raising of children. Recent college graduates Karen Wright and Martha Dobie have opened a school for girls. Helping them is an elderly, socially prominent woman in the local community, Mrs. Amelia Tilford, who by placing her orphaned granddaughter Mary in the school gives it her stamp of approval and makes it fashionable. As the plot will later prove, though, this puts the establishment and its proprietors in a vulnerable position.

The role of Amelia Tilford is one of the most challenging and exciting roles for an older woman in the American theater. There were many opportunities to play powerful dowagers and matriarchs on stage and screen in the years between the world wars, but few delved so deeply into the psychology of the grandmother-cum-leading citizen as *The Children's Hour*. The role of Mrs. Tilford first belonged to Katharine Emmett, who created and played her in the original Broadway production at Maxine Elliott's Theatre from 1934 to 1936. Emmett missed out on reprising her greatest role on the screen, because she was still doing the stage version while the film was being produced in late 1935 and early 1936.[16] (The play was *still* running when the film was released on March 18, 1936.)

Physically, Kruger was not all that different from Emmett. Mrs. Tilford is described in the play as "a large, dignified woman in her sixties, with a pleasant, strong face."[17] Both Emmett and Kruger fit the physical description of Mrs. Tilford to a tee, being large, imposing women with a distinguished though fairly homely appearance. Kruger's characteristic goiter, pointy nose, and dentured grin are evident in her debut film, as is her deep, cultivated, "inimitable viola speaking voice."[18] Future *Citizen Kane* cinematographer Gregg Toland often chooses to shoot her from below, not the most flattering angle, but one that suggests her high station and, at times, the point of view of the child Mary.

Dowagers served many functions in the plays and films of the era, both to help and to harm the protagonists, but seldom was the story much interested in these domineering or self-sacrificing women's deeper motivations and responsibilities. They were a hindrance for the hero and heroine to overcome or a helpmeet in their quest, and once the goal was reached, they disappeared as quickly and silently as they had come. *The Children's Hour* was one of the first plays to examine the kinds of power these women had and what they did with it for good and for evil. In both the play and the film, the protagonists' biggest helper turns into their chief antagonist. In both the play and the film, too, pride goeth before a

Playing Mrs. Amelia Tilford in *These Three* (Samuel Goldwyn Company, 1936), the self-righteous grandmother and community leader who feels duty-bound to blow the whistle on a couple of school-teachers suspected of sexual misconduct, would turn out to be not just Alma Kruger's first film role but also her best role during her eleven years and forty-six films in Hollywood. Here we see her coming to grips with her troublemaker granddaughter, played by Bonita Granville, who was Oscar nominated for her efforts.

fall. If there is anyone in the story who has to come to grips with her own fallibility, it is Amelia Tilford. She must ultimately recognize her guilt, humble herself before her victims, and ask forgiveness.

The power of the film's finale is, of course, considerably weakened by the fact that Martha Dobie in *These Three* does not take her own life. "Having the lesbian pass for straight in this film," writes Patricia White sardonically, "saves her life."[19] Indeed, the big confrontation scene towards the end of the play now takes place in Mrs. Tilford's elegant drawing room, rather than in the empty school. Most of the original dialogue from the showdown between Mrs. Tilford and Karen in *The Children's Hour* has been given to Mrs. Tilford and Martha in *These Three*. Rather than being dead, Martha ends up as an amateur detective, who solves the mystery and proves their innocence by getting Rosalie Wells to admit she lied under pressure from Mary.

Despite the fact that her actions don't actually kill anyone in *These Three*, Mrs. Tilford remains a highly ambiguous figure and ultimately a symbol of the failure of conservative values, respectability, gentility, and the American establishment. White notes that what got past the censors was the film's "rather unflattering portrait of so-called guardians of morality."[20] A large part of the power of the social and ideological critique Hellman channels through Mrs. Tilford comes from the fact that she is not some kind of psychopathic or evil monster. She is a good, upstanding, Christian woman and, as such, representative of a mass of American women of wealth and social position in society of the day, whose limited experience with and perspective on life could lead them to do more harm than good.

Richard Moody points out that women like Mrs. Tilford are common in Hellman's plays: "Many of the later plays feature ladies who speak with assurance and authority, who are comfortable with their wealth, who recognize and trade on their superiority, yet without arrogance. Most of them are less gullible than Grandma Tilford."[21] The point with these powerful older women characters, though, is that they are wrong. However much privileged and protected and educated and knowledgeable about the politer ways of the world, they all come to the limit of their intellectual and human resources in the course of the play. If they don't recognize this in time, the results, as in *The Children's Hour*, can be disastrous. Fanny Farrelly in *Watch on the Rhine* (1941) is another good example of this character type, only she is more a passive witness than an active participant in the danger and persecution taking place inside her own comfortable mansion. She must learn to see what is happening right before her eyes. Mrs. Tilford, by taking the fate of two fellow human beings into her own hands and effectively destroying their lives, herself becomes the instrument of active wrongdoing, though the basis and root cause is her love for her own flesh and blood. Both women confront evil, though it takes the very different forms of fascist ideology in *Watch on the Rhine* and an emotionally disturbed child in *The Children's Hour*.

Katherine Lederer feels that later incarnations of the powerful dowager in Hellmann's plays are better developed characters than Mrs. Tilford: "The grandmother does speak with an authority anticipatory of Mrs. Farrelly in *Watch on the Rhine* and Mrs. Ellis in *The Autumn Garden*, but she remains a type rather than an individual." This is because Lederer finds that "with the exceptions of the child, Mary, and the old actress, Lily Mortar, there is little concrete detail in the characters' speeches" in *The Children's Hour*.[22] Be that as it may, the lesson to be learned by the audience from the action of the play is part and parcel of the lesson to be learned by these older women characters.

Much ink has been spilled on the relative merits of *These Three vis-à-vis* the original play and William Wyler's 1961 remake. Each version of the story deserves to be judged on its own merits. This means that even though *These Three* is an adaptation of a play, it has to be able to stand on its own feet as a film and so, I think, it does on the whole. We can regret the loss of the same-sex dynamics of the original love triangle — some critics both then and now seem almost relieved at how easily it was expurgated — but I don't think Hellman was being disingenuous or homophobic when she said in an interview in connection with the Broadway revival in 1952, that "this is really not a play about lesbianism, but about a lie. The bigger the lie the better, as always."[23] It isn't wrong to point out, as Mark Estrin does, that at its thematic core the play is about "the destructive power of gossip, the easy acceptability of lies as truth, the cowardly reluctance of 'good' people to challenge evil directly."[24] While most of the time gay men and lesbians rightfully cringe when hearing that some artistic product with gay or lesbian characters is "not really" about them, I think in this case Hellman has the courage of her convictions. Given the logic of her argument here, though, changing the lie, making it in her terms "smaller," would necessarily change the film and potentially diminish its power and effect. Had she originally wanted to write about a conventional love triangle between two women and a man, one assumes she would have done so.[25]

While the cause of the scandal in *These Three* may seem considerably tamer by any standards, past or present, than in *The Children's Hour*, the film nevertheless works to a certain extent and on its own terms. It was received by the original audience "as a work in its own right," according to Carl Rollyson.[26] Frank Nugent in the *New York Times* revealed that producer Samuel Goldwyn had bought the film rights to the play knowing full well that, if he was ever to win the approval of the Hays office, "he could not use its title or its plot or even mention the fact that he had acquired it": "*The Children's Hour*, in Hollywood's eyes, was a dead horse, and Mr. Goldwyn, much to everyone's amusement, donated $50,000 for the privilege of carting it away under the cover of night." Nugent was of the opinion that *These Three* "may be judged — we had almost said 'should be judged' — as a separate entity, apart from any consideration of *The Children's Hour*."[27] Nugent was among the many reviewers who praised the film, writing, "Miss Hellman's job of literary carpentry is little short of brilliant.... In its totality, the picture emerges as one of the finest screen dramas in recent years." He thought, though, that *These Three* "lacks the biting, bitter tragedy of *The Children's Hour*." And Kruger, he found, "plays Mrs. Tilford with the proper dignity and outraged respectability."[28]

If *These Three* is still enjoyable, and I think it is, it is due to the beauty of the cinematography, the fine production values, the perfect casting, and the excellent performances. For her performance as Mary Tilford, Bonita Granville was nominated for an Academy Award at the tender age of 14. Merle Oberon gave one of the best performances of her career as Karen, despite sounding more British than Queen Elizabeth II; while Miriam Hopkins, with her hardness just below the feminine surface, and Joel McCrea, with his usual man-next-door earnestness, made an attractive and believable Martha and Joe. Catherine Doucet was "flawless" as the irritating but vastly entertaining and in every way dramatic Aunt Lily Mortar.[29] For Doucet, this was *the* performance of her film career. *These Three* marked the first collaboration of a creative team consisting of director Wyler, cinematographer Toland, and screenwriter Hellman, in addition to producer Goldwyn, which would also result in *Dead End* (1937) and *The Little Foxes* (1941). Neither Wyler nor Goldwyn ever used Kruger again. She died the year before *The Children's Hour* was remade in 1961, where Amelia Tilford was played beautifully by Fay Bainter in what would prove her final screen role.[30]

At age 64, then, and like so many stage-trained, veteran Broadway character actresses before her, Kruger had staked her future on a career in films. That future must have seemed promising, when such a plum role as Mrs. Tilford had landed so squarely and unexpectedly in her lap. Kruger could fortunately not have known, or even suspected, that her role in this film would be the best of the lot. Though she had 45 films yet to make after *These Three*, nothing she was offered or acted in could ever compare with her screen debut.

This is the sad fate that character actresses in Hollywood sometimes suffered. Sara Allgood is another example; Judith Anderson, Gale Sondergaard, and Blanche Yurka as well; and even Agnes Moorehead arguably belongs in this group of actresses who started on a high note and then petered out in steadily smaller or less interesting parts. Allgood made her bow in American films with a terrific role as Vivien Leigh's bumptious mother in *That Hamilton Woman*, got an Oscar nomination for her fourth film *How Green Was My Valley*, and then languished as a contract player at Twentieth Century–Fox for the duration. Judith Anderson is deservedly well known for *Rebecca*, but for what else? Gale Sondergaard won the first ever Academy Award for Best Actress in a Supporting Role for *Anthony Adverse* (beating Bonita Granville in *These Three*), but ended up mostly playing exotic villainesses in thrillers. Blanche Yurka was brought to Hollywood to play a terrifically terrifying Madame

De Farge in MGM's *A Tale of Two Cities*, but nothing that followed could compare to that sterling opportunity. Despite the distinction of Agnes Moorehead's long and varied film career, she was never able to top playing Fanny Minafer in Orson Welles's *The Magnificent Ambersons*, her second film.

Kruger's next film was *Craig's Wife* (D. Arzner, 1936) at Columbia, starring Rosalind Russell as the anti-heroine Harriet Craig, who is in love with her house, and John Boles as her beleaguered husband Walter. Kruger was billed sixth as Walter's live-in aunt, Ellen Austen, who opens his eyes to his wife's machinations and ultimately goes to live elsewhere. The movie was based on a 1925 Pulitzer Prize–winning Broadway play by George Kelly; Kruger's role had been created on stage a decade earlier by Anne Sutherland. Kruger was herself a George Kelly alumna, having done Kelly's next Broadway play after *Craig's Wife*, *Daisy Mayme*. It was not as large a critical and commercial success as its predecessor, but it lasted 112 performances at the Playhouse Theatre in 1926–27. One critic called it "a remorseless, unpleasant drama of the suburbs and middle-class life, brittle, searching and drab." He regretted that the play "seems determined to see truth merely in terms of bit-

Alma Kruger may be best remembered today as Nurse Molly Byrd in more than a dozen hospital dramas between 1939 and 1947 starring Lew Ayres as Dr. Kildare and Lionel Barrymore as Dr. Gillespie. Her film career started in 1936 with *These Three*, the focus of this chapter. This publicity shot is also from 1936.

terness."[31] Kruger played one of two selfish sisters trying to prevent their bachelor brother from marrying, afraid that they will no longer be able to sponge off him if he has a family of his own. The other sister was played by Josephine Hull. Zelda Sears played the title character.

Kruger ultimately made 46 films in Hollywood between 1936 and her retirement in 1947. She worked for all the major studios, but her home studio starting in 1938 was MGM, where she made a total of 21 films. In the long run, her most important role, quantitatively if not qualitatively, and the one for which she is best known, would be her portrayal of head nurse Molly Byrd in 14 of the 16 films of the Dr. Kildare–Dr. Gillespie series. It started for her with the third and fourth films, *Calling Dr. Kildare* (H.S. Bucquet, MGM) and *The Secret of Dr. Kildare* (H.S. Bucquet, MGM), both from 1939, and ended with the final film in the series, *Dark Delusion* (W. Goldbeck, MGM), in 1947. Lew Ayres starred as Dr. Kildare in eight of these films, Lionel Barrymore played his older mentor Dr. Gillespie, and when Ayres quit, Barrymore went on in turn to get Van Johnson as his new junior, Dr. Randall "Red" Adams. As Molly Byrd, Kruger was stern yet not unsympathetic, strict yet caring, and we suspect she's been nursing an unrequited love for Dr. Gillespie for quite some time. By this late date, performing unrequited love had become routine for Kruger. Perhaps the unmarried and childless actress knew something about this feeling from her own life.

Dignity, the "d" word, would follow Kruger from the beginning to the end of her career. There are worse qualities to project as an actress, certainly, but I wonder if Kruger ever tired both of playing and being described as "dignified." If she did, her role in *His Girl Friday* (H. Hawks, Columbia, 1940) must have been a refreshing change of pace. This famous adaptation of the Ben Hecht–Charles MacArthur comedy *The Front Page* (1928), originally filmed in 1931, is today Kruger's most popular film by a landslide.[32] She played the role of Rosalind Russell's soon-to-be mother-in-law, Mrs. Baldwin, who certainly is not able to maintain her dignity at all times amidst the chaos and furor of the press room of the Criminal Courts building. Among Kruger's more familiar film titles, we also find *Marie Antoinette* (W.S. Van Dyke, MGM, 1938), where she played the ill-fated queen's mother, Austrian empress Maria Theresa; *Made for Each Other* (J. Cromwell, Selznick International, 1939), where she made only the briefest of appearances as a nun; and *Mrs. Parkington* (T. Garnett, MGM, 1944), as old-moneyed Mrs. Jacob Livingstone, who at first snubs Greer Garson, but later comes to regret it when Walter Pidgeon sets out to ruin her husband.

After her fourteenth and final film in the Kildare-Gillespie series, *Dark Delusion* (1947), and a small role as a dull noblewoman, Lady Redmond, in *Forever Amber* (O. Preminger, Twentieth Century–Fox, 1947) with Linda Darnell and Cornel Wilde, Alma Kruger retired. She died in a nursing home in Seattle on April 8, 1960, at the age of 88. She had moved to Seattle from Stamford, Connecticut, in 1955 and was even then in ill health.[33] Kruger was cremated. Her place of burial is unknown.[34]

The Real Thing: Aline MacMahon in *Side Streets* (1934)

*I believe she is a fine and a very nice woman —
an unusual combination of talents!*

Paradoxically, because she didn't look like anyone, she could play everyone. Her tall, erect figure and round, placid face lent themselves to portraying characters ranging from pioneer women and Chinese peasants to beleaguered housewives and quick-witted sidekicks. Aline MacMahon was one of the most versatile screen actresses of the 1930s and beyond.

The actress who would be known throughout her life by her maiden name was born Aline Laveen MacMahon on May 3, 1899, in McKeesport, a small town on the Monongahela River in western Pennsylvania, just southeast of Pittsburgh. Her father was William Marcus MacMahon, born in 1877, at one time the editor of *Munsey's Magazine* and for many years Associate Press editor in New York. He was also "a widely known writer of short stories."[1] Her mother was Jennie Simon MacMahon, born on January 19, 1878.[2] Aline was the couple's only child. Interviewed during the 1926 Broadway revival of Eugene O'Neill's *Beyond the Horizon*, MacMahon had "no startling childhood experiences to relate."[3] She was raised in Brooklyn and Manhattan and got her education at P.S. 103 and Erasmus Hall High School on Flatbush Ave. in Brooklyn and Barnard College of Columbia University in Morningside Heights, Manhattan.[4]

MacMahon had a remarkably long, varied, and productive career both on stage and screen. She had wanted to act since she was a child and started her professional training with the Yorkville Stock Company on the Upper East Side after graduating from college in 1920.[5] She was seen on Broadway in no less than 31 productions between 1921 and 1975. Most of these plays have long since been forgotten, but among the titles that still ring a bell we find O'Neill's *Beyond the Horizon* (1926–27), Ben Jonson's *The Alchemist* (1966), Garcia Lorca's *Yerma* (1966–67), Brecht's *Galileo* (1967), Schiller's *Mary Stuart* (1971), and Arthur Miller's *The Crucible* (1972).

MacMahon's busiest period on Broadway was the 10 years following her debut in 1921, when she was almost continuously employed in various shows. During her first two seasons, she was associated with the Neighborhood Playhouse, housed in a theater at 466 Grand St. on the Lower East Side, in plays such as Harley Granville-Barker's *The Madras House* (1921), *The Green Ring* (1922), and Yeats's *The Player Queen* (1923). Her imitation of Gertrude Lawrence in the successful *Grand Street Follies of 1924* "attracted considerable attention" and resulted in a contract with Lee Shubert.[6] He started her off in another musical revue, *Artists and Models* (1925–26), which played 416 performances at the Winter Garden. After a summer spent in Europe "visiting the Continental theatres,"[7] MacMahon opened in *Beyond the Horizon* on November 30, 1926. Playing the frustrated farmer's wife Ruth Atkins was her breakthrough role on Broadway. The role had been created by Elsie Rizer in the original production seven years earlier. MacMahon got rave reviews; *The New Yorker* wrote that she "tempted one to rank her immediately as among the Olympians," and Noël Coward described her performance as "astonishing, moving and beautiful."[8] The *New York Times* felt that the play "has lost none of its power" and said "Aline MacMahon in particular is a fortunate choice for the wife."[9] *Beyond the Horizon* has not been seen on Broadway since this production.

MacMahon was never one to shy away from controversial roles or plays; her 1928 show *Maya*, in translation from the French original of Simon Gantillon, dealt with prostitution. In the lead role as a Marseilles streetwalker, wrote Brooks Atkinson, "Aline MacMahon catches all the preternatural patience of Bella in a splendid performance that likewise reveals her pitiful ignorance and her gaucheries. Hers is notable character acting."[10] *Maya* was taken off by the producers after only 15 performances rather than risking a shutdown by the police under the new Wales padlock law, which could have left the Comedy Theatre dark for a year.[11]

On Tuesday, March 27, 1928, not long after the forced closing of *Maya*, MacMahon married the noted architect and urban planner Clarence S. Stein in the chambers of Judge Peter Schmuck in City Court, New York. She was 28 and he 45 and it was the first marriage for both. The *New York Times* wrote that MacMahon would continue on the stage.[12] During the years when MacMahon worked in Hollywood, she made frequent trips between pictures to her husband in New York.[13] The Steins would be married for 47 years, until his death after a long illness on February 7, 1975, at the age of 92.[14] To her regret, they remained childless.[15] A recent chairman of the State Housing and Regional Planning Commission (1923–26), in 1929 Stein completed his most famous building, the Temple Emanu-El on Fifth Avenue and East 65th Street, directly across Central Park from where the couple would make their home at 1 West 64th Street. The Steins also owned a large property in Westchester County.[16] Described as a "pioneering town planner" on his death, by the time he married Stein had already designed two of the communities that would be his most celebrated and lasting legacy: the garden city Sunnyside Gardens in Queens (1924–28) and the planned suburb of Radburn, New Jersey (completed in 1928).[17]

On November 12, 1929, just after the stock market crashed, MacMahon opened in retired English professor Thomas H. Dickinson's drama *Winter Bound* at the Garrick Theatre.[18] In this early lesbian play, MacMahon played mannish Tony Ambler, described by one reviewer as a "Sappho in Overalls." According to Kaier Curtin, this was a Broadway audience's "first look at a female character who might have been crudely called a 'bull dyke.'"[19] With a plot strongly reminiscent of D.H. Lawrence's novella "The Fox," Ambler and her girlfriend are involved in a love triangle with a man who invades their farmhouse retreat in rural Connecticut. The *New York Times*'s critic wrote that the play had "a theme of twisted impulses that wandered vaguely along the path of *The Captive*": "To the role of Tony, the pivotal point of the play, Miss MacMahon brings a well-molded and decisive assurance that illuminates, at least in part, a character that is as ill-defined as the play itself."[20] Curtin, who interviewed MacMahon in 1977, writes: "Almost half a century later, MacMahon was enraged at the suggestion that Tony might in any way be related to the emergence of lesbians in American drama."[21] Both *Beyond the Horizon* and *Winter Bound* were staged by James Light, who had originally offered MacMahon a job when she was a senior in college, but she had opted to finish her degree.

MacMahon was absent from Broadway during most of the 1930s, devoting herself to her film career. She did two shows in the '40s (one of them was Maxwell Anderson's hit *The Eve of St. Mark*, 1942–43) and was seen regularly, if not often, on the New York stage between 1955 and her retirement 20 years later. During her later Broadway career, she was associated with the Repertory Theatre of Lincoln Center, which was housed at the Vivian Beaumont Theatre, just a block from MacMahon's home on the corner of West 64th Street and Central Park West. Her final stage role was playing Miss Trafalgar Gower in a celebrated 1975 revival of Arthur Wing Pinero's classic *Trelawny of the Wells* with Mary Beth Hurt as Rose Trelawney. This production was 26-year-old Meryl Streep's Broadway debut. Fifty-five years earlier, Mac-Mahon had acted in the same play while a student at Barnard.[22]

Whether in comedy or drama, MacMahon was uniformly excellent: "Rarely did she get a bad notice, even in productions that were otherwise panned."[23] Legendary *New York Times* critic

A soulful Aline MacMahon in a 1934 Warner Bros. publicity shot, wearing an exotic top of possibly North African origin. MacMahon did a string of films at Warner Bros. and First National during the first half of the 1930s.

Walter Kerr observed in 1967: "I have been seeing Aline MacMahon for more years than I'm going to be honest enough or ungentlemanly enough to count. Always she has pleased me, sometimes more, sometimes less, nevertheless always."[24]

MacMahon is one of the unsung heroines of 1930s films. Both in the way she looked and the way she sounded, she was different from anyone else in movies at this time and this was reflected in the roles she played and the stories she helped bring to life. She was 5'7" tall and had blue eyes.[25] David Quinlan writes that "her horsey, mournful face was obviously destined for more interesting things than straight leads, and she proved as adept with wise-cracks as with wisdom."[26] This is an apt description with the exception of the word "horsey." If anything, MacMahon's visage was circular and moonlike. John Springer and Jack Hamilton liken it to "a tragic mask."[27] A journalist describing her in 1942 wrote,

[T]here is something strangely refreshing in the untampered with and faintly acerbic appearance of an Aline MacMahon.... The suit is usually tweedy and tailored. There is no flagrant makeup.

The dark hair is that of a woman who has known no permanent; it is drawn back into a knot that would be spinsterish on a spinster but on MacMahon gives the impression of a bachelor girl who scorns beauticians.[28]

My "Top Five" list of MacMahon's films would include (in chronological order) *One Way Passage*, *Gold Diggers of 1933*, *Heroes for Sale*, *The World Changes*, and *Side Streets*. There are such riches here, a whole "alternative" history of Golden Age Hollywood films could be written just based on MacMahon's collected works. In *One Way Passage* (T. Garnett, Warner Bros., 1932) she plays "Barrel House" Betty (*aka* Countess Barilhaus), a con woman posing as a Central European countess on a cruise ship that is also carrying William Powell, a murderer being transported home to the gallows in San Francisco, and mortally ill Kay Francis. MacMahon gets involved with Steve (Warren Hymer), the police sergeant escorting Powell, and does all she can to help Powell escape, though ultimately to no avail. She also finds herself falling in love with the copper, who it turns out has the chicken ranch back home she's been pining for. MacMahon looks sultry and attractive, even with the characteristically dark rings under her eyes, and in one scene is seen brushing out her long hair. The screenplay to this Pacific Ocean "brief encounter" won Robert Lord an Oscar. The *New York Times* once wrote that MacMahon played sidekicks with "kindly acerbity and sardonic understanding": "[S]he hurls the barbed mot like a knife-thrower at a circus and never nicks the skin; simultaneously, by her own quiet nuance of technique, she is as soothing as the insomniac's glass of warm milk at bedtime."[29]

MacMahon was also billed third in the classic backstage musical film *Gold Diggers of 1933* (M. LeRoy, Warner Bros., 1933), as Trixie, one of a trio of performers sharing an apartment and hoping for a part in a new show. Her two roomies were Joan Blondell and Ruby Keeler. Trixie is a comic lead, like Helen Broderick, Hope Emerson, or Esther Howard in real life. She is paired with the "angel" Mr. Peabody, played by Guy Kibbee, in the first of his and MacMahon's 10 films together. Some dames get Gary Cooper or Cary Grant, MacMahon got Kibbee...

Heroes for Sale (W.A. Wellman, First National, 1933) was the first of 10 films in which MacMahon got top billing. As Mary Dennis, she plays the girl who doesn't get the guy, unhappily devoted to her idealistic lodger Richard Barthelmess. Barthelmess falls for and marries Loretta Young and they have a son. Even after Young is killed in a demonstration and MacMahon has cared for his boy while he has served time in jail, they don't become a couple. In the final scene, as Barthelmess is about to go off yet again, leaving his child behind, MacMahon asks if she can kiss him. Barthelmess assents. It is a fine moment in a long and tortuous film, which must be one of the most astonishingly forthright critiques of capitalism ever produced in Hollywood.

There was yet another change of pace in *The World Changes* (M. LeRoy, First National, 1933), a long-winded but absorbing western family saga, where MacMahon starred with no less a figure than Paul Muni in his follow-up film to *Scarface* and *I Am a Fugitive from a Chain Gang* (both 1932). She plays Anna Nordholm, a western pioneer woman who with her husband Orin Nordholm (Muni) founds the community of Orinville. Ultimately, she becomes a great-grandmother and the matriarch of a large clan based in decadent New York. As the family fortune is about to be lost and her great-granddaughter marry an effete English nobleman, the still resolutely rural Mrs. Nordholm reluctantly shows up on the urban scene to sets things right. MacMahon's role is a precursor of Mrs. Parkington; *The World Changes* has shades of *Cimarron* as well.

Today *Gold Diggers of 1933* (Warner Bros., 1933) is the highest-rated of Aline MacMahon's more than fifty feature films. MacMahon is seen far right in a police uniform with several members of this backstage musical's talented cast, including (from left) Warren William, Fred Kelsey, Dick Powell, Ruby Keeler, Wallace MacDonald, Joan Blondell, and Guy Kibbee.

If I had to choose one favorite out of these five, it would be *Side Streets* (A.E. Green, First National, 1934), because to my mind it is the quintessential Aline MacMahon film. It is aptly named, for it deals with a totally ordinary and unglamorous segment of the urban population. *Side Streets* was originally entitled "A Woman in Her Thirties," and the heroine, Bertha Krasnoff, is indeed no longer young and has probably never been much to look at. MacMahon's Bertha is a fully realized, stunningly real character. A furrier with a small but thriving business, Bertha calls herself "Madame Valery," because it sounds better. A consummate saleswoman, she is full of the period's marketing buzz words and loves to use superlatives like "slenderizing," "gorgeous," and "delicious." In creating the role, MacMahon uses her characteristically folksy, squeaky dry voice with a Brooklyn inflection and, indeed, we are told that Bertha came to San Francisco from New York with nothing seven years ago.

At the opening of the film, Bertha encounters down-on-his-luck sailor Tim O'Hara (Paul Kelly) while feeding the squirrels in the park. She ends up feeding him, too, and giving him a job. One thing leads to another, they marry and have a child, who dies. We follow the couple through some fairly tortuous plot twists involving "other woman" Marguerite Gilbert (Ann Dvorak) and Bertha's man-loving niece Ilka (Dorothy Tree). Another film about marriage and fidelity, adultery and forgiveness, in other words, yet these conventional dramatic ingredients are given a novel twist by Manuel Seff's fine screenplay based on a short story by Ann Garrick and Ethel Hill called "Fur Coats." The storyline comes to life not least of all through the united efforts of a splendid ensemble cast, that in addition to the leads includes Henry O'Neill, Mayo Methot, and Marjorie Gateson.

Side Streets has a particularly good supporting role for MacMahon's frequent co-star Helen Lowell, as Tillie, the faded and wrinkled forewoman in Bertha's shop. Tillie is seen working on something in almost all her scenes. Still, she keeps a watchful eye on her employer and friend, even if it isn't always appreciated. Bertha repeatedly tells her to butt out when Tillie tries to make her see her marriage is on the rocks, including admonishing her to "dress up" so that she will stay attractive to her husband. Bertha's trials and tribulations lead Tillie to conclude, "Maybe I'm lucky I never had a husband." Tillie is a touching monument to older, self-supporting, unmarried working women.

For the first decade of her film career, MacMahon found a congenial home studio at Warner Bros., where she was given many fine opportunities and was, in the words of Larry

MacMahon moved from Warner Bros. to MGM in 1935 and starred in the original version of *Kind Lady*. Based on a drama by Edward Chodorov, the film was remade in 1951 with Ethel Barrymore in the lead. Here we see MacMahon (left) with the villain of the piece, Basil Rathbone (center), an impecunious painter who inveigles himself into MacMahon's home and affections; and one of her skeptical relatives, played by Doris Lloyd. Lloyd was also in the remake, as Barrymore's murdered maid.

Swindell, a "hard-boiled egg in the Warner salad."[30] Mervyn LeRoy gave her her start when he cast her as Edward G. Robinson's secretary in *Five Star Final* (First National, 1931). The story goes that he saw her in a road company production of *Once in a Lifetime* in Los Angeles.[31] LeRoy, who some years later would bring another exotic-looking, multi-talented actress to Hollywood, Gale Sondergaard, would be MacMahon's five-time and most frequent director. According to modern sources, MacMahon had originally been "intended for stardom" at the studio, "but then shunted to top featured leads."[32] She made 21 films for First National and Warner Bros. between her debut in *Five Star Final* and *The Eddie Cantor Story* (A.E. Green) in 1953 and got top billing in nine of them.

Her second most important studio was MGM, where she worked intermittently between 1935 and 1960, starred in the original version of *Kind Lady* (G.B. Seitz, 1935), and made films such as *I Live My Life* (W.S. Van Dyke, 1935), *Ah, Wilderness!* (C. Brown, 1935), *Dragon Seed* (H.S. Bucquet and J. Conway, 1944), and *Cimarron* (A. Mann, 1960). She also made four films at Columbia, including her most popular film today, *The Man from Laramie* (A. Mann, 1955), starring James Stewart.[33] MacMahon's film career slowed down considerably in the 1940s, when she made 10 films, and even more so in the '50s, with only three feature films. Her final five features were produced in the early 1960s, the last to be released being *I Could Go On Singing* (R. Neame, Barbican Films, 1963), with MacMahon playing Judy Garland's sidekick in the troubled star's final film; and *All the Way Home* (A. Segal, Paramount, 1963), reprising a role she'd played on Broadway in a hit play by Tad Mosel, which won the 1961 Pulitzer Prize for Drama. She was only 64 years old and would keep on acting on the stage for another dozen years, but her film career was over.

In 1977, two years after her retirement from the stage, MacMahon told David Ragan that she was living on investments, her monthly Social Security check, and pensions from the Screen Actors Guild and Actors Equity. Forty years after the film was released, she still lamented losing the role of O-Lan in *The Good Earth* (1937) to Luise Rainer.[34] The film garnered Rainer her second Oscar. MacMahon had to be satisfied with a nomination, ironically for another mock–Chinese film, *Dragon Seed* (H.S. Bucquet and J. Conway, MGM, 1944), where she played Katharine Hepburn's mother and Walter Huston's wife. The award that year for Best Actress in a Supporting Role went to Ethel Barrymore for *None but the Lonely Heart*.

Another missed opportunity was playing the nurse to Judith Anderson's Medea at the National Theatre (and later the Royale) in 1947 and '48. The director was none other than John Gielgud, who also played Jason. With rehearsals well underway, Gielgud wrote his mother on September 12, 1947: "Aline MacMahon, who plays the Nurse, does not arrive till next week. I believe she is a fine and a very nice woman — an unusual combination of talents!"[35] MacMahon was filming *The Search* (F. Zinnemann, MGM, 1948) with Montgomery Clift at this time and clearly there was some delay that meant she had to withdraw from *Medea*. The play opened on October 20 and production on *The Search* didn't close down until November 5. The show was a sensational success and the nurse was played by Florence Reed, who was 16 years older than MacMahon.

Gielgud called her "a fine and very nice woman" without ever having met her. Clearly, MacMahon had a sterling reputation in the business. In a lengthy interview in the *New York Times* in 1942, when she was 43 years old and the major phase of her film career was nearing its end, the journalist refers to "[t]he faint humorous bitterness" with which her personality is tinged, ascribed by some, he added, "to the fact that she was brought up in Brooklyn." MacMahon didn't agree with that, saying it might be "more a matter of scrambled

Aline MacMahon at the New York premiere of *The Eddie Cantor Story* (Warner Bros.) on Christmas Day 1953 with Keefe Brasselle, who played songster Cantor in this Technicolor musical biopic. Though MacMahon was twenty-four years his senior and played his grandmother in the film, Brasselle predeceased her by a decade, dying from cirrhosis of the liver in 1981.

nationalities: Irish, English, and Russian, 'well mixed' ... but nevertheless a cocktail of hereditary components essentially incompatible." Among the interests, MacMahon mentions "authors as widely diversified as Proust and Louisa M. Alcott." She admits to being frugal ("gets everything possible from the five and dime"; "never buys anything if she hasn't the money to pay on the spot"; "wears forever any frock or hat she likes, no matter how often friends raise their eyebrows") and is "a confessed gourmet" who intends to learn to cook "in some shadowy time of future leisure." She also likes to walk in the country, is good at bridge and "scaling Fifth Avenue buses," and collects old china, oriental jewelry and Chinese art.[36]

Aline MacMahon died in her New York apartment from what appeared to be pneumonia on Saturday, October 12, 1991, at the age of 92.[37] She was buried in Mount Pleasant Cemetery in Hawthorne, New York.[38]

Woman of the People: Beryl Mercer in *Outward Bound* (1930)

Mother-love never had such a staunch screen representative as this little dumpling.[1]

"Blessed are the meek, for they shall inherit the earth." Small, gray, and mousy Beryl Mercer certainly gave the impression of being meek, but whether she really was I cannot say. She died in 1939, so there are unlikely to be many people around to enlighten us. For our purposes, though, it is primarily important to point out that she was very good at *acting* meek and did so in a number of films in the 1930s, before her life and film career were cut short all too soon at age 56.

Mercer also had an "Everywoman" quality, which stood her in good stead in a series of important but hardly flashy roles as mothers, housekeepers, cooks, cleaning ladies, and landladies. John Springer and Jack Hamilton describe her as "an absolute darling, with her great mournful eyes, her shy smile, and her fetching little waddle of a walk. She was very capable of pouring on lots of extra syrup — Mercer mothers could be as gooey as a caramel-fudge sundae smothered in whipped cream."[2] No dried-out spinsters for Mercer, no imperious dowagers either, though I may have missed one or two (and not forgetting that on Broadway she once played the greatest dowager of them all, Queen Victoria). Mercer was a tiny brown Cockney sparrow. With her down-to-earth, folksy demeanor, homely Munchkin face, and dumpy body, there was a limit to how far producers wanted to stretch the audience's imagination. I can't think of many examples of Mercer being cast against type, though it would have been interesting to see if she could surprise us. Beryl Mercer as a meanie. How about that?

Where do we place her in the character actress landscape? Another Clara Blandick? No, Blandick had fiery dark eyes that could pierce you — and those pince-nez her characters favored, imagine them on Mercer's little button nose! Kin to Jane Darwell, then? How is that for a comparison? Hmm, not much better. Darwell could be bellows loud, fractious, bumptious, and belligerent and she was about as American as Mercer was British. Wait, I've got it, Mercer was another Sara Allgood. Well, then again, no. Allgood didn't arrive in Hollywood until two years after Mercer was dead so, if anything, Allgood was another Beryl Mercer. That comparison only goes a certain distance, too. Allgood may have played mostly proletarian roles, like Mercer, and been a plain Jane like Mercer, but she was a much larger woman, a much louder woman, and an Irishwoman.

Then you have the May Beattys, Dorothy Vaughans, Mary Gordons, and Emma Dunns, "those darling, dumpy women of the early 1930s who played the mothers of scrapping brothers, Irish cops, and slum-bred hoodlums."[3] But they weren't quite like Mercer either. For all her timidity and modesty on the big screen, Mercer was a first-rank character actress. She only played named, credited roles at major studios, however small some of those parts were by the time the editor had done with them. So, am I trying to suggest Mercer was unique? Of course she was. They all were. It is just a question of being able to see them and appreciate them in their individual glory. They all so dearly wanted to impress us, to be seen, to be recognized — and so very few of them ever were. It's sad, when you think about it.

Mercer's family background is a bit of a mystery. Some of what has come down to us sounds like the invention of a studio publicity department. According to the most detailed version, which is to be found in an interview in the *New York Times* in 1917 (albeit long before her film career), we can read that Mercer's father, Edward Sheppard Mercer, was Spanish and "attached to the Spanish Embassy in London in the '80s": "At an embassy ball in London he met Beryl Montague, the famous leading woman of the Bancroft Robertson productions of the period, and shortly afterward the two were married and went to Seville, Spain, to live. There Beryl, their first child, was born, in 1882."[4] On August 13, 1882, to be exact. About that there is no question.[5] But how many Spaniards are baptized Edward Sheppard Mercer? And why does John Parker's *Who's Who in the Theatre* tell us that Beryl Mercer's mother was called Effie Martin? Maybe it was the other way around, and Mr. Mercer was a British diplomat in Spain. Maybe Beryl's mother wasn't a leading lady at all, but just plain old Effie Martin Mercer.

Mercer was one of the busiest child actors of her day. Who would have thought that the long-suffering and self-sacrificing maternal presence, this "symbol of respectable motherhood" in so many 1930s films was, once upon a time, between the age of 10 and 15, "one of the most popular impersonator of boys' roles in London and the provinces"?[6]

Mercer made her stage debut at the Theatre Royal, Yarmouth, on August 14, 1886, when she replaced a sick boy slated to play Willie Carlyle in the classic nineteenth-century melodrama *East Lynne*. Astute mathematicians will be able to calculate that she was then four years old. Her parents tried to stem this early histrionic impulse by sending her away to school in the Channel Islands. By the age of ten, though, Beryl was back in the limelight and would stay there till she died. Among her celebrated roles as a child were Shakespeare Jarvis in *The Lights o' London*, Dick the crippled acrobat in *The Scarlet Sin*, Wally in *The Two Little Vagabonds* (her London stage debut in 1896), and Micah Dow in *The Little Minister*. She had some notable successes in her late teens as well. Under the guidance of Herbert Beerbohm Tree she played It, the shadow, in *The Darling of the Gods* and Puck in Oscar Asche's production of *A Midsummer Night's Dream*, "styled by some London critics as the most sprightly and unearthly the London stage had ever seen."[7]

Mercer's New York debut was in a 1906 play called *The Shulamite* at the Lyric Theatre. It ran for a less than stunning 25 performances. The critic for the *New York Times* was not impressed by this domestic melodrama set in Boer South Africa and based on a novel of the same name by Claude Askew and his collaborator Edward Knoblock. He wrote that the London star Lena Ashwell "had been rather badly handicapped on her first visit here by a bad play." Next to Ashwell, he added, "Miss Beryl Mercer, who appeared as a little Kaffir slave, is most to be commended for a bit of character that is pathetically appealing."[8] "Little" and "pathetic" were epithets that would follow her throughout her career. This role as the slave Meinke marked the first time Mercer played a role considerably older than her years.[9] She was 24 years old and fully grown stood only 4'11" tall.[10] She wouldn't appear on Broadway again for another 10 years.

Lena Ashwell signed Mercer to a three-year contract on their return to London.[11] Among several of her West End shows, she reprised her childhood role as Wally in *Two Little Vagabonds* when she was 27 years old.[12] During her final years in her native England, she also performed in variety theatres and became known to music hall patrons throughout the British Isles.[13]

Mercer returned to Broadway in 1916, this time for good, in support of Marie Tempest in a play called *A Lady's Name*, which ran for 56 performances at Maxine Elliott's Theatre. She stayed on for *Somebody's Luggage* in the fall of that year and *The Lodger*, in which she made her first major impression on the critics. The *New York Times*'s headline read "*The Lodger* Proves Highly Amusing: Beryl Mercer Makes Off with the Honors of a New English Comedy." Mercer played Mrs. Bunting, a landlady who mistakenly believes her lodger, played by later horror film standby Lionel Atwill, is a murderer wreaking havoc in the neighborhood. According to the *New York Times*, Mercer "calmly made off with all the honors of the first night," concluding that "Mr. Atwill took last evening the curtain calls evidently intended by the audience for Miss Mercer, who has always amused New York playgoers and who is enormously laughable as the tender-hearted but suspicious landlady."[14] It's is doubtful if Atwill was equally enthusiastic about his co-star after this verbal slap.

Her critical success in *The Lodger* was followed by an even greater success when Mercer starred in a "playlet" by J.M. Barrie called *The Old Lady Shows Her Medals* at the Empire Theatre in the spring of 1917. Here she combined her penchant for old lady roles with "her other specialty," one-act plays.[15] To alleviate her loneliness and isolation, her character Mrs. Dowey invents a son at the front during World War I by picking a soldier with her name out of the newspaper. When the young man in question shows up to confront her with her lie, she charms him into submission. On his subsequent death, she receives his medals. Mercer's performance was described as "ineffably touching" and "heartbreakingly tender and true."[16]

On the day of her last performance as Mrs. Dowey, the *New York Times* carried an interview with Mercer under the heading "The Young 'Old Lady' of Mr. Barrie's Play." The journalist started by pointing out that many audience members mistaking the 35-year-old Mercer for a much older woman after having seen her in *The Old Lady Shows Her Medals* "was an unconscious tribute to the actress's art." The journalist continued,

> The general excellence of the four characterizations she has given in New York refutes the oft-uttered assertion that English actresses of character parts cannot approach their American cousins. Surely the American stage can boast of no more gifted interpreter of roles of this type.... She had always had the ambition to portray the unfortunate of her sex and the realization of her ambition came when Lena Ashwell recognized her aptitude and engaged her for the part of Meinke in *The Shulamite*.[17]

Almost four years later, in the *New York Times* for March 25, 1921, we can read this melancholy announcement under "Died": "HERBERT — On March 21, 1921, at Beechhurst, L.I., David, the dearly beloved son of Beryl and Holmes E. Herbert, aged 8 months."[18] It was poignant that an actress who would play so many mothers of sons good, bad, and indifferent, would herself lose her only son when he was just eight months old. David Herbert would have been born in July 1920, when his mother was nearly 38 years old. Only two months after David's birth, Mercer went into a new comedy called *Three Live Ghosts*, which was her biggest commercial success on Broadway and was still running at the Greenwich Village Theatre when the baby boy died. If Mercer's marriage to Holmes Herbert fell apart at this point is hard to know, but they were divorced sometime between their infant son's death in 1921 and Herbert's marriage to the pioneering film producer Thomas Ince's widow, Elinor "Nellie" Kershaw Ince, on May 3, 1930.[19] Herbert, born Horace Edward Jenner in Mansfield, Nottinghamshire, in 1882, was a handsome leading man type, who moved to the United States in 1912. He later came to have a prolific career as a character actor in Hollywood films, racking up more than 200 roles (if not screen credits) during his years in the industry between 1915 and his retirement in 1952.[20] Mercer was also married at one point to a man with the unlikely moniker Maitland Sabrina Pasley, but when, where, and how she parted from him is not known.[21] She had a daughter with Holmes Herbert called Joan, born in 1918, who survived her.[22]

The two personal triumphs of Mercer's later Broadway career were *Queen Victoria* (1923) and *Outward Bound* (1924). Not so famous as Helen Hayes's later starring vehicle *Victoria Regina* (1935), the biographical play *Queen Victoria* by David Carb and Walter Prichard Eaton was built on somewhat similar lines, following Queen Victoria's life from her accession into old age. This was a perfect opportunity for Mercer to play both younger and

Judging from the style of her cloche hat, this portrait of Beryl Mercer was probably taken in the 1920s. A pleasantly plump, doe-eyed, and dark-browed woman with a mass of curly hair, Mercer stood only 4'11" tall in her stocking feet.

older than her 41 years. Drama critic John Corbin found "the slight let-down occurred in the episodes of middle age." There was a "marvelous girlish quality" in the youthful scenes, and in the final episode Mercer "again reached the heights of her sensitive imaginative art." Even as a queen and empress, Mercer couldn't escape being characterized as "a ragbag for all her imperial finery."[23]

The single role for which Mercer was best known was the poor, pathetic scrubwoman Mrs. Midget in Sutton Vane's metaphysical mystery play about what happens after we die, *Outward Bound*. However melodramatic and sentimental by today's standards, *Outward Bound* was an original, well crafted, and thought-provoking play in its day. A small company of strangers find themselves on a ship with only one visible crew member, Scrubby (J.M. Kerrigan), whom we later learn is a "half-way," doomed to sail endlessly between life and death because he committed suicide. Among the passengers bound for the great unknown, who do not initially realize they are dead, is the snobbish and insincere dowager, Mrs. Cliveden-Banks (Charlotte Granville); the "amiably bibulous and inwardly distracted" observer figure, Tom Prior (Alfred Lunt); the "pompous and hard boiled" businessman, Mr. Lingley (Eugene Powers); and the lapsed clergyman, William Duke (Lyonel Watts), in addition to Mrs. Midget. Each receives their just reward when they come face to face with the "Examiner," played by Dudley Digges. It turns out that Tom Prior is Mrs. Midget's long lost son, whom she gave up so that he could have a better future than she could give him. They are reunited in death, where Mrs. Midget will spend eternity as an unpaid housekeeper for her boy. *Outward Bound* opened at the Ritz Theatre on January 7, 1924, and ran for 144 performances.[24] The play, according to one reviewer, stirred the audience "to very considerable depths of human pity and mortal terror." He wrote of Mercer that she "has never been more seraphically maternal, more racily human."[25]

Of the 19 plays Mercer did on Broadway, the only one to remain in the modern repertoire is George Bernard Shaw's *Pygmalion*. Mercer played Professor Higgins's housekeeper, Mrs. Pearce, in a successful Theatre Guild revival at the Guild Theatre in 1926 and 1927, starring Reginald Mason as Higgins and Lynn Fontanne as Eliza Doolittle, with Helen Westley as Mrs. Higgins and Henry Travers as Alfred Doolittle. There were notable failures, too, towards the end of her dozen years on Broadway. *A Bit of Love* (1925), a drama by John Galsworthy with O.P. Heggie and Chrystal Herne, was taken off almost before it opened. *Fool's Bells* (1925), an A.E. Thomas comedy, lasted only five performances. *Brass Buttons* (1927), a drama by John Hunter Booth, lasted eight and was Mercer's last show on Broadway. These flops may have been instrumental in convincing her that her future lay in the west.

Mercer had made a handful of silent films, so she wasn't a total stranger to the medium. In the late 1920s, there was a brave new world opening for talented character players who could speak the King's English and adapt themselves to the requirements of the "talkies." But Hollywood wasn't just importing actors from the stages of Broadway. This was the period when the introduction of sound made necessary a whole new approach to storytelling in film. The studios needed new, more sophisticated stories and complex dramas and they found them to a great extent in the hit plays of the day. These early sound versions of Broadway successes like *Common Clay*, *Cavalcade*, *Outward Bound*, and *Smilin' Through*, however studio-bound and stagey they may seem today, are the closest we can ever come to what it would have been like being in the original Broadway audience of these famous shows.

Mercer was on hand from the first days of sound and among character actresses was thus a pioneer of sorts, setting a high standard for the many who would follow her. Her sound film debut was in a film called *Mother's Boy* (B. Barker, Pathé Exchange, 1929), where she and her "boy," 28-year-old Morton Downey, received top billing playing a golden-voiced Irish lad, Tommy O'Day, who runs away from home and becomes a professional singer. His devoted mother (Mercer) is saved from the jaws of death by her prodigal son's returning to sing a rousing tune at her sick bed.

Several of Mercer's early film roles were reprises of performances she had given on the stage. She had the chance to repeat her Broadway role as the greedy landlady Mrs. Gubbins in *Three Live Ghosts* (T. Freeland, Joseph M. Schenk Productions, 1930), a story about what happens when three World War I soldiers believed dead return to London very much alive. This was the comedy she was performing in when her son died and, ironically, was her biggest commercial success with 250 performances. Mercer's celebrated role as Mrs. Dowey in the one-act J.M. Barrie play *The Old Lady Shows Her Medals* was also fixed forever on celluloid when she starred in a film version called *Seven Days' Leave* (R. Wallace, Paramount, 1930) with a 29-year-old Gary Cooper as the son of her hopes and dreams.

Another of Mercer's early assignments was replacing ZaSu Pitts as the hero's mother, Mrs. Bäumer, in *All Quiet on the Western Front* (L. Milestone, 1930). Preview audiences had not been able to take zany comedienne Pitts seriously in a straight role and "hooted with laughter at her deathbed scene."[26] Her scenes were reshot with an actress more likely to evoke an appropriately lachrymose response. It's telling that when Universal had to find an actress guaranteed to strike the right note of pathos and sentimentality, they chose Mercer. For her efforts, Mercer was billed fifteenth, but she was credited, as always. *All Quiet on the Western Front* is Mercer's most popular and highly rated film among today's viewers.[27]

Mercer's first film for Fox, the closest she would come to a home studio (she made 13 films there between 1930 and 1939) was the first sound version of Cleves Kinkead's hit play *Common Clay* (V. Fleming, 1930), starring Constance Bennett as the hard-done-by but inwardly noble and untarnished heroine Ellen Neal. Mercer played Ellen's adoptive mother, who comes to her defense in the big climactic trial scene. The role of Mrs. Neal was created on Broadway in 1915 by Mabel Colcord.

Outward Bound (R. Milton, Warner Bros., 1930) was Mercer's ninth sound film when it premiered at the Hollywood Theatre in New York on September 17, 1930. The Warner Bros.–owned theater at Broadway and W. 51st St. had opened on April 22 that year, as the first movie theater especially designed for talkies. The studio had hired Robert Milton, who also staged the play on Broadway, to direct the film. An extremely productive director on Broadway between 1908 and 1941, the Russian-born Milton also directed a handful of films between 1929 and 1934. The producers had gone to great lengths in filming the play, Mordaunt Hall told his readers, and wherever it was possible they obtained the services of

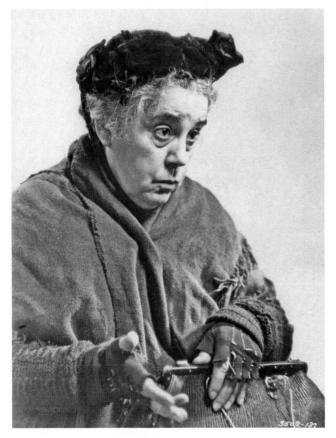

players who had acted in the stage production.[28] Thus, Mercer, Dudley Digges, and Lyonel Watts reprised their stage roles. Leslie Howard, who had played one of a young pair of potential half-ways who are saved at the last moment, made his sound film debut here in Alfred Lunt's part of Tom Prior, while Douglas Fairbanks, Jr., took over Howard's role as Henry.

Maybe the most important change in casting was that veteran British character actress Alison Skipworth, 20 years Mercer's senior, took over the role of the "haughty Mrs. Cliveden-Banks, who dotes on her hyphen."[29] The scenes between her and Cockney Mrs. Midget, who in her own characteristic phrase has been "struck all of a 'eap" by the latest events, are among the most amusing and incongruous encounters between older women ever filmed. Mrs. Cliveden-Banks is alternately patronizing towards the little charwoman ("No one could possibly be called Midget") and appalled to discover that there is only one class on the boat ("How am I to

Beryl Mercer in her signature role as the humble charwoman Mrs. Midget in the supernatural drama *Outward Bound.* Mercer created this little Cockney sparrow of a woman on Broadway, where the play by Sutton Vane ran for 144 performances. In 1930 Warner Bros. produced a film retaining some of the original cast, including Mercer, Leslie Howard (in a different role), Dudley Digges, and Lyonel Watts.

know who are the ladies and gentlemen, and who are not?"). She insists "It would be quite impossible for me to lunch at the same table with a woman who has been struck all of a heap."[30] According to the *New York Times*, "It was a memorable evening in more ways than one." Hall thought Mercer gave "as fine a performance as Mrs. Midget as she did on the stage."[31]

Mercer's glory days on the big screen were the early 1930s. Things began to slow down after 1933, as her roles became smaller and less interesting and her name moved further down the credits list. In the early days of sound, telling stories with older women in the lead was nothing out of the ordinary and there was an influx of older actresses to satisfy the demand. Marie Dressler was only the most stunningly successful example, but character actresses like May Robson and Alison Skipworth also starred in their own vehicles, as did Beryl Mercer in her first three sound films. This situation didn't last, though the studios didn't give up trying to create a new Dressler until the 1940s. Mercer was 20 years younger than the first generation of actresses to make a major impact in sound films, but then she'd always played older than her years (or younger).

Among Mercer's more familiar film titles, we find *Inspiration*, *The Public Enemy*, *The Miracle Woman*, *Cavalcade*, *Jane Eyre*, *Night Must Fall*, and *The Hound of the Baskervilles*. Her roles here ranged from gangster mothers (*The Public Enemy*, W.A. Wellman, Warner Bros., 1931) to maids (*Inspiration*, C. Brown, MGM, 1931), cooks (*Cavalcade*, F. Lloyd, Fox, 1933), housekeepers (*Jane Eyre*, C. Cabanne, Monogram, 1934), landladies (*The Miracle Woman*, F. Capra, Columbia, 1931), and salesladies (*Night Must Fall*, R. Thorpe, MGM, 1937). In *The Hound of the Baskervilles* (S. Lanfield, Twentieth Century–Fox, 1939), she was surprisingly not cast as Sherlock Holmes's housekeeper Mrs. Hudson, that role belonged to Mary Gordon, but got to play a psychic medium who stirs up the action at a weekend party on the Baskerville family's estate.

Sometimes Mercer found herself playing adult roles in filmatizations of plays she'd performed in as a child. This was the case with *East Lynne* (F. Lloyd, Fox Film, 1931) and *The Little Minister* (R. Wallace, RKO, 1934). In the former, she now played Joyce Hallijohn, a maid at East Lynne. In the latter, she was billed seventh as "little minister" Gavin Dishart's angelic mother, who has sacrificed much to see her son in the pulpit and is finally rewarded when he gets his first congregation. Even though their entire future is threatened by his liaison with gypsy temptress "Babbie," Mrs. Dishart welcomes her into the family with open arms. The film starred bland John Beal and spicy Katharine Hepburn.

Towards the end of her career, Mercer was called on to play her specialty role, Queen Victoria, twice: in *The Little Princess* (W. Lang, Twentieth Century–Fox, 1939), starring Shirley Temple, and *The Story of Alexander Graham Bell* (I. Cummings, Twentieth Century–Fox, 1939).

During her years in Hollywood, Mercer first made her home at the Aloha Apartment Hotel at 6735 Leland Way, a one-block street in Hollywood which runs parallel to Sunset Boulevard between McCadden Place and Las Palmas Avenue.[32] By 1933, she was living at 5051 Almaden Drive, which is four blocks north of York Boulevard in a residential neighborhood in northern Highland Park about midway between Glendale and Pasadena, not far from Anderson Field. Mercer's modest, four-bedroom, two-bathroom, 1180 square foot bungalow from 1921 is still standing on its tiny sliver of land with just enough space for a garage, a driveway, and a postage stamp–sized front yard. In fact, her cozy, quiet block seems to be little changed since her day, consisting of small, closely built houses from the 1910s and '20s with the odd palm and jacaranda tree to break the monotony.[33]

Mercer's final film, *A Woman Is the Judge* (N. Grinde, Columbia, 1939), a one-hour crime and justice drama starring Frieda Inescort and Otto Kruger, was released two months after her death. Ironically, Mercer, who had played little old ladies for much of her career, would not live to become a little old lady herself. She died on July 28, 1939, at Santa Monica Hospital at the age of 56. The *New York Times* reported, "Little hope had been held for her recovery since she had undergone a major operation earlier this month."[34] Apart from her name, given as "Beryl Mercer Herbert," and dates, the plaque on her modest grave on the Sunrise Slope of Forest Lawn Memorial Park in Glendale reads "Beloved by all."[35]

Her Girl Friday: Juanita Moore
in *Imitation of Life* (1959)

"Miss Lora, you never asked."

In 1960, Juanita Moore became only the third African American to be nominated for an Academy Award in the supporting actress category for her performance as Annie Johnson in *Imitation of Life* (1959). Her competitors were Shelley Winters for *The Diary of Anne Frank*, Hermione Baddeley for *Room at the Top*, Thelma Ritter for *Pillow Talk*, and her own onscreen daughter, Susan Kohner, for *Imitation of Life*. Winters won.

Ross Hunter originally had the wild idea to cast Mahalia Jackson as the soft-spoken, shy, and retiring Annie, who as a widowed, homeless mother with a young child to support inveigles herself into the affections of Lora Meredith (Lana Turner), also a widow with a young daughter and barely more financially secure than Annie. Pearl Bailey was also in the running in what was described as "the greatest search of all in the casting of *Imitation of Life*."[1] As Moore herself recalled 50 years later, "They wanted everybody but me. Only the director and Ross Hunter liked me."[2]

Mahalia Jackson had wisely declined, saying, "I'm a singer, not an actress." She suggested Hunter get in touch with her friend Juanita Moore. Moore hadn't been seen on the big screen in 1958 and her uncredited bit parts in five films in 1957 would hardly have made the high-powered Hunter sit up and take notice. Their meeting, though, was a success and the producer was sold on the idea of Moore as Annie Johnson.[3] Ironically, he would spend more money on Lana Turner's wardrobe ($23,645) than he would pay Moore in salary ($5,500).[4] She was 35 years old when filming started at Warner Bros. Studios on August 5, 1958, and had been acting in films for 10 years. *Imitation of Life* would be her twentieth film, but only the sixth where she was given screen credit.

No argument can be made for Douglas Sirk's final film as a breakthrough or a pioneering film in its treatment of African Americans in general or Annie Johnson in particular. It was probably the end of something, rather than a new beginning. But Annie Johnson is a significant figure in the history of black women in films and her creator, Juanita Moore, is now one of the few living connections with a tradition of African American actresses in Hollywood films, which goes back to the heady days of Hattie McDaniel and Louise Beavers and scores of others whose names have been lost to us. This is not to suggest that Moore is as old as all that. She was born in Los Angeles on October 19, 1922, as the youngest of eight children. Her parents, Harrison and Ella Moore, had come to California from Greenwood, Mississippi, in the final years of World War I and prospered in South Central Los Angeles, where Juanita's mother opened a laundry.[5]

In the African American actress genealogy, there is a direct line of descent from McDaniel, Beavers, Libby Taylor, Gertrude Howard, Marietta Canty, Theresa Harris, and Ethel Waters, all born in the 1890s and early 1900s, down through the second generation of Pearl Bailey, Nina Mae McKinney, Claudia McNeil, Butterfly McQueen, Maidie Norman, Isabel Sanford, Beah Richards, Ruby Dee, and Juanita Moore to the third generation of the 1930s and '40s and so on. As I write, among these talented actresses, only Dee and Moore are still alive, at age 86 and 88 respectively.

The second generation, as I call them, faced somewhat different challenges and limitations in their careers than the pioneers in the 1930s and '40s. They came of age and started their careers during one of the most oppressive periods in American race relations and, arguably, the worst possible time to be an African American in the movie industry, at least with regard to job opportunities and the restrictions on what blacks could do and say on screen. For all its racial myopia and basic refusal even to suggest racial tension on the screen, during the 1930s there was at least plenty of work to be had. However briefly and superficially, there was a very real African American presence in a vast number of films. As in American society, where black domestic workers oiled the social machinery, in American films of the era, they kept the wheels of the plot turning. They could also be funny. By the 1950s, the pall of seriousness had descended, if African American actors were seen on film at all. Often it was easier to evade the race question entirely by dropping black bit players and extras, resulting in an even more oppressive and exclusionary atmosphere than before.

Moore had no Broadway shows to her credit when she started in films, unlike everyone else in this book, but that was not uncommon for African American actors. After graduating from Jefferson High School, she had spent "just long enough to take a deep breath" at Los Angeles City College, before decamping to New York and becoming a chorus girl.[6] Her first dramatic role was in Sartre's *No Exit*, an Ebony Showcase production in Los Angeles with James Edwards and Maidie Norman.[7] She had also been a successful singer in night clubs in New York, London, and Paris.[8] That was how she was presented when she was cast in *Imitation of Life*, as "a former singer who had headlined at Paris' Moulin Rouge and London's Palladium."[9]

If we look at the opportunities Moore was given in the decade she spent in the movies before *Imitation of Life* came along, you can get some idea of the professional desert the movie industry had become for African American actors by this time. Moore's feature film debut was in Elia Kazan's famous film about passing and interracial romance, *Pinky* (Twentieth Century–Fox, 1949), starring Jeanne Crain and the two Ethels, Barrymore and Waters. Moore has a brief exchange with Crain on the stairs as a nursing student at the close of the film, when Crain has turned Ethel Barrymore's palatial plantation home into a college for nurses. *Pinky* was followed by half a dozen small roles in forgotten films of the early 1950s. In the mid–1950s, Moore played maids in four of her more familiar titles: *Not as a Stranger* (S. Kramer, Stanley Kramer Productions, 1955), as Gloria Grahame's maid married to the stableman; *Queen Bee* (R. MacDougall, Columbia, 1955), as Joan Crawford's maid; *Ransom!* (A. Segal, MGM, 1956), as Glenn Ford and Donna Reed's maid; and *The Opposite Sex* (D. Miller, MGM, 1956), as a powder room attendant in the big final showdown scene of this remake of *The Women*. Moore's participation in these films was modest, to say the least.

Prior to playing Annie Johnson, the most significant character Moore had portrayed was Polyclinic "Polly" Jones in *Women's Prison* (L. Seiler, Columbia, 1955). A sympathetic inmate with a word of good cheer for everyone, Polly is first seen scrubbing the floor of the cell block when Jan Sterling and Phyllis Thaxter arrive at the prison. She prays for Audrey

Totter's recovery after she is beaten by the sadistic and psychopathic superintendent played by Ida Lupino. Harkening back to her days as a singer, Moore performs a serenade with her three black cellmates for a fellow prisoner who is about to be released.

Then along came Ross Hunter, Douglas Sirk, Annie Johnson, and *Imitation of Life*. There is no simple, uncomplicated way to respond to a character like Annie. On the one hand, you could argue that she is one of the most egregious examples of 1950s Uncle Tomism and, seen from a racial point of view, the narrative of which she is a part is reactionary at best, if not outright racist. On the other hand, she might be viewed as a rare opportunity for an older African American woman to come more sharply into focus and have at least part of the story be about her.

What strikes me first about Annie is how utterly genteel and middle-class she is. She looks like a woman who never had sex. Was Sarah Jane conceived through immaculate conception? How this prim and proper matron ever found herself without friends and family and any viable means of support is, of course, one of the many implausibilities of this version that we are forced to accept. If Annie were to be seen at any moment in dishabille or with a hair out of place, it would have been more shocking than her daughter disavowing her. For better or worse, we need never contemplate Annie as a sexual being. Her husband is long gone and she doesn't have anything remotely approaching a love interest in the film. Like so many film mothers, mammies, and maids, she is sexually *hors de combat*, as the French say — completely out of the running.

Moore claimed to have based her characterization on her devout, college-educated sister, who worked as a maid and companion like Annie Johnson.[10] Unlike Annie and apparently her sister, Moore herself has been married for most of her life. Moore's first husband was Nyas Berry (b. ca. 1912), part of the team of acrobatic dancers called the Berry Brothers. He died of cancer in 1951. Her second husband was bus driver Charles Burris. When he died in 2001, the couple had been married for half a century.[11]

Jeremy G. Butler writes that Annie is "much less conventionally 'black' than Delilah" in the original 1934 version of the film. She no longer speaks in dialect, for example.[12] The changes in the names of the characters from the novel and the first film version to this remake are also significant. Delilah becomes Annie Johnson. Her daughter Peola becomes Sarah Jane. Bea Pullman, the white heroine, becomes Lora Meredith. Her daughter Jessie is renamed Susie. It's as if all the characters are being gentrified with English- and Scandinavian-sounding names.

Both the standardization of the African American characters' speech and the name changes are part of the way in which racial markers of difference are being wiped out to a great extent in the 1959 version of the film. What happens when these markers are removed, which might initially seem like a progressive and liberal revision, is not that everyone becomes blacker, more ethnic, more diverse. No, what happens is that everyone becomes whiter, which means more conventional, middle-class, and heterosexual. Annie Johnson, then, not just in name, but in appearance and demeanor, is a whitewashed version of Delilah. Clearly, Annie in the person of Juanita Moore bears some physical traits racially specific to African Americans, but they really make little or no difference to who she is as an individual in this narrative.

As a story with a 25-year history by the time this final version was made, *Imitation of Life* can tell us a lot about changing ideologies, priorities, and possibilities in American culture from the mid–1930s till the late 1950s. It was impossible in 1959, for example, to imagine Delilah-Annie being played the way Louise Beavers portrayed her in 1934. The biggest difference between the two film versions is that the latter discards the whole storyline so central to the novel and first film, where Bea Pullman and her devoted Delilah build an empire on syrup and pancakes. In the remake, there is a huge, gaping hole in the middle where a plot used to be. Where Delilah is an idiosyncratic yet industrious and successful entrepreneur with a life lived both in the public sphere and the home environment, Annie is reduced to being a mostly unpaid domestic worker and stay-at-home mom in a cloistered, all-female household. While Delilah may be uneducated and folksy in speech compared to Annie, she is the successful partner in a major business venture. Annie, on the other hand, for all her airs and graces, exists only to serve others, with no marketable skills, no independent income, and no identity separate from her biological and elective families. Is this progress?

Donald Bogle explains the difference the plot change makes to the character of Delilah-Annie: "Ironically, by stripping away the pancake business, the filmmakers have also stripped away the black woman's basic individuality and her personal tragedy. In the earlier version, we assumed the two women remained together partly because they were in business together. Here the black woman simply seems to be *hanging around*. She's an understanding maid but little more." He concludes that she "has almost nothing going for her."[13]

The question is whether these changes in the Delilah-Annie character primarily have to do with her race at all, or if it is rather a case of the producers taking a thoroughly original African American protagonist, Delilah, who in an unprecedented way dominates the film with her charm and charisma, and turning her into a self-effacing, conventional and dull supporting figure, who doesn't even dominate her own life. To put it another way, Delilah (Louise Beavers) is original and important because she is an African American woman who is both a mother and a businesswoman and plot-wise on a level with her friend and business partner, Bea Pullman (Claudette Colbert). Annie on the other hand is clearly reduced substantially in significance to a point where, as I've suggested, she fulfills many functions, but only secondary and supporting ones, and where her race has been almost entirely effaced.

Annie Johnson is the female supporting character taken to an almost parodic extreme. She doesn't just have one mistress, daughter, friend; she has three. She isn't just self-effacing, self-sacrificing, and motherly in relation to one heroine, but three. It really makes little difference whether the protagonist in question is her employer, her employer's daughter, or her own daughter. Annie is there to serve, to be available to others, to help, give advice, and lend a sympathetic ear. Lucy Fischer calls her a "wish fulfillment fantasy" for white women: "a double who appears at the door, offering, *gratis*, the custodial services they require."[14] According to Fischer, the film "fabricates a suspect solution to the dilemma of the middle-class professional woman: a deferent black double who assumes the position she vacates."[15] You could say that Lora has a wife and Annie has a female husband.

To make matters worse, Annie is completely devoid of the element of irony that has always been the prerogative of second leads in general and maids and other servants in particular, whether black or white. In *Slow Fade to Black: The Negro in American Film, 1900–1942*, Thomas Cripps discusses how black actors in the 1930s "played servants or foils who were faithful *and* flippant, mannered *and* casual, distant *and* familiar," and who "brought a querulous stubbornness to their job."[16] There isn't much of this tradition left by the time the *Imitation of Life* remake comes along. As Annie Johnson, Moore is hardly joining the ranks of Hattie Noel, Dorothy Dandridge, Hilda Simms, and Theresa Harris as "wisecracking, fey, abrasive rebels against caste": "With sly winks they proffered advice or raised eyebrows at their employers' follies as though following the path laid down by Hattie McDaniel in *Alice Adams*."[17] There are no raised eyebrows here, no amusing asides on the feats and

This iconic photograph from *Imitation of Life* (Universal International Pictures, 1959) says a lot about the relationships in this classic melodrama. In her signature role of Annie Johnson, prim and proper Juanita Moore gazes up adoringly at her employer and friend, soon-to-be star Lora Meredith (Lana Turner). Ms. Meredith stands self-importantly with a script in her hand, acknowledging her friend's admiration with a Mona Lisa smile, her image reflected in the mirror behind her. On Annie's lap, her arm protectively around her, sits Lora's daughter Susie (Terry Burnham), while Annie's own daughter Sarah Jane (Karen Dicker) stands pensively behind her mother's chair.

foibles of the heroine(s), no archness or ironic distance. This is partly why commentators have found Annie to be, in the words of a writer in *Cue* magazine, "insufferably saintly."[18] And, of course, she is. To be otherwise would be to attract attention to oneself and there isn't room for that in a story with not one but three heroines.

"You never asked." That brief comment is the closest Annie ever comes to criticizing Lora. In those three words, we see telescoped and summarized three decades of Hollywood's willed ignorance about, lack of interest in, or downright prejudice towards anyone who was not young, white, middle-class, and heterosexual. The racial difference between Annie and Lora is the elephant in the room. It is really quite remarkable that the entire film basically ignores this difference. Marina Heung explains: "What is at stake in this film, I would argue, is the need to suppress the true location of potential conflict: that between white mistress and black servant.... As a result, it is mother and daughter who are each other's antagonists, not two black women and a racist society."[19] This is not a case of Lora Meredith being "color blind," as Moore has described director Douglas Sirk.[20] Rather, in her self-absorption Lora is not capable of summoning enough interest in Annie to consider that she is African American, what that means to Annie, and the difference it might make to their relationship. As Donald Bogle tersely puts it: "Lana Turner doesn't seem aware that Juanita Moore exists."[21] Had Annie been a genteel-yet-homeless white woman with a daughter, it would have made little difference to her relationship with Lora, though obviously it would have made a big difference to her relationship with her daughter Sarah Jane. This is not to suggest that *Imitation of Life* is not about race, clearly it is on some levels, but only to suggest that Lora Meredith's obliviousness about who her ostensibly closest friend really is becomes the blindness of the film as a whole.

In the Annie-Lora relationship, apart from the obvious parallels to the original Delilah and Bea, there are also echoes of other white mistress–black maid relationships in films as diverse as *Finishing School* (1934) and *Gone with the Wind* (1939). What Annie seems to share with Mammy in *Gone with the Wind* is a keen eye for the proprieties. The moment early in the film when Annie says "It just ain't seemly, Miss Lora" (about lover boy John Gavin's photo of the girls and the fat man at Coney Island) takes me right back to Mammy telling Scarlett "It ain't fittin', it just ain't fittin'." There is an interesting difference here, too, though. I've suggested before that Mammy in *Gone with the Wind* functions to mediate the audience's relationship with a highly ambiguous heroine, someone who throughout the film can be hard to take.[22] While Mammy serves to make Scarlett more likable by virtue of her ability to inspire love and loyalty in an upstanding black Christian woman, one can hardly say that Annie's dogged devotion to Lora has the same effect. Lana Turner's Lora Meredith remains an effigy, shellacked, powdered, painted, and corseted into place. Like an automaton in haute couture, she moves unblinkingly through the narrative, oblivious to everyone around her, dedicated only to her image of herself. Even to call her self-absorbed may be investing her with more personality than she actually has. To be self-absorbed, you have to have a self to be absorbed in.

I'm also reminded of Theresa Harris, who plays Billie Burke's maid Evelyn in *Finishing School*. Though Burke's portrayal of the selfish socialite and Frances Dee's neglectful mother, Helen Crawford Radcliff, is positively enthralling compared to Turner's whited sepulcher of a performance, there is something in the entirely one-sided dynamic of Mrs. Radcliff and Evelyn, mistress and maid, where Evelyn has to listen to endless monologues on Mrs. Radcliff's difficult life, that is not so different from Annie and Lora's one-sided friendship.

I'm reminded, too, of *In This Our Life* (1942), because it was one of the first films within a straight dramatic format and a realistic genre to give audiences some insight into "how the other half lived," i.e., the African American servants in their off hours. Hattie McDaniel portrays a housekeeper and mother, who must fight for her son when he is falsely accused of a hit-and-run accident that has actually been perpetrated by the daughter of her employers. For the black paid help to have their own storyline was something quite out of the ordinary, so much so in fact that it would be several years before it happened again, in *Pinky* (1949), and there the mixed race heroine had to be played by a white actress.

As far as the troubled Annie-Sarah Jane relationship is concerned, there is of course a precedent in the original 1934 version. The portrayal of the demise of the mother-daughter relationship is not that different from one film to another. The fact of daughters being ashamed of their mothers and their background is not the exclusive province, though, of African American families. Anne Shirley and screen mother Barbara Stanwyck in *Stella Dallas* (1937) and Ann Blyth and Joan Crawford in *Mildred Pierce* (1945) are only two of the more prominent examples of daughters disavowing their mothers, moving on by jettisoning the past, only here it is not to pass into another race, but rather into another class.

Having attained her success meteorically and early on in the film, Lora Meredith is really left without a story for the remainder of the narrative, except the contrived subplot of her daughter Susie (Sandra Dee) falling in love with Lora's would-be husband Steve Archer (John Gavin). Stephen Handzo writes that "she is at once the central character, yet extraneous to the narrative."[23] What little spark of genuine life there is in this film is, of course, struck by the drama between Annie and her rebellious daughter Sarah Jane (Susan Kohner), who chooses to pass for white. Critics have pointed out that their story dominates the second half of the film. Paul V. Beckley writes: "It may not be that the acting talents of Miss Kohner and Miss Moore alone lift this part of the story so high above the rest of the picture as to leave it in a kind of shadowy, powdered vacuum. It is more probable that the genuine drama of their conflict stung director and screenplay writers alive."[24]

As the film progresses and Annie seems more and more to be stalking her own daughter, we begin to understand Sarah Jane's frustration, which finally explodes in the question: "Why can't you leave me alone?" The final scene between them, terribly affecting and beautifully played by both Moore and Susan Kohner, is the finest and truest in the film, though in a film where "nothing is natural," that may not be saying a lot.[25] According to Rainer Maria Fassbinder, "It is the mother who is brutal, wanting to possess her child because she loves her.... Sarah Jane defends herself against her mother's terrorism, against the terrorism of the world. The cruelty is that we can understand them both, both are right and no one will be able to help them."[26]

Hollywood films have never been democratic in the sense that they give equal time to the whole spectrum of humanity across differences and divides of age, race, class, and sexual orientation. They are heavily weighted towards the young, white, heterosexual, middle-class, and, one might add, physically attractive. Any character not sharing some of these demographics is likely to find him- or herself being eccentric to the core of the narrative. It would be nice to say that Annie gets the last laugh. She doesn't. Pointing out that "It is her coffin at the end before which all other characters supplicate"[27] is a bit like saying that going to prison for two years is the best thing Oscar Wilde did for his career. "The fundamental irony," writes Marina Heung, "lies in the suggestion that for Annie, her annihilation is the prerequisite for recognition."[28] Funerals are not for the dead, they are for the living. This funeral is not a final, long-awaited act of self-assertion on Annie's part, but rather yet another attempt to make her selfish friends and next of kin feel a little better about themselves and Annie's wasted life.

Unfortunately, then, the finale to *Imitation of Life* cannot be regarded as "the revenge of the supporting players," where all the overlooked maids, mammies, and confidantes come back to demand that "attention must be paid." The finale does highlight, though, the artificiality and one-sidedness of the film, despite the fact that it gives the African American maid more screen time than any other. Donald Bogle writes that "there is no sense whatsoever of a black community here. Don't this black mother and daughter have black friends with whom they mix? Consequently, at the climactic funeral, which is attended by every black extra Central Casting was able to scrounge up, we're a bit startled. Suddenly, it hits us that the entire film has been told to us from the white woman's point of view."[29]

The whole concluding funeral segment is so ridiculously over-the-top, one would have to have a heart of stone not to break out laughing. Bosley Crowther called it "a splurge of garish ostentation and sentimentality."[30] Donald Bogle wrote that is was "grossly overdone," but "fun all the same."[31] According to the reviewer for *Time*, this "Hollywood reconstruction of the little old neighborhood Baptist church" looked "suspiciously like Westminster Abbey on coronation day."[32]

The intentions of the filmmakers and the obvious elements of sexism, racism, homophobia, or ageism in a work, need not prevent us from appropriating the film and using it for our own purposes. Ironically, they don't even necessarily preclude enjoyment. That is what camp is: Active enjoyment of the awful, the inappropriate, the politically incorrect, primarily by those groups who themselves are the "victims" of the portrayal, but also by their friends and allies. To the extent that *Imitation of Life* falls apart under the weight of its own improbabilities and utter humorlessness, to the extent that it cannot be taken seriously as a story, it is pure, unadulterated camp. In other words, even though what gets put into a Hollywood film may be highly predictable, controlled, and limited, what we take out of it need have none of those limitations.

As a camp extravaganza, *Imitation of Life* is really the end of something. I see it as the death throes of the classic Hollywood narrative, with its relentless absorption in certain kinds of people, certain kinds of stories, certain kinds of beginnings, middles, and ends. *Imitation of Life* is decadent to the extent that it marks the point where certain narrative conventions have become ridiculous, where certain film clichés begin, however subtly, to draw attention to their own absurdity. In other words, this is a serious film it is impossible to take seriously.

I'm not suggesting that Sirk's version is more racist than the original, but it isn't less either. Personally, I find Annie Johnson a more offensive figment of the white imagination than Delilah for many of the reasons I've already outlined; this despite the fact that Juanita Moore undoubtedly does everything humanly possible to endow her character with dignity and authenticity. It is a fine performance in a thankless role. The reviewer for the *New York Herald Tribune* said he "could wish the mother's point of view were clearer," but hastened to add that it "isn't the fault of Miss Moore's acting, which is both restrained and palpable."[33] Donald Bogle wrote in 1988 that "Moore projects an *intelligent* brand of warmth that the more instinctual Louise Beavers lacked in the original.... It's Moore's fundamental intelligence in all her roles that always makes her seem much too good for them," something he also finds to have been the case with Theresa Harris.[34] More recently he has called Moore's Annie "a touching and now underrated performance."[35] Bosley Crowther wasn't impressed with any of the actors; the *New York Times* critic wrote in his April 18, 1959, review that they "do not give an imitation of life, [t]hey give an imitation of movie acting at its less graceful level twenty-five years ago."[36]

Unlike her co-star Susan Kohner, Moore has only fond memories of Douglas Sirk. Interviewed on the fiftieth anniversary of the film's release, she recalled that he was "right there to help me." He would tell her "you have such a wonderful face." "If he could see it now!" Moore added ruefully in 2009.[37] She told Sam Staggs that she spent most of her time between scenes in her dressing room: "I was not being unsociable. It was just my way of sustaining whatever mood I need for my scenes. I think my part in *Imitation of Life* is the greatest dramatic role ever given to an actress of my race, and I was determined to do it complete justice. My dressing room is my study hall, and for me there is no recess."[38] Still in shock after her daughter Cheryl Crane's trial for the murder of Johnny Stompanato, Lana Turner would not infrequently come knocking on Moore's dressing room door.[39]

Moore and Susan Kohner (b. 1936), now living in New York, have stayed in touch down through the years.[40] With John Gavin (b. 1928) and the child actors Karin Dicker (Sarah Jane) and Terry Burnham (Susie), they are now the only survivors among the film's principal cast. Robert Alda (agent Allen Loomis) died in 1986, Lana Turner in 1995, Troy Donahue (Sarah Jane's abusive boyfriend Frankie) in 2001, and Sandra Dee and Dan O'Herlihy (playwright David Edwards) in 2005.

The Oscar nomination had no substantial effect on Moore's later career. She remained like other African American character actors, in Sidney Poitier's words, "terribly boxed in."[41] Lucy Fischer draws a parallel between actress and role when she writes that "Juanita Moore's career seemed as limited as Annie Johnson's."[42] Among her films following *Imitation of Life*, we find titles such as *Tammy Tell Me True* (H. Keller, Universal, 1961), *Walk on the Wild Side* (E. Dmytryk, Famous Artists, 1962), *The Singing Nun* (H. Koster, MGM, 1966), and *Rosie!* (D.L. Rich, Universal, 1967), but no roles that can remotely compare with Annie Johnson.

Two highlights of Moore's stage career were playing Lena Younger in *A Raisin in the Sun* at the Adelphi Theatre in London in 1959 and her only show on Broadway, a production of James Baldwin's *The Amen Corner* at the Ethel Barrymore Theatre in 1965. Under the heading "London Critics Cool to *Raisin in the Sun*," the *New York Times* reported that the production was "warmly applauded by the audience and coolly received by the press": "Most of the reviewers found its pace too slow, although most of them liked the theme and the acting, particularly of Juanita Moore as the mother and Earle Hyman as the son."[43] Moore could read in the *New York Times* in connection with the first and hitherto only Broadway

Though still a maid, three years after *Imitation of Life* the setting for Juanita Moore's domestic duties could not have been more different. In this still from *Walk on the Wild Side* (Columbia, 1962), we find Moore, hands on hips (center), amidst a bevy of beauties in a New Orleans brothel run by none other than Barbara Stanwyck. Opportunities for African Americans in film and television would soon begin to broaden, but not for Juanita Moore, who would nevertheless still be working in the early twenty-first century.

production of *The Amen Corner*, a satire on the role of religion in African American life in which she and Whitman Mayo played a married couple of hypocritical church elders, that they "know how to convey fraudulent piety with relish."[44] The show lasted 84 performances.

Sam Staggs describes Moore's personality in his book *Born to Be Hurt: The Untold Story of* Imitation of Life: "In her you'll find no trace of the sanctimonious self-righteousness of Ethel Waters in those Billy Graham crusades, nor is she self-absorbed like many in show business. More than any Hollywood actor I've known, Juanita sees herself clearly — meaning that she views the rest of us clearly, too." He adds that "there isn't room enough for Juanita and stress in the same place."[45]

Today Juanita Moore is a producer with the Cambridge Players, a Los Angeles theater company headed by her grandson.[46] She lives in a modest apartment building on South Bronson Avenue in the city's Crenshaw section, not far from the Museum of African American Art. Her final film to date is also her most popular with contemporary audiences: *The Kid* (J. Turteltaub, Walt Disney, 2000), where she plays a grandmother. Moore, who has worked in television since 1953, was last seen on the small screen on February 20, 2001, in an episode of the second season of *Judging Amy* entitled "One for the Road." There she played one of Tyne Daly's clients, Katerine Barrantes, a bedridden elderly woman who pretends to be a holly bush so she will be taken away to an old age home. Her performance showed that Moore was still at the top of her game.

Killing Your Babies:
Marjorie Rambeau in *Slander* (1957)

"I don't want to be ashamed of my son."

I'm tempted to call this story "The Mad Miss Manton," though it has no connection with the 1938 movie starring Barbara Stanwyck and Henry Fonda. That film was a comedy, this is a melodrama, so you have to imagine appropriately surging music to accompany the action. Setting: New York City, night. We are following a determined-looking young woman, her two female friends, and a detective down a dimly lit, luxuriously appointed hotel corridor. The young woman finds the number of the room she is looking for, takes a key from her purse, unlocks the door, and the group enters. Cut to the interior of the hotel suite. In the bedroom, a middle-aged, attractive but slightly blowsy, curly-haired blonde in a state of dishabille is reclining on an unmade bed. Sitting on the bed is a partly undressed man, balding, about 45. The blonde woman seems completely unperturbed at this sudden intrusion of four complete strangers. After shaking hands with the private investigator, she continues rehearsing what sounds like lines from a play. The group of intruders leaves after about 15 minutes. There is no unpleasantness or altercation.

Cut and print. What sounds like a scene from one of Marjorie Rambeau's films is rather a scene taken from her own life. As you have probably already guessed, Rambeau was the blonde woman in the bed. What I have described is what happened in her suite on the night of August 29, 1925, at the exclusive Endicott Hotel on Columbus Ave. between 81st and 82nd Street on the Upper West Side. The young woman with the key was called Mabel Manton and the man on the bed was her husband, William Kevitt Manton, a 45-year-old Canadian-born actor known as Kevitt Manton. The Mantons had been married eight years at this point and had two children aged five and six.[1] When in August 1925, Mabel Manton discovered an extra key to Rambeau's suite and what she considered an incriminating telegram in her husband's room at the Remington Hotel, she took drastic action. At 2:20 A.M. on the night in question, she "raided" the apartment accompanied by two women friends and a detective, Israel Rourke. They found Rambeau, according to the testimony of one of the women at the Mantons' divorce trial in late February 1926, with "nothing on," as far as she could see, and Manton in only his B.V.D.s. She had to admit under cross-examination, though, that "the raiding party found the actress very polite and pleasant" and that "she even shook hands with the detective as he went out."[2]

In her defense at the trial, where Rambeau was named as co-respondent, her lawyer Bernard H. Sandler made reference to "a sort of childlike disregard for convention to which great artists are prone in the press of rehearsals and the memorizing of unfamiliar lines."

He described Rambeau as "a distinguished actress of the highest order," while Manton was nothing more than "a lackey, an employee, a paid 'cueist' whom she had hired to assist her in the study of a part."[3] The part was the titular role in *Antonia*, which opened at the Empire Theatre October 20, 1925, and was co-directed by 26-year-old George Cukor.[4] Manton himself testified that he had been hired as a cueist at $50 a week, that he was "ready for Miss Rambeau at all hours," and that "she often called him to her room at late hours, after rehearsals, to help her with her lines." According to Manton, Rambeau was wearing "a blue wrap, a negligee." He insisted that he still loved his wife and "no other woman shared his affections."[5]

After the second day of the trial, the *New York Times* reported that "the unconventional replies made by the actress in her examination and the 'asides' with which she punctuated much of the testimony of other witnesses continually brought impatient admonishments from Justice Wasservogel and the lawyers."[6] Rambeau took the stand with an attitude of "amused contempt and condescension toward the entire affair" and explained that she had met Manton in 1925 through her fiancé A.E. Anson, an actor, and had employed him immediately as a cueist, stage director, and private secretary.[7] Rambeau dismissed the telegram which her fiancé had sent Manton on her behalf as a joke. Dated May 28, 1925, it read: "Darling, I love you and nothing can keep us apart but the Harlem [River]. As the old conniver says, don't be carnivorous. Your old pal in crime, Marjorie Rambeau." The old conniver referred to was Anson. He corroborated his fiancée's evidence and said they hoped to be married "before June."[8]

On February 26, 1926, after all the testimony had been heard and the jury had been deliberating for seven hours, the Mantons surprisingly reconciled. The headline in the *New York Times* the next day read, "Mantons Reunited; Actress Cleared," and the story reported that the divorce suit had been called off and the alienation case against Rambeau dropped. Rambeau received the news by telephone at the Mansfield Theatre, where she was performing in *The Night Duel*. The actress reportedly "bubbled with joy at the news and wished the Mantons a future full of 'blessed happiness.'"[9]

That was not to be. The Manton divorce case would haunt Rambeau for the next 10 years and beyond. The reconciliation between the couple had apparently been forced on Mrs. Manton, or so she would later claim, and they never lived together again. Mrs. Manton attempted to have the divorce suit reopened in late June 1926, but met with difficulties when the presiding judge learned that "all attempts to locate Manton had failed."[10] On December 2, 1926, she was finally granted a divorce, receiving custody of the couple's two children and alimony amounting to $30 a week. Manton did not defend the suit. Rambeau was again named as co-respondent.[11]

On February 19, 1927, Mabel Manton instigated a suit against Rambeau for $100,000 damages "for alleged alienation of the affections of William Kevitt Manton."[12] When the trial came up in the Supreme Court of New York, Rambeau was unable to witness as, according to her lawyers, "she did not have the carfare from Los Angeles." She was also needed at the bedside of her seriously ill mother.[13] It was not until March 21, 1932, that Mrs. Manton was finally awarded damages amounting to $40,000 for alienation of affections, after the jury had deliberated less than half an hour. Rambeau did not defend the action. Meanwhile, Kevitt Manton had died a suicide on July 30, 1931. I do not know if Mrs. Manton ever received her damages, which by 1935, when the default judgment was transferred to the Supreme Court of Los Angeles, had risen to $48,296.[14]

This was not the first time Rambeau had been the co-respondent in a divorce case. In

1925 the actress Blanche Yurka had been forced to name her as the "other woman" who had alienated the affections of Yurka's husband of three years, Ian Keith Ross. According to the *New York Times'* summary of the divorce trial on March 4, 1925, "Miss Yurka contended that her husband had been attentive to Miss Marjorie Rambeau, but did not intend to name Miss Rambeau until Justice Lydon insisted that the identity of the woman that she alleged had succeeded her in the actor's attentions be known."[15] Born in 1899, the stunningly handsome blond actor known as Ian Keith had played Orlando to Rambeau's Rosalind in a brief revival of *As You Like It* at the 48th Street Theatre in April 1923, when according to Yurka their affair led to an estrangement from his wife; "They were guests at a dinner party at which her husband became intoxicated and made love conspicuously to Miss Rambeau." Yurka was also "subjected to the annoyance of seeing large autographed photographs of Miss Rambeau on her husband's dressing table." Keith did not appear at the trial."[16] Yurka got her divorce and never saw her husband again.

In her 1970 autobiography *Bohemian Girl*, written while Rambeau was still alive and published in the year of her death, Yurka diplomatically does not name Rambeau as her rival. She only makes veiled reference to "all the gossip circulating about [Ian Keith's] attentions to his leading lady" and their disgraceful behavior at a dinner party she threw in their honor. Yurka mainly blames her domineering mother-in-law for being determined to break up the marriage. She does point out, though, the irony in the fact that she had used one of her connections to get Keith the role in *As You Like It*, after he had flubbed the audition. "Left free to follow his own desires," writes Yurka with evident satisfaction, he "apparently tired of his new attachment almost as quickly as he had involved himself in it." Though he later asked to be reconciled with Yurka, "what I had felt for him as my lover and husband was dead."[17] Yurka was four years younger than Rambeau and died in 1974. She was best known for playing Madame De Farge with stunning malevolence in the 1935 film of Dickens's novel *A Tale of Two Cities* and for her many Ibsen roles on Broadway. Keith died in 1960.

Clearly, Marjorie Rambeau was news and the news was often scandalous. She made Tallulah Bankhead look like Lillian Gish. Here is just a handful of *New York Times* headlines from a life filled with incident: "Actresses's Auto Kills Boy: Six-Year-Old Lad Runs in Front of Miss Rambeau's Car" (Sept. 4, 1917); "Marjorie Rambeau Hurt: Star of *Eyes of Youth* Breaks Her Leg While Skating" (Feb. 27, 1918); "Miss Rambeau Denies Sending Love Wire" (Feb. 25, 1926); "Marjorie Rambeau Sued: Tax Liens of $10,832 Filed in Los Angeles by Government" (Oct. 16, 1929); "Marjorie Rambeau Sues: Screen Star, Idle, Wants Contract with Managers Canceled" (June 10, 1930); "Marjorie Rambeau Hurt: She Suffers Possible Skull Fracture in Coast Auto Accident" (Feb. 17, 1945).

Rambeau had been a star on Broadway from the moment she first set foot on the stage of the Longacre Theatre on December 2, 1914, at the age of 25. The play was a new drama written by and co-starring her first husband, Willard Mack, called *So Much for So Much*. "Miss Rambeau Excellent" read the *New York Times* headline. In the review, Mack could read that he had acquitted himself "most creditably" in his role, "but the chief acting honors of last evening fell to Marjorie Rambeau, an actress of no Broadway fame": "In all her performance there is not one false note. Her work is simple, direct, and charming."[18]

Rambeau and Mack had married in 1912, the same year they first hit New York and spent nine weeks in vaudeville in a sketch called "Kick In," which Mack later turned into a full-length play.[19] "Now I hope we are here to stay," said Rambeau in an interview during the run of *So Much for So Much*.[20] She stayed, indeed, for a dozen years. "So much beauty and charm and talent rolled into one personality is not meant to blush comparatively unseen in the glow of California's sun."[21]

Rambeau continued to be a favorite of the critics, though her vehicles did not always meet with their approval. In her second Broadway show, the Avery Hopgood farce *Sadie Love* (1915–16), she was "charming, gifted, and expert."[22] In *Cheating Cheaters* (1916–17), "the lovely and gifted Marjorie Rambeau quite naturally leads all the rest."[23] In *Eyes of Youth* (1917–18), she gave "a vivid and highly vitalized performance" in "the best acting opportunity which she has yet had."[24] In the World War I French melodrama *Where Poppies Bloom* (1918), she was "bewitchingly lovely in her mourning."[25]

Rambeau was even a favorite of the notoriously acerbic Alexander Woollcott. While he might pan the production as a whole, he always had a good word for "the beauteous and accomplished Marjorie Rambeau."[26] Reviewing *The Unknown Woman* in 1919, Woollcott wrote, "It is doubtful if Miss Rambeau, even in her early barn-storming days in Alaska, was ever before called upon to breathe life into as mechanical and grotesquely improbable a melodrama as the highly-colored effort at sensationalism which had its New York premiere last night." Woollcott concluded by saying, though, that "there really is no kind of play that is beyond Marjorie Rambeau's reach. She has such a collection of old stock company tricks of histrionism that the playwright does not live who could baffle her for a moment."[27] In *The Goldfish* (1922) at Maxine Elliot's Theatre, Woollcott found her "more beautiful than ever."[28]

In addition to the frequent mentions of her physical beauty and fine technique, Rambeau was commended for her voice: "Next to the light that lies and Lies and LIES in Miss Rambeau's eyes her chief charm is her voice — a voice of infinite variety that sings and chuckles in a whimsical way by turns."[29] In summing up the theatrical year 1914, the *New York Times* drama critic dwelt on Rambeau's "several valuable assets": "She has youth and she has considerable good looks. She is pretty but she has more than prettiness. Her face is bright and it lights up with that responsiveness which is priceless. And, above all, she knows how to act."[30] It speaks volumes for her initial impact, that this encomium was written after she had spent only 10 days on Broadway.

The *New York Times* writer was correct in pointing out that "Marjorie Rambeau is no novice": "Save for an unchronicled vaudeville visit some two years back, she is new to New York, but what passes for the Rialto in Alaska knows her well and she is known in Denver and along the coastline where Oliver Morosco dwells and flourishes."[31] A later review, sub-titled "Marjorie Rambeau Shines," pointed out that she "has had a training few of her contemporaries can boast, and the complete skill of her performance is a joy to behold. You feel that here is a highly competent actress, who is scarcely a specialist in farce, but who can turn her hand to any work the theatre is likely to give her." Her comic method "suggests Ethel Barrymore, but the memory that haunts you while she plays is the memory of Maude Adams."[32]

Rambeau had been on the stage since she was 12 years old. She claimed in an interview in 1915 to be from Ohio, though "most of her life has been spent in the Far West."[33] She was born in San Francisco on July 15, 1889, the daughter of the French-born businessman Marcel Burnette Rambeau and Lillian Garlinda Kindelberger.[34] Her parents divorced when she was "very young" and Rambeau stayed with her mother: "Mother's people were army folks and as a kiddie I lived in the Presidio in San Francisco."[35] Being big for her age, "all hands and feet and arms and legs," she was sent to dancing school in the hope that she "might acquire some grace." It was there, according to her own account, that she was discovered as a young teenager and got her start in a vaudeville sketch called "The Lady and the Tramp."[36]

Rambeau claimed in a 1914 interview never to have played anything but leading roles since her first days in the theater. "I think it did me more good than if I had put in many years playing little bits," she said.[37] At age 13, she found herself "playing Camille and all the sorrowful sisters of her kind" in a stock company in Portland, Oregon.[38] Rambeau's mother joined her daughter, playing bit parts and sometimes managing the company. "Mother had been studying to be a physician, but she wanted to be with me and so I made an actress out of her."[39] In her early interviews, Rambeau made much of a trip to Alaska she and her mother had made in 1906. The dispersal of the touring company had left them stranded in Dawson City and the two enterprising women started a drama school that soon became popular.[40]

On March 4, 1917, while playing in *Cheating Cheaters* at the Eltinge 42nd Street Theatre, Rambeau sued Willard Mack for divorce, accusing her husband of "misconduct with 'a certain young woman,' whom she says has been living with the defendant at Mountain Lakes, New Jersey, since Feb. 1 last."[41] Two years later, on March 8, 1919, she married fellow actor Hugh Dillman, who was currently playing her son in *The Fortune Teller* despite being four years her senior. Born Hugh Dillman McGaughey in Ohio in 1885, Dillman had made his Broadway debut in 1913, joined the Navy in 1917 and served in World War I, but was back on the New York stage by the spring of 1918.[42] Dillman was also seen in support of Rambeau in *The Unknown Woman* (1919–20), which was his last show on Broadway. By the spring of 1923 the marriage had soured. In filing for divorce in San Francisco on August 8, 1923, Rambeau claimed Dillman had deserted her in April of that year, the very month she was involved with Ian Keith in *As You Like It* and, apparently, elsewhere. She also claimed that Dillman had struck her "on several occasions" and "failed to contribute to her support for nearly a year, although he earned approximately $1,000 a month."[43] She was granted an interlocutory decree of divorce from Dillman in San Francisco on Nov. 13, 1923. The *New York Times* wrote that a property settlement, "said to have been for $60,000," was settled out of court.[44]

We have seen that Rambeau was engaged to fellow actor A.E. Anson when the Manton trial came up in February 1926. Anson was born in London in 1879 and was greatly in demand as a character actor on Broadway between 1902 and 1930. He and Rambeau were in two shows together: the ill-fated *As You Like It* revival in 1923 and Rambeau's next Broadway outing, *The Road Together* in early 1924. The engagement with Anson was broken and he died in California in 1936. Rambeau married for the third and final time on November 10, 1931, when she was 42 years old. The groom was 54-year-old Francis A. Gudger, a widower and retired businessman resident in Sebring, Florida. The ceremony took place in Yuma, Arizona, and was performed by justice of the peace Earl E. Freeman, who the day before had married Gloria Swanson and Michael Farmer. Gudger had previously been "an official of the du Pont Company" and a vice-president at Goldwyn Studios.[45]

After her last show on Broadway, *Just Life*, ended in November 1926, Rambeau had played Amy in Sidney Howard's *They Knew What they Wanted* in Los Angeles and taken leading roles in California stock productions of plays like *The Pelican*, Noël Coward's *The Vortex*, and *What a Woman Wants*.[46] During the two years prior to her marriage, she had spent a busy period in Hollywood and had no less than 14 films released between September 1930 and January 1932, including two of her best: *Min and Bill* (1930) and *The Easiest Way* (1931). Now she announced her retirement from stage and screen.

An early gender-bending comedy, *The Warrior's Husband*, was first a 1924 Broadway play by Julian F. Thompson, which was revived there in 1932. The following year a film was produced by Fox Film Corporation, starring Marjorie Rambeau (left) as the warrior of the title and Ernest Truex (right) as her husband. Though she had a background in silent films, Broadway star Rambeau did not move to Hollywood until the early 1930s and would work in films until 1957.

Hardly more than a year had passed, though, when the newspapers could relate that Rambeau had signed a contract with Paramount and was returning to the big screen; "Her decision to return came as a surprise to her friends."[47] She had been living in Sebring, Florida, with her husband, but was scheduled to arrive in Los Angeles on December 23, 1932, to start filming *Strictly Personal* (R. Murphy, 1933), co-written by her ex-husband Willard Mack, where she would star.[48]

Rambeau's 27-year film career was varied and interesting and, in retrospect, at least as important as her stage career. While all her 15 Broadway plays, save Shakespeare's *As You Like It*, have dropped into a well deserved oblivion, many of her films are not just readily available but well worth a look. David Quinlan has suggested that "her characters were perhaps summed up by the title of her 1931 release *Leftover Ladies*."[49] Producers thought in terms of "Marjorie Rambeau type of roles" according to her obituary,[50] yet Rambeau had a broad range of characters she could play.

Her quintessential type was the life-hardened yet eternally optimistic and cheerful good-time girl, a little worse for wear, no saint, but no repentant sinner either, who could be "just one of the boys" and clean up as nicely as any of the girls. The most significant example of this type is Mamie Adams, Ginger Rogers's gutsy, brassy, and joyful mother in *Primrose Path* (G. La Cava, RKO, 1940), doggedly carrying on the proud family tradition of prostitution, though the film does all it can to cloud the issue. With the exception of an overwrought deathbed scene, Rambeau gives a stunningly real performance in a role where she can make full use of her electrical energy and vivacity. Rambeau's huge, expressive, saucer eyes are used to their full effect and she has just the right combination of attractiveness and vulgarity to suit the part. Mamie strives to appear genteel and to instill manners in her youngest daughter, Honeybell (Joan Carroll), though Mamie's old hag of a mother (Queenie Vassar) does her best to sabotage her by teaching the little girl dubious doggerel verses and old vaudeville show tunes. Rambeau is accidentally shot by her alcoholic husband Homer (Miles Mander), as he tries to do away with himself. She expires, but not before asking Ellie May (Rogers) to care for the family in a "some are born to be taken care of and some to care for them" deathbed monologue.

Other Rambeau demimondaines to delight in are Lulu in *Inspiration* (C. Brown, MGM, 1931) and Elfie St. Clair in *The Easiest Way* (J. Conway, MGM, 1931). As Lulu, Rambeau ducks in and out as the most sympathetic member of the bohemian crowd that heroine Greta Garbo runs with, consisting of mature male artists and their model mistresses. Apart from lending support to Garbo, Rambeau is chiefly preoccupied with her Pekingese Boo-boo, who it is finally reported has had a litter of puppies that look like police dogs. Rambeau is beautifully dressed, as usual, fairly fat and 40, but her brilliant eyes shine forth as ever.

Inspiration has parallels to *The Easiest Way*, where Robert Montgomery also falls for a "fallen" woman, Constance Bennett this time, and the plot turns on the unequal awareness of her past of the various parties involved. Here Rambeau has an amusing role as Elfie, a rapidly aging, hard-bitten commercial artist's model whom Bennett encounters during her brief modeling career. Rambeau acts as a guide to Bennett's character, Laura "Lolly" Murdock, and later shows up when Bennett is down on her luck in a fleabag hotel after boyfriend Montgomery has gone to revive his journalism career in Mexico. Honest work is hard to find, as all the modeling jobs have been taken by chorus girls, but Bennett is determined that she will not be kept again by Adolphe Menjou. She rates Rambeau's ire when she asks to borrow $100; Rambeau resents that Bennett is now too holier than thou to get it the usual way, but prefers to chisel it from her instead. Rambeau leaves the hotel room in high dudgeon with her raccoon coat aflutter. Her best scene, though, is her third and last. Penniless after her Sugar Daddy "Jerry" has been incapacitated by a stroke without leaving provision for his mistress, Rambeau is the one asking Bennett for money this time. She goes out guns ablazing in a scenery-chewing monologue about men having all the cards in their hands and not being hurt by what they don't know.

Rambeau also played plenty of straight-laced dowager roles during her years in Hollywood. For some reason, getting cast in films set in the India of the British Raj often had this gentrifying effect on her. In the overwrought interracial romance *Son of India* (J. Feyder, MGM, 1931), she has a fairly small role as Madge Evans's straight-laced, conventional aunt, a shocked witness to her niece's romance with Indian Ramon Novarro. Rambeau has a British accent and says "Really, my dear" a lot, despite being as American as Evans. There is a faintly amusing scene with a leopard and some double entendres, when Rambeau comes to fetch Evans after she has been looking at Novarro's jewels. Eight years later, she was back in India in *The Rains Came* (C. Brown, Twentieth Century–Fox, 1939), this time in support of Tyrone Power, Myrna Loy, and George Brent. Rambeau plays Mrs. Simon, a socially

Candid photographs showing older actresses in their home environment were par for the course when a studio signed a new contract player and were a far cry from the "cheesecake" photographs young starlets were subjected to. Wearing a modest print dress and minimal makeup, Marjorie Rambeau shows off her collection of bric-a-brac in this undated image.

ambitious wife of an American missionary; she practically throws her daughter, "our little Fern," into Brent's arms at a party.

Rambeau wasn't too fussy about how large the part needed to be to interest her. When Marie Dressler had suggested her for a supporting role in *Min and Bill* (G.W. Hill, MGM, 1931), producer Harry Rapf had been skeptical, saying Rambeau had been a Broadway star for years and would never be interested in such a relatively modest part. Yet she grasped the opportunity eagerly. The rapacious, long-lost mother Bella Pringle, who gets murdered by Min to prevent her from ruining her daughter's future, became her first important role in talkies. As Frances Marion recalled, "All of us had fun during the shooting of this riotous film for never were there better-matched personalities than Dressler, Beery, and Rambeau."[51]

Naturally, among Rambeau's 50 and some odd feature films, there are some real corkers. In the turkey category, I would nominate *Tugboat Annie Sails Again* (L. Seiler, Warner Bros., 1940) and *Three Sons o' Guns* (B. Stoloff, Warner Bros., 1941). In the sequel to a big 1933 Marie Dressler hit, Rambeau stars as Annie Brennan, an Irish brogue Miss Malaprop (e.g., "Both my parents lived to be octoroons!") and captain of the *Narcissus* of Secoma, locked in mortal "to the death" rivalry with competing tugboat captain Alan Hale. It falls to Rambeau to try to save her employer, the Secoma Towing and Salvage Co., after the boss goes away to secure financing and she is left in charge. *Three Sons o' Guns* is a trying domestic comedy about an impoverished but genteel widow (Irene Rich) and her three ne'er-do-well sons. Rambeau is the live-in aunt and sister-in-law, who provides a running ironic commentary on the boys' antics and interrupts the final draft board meeting to tell the officers these boys really need to go into the army. Rambeau delivers her standard hands on hips, folksy, gravelly-voiced performance.

The beautifully produced, finely cast, and perfectly performed drama *Slander* (R. Rowland, MGM, 1957) offered Rambeau one of the most interesting dramatic roles of her career and her last. Billed fourth after the stars Van Johnson, Ann Blyth, and Steve Cochran, Rambeau plays the semi-invalid, disenchanted mother of an enterprising yet unscrupulous Manhattan magazine publisher and editor, H.R. Manley, who has built his career and fortune on destroying the reputations of others. Formerly from Washington Heights, Mrs. Manley now lives in the lap of luxury in a sumptuous Park Avenue penthouse and has her own paid companion to keep her company, yet she is dissatisfied and listless. Her overly solicitous, confirmed bachelor son has imprisoned her in a gilded cage, where she wants for nothing materially, but lacks everything spiritually. Under her son's watchful eye, she can't even enjoy her only remaining pleasure, alcohol.

Slander is an interesting inversion of the "monster mom" paradigm. Rather than the bad mother dominating her good son, we here understand in the course of the film that it's the other way around: the not-perfect but basically good-hearted mother would like to reform her "monster" son. When Manley indirectly becomes responsible for the accidental death of a young boy whose father he has outed as a former criminal in his tabloid *Real Truth Magazine*, his mother shoots and kills him with his own gun. This may seem like drastic action on the part of the old biddy, but the film has shown step by step how immune Manley is to all his mother's attempts to reform him by other means. "I don't want to be ashamed of my son," she says. Despite the "queer" resonances of this intense mother-son relationship, there is nothing fey or effete about H.R. Manley, played with repulsive charm and "a fine flow of oiliness and sneers" by macho Steve Cochran.[52]

Rambeau has aged drastically in the 15 years since *Primrose Path* and at age 67 is now a frail, slightly stooped old lady, with fluffy hair and hollow cheeks. Her signature black eyes are haunting when set in such a gaunt and grizzled face. It was ironic that an actress who had been so often in the headlines would bow out with this film about celebrity and the price to be paid for fame. In Rambeau's heyday, though, in the teens and twenties, there had been no "smear" magazines like *Confidential* to dig up dirt on the stars or invent it if they couldn't find it.

Ann Blyth (right) has every reason to look nonplussed by the uninvited appearance by the mother of the gossip rag editor who has indirectly caused the accident that killed Blyth's son. Rambeau's final years on the big screen gave her some prime acting opportunities, and the gin-loving Mrs. Manley in *Slander* (Metro-Goldwyn-Mayer, 1957) was one of them.

Marjorie Rambeau is the only actress in this book to have been Oscar-nominated twice as Best Actress in a Supporting Role. The first time was in 1941 for *Primrose Path*. She lost to Jane Darwell in *The Grapes of Wrath*. She was nominated a second time in 1954 for her sterling performance as Joan Crawford's chain-smoking, beer-loving, grasping but not unsympathetic mother in *Torch Song* (C. Walters, MGM, 1953). That year Donna Reed won the Academy Award for Best Supporting Actress for *From Here to Eternity*. Rambeau has a star on the Walk of Fame at 6336 Hollywood Boulevard, near the corner of Ivar Avenue and across the street from the Church of Scientology International.

As far as married happiness is concerned, it was third time lucky for Rambeau. She was married to Francis Gudger for 45 years, until his death in February 1967 at the age of 89.[53] Rambeau herself died at her home in Palm Springs, California, on July 6, 1970, at the age of 80. She was laid to rest next to her husband in the small, celebrity-laden cemetery Desert Memorial Park near Palm Springs.[54]

Big Mama: Evelyn Varden
in *Hilda Crane* (1956)

"I live for nothing but that boy."

Evelyn Varden was born in Adair, Oklahoma, a small town in the northeastern corner of the state at the crossing of State Highway 28 and U.S. Highway 69. Varden is the only successful performer ever to have come out of Adair, though no one seems to remember.[1] She was on the stage from an early age, acting in the company of her aunts Blanche Hall and Jessie Mae Hall, which toured throughout the West. She came to New York when she was only 15.[2]

Varden's Broadway career as "a top-drawer character actress in dramatic and comic roles"[3] can bear comparison with any actress of her generation. Actually, she had two Broadway careers. The first was of brief duration and proved a false start, though it brought her some attention and no doubt valuable experience. She debuted on November 22, 1910, at the Bijou Theatre when she was only 17, in support of Zelda Sears in the Anne Caldwell comedy *The Nest Egg*, about the consequence of a "poor seamstress with a passion for romance" writing her name and address on one of the eggs she was sending to market. For her fledgling efforts, Varden had the satisfaction of being "noticed" by the *New York Times*, who wrote that she was "a very pretty girl" and "played sweetly and sympathetically."[4] Her aunt Blanche Hall was also in the show.

In 1918, Varden was at the Park Theatre in the hit *Seven Days' Leave*, a military melodrama which starred William J. Kelly and Elisabeth Risdon; and in *Allegiance* later that same year, a play about three generations of a German American family and their response to World War I. The latter production opened William Faversham's first season as manager of the Maxine Elliott Theatre.[5] Varden's fourth and final play on Broadway during this early phase of her career was *The Honor of the Family*, a revival of a French play based on a novel by Balzac. At age 26, Varden found herself acting opposite the legendary Otis Skinner, who was 35 years her senior. Skinner was reprising his celebrated role as the dashing Colonel Philippe Bridau, who must wrest his wealthy, aged uncle away from the avaricious arms of Flora Brazier (Varden) and later finds out "he would like the fair Flora" for himself. Varden was mentioned among the cast members who supported Skinner "to good effect."[6]

After this, Varden married hotel operator William J. Quinn and retired from the stage. What followed was 15 years out of the limelight and, one assumes, happily married life. Varden's doings during these years are momentarily illuminated by a news item from Los Angeles in the *New York Times* on August 14, 1926, when she was 33. It says that Blanche Hall, "a prominent actress on the New York stage of several years ago," is critically ill at her home in Los Angeles: "Her niece, Mrs. P.W. Quinn, who as Evelyn Varden was also a stage star, is with her here."[7] We also know that Varden lived in Baltimore and was involved as an actress and director with the Vagabond Players. Her first character role, according to the *New York Times*, was in the Clare Kummer comedy *Her Master's Voice*, probably in the role of Aunt Minnie Stickney created on Broadway in 1933 and on film by Laura Hope Crews, an actress Varden somewhat resembled. Florence Reed saw her performance and persuaded her to relaunch her New York stage career.

By the time Varden returned to Broadway as a character actress in September 1934, potential competitors like Beulah Bondi and Marjorie Main had already made their move to Hollywood, leaving the field clear. There were plenty of now forgotten plays during her two decades of continuous work on Broadway, like the Group Theatre's production of *Weep for the Virgins* (1935) with Phoebe Brand and John Garfield; the Theatre Guild's *Prelude to Exile* (1936–37) with Eva Le Gallienne, Leo G. Carroll and Lucile Watson and *To Quito and Back* (1937) with Sylvia Sidney; *Family Portrait* (1939) with Judith Anderson; Ben Hecht and Charles MacArthur's *Ladies and Gentlemen* (1939–40) and Maxwell Anderson's *Candle in the Wind* (1941–42), both with Helen Hayes; and Elmer Rice's huge hit *Dream Girl* (1945–46), starring his wife Betty Field. More importantly, though, there was *Our Town*, not just once, but twice; the 1951 revival of *Romeo and Juliet*, starring Douglas Watson and Olivia de Havilland; the original production of Noël Coward's autobiographical *Present Laughter* (1946–47), with Clifton Webb as Gary Essendine and Varden as his secretary Monica Reed; and Oliver Goldsmith's *She Stoops to Conquer* (1949–50) at the City Center with Varden as Mrs. Hardcastle.

The sober *New York Times* critic Brooks Atkinson was being wildly enthusiastic when he wrote after the premiere of Thornton Wilder's first play and instant classic *Our Town* that it was "one of the finest achievements of the current stage." "Under the leisurely monotone of the production there is a fragment of the immortal truth," he opined. Varden created the role of the doctor's wife, Mrs. Gibbs. She is the mother of the young bridegroom and husband, George Gibbs (John Craven), and after her death serves as a guide to Emily Webb (Martha Scott) after she, too, dies. Atkinson thought she played the role "with an honesty that is enriching."[8] The legendary critic Alexander Woollcott was prompted to write Varden a personal letter after seeing the show: "I shall not feel comfortable until I have written a note to you telling how superbly right you seem to me in your part of the proceedings... You are now part and parcel of one of the richest memories in my long life as a playgoer."[9] Fay Bainter played Mrs. Webb in Sam Wood's finely realized film version from 1940. Varden was back on Broadway for the first revival of *Our Town* in 1944, where Montgomery Clift played her son George.

On March 10, 1951, at the Broadhurst Theatre, Varden became one of more than a score of twentieth century character actresses to play Shakespeare's Nurse in *Romeo and Juliet* on Broadway, some of her more noted predecessors being Mrs. Sol Smith in support of Julia Marlowe (1904, 1905), Charlotte Granville to Ethel Barrymore (1922–23), Jessie Ralph to Jane Cowl (1923), Leona Roberts to Eva Le Gallienne (1930), Edith Evans to Katharine Cornell (1934–35), Florence Reed to Katharine Cornell (1935–36), and Dame May Whitty to Vivien Leigh (1940). "Evelyn Varden's raffish Nurse, groaning, whimsical and unscrupulous, is thoroughly delightful," wrote Atkinson.[10]

For more than 20 years, Varden and her husband made their home at the Gorham Hotel at 136 W. 55th St. between 6th and 7th Ave. in New York.[11] In addition to her stage work, she was also kept very busy in radio, at one time playing four different characters on as many NBC radio serials.[12] She also worked occasionally in television from 1952 till her death. Varden was never more than a visitor to Hollywood during the years of her brief, intermittent film career between 1949 and 1957 and only acted in 14 films. Among these, we find three unique performances: Melba Wooley in *Pinky*, Sallie Carr in *Phone Call from a Stranger*, and Mrs. Burns in *Hilda Crane*. Some would also include in this list her Icey Spoon in the cult classic *The Night of the Hunter* (C. Laughton, Paul Gregory Productions, 1955), who precipitates single mother of two Shelley Winters into madman minister Robert Mitchum's arms, only to turn against him with the vengeance of a woman scorned when it is discovered that he has murdered her; and Monica Breedlove, the landlady and amateur psychologist who calls herself an "over-sized analyst" in *The Bad Seed* (M. LeRoy, Warner Bros., 1956), a role she had originated on Broadway in 1954. Varden also played more modest and less interesting roles, such as the school principal in *Cheaper by the Dozen* (W. Lang, Twentieth Century–Fox, 1950), who is impressed by Clifton Webb's regimen for his large brood of children; and Marie in *Desirée* (H. Koster, Twentieth Century–Fox, 1954), playing Jean Simmons's maid in the film about the rise and fall of Napoleon, played by Marlon Brando.

Marlon Brando looks every inch the Emperor Napoleon and Jean Simmons is suitably sweet as his love interest Desirée in the film of that title (Twentieth Century–Fox, 1955), but who is the dumpy woman kneeling between them? Napoleon's ma? His podiatrist? No, the woman with the curiously two-toned hair and the fancy bathrobe is Simmons's maid Marie (Evelyn Varden) inquiring about the fate of her nephew, who has fought in the disastrous Russian campaign with Napoleon.

The race-conscious and controversial film *Pinky* (Twentieth Century–Fox, 1949), that Elia Kazan took over directing from ailing John Ford, offered Varden a standout debut film role as Melba Wooley, the grasping, insincere, racist, and thoroughly unpleasant wife of Miss Em's first cousin once removed, Jeffers Wooley (Everett Glass). In her first scene, she forces her attentions on the ailing and bedridden, patrician Miss Em (Ethel Barrymore), who tells her nurse, Pinky (Jeanne Crain), not to leave the room under any circumstances. After Pinky nevertheless exits and Melba comments that she is "whiter than I am," she adds that she has come to warn her against the mixed-race girl. Varden's second big scene is in the general store, when she raises a fuss over the shop assistant making her wait while she is serving Pinky. She demands to know if it is the store's policy to serve "nigras" ahead of white folks. Finally, Mrs. Wooley witnesses at the trial during the suit she and her husband have brought against Pinky to wrest her inheritance from Miss Em away from her. Her testimony is a caution and a mendacious masterpiece of imaginative embellishment.

The little known but excellent film *Phone Call from a Stranger* (J. Negulesco, Twentieth Century–Fox, 1952) has three parts united by the figure of Gary Merrill, who befriends three strangers on a flight from Midland, Iowa, to Los Angeles. After a layover due to bad weather, the plane crashes. Eighteen passengers die, including Merrill's three new companions. As one of only three passengers to survive, he escapes with no serious injuries,

Given half a chance, Evelyn Varden was devastatingly good at being devilishly bad, as here in *Phone Call from a Stranger* (Twentieth Century–Fox, 1952), a little-known ensemble film. Varden plays a dragonic night club owner, Sallie Carr, who keeps a firm grip on her son and suspects that Gary Merrill (left) is a lawyer seeking alimony on behalf of her despised daughter-in-law (Shelley Winters).

books himself into the Wilshire Hotel and starts contacting the survivors of his three dead friends. One of the dead is down-on-her-luck, troubled actress Bianca Carr (aka Binky Gay), played by Shelley Winters. In the second segment, Varden gives a bravura performance as Winters's mother-in-law from Hell, Sallie Carr, former vaudevillian and star at the Palace, who is now running a fleabitten Hollywood nightclub, Club Carr, where she is the emcee and star attraction. When Merrill arrives, she is performing. Taking Merrill into her inner office, she spins a yarn about how she did all she could for her daughter-in-law, but Binky had only married her son Mike to get the Carr name and advance her stage career.

There is an amusing fantasy flashback sequence ironically colored by Mrs. Carr's mendacious point of view, where she is dressed in an early 1950s Hollywood version of Biblically inspired widow's weeds and speaks with elevated diction, while Winters, whom she refers to as a "dame" and a "rip," is painted as a vulgar, slangy, grasping tart. Varden does not know Winters is dead and thinks she has engaged Merrill to get her alimony after her husband has recently sought a divorce. To avenge Winters, Merrill spins a yarn back about how she was up for the Mary Martin part in Rodgers and Hammerstein's *South Pacific* and wanted her mother-in-law to play Bloody Mary, a part that only comes along once in a generation. "For an old doll, that's dream stuff," he says.[13] Varden's evil ways are emphasized by her yelling at a janitor for vacuuming while she is on the phone and having her maitre d' fire a waiter for waiting on tables during her performance.

The vast sisterhood of dowager-playing actresses in Hollywood was nearly gone by the time Varden appeared on the scene, but so were also most of the dowager roles. Those who remained among the more prominent names from the 1930s or '40s were Florence Bates (until 1953), Ethel Barrymore, Beulah Bondi, Isobel Elsom, and Cora Witherspoon (until 1954), all rather different types from Varden. Jessie Royce Landis, Mildred Dunnock, and Mildred Natwick started playing film matrons about the same time as Varden, but they too were all quite different physically from her and, like her, were chiefly devoted to the stage.

If there was only one quality Varden had that was unique to her, I would say it was her ordinariness. It wasn't just an "Everywoman" quality necessarily, but it was a quality of being sufficiently average-looking in her face and figure, voice and dialect to be able to represent a wide range of "middle American" women with spirit and conviction. Varden was particularly expert at portraying a certain type of proud, pigheaded, and conventional middle-class matron, who often reveals a deeper strain of vulgarity, materialism, and outright malevolence when she is cornered or put to the test. Varden's was tall enough and sufficiently padded to give her roles the necessary weight both literally and metaphorically. Her doughy face with blue eyes that could narrow to slits like no others was capable of registering a myriad of evanescent, momentary, and often conflicting emotions, that only the camera can capture. Hers was not the imperiousness born of great wealth, fine breeding, and high station, like so many of the dowagers of Lucile Watson or Gladys Cooper. Nor was she simply the paper cutout, one-dimensional and one-ideaed mother or mother-in-law from Hell of so many 1930s and '40s comedies and melodramas. Her characters revealed the development and impact of Freudian psychology on American play- and screenwriting in the post–World War II era and nowhere more so than in her portrayal of the titular heroine's mother-in-law both in the Broadway production and the later film version of Samson Raphaelson's *Hilda Crane* (P. Dunne, Twentieth Century–Fox, 1956).[14]

In the movie Hilda (Jean Simmons) is a twice-divorced career woman who has come to the end of her rope both personally and professionally. She makes a visit of uncertain duration to her hometown in Illinois, where her dead father was a college professor and

Evelyn Varden (left) reached new pinnacles of rapacious fury and over-protective mother histrionics in *Hilda Crane* (Twentieth Century–Fox, 1956), where she played the *nouveau riche* ma of a self-made man. Jean Simmons has done little or nothing to hook this eligible bachelor, but Varden does what she can to scotch the deal. In this photograph, she smugly presents damning evidence of Simmon's scarlet past in the church after the wedding rehearsal.

where her genteel, conventional mother, Stella Crane (Judith Evelyn), still lives in Hilda's childhood home. While there, Hilda is reunited with a former flame, Jacque De Lisle (Jean-Pierre Aumont), a dashing French professor turned best-selling author, and Russell Burns (Guy Madison), an eminently respectable, successful, and eligible bachelor, who through hell and high water remains determined to marry her, despite both Hilda's own doubts and his domineering mother's adamant opposition. Mrs. Burns (Evelyn Varden) is described in the play as "a heavy, coarse woman, somewhat overdressed"[15] with a determination to match her son's; in the course of the film she does everything in her power to prevent a marriage she considers beneath her and Russell. Like so many mothers of sons who have lived the American Dream, she has sacrificed all her life to help get him where he is. There is no way she is going to stand idly by, while he squanders both his wealth and affections on a woman she considers entirely unworthy of him. "I live for nothing but that boy," she says. Along with Beulah Bondi in *Track of the Cat* (1954), Mildred Dunnock in *The Story on Page One* (1959) and Varden's own *Phone Call from a Stranger*, *Hilda Crane* is an interesting, late example of the "silver cord," possessive mother tradition.

As Mrs. Burns, Varden has three big scenes in the film. In the first, she comes on a tour of inspection of the Crane home to see who her son has gotten himself involved with and is none too impressed by the timeworn aspect of the house and, she already suspects, the equally "shopworn" character of her potential daughter-in-law. The second scene, even more confrontational, takes place between her and Hilda in the church after the wedding rehearsal, when Mrs. Burns tries to blackmail Hilda into jilting Russell, by revealing what she has discovered (with the aid of a detective) about Hilda's checkered past. Finally, on the day of the wedding, Mrs. Burns makes one last, no-holds-barred attempt to prevent the marriage by buying Hilda off, once again to no avail. In the most highly charged moment of a volatile, involuntary relationship, she calls Hilda a "tramp," tears the wedding bouquet out of her hands and promptly has an attack. In the stage version, she rallies sufficiently to leave the house ahead of the bride, but later dies while the couple is on their honeymoon, casting a pall of guilt over the marriage, while in the film Hilda and her mother leave her to go to the church. The wedding party learns immediately after the ceremony that Mrs. Burns is in the hospital, where she later dies.

Varden is stunningly well cast in this role, which capitalizes on her ability to be tough, crass, and pull no punches with only the thinnest veneer of gentility. As "a big, overdressed, and uncouth person,"[16] she is a stunning contrast to Hilda's slender, overly polite, and controlled mother, Mrs. Crane, played by Judith Evelyn, Miss Lonelyhearts in *Rear Window* (1954). After the play premiered on November 1, 1950, Atkinson had written that it was "admirably acted by a well-selected cast," which included Jessica Tandy in the title role and Beulah Bondi as her mother, but he found the heroine "a tiresome, irritating egotist," who "does not seem to be worth the trouble." It was unfortunate that Bondi did not reprise her stage role in the film version, as Judith Evelyn seems miscast in the role, which has been expanded to make her one of the root causes of her daughter's unrest and unhappiness. "Evelyn Varden," Atkinson wrote, "leaves her mark on a character by playing the part of an old harridan with versatility and integrity."[17]

Expressing the casual sexism of the 1950s, Bosley Crowther thought the film "certainly not for men," found Jean Simmons so lovely that "if this is how trouble affects a woman, all women should have some of the same," but found Hilda "still a tough one to understand." He blamed Raphaelson and the writer-director Philip Dunne, who had made matters worse by tacking on a happy ending not in the play (where the curtain goes down after Hilda has taken an overdose of sleeping pills). Crowther wrote that Varden and the other supporting players "behave like artificial characters in a gaudy CinemaScope soap-opera, which this is."[18]

Varden had the satisfaction of ending her career on a high note both on Broadway and in the West End of London. Her last Broadway show, *The Bad Seed*, was her biggest commercial success with 334 performances at the 46th Street and Coronet theatres in 1954 and 1955. Varden made her London debut at the Phoenix Theatre on September 26, 1957, when she was 64 years old, in what would prove her final role on stage or screen. The play was Lesley Storm's new comedy *Roar Like a Dove*. A playwright of some repute in her own day, though now forgotten, Storm was known on Broadway for the plays *Heart of a City* (1942) and *Black Chiffon* (1950). Doing what she did best, Varden played Muriel Chadwick, an opinionated, house-proud, self-satisfied, and "carefully groomed American matron in her fifties," who with her predictably more sympathetic and low-key husband Tom goes on a rescue mission to their daughter in Scotland. Emma is married to a nobleman, Lord Dungavel, and has produced six daughters, but her husband is still not willing to give up on the dream of having a son and heir. As Mrs. Murdock says to her son-in-law in one of "a series of blasting comments on the British upper class way of life, which reduces the audience to helpless laughter": "Emma was never obligated to form a colony ... she never undertook to turn herself into a family tree for you to swing on."[19] The play turns into a modern-day, miniature *Lysistrata* when mother and daughter take off for the continent, leaving their menfolk to fend for themselves at Dungavel Castle in the Western Highlands. A tremendous hit, *Roar Like a Dove* ran for more than 1,000 performances between its premiere and March 1960.[20] After the premiere, W.A. Darlington reported from London that the playwright was particularly indebted to "three American guests who made their first London appearances as Lady Dungavel and her parents—Anne Kimbell, Evelyn Varden and Paul McGrath."[21]

Varden stayed in the show for nine months. Not feeling well enough to continue in the role, she withdrew at the end of June 1958 and returned to New York. There she entered the Flower and Fifth Avenue Hospitals on the Upper East Side between 105th and 106th St. She died there two weeks later, on Friday, July 11, 1958, of undisclosed causes. Varden was survived by her husband and three married sisters. A week before she died, she received word that the London drama critics had cited her work in *Roar Like a Dove* as the best supporting role of the season.[22]

Grandma from Hell:
Queenie Vassar
in *Primrose Path* (1940)

"Honeybell, you know I don't think that fella's all there."

One-hit wonders. The term is commonly used about authors who write one good novel or play and then are never heard from again or, in other cases, who never again achieve the success of their debut work. Here I want to apply this expression to certain Hollywood character actresses who, for various reasons, acted in only one or two or three films, even though they acquitted themselves admirably. One example of this is Grace George (1879–1961), a star on Broadway for decades, the wife of fabled producer William A. Brady and stepmother of Alice Brady. In 1943, at the age of 64, George starred with James Cagney in the excellent *Johnny Come Lately*, based on a Louis Bromfield novel, and then she was never seen on the big screen again. Minnie Dupree (1873–1947) is another example. She was only in two films, but her efforts as Miss Ellen Fortune in the comedy *The Young in Heart* (1938), in excellent company with Janet Gaynor, Douglas Fairbanks, Jr., Paulette Goddard, Roland Young, and Billie Burke, make one want to see more. Florence Reed (1883–1967), another star on Broadway and famous for creating the role of Mother Goddam in John Colton's *The Shanghai Gesture* (1926), was in three films, but qualifies as a one-hit wonder for her interesting interpretation of Miss Havisham in the first sound version of Dickens's classic *Great Expectations* (Universal, 1934).

The greatest one-hit wonder of them all, though, is Queenie Vassar. "Queenie who?" you ask. The vaudeville entertainer born Cecilia Vassar in Glasgow, Scotland, on October 18, 1870, known throughout her career as "Queenie Vassar" and in private life variously as Mrs. Henry Kernell, Mrs. William Lynch, and Mrs. Joseph B. Cawthorn, who left her small but indelible mark on American film history when in 1940, at the age of 70, she portrayed Ginger Rogers' grandmother in *Primrose Path*.

I imagined it would be difficult to find out anything about Queenie at this late date. There I was mistaken. Under her various cognomens, she crops up regularly in the New York papers of the 1890s and early years of the twentieth century, both because of her professional activities and her stormy personal life. On March 11, 1892, when she was 22, one of Vassar's earliest headlines read "Mrs. Kernell Wants a Divorce." Buyers of the *New York Times* that day could read that Mrs. Kernell, "known on the stage as 'Queenie Vassar,'" was suing for a "limited divorce," alleging cruelty, from fellow actor Harry Kernell. A limited divorce, as opposed to an absolute divorce, was the equivalent of legal separation and meant that the couple would remain legally married, but would establish separate households and could divide their assets. Mrs. Kernell also wanted a restraining order against her husband. She alleged he was worth $40,000 and earned $300 to $800 a week.[1]

In all, Queenie Vassar was married three times. She married her first husband, Harry Kernell, after the impresario Tony Pastor brought her to the United States from England in 1887. The Kernells had two sons, born in 1888 and 1891. Kernell himself was born in Philadelphia in 1850 and was thus 20 years older than his wife. He was said to have begun his performing career as a drummer boy in the Union Army during the Civil War. As an adult, he became one of the best-known Irish comedians of his day, which meant that he specialized in comical impersonations of the "sedate Irishman in store clothes, silk hat, high collar, and 'ribbon' whiskers": "His North of Ireland dialect was pronounced by experts to be remarkably true." Kernell traveled for many years with Pastor's road company, which is no doubt where he met Vassar. His special act was a "droll monologue with a song-and-dance accompaniment." He also "double teamed" with his younger brother John and "achieved an exceptional success."[2]

In early October 1892, seven months after his wife filed for divorce, Kernell was pronounced legally insane and committed to Bloomingdale Asylum, a private mental hospital in Morningside Heights on the site now occupied by Columbia University. "The doctors are inclined to think that Kernell's mind is hopelessly impaired," the *New York Times* reported.[3] He was described as "thin and haggard" four months later in an article entitled "Actors Entertain Lunatics." It turns out Vassar had taken the initiative to put on a show for the patients at Bloomingdale Asylum on February 9, 1893. In the audience of 300 "lunatics" were several well-known performers of the day, including Kernell and another Irish comedian, W.J. Scanlan, whom the reporter gleefully and painstakingly described in all their mental and physical decay. Vassar sang "Shadowland" and a yodel song.[4]

A little over a month later, Kernell was dead. He had "failed steadily" from the time of his committal and had a "severe sinking spell" on Saturday, March 11, 1893. His wife was sent for at the Madison Square Theatre. She came up after the performance and stayed with Kernell till he died. The *New York Times* reported, "He was conscious when his wife arrived and whispered 'Queenie,' but soon after lost the power to speak. Mrs. Kernell was completely prostrated by her long vigil and her grief, and was removed from the asylum soon after her husband's death." The cause of death was given in Kernell's *New York Times* obituary as "paresis."[5] Paresis, known as general paresis of the insane or paralytic dementia, is a serious and ultimately fatal disorder affecting the brain and central nervous system and is caused by syphilis infection. In Kernell's obituary, it was strongly suggested that Vassar had driven her husband crazy. "This marriage was not a smoothly happy one, through incompatibility of temper," wrote the *New York Times*: "His domestic troubles are said to have contributed much toward unsettling his reason." The Kernells' divorce had been "discontinued" prior to his being declared insane. It was believed that Kernell left "considerable property" to his wife and two small children, Harry and William.[6]

This was not the last time Queenie Vassar's marital woes would get her into the papers. She married again on June 22, 1893, only three months after Kernell's death, in the Church of the Holy Innocents, Manhattan. Her second husband was William Lynch, "a son of Mrs. Theresa Lynch, diamond merchant of 1 Union Square, Manhattan."[7] In early November 1900, while she was performing in *The Belle of Bridgeport* at the Bijou Theatre, she was granted an absolute divorce from Lynch. She testified that she and her husband had not lived under the same roof since May 3, 1897, when the couple had a "violent quarrel" and

Lynch left the house for good. She decided to file for divorce after he had "persistently refused" to return to his home. Vassar and Lynch had a daughter together. The divorce was uncontested.[8]

Vassar's name crops up frequently in news articles in the first decades of the last century in connection with the activities of the Professional Women's League and the frequent benefit performances being given for indigent actors or other persons or groups in need. Vassar spent most of her stage career in what in Great Britain was known as the music hall and in America as vaudeville. She also did a handful of Broadway shows, including *The Passing Show* (1894); *The Toreador* (1902), where she had "little to do" as the owner of a flower shop; and *The Girl from Utah* (1915).[9] She supported the star comedienne May Irwin, another former Tony Pastor protégée, in the farces *Sister Mary* (1899–1900) and *The Belle of Bridgeport* (1900), both at the Bijou Theatre.[10] In September 1901, Vassar starred herself in a short-lived musical comedy called *The Ladies Paradise* by George Dance and Ivan Caryll at the Metropolitan Opera House at Broadway and 39th St. In *The Slim Princess* (1911) and *The*

Queenie Vassar's performance as the matriarch in a multi-generational family of prostitutes in *Primrose Path* (RKO, 1940) is one of the most stunningly naturalistic performances by any character actress on record. Vassar, who had only the briefest of film careers, had an extensive performing background in vaudeville, but one would have thought little to prepare her for the more subtle requirements of the film medium. It is regrettable that she wasn't given more opportunities of this kind for she is a wicked joy to behold. From left: Vassar, Joan Carroll, Ginger Rogers, and Miles Mander.

Lady of the Slipper (1912–13), she supported the former child star Elsie Janis. *The Lady of the Slipper* was a "musical fantasy" inspired by "Cinderella." With Lillian Lee, Vassar made "about as grotesque a pair of wicked step-sisters as anyone would care to see."[11]

Playing the role of Herr Louis von Schloppenhauer in *The Slim Princess* was a 42-year-old actor called Joe Cawthorn. Cawthorn had for the past eight and a half years been Queenie Vassar's third and last husband. The couple had been married by the Rev. H.M. Warren at the Criterion Hotel on June 1, 1902.[12] Born Joseph B. Cawthorn on March 29, 1867, or 1868, in New York City of English parentage, he made his stage debut when he was only three or four years old. When he was nine, Cawthorn was taken to England and performed there for four years. As an adult performer, he became famous as "the most outstanding of 'German' comedians." He spent 47 years in musical comedies on Broadway and elsewhere under such celebrated producers as Klaw and Erlanger, Charles Frohman, Charles Dillingham, Al Woods, and Oscar Hammerstein and supported the star Julia Sanderson for eight years. A favorite of President Woodrow Wilson, he was once invited to the White House "to see the nation's first vaudeville lover, and to talk with him."[13]

The *New York Times* wrote in their review of *The Slim Princess* that Cawthorn was "genuinely funny as the German tutor," while Vassar was "lost in a part that demanded little."[14] The Cawthorns were also together in the Charles Frohman–produced musical comedy *The Girl from Utah* at the Knickerbocker Theatre in August 1915; it was Vassar's last Broadway show. Cawthorn continued to act on Broadway off and on until 1922. In 1926, he signed a motion picture contract with RKO and he and his wife moved to California, where they would remain until their deaths. They made their home in a beautiful brick house at 721 N. Linden Dr. in Beverly Hills.[15] Cawthorn acted in over 50 films between his arrival in Hollywood and his retirement in 1942, including *Love Me Tonight* (1932), *Naughty Marietta* (1935), *Gold Diggers of 1935* (1935), *Page Miss Glory* (1935), *The Great Ziegfeld* (1936), and *Lillian Russell* (1940). Cawthorn died of a stroke at his home in Beverly Hills on January 21, 1949, at the age of 81.[16]

It seems somewhat strange that Vassar didn't start working in the movies herself, but maybe she didn't need to or want to. Then on October 23, 1939, after the couple had been in Los Angeles for 13 years, the *New York Times* announced that RKO was testing Vassar for the grandmother role in *Primrose Path*.[17] Based on Robert Buckner and Walter Hart's hit Broadway play of the same title from 1939, the film was a fairly free adaptation of their story of three generations of a matriarchal family of prostitutes living in a shack in a poor section of Monterey (in the play, it was upstate New York). Naturally, the producers did all that was necessary to obscure the nature of the family business and turned what had been a play focusing on the mother figure into a film focusing on the daughter and her love affair and subsequent troubled marriage with a clean-cut, boy-next-door type. Ginger Rogers starred as the daughter and heroine Ellie May Adams, Joel McCrea played her love interest Ed Wallace, Marjorie Rambeau her always cheerful, optimistic, and hard-working mother Mamie, and Miles Mander her alcoholic and ineffectual, gentleman-scholar father, Horace.

It was the grandmother figure, though, who walked off with the show both in the stage and screen versions of the story. In the play, which opened at the Biltmore Theatre on January 4, 1939, the role of Grandma was taken by the veteran character actress Helen Westley. It marked a return for her to Broadway after an absence of four years, which she had spent filming in Hollywood, and would be her final Broadway show. Normally, Westley would have been a shoo-in to reprise her acclaimed performance in the film version. Yet she was a very busy contract player at a rival studio, Twentieth Century–Fox. Chances are

First meetings with potential in-laws can be nerve-wracking and never more so than in *Primrose Path* (RKO, 1940). Here Ginger Rogers's beau Joel McCrea (center) comes to meet her family, represented in this photograph by "Grandma" Queenie Vassar and Rogers's little sister Honeybell (Joan Carroll, far right).

they wouldn't loan her out or there was a scheduling conflict. This left the plum old lady part up for grabs. Vassar, despite being entirely untried in films and to all intents and purposes retired, got the role of a lifetime. Only four days after her screen test, one could read "Queenie Vassar to Make Debut" in *Primrose Path*. Henry Travers would round out the main cast, as McCrea's genial, diner-owning grandfather.[18] The production got underway almost immediately, in early November 1939, under the capable direction of 47-year-old Gregory La Cava. A director since 1916, La Cava is best remembered today for classy comedies like *My Man Godfrey* (1936) and *Stage Door* (1937), both of which garnered him Oscar nominations for Best Director. He also co-wrote the screenplay to *Primrose Path* with Allan Scott, who had previously written films like *Top Hat*, *Swing Time*, *Quality Street*, and the original *Imitation of Life*.

There are certain rare occasions when an actor and a role, a performer's personality and lived experience and those of the fictional creation she is portraying are such a perfect fit that not a single false note can be heard, not a drop of histrionics can squeeze through. Such an occasion is Vassar's *tour de force* performance as Ellie May's evil-minded, grasping, and mendacious grandmother. Her plot function is to create as much trouble for her granddaughter and her husband Ed as humanly possible, so that their love can be tried and tested in the timeworn Hollywood fashion. On the level of character motivation, Grandma's behavior is explained by her fear that Ellie May's marriage will reduce the family's income. She does her level best to scare Ed off when he comes to visit for the first time in a dinner scene that makes *Alice Adams* look like *Dinner at Eight*. Later, she lies to him about Ellie May's whereabouts, when he tries to see her after their separation. Grandma's "dramatic need" is to have food on the table and her machinations may ultimately be explained by her fear of starvation. It would appear, though, that she is basically incapable of wishing anyone well, including her own flesh and blood.

Grandma dresses like a "Belle of the '90s" way past her "sell by" date. Vassar makes full use of her vaudeville background in creating the role, as she sings show tunes and teaches off-color verses to her youngest granddaughter, Honeybell (Joan Carroll). Her permanently sour expression is perfect for the role, as is her small stature. McCrea towers over Vassar's tiny and wizened, yet strangely resilient figure in their scenes together, making the contrast between her more or less inexplicable animosity and ingrown skepticism and his innocence and guilelessness all the more striking. She is the one who cooks for the family and is often seen stirring a pot, like a witch over a cauldron. She continually makes disparaging remarks about almost everyone, particularly her bookish, impractical, and drunken son-in-law Homer. When daughter Mamie returns from a "date" with gifts and money for the whole family, and Homer goes into a blue funk, Grandma ejaculates: "Let him cry! Maybe some of the gin will run out of his eyes." Fittingly, Grandma gets the last line in the film, directed to her youngest granddaughter as she counts the wad of bills Ed has given her: "Honeybell, you know I don't think that fella's all there."

Primrose Path premiered on March 22, 1940. Frank S. Nugent wrote in the *New York Times*, "The performance is generally good ... Miss Rogers is variably effective and never less convincing than as the tomboy broken to harness by Mr. McCrea's first kiss. Much better are Queenie Vassar's rouged, bewigged, thoroughly evil old Grannie ... and little Joan Carroll's amazingly precocious Honeybell, who obviously was going to be a chippie off the old block.... Any resemblance between this *Primrose Path* and that staged on Broadway last season is purely coincidental."[19]

Maybe not surprisingly, Vassar played a grandmother in her next film as well, which was also helmed by Gregory La Cava. In *Lady in a Jam* (Universal, 1942), she is flibbertigibbet heroine Irene Dunne's fast-talking, no-nonsense Arizona gold-miner granny "Cactus Kate," who still lives in a rustic cabin and is rumored to be sitting on a mother lode in the "Lost Hope" mine. When Dunne is down on her luck, she returns to her grandmother's rural home on psychiatrist Patric Knowles's recommendation. Vassar then gets involved in Dunne's attempt to ensnare Knowles, whom Dunne has inexplicably employed as her chauffeur (despite having lost all her money). Due to an unhappy love affair, Knowles "won't vibrate" according to Dunne. According to Vassar, "There ain't no cure for what she's got" (Dunne, that is). She calls Knowles a "big galoot," and goes around continuously singing "My Darling Clementine." Dunne looms over her just like McCrea did, though there is precious little else to compare with *Primrose Path* in this "farce without mirth, screwball comedy with the pace of a slug."[20]

Vassar only has one scene in her third and final film, *None But the Lonely Heart* (C. Odets, RKO, 1944), starring Cary Grant and Ethel Barrymore. She plays Jane Snowden, a marvelously shady leader of a gang of shoplifters, who tries to get Barrymore's Ma Mott to sell stolen goods in her shop. She keeps repeating the financial incentives ("Five hundred pounds, I says, not less") and, unlike the principals, actually sounds like a Cockney. Vassar endows her character with a strut that, coupled with her ostrich boa, penciled-in eyebrows, and artfully curled hair, make her look like a munchkin Mae West. Verbally sparring like two seasoned pros, Vassar and Barrymore are an electric combination in what was the debut film of Barrymore's character actress career and a role which garnered her an Oscar.

Barrymore would go on to 19 more films before her death in 1959, but for Vassar this was the end of the road. Retiring at age 74, she lived on for another 16 years. Cecilia "Queenie" Vassar Kernell Lynch Cawthorn died in her home from complications following surgery on September 11, 1960, and was buried with her husband in the Sanctuary of Refuge, Abbey of the Psalms, Hollywood Forever Cemetery. Only one of her three children, a son, survived her.[21]

Thoroughly Modern Mammy: Ethel Waters in *The Member of the Wedding* (1952)

"Oh my, Ethel Waters—she was the bitch of all time."[1]

As a trailblazer and pioneer, there were few twentieth century African American artists who could compare with Ethel Waters. From the most unpromising of beginnings, as the illegitimate child of a raped, unwed teenage mother, Waters, born in Chester, Pennsylvania, on October 31, 1896, rose to heights of fame and fortune unparalleled by any other black performer of her day. Waters was the first African American to move successfully from black vaudeville and nightclubs to "the white time," the first to co-star with whites in the South, the first black woman artist to have a regular radio show over a major network (that was in 1933), and only the fourth black woman to record her songs in the 1920s. The year she starred with Helen Broderick, Marilyn Miller, and Clifton Webb in *As Thousands Cheer* (1933–34) at the Music Box Theatre, she became the highest paid woman performer on Broadway. The show also made her the first black performer to appear on Broadway in an otherwise all-white cast.

In 1939, Waters became the first African American woman to star in a drama on Broadway: *Mamba's Daughters*, a melodrama of murder and mayhem in three generations of a matriarchal African American family, written by Dorothy and DuBose Heyward, authors of *Porgy*. It ran for 162 performances at the historic Empire Theatre with Georgette Harvey, Anne Brown, Alberta Hunter, Canada Lee, Fredi Washington, and José Ferrer in supporting roles. Hagar, wrote Waters, was "the part that made my reputation on the American legitimate stage."[2] Waters conquered television, too, when *Beulah* became the first nationally broadcast weekly television series starring an African American on its premiere October 3, 1950. Waters was the first actress to play the title role on television, which was taken over briefly by Hattie McDaniel and later by Louise Beavers. In 1962, Waters became the first black actress to be nominated for an Emmy and the first to be nominated in a dramatic role, rather than in a musical or variety show. Last but not least, Waters was the first genuine black female movie star in America and the first to receive top billing in films.[3]

Carson McCullers's play *The Member of the Wedding* gave Waters her biggest commercial and critical success on Broadway.[4] For 501 performances at the Empire Theatre, where she had starred in *Mamba's Daughters* a decade earlier, Waters portrayed Berenice Sadie Brown, a many-times-married, now widowed, middle-aged housekeeper in a white Southern family, with only one good eye, a few extra pounds, and a whole lot of wisdom. With her in this

191

enterprise, Waters had the brilliant young actress Julie Harris, playing the troubled teenager Frances "Frankie" Addams, and the talented child actor Brandon De Wilde, as Frankie's unusual cousin John Henry. Waters described the play as "all mood and loveliness, but not too much plot."[5] Poised between life and death, childhood and adulthood, we briefly encounter "an adolescent girl, a warm-hearted Negro mammy and an amiable little boy"[6] thrown together by circumstance in a simple kitchen setting, where they try as best they can to help each other understand how to deal with life's large and small challenges. To help Frankie accept that she cannot become a part of her older brother's marriage, "a member of the wedding" in the way she fantasizes about, Berenice must relive one of the most difficult times of her life, the death of her one true love, her first husband Ludie. By the play's end, Frankie is ready to adapt to the demands of adult life, John Henry is dead, and Berenice must make a new beginning somewhere else.

The three leading players were respectively 53, 24, and 7 when they started on this journey, which would include a lengthy road tour and a film version where all three leading actors reprised their stage roles. The play opened on January 5, 1950, while the film premiered in Los Angeles on Christmas Day 1952. Bosley Crowther wrote of Waters' performance in the film, which he found "repeated on the screen in a manner indistinguishable from her delivery of it on the stage," that it "glows with a warmth of personality and understanding that transmits a wonderful incidental concept of the pathos of the transient nurse." Of the film as a whole, he wrote, "[T]he earnestness and fidelity of everyone concerned have not been able to conceal or alter the basic staticness of a tender play."[7]

As "the first studio film to be carried by a black woman star,"[8] *The Member of the Wedding* represents nothing less than the revolt of the supporting players. Here the characters who usually are rendered in the background are permitted to take center stage and to be what the story is all about. A tomboy, an African American servant, and a queer little boy share the limelight in a film that was unique in Golden Age Hollywood for focusing on characters and storylines the likes of which had never been seen on the screen before. Frankie's older brother Jarvis's romance and wedding is a subplot in the film at best and is only important for the impact it has on Frankie and, more indirectly, on Berenice. Because the narrative sidesteps the regular, relentless emphasis of the classical Hollywood plot on white, heterosexual, middle-class and young adult romance, it makes us aware how artificial, limited, and monotonous this plot really is.

The Member of the Wedding gives us a rare opportunity as well to examine how power and significance are allotted to characters in film. There are various vectors that allow us to gauge a film character's importance. Primary, of course, is screen time: In how many scenes and for how long in each is the character shown on the screen? Beyond that, there is the question of prominence. A character can be in the background in a large part of the film without coming to prominence at all. Lillian Yarbo, for example, flits in and out of most of the scenes from the chaotic Sycamore home in *You Can't Take It with You* (1938), but that doesn't make her a major character. Thus, we need to ask about the character's relation to the story and to the storytelling, the plot and the camera: How central is the character to the plot? Does she have her own storyline or is she only there to support another character in her storyline? Does she get any close-ups or is she only visible in two-shots or group shots?

Though the camera, certainly, suggests point of view, it is only rarely that a film consistently employs only one character's visual point of view, as in the opening of *Dark Passage* (1947) or *Lady in the Lake* (1947). This being said, there is an informal hierarchy formed among the characters in a film depending on the extent to which they operate on their own or in combination with other characters. In the case of *The Member of the Wedding*, we find a significant difference between the three leads Frankie, Berenice, and John Henry in that Frankie goes off on jaunts into town without Berenice and John Henry, while we never follow the latter two on any excursions of their own outside the Addams house. It is true, as well, that even in the house, we seldom if ever see Berenice without Frankie or John Henry without Frankie and Berenice. This is a remnant of the original novel, which in addition to giving prominence to Frankie's experiences at home and abroad, also privileges her cognitive point of view by making her the filter through which the other characters and events are perceived. The privileging of Frankie here remaining from the novel is counterweighted in the film version by casting Waters, the film's only star, in the role of Berenice. Patricia White, reflecting on Waters' film roles in general, writes: "Her performances combined the individuality of the realist characters she portrayed with her individuality as a star — with a history as a sensual, talented, and famous singer."[9] Casting is thus another way of influencing the relative importance of the various characters in a film narrative.

According to most of the criteria for determining a character's significance I have discussed, Berenice Sadie Brown emerges as a more individualized, important, and meaningful African American character than had hitherto been seen on the big screen. Berenice incorporates most of the positive aspects of her predecessors without the often concomitant negative or dehumanizing character traits. In a sense, she is a supreme mammy figure, yet not subservient, one-sidedly nurturing and self-effacing, or comical. She incorporates the "black Christian stoicism"[10] of many of Louise Beavers' mammies and maids, yet she has a life and concerns of her own as an individual. She is opinionated, wise, and strong like Hattie McDaniel's more developed characters, particularly Mammy in *Gone with the Wind* (1939), yet she is never ridiculed for an oversize physique or rendered sexless due to her age and girth.

Thus, Waters' Berenice is about as far from a "handkerchief head" or "Aunt Jemima" as Frankie is from a nubile starlet. Even down to the details of her clothing, Berenice looks like someone who has gone into her own closet and dressed for the day, rather than a product of the costume department's idea of what the African American mammy or maid should look like. She has her work clothes and her Sunday best, like generations of real, hardworking yet eternally impoverished African American women, attempting on whatever slender means to always appear neat, tidy, even elegant, in public.

Berenice also incorporates aspects of the tradition of the comic black maid as the knowing and tongue-in-cheek commentator on her white mistress's doings and sayings. I'm thinking of the type of maid played in the thirties by Madame Sul-Te-Wan, Libby Taylor, and Gertrude Howard. We see this illustrated by the scene where Frankie shows Berenice what she considers appropriate wedding attire, a ludicrously overblown satin gown she has just purchased, that in no way suits her age or androgynous body type.

Berenice is also the black matriarch who must fuss and fret over her male dependents, represented here by foster brother Honey Camden Brown. While in the fictional world, Berenice supports Honey, on a higher level of structural analysis of the narrative as a whole, Honey, like Berenice's unsuitable suitor T.T. Williams, is really there to support her; that is, to give us further insight into who Berenice is and the circumstances of her life separate from the Addams family. Unlike so many of her predecessors, Berenice has her own family, her own kith and kin to care for and worry about. She has her own life. This does not prevent her, though, from also fulfilling some of the traditional functions of the mammy, maid, and confidante. While Frankie is in several ways a parody of the traditional Southern

The rapport between Julie Harris (left) and Ethel Waters both on screen and off is evident from this photograph from *The Member of the Wedding* (Stanley Kramer Productions, 1952). The story of a young Southern tomboy's coming of age was unlikely material for a commercial Hollywood film.

belle, Berenice retains the authority of the African American mammy without being reduced to or limited by that often stereotypical role. She is engaged in domestic duties of cooking and child care, yes, but we get a full sense throughout the film of how little these mundane, income-generating and thus necessary activities define who she is as an individual.

I can only think of one other example up to this point, where a black female character's non-working and private life apart from the white family becomes the focus of film's action and that is Hattie McDaniel as Minerva Clay in *In This Our Life*. In that Warner Bros. film from 1942, McDaniel plays the housekeeper in the upper-class Timberlake family, consisting of Frank Craven, Billie Burke, and their two daughters Olivia de Havilland and Bette Davis, but has family of her own in the form of her talented, hard-working son Parry (Ernest Anderson). When his future is threatened by being falsely accused of a hit-and-run accident Davis has committed, the film opens up in a new way to reveal aspects of the African American's domestic life that were seldom if ever seen. This is also the case in a comic vein in *The Great Lie* (1941), where Bette Davis and Hattie McDaniel are paired as headstrong mistress and devoted mammy. The film is unusual in the degree to which is shows everyday life among the African Americans in the servants' quarters of Davis's estate.

In addition to McDaniel, an important precursor for Waters is the aforementioned

Louise Beavers, who effectively starred in at least a couple of pictures in the 1930s, though without star billing. Even in the original version of *Imitation of Life* (1934), though, and the somewhat later drama *Rainbow on the River* (aka *It Happened in New Orleans*; 1936), Beavers's character is defined to a great extent in relation to the needs of the white protagonist: Claudette Colbert in the first case and the little orphaned boy played by Bobby Breen in the second. "She was always happy, always kind, always intricately involved in the private lives of her employers," writes Donald Bogle, "so much so that she usually completely lacked a private life of her own."[11]

This is not to suggest that the original version of *Imitation of Life* is not a milestone, particularly in its suggestion of the challenges facing African Americans in white-dominated society and the then unexplored theme of passing. Nevertheless, if we compare Delilah in *Imitation of Life* and Berenice in *The Member of the Wedding*, we can see in the 18 intervening years a quantum leap in character development, sophistication, and depth. Berenice has the power and the ability to reflect on her own life and experience that is not just unique in the annals of Hollywood's black characters, but which is rare in American film history taken as a whole. How often do we find film characters with the rhetoric and the occasion to enthrall us with a lyrical and poignant monologue of the kind we hear in the modest kitchen when Berenice relives the night her husband Ludie died? Her story is a gift to Frankie and little John Henry, but ultimately to the film audience. It shows us Berenice as a woman who has come through terrible times and deep bereavement and has not only survived, but been ennobled by her suffering.

In addition to McDaniel and Beavers, Waters was her own precursor by the time she played Berenice on the big screen. Though she made an appearance in the musical film *On with the Show!* (A. Crosland, Warner Bros., 1929), where her numbers "Am I Blue?" and "Birmingham Bertha" were as carefully segregated from the white performances as they had been in *As Thousands Cheer*; and in the musical comedy *Gift of Gab* (K. Freund, Universal, 1934), starring Edmund Lowe and Gloria Stuart, Waters' film career didn't begin in earnest till *Tales of Manhattan* (J. Duvivier, Twentieth Century–Fox, 1942). It was an anthology film about a dress coat and the various people who own it. Waters appeared in the final sequence as a devout sharecropper, Esther, married to Luke (Paul Robeson in his last film role), who finds the coat full of stolen money after a robber has dropped it from a plane and views this as manna from heaven. Robeson got to sing in the film's finale, Waters did not. The segment was controversial. In *The Negro in Films* (1949), Peter Noble refers to it as "a Jim Crow scene amid half a dozen ordinary American episodes [that] showed the Negro as a superstitious, hymn-singing, gullible, good-natured dolt."[12] Thomas Cripps took a less critical view, writing in 1977, "If the sequence was broadly stylized, so too were the white parts of the picture."[13]

Waters's next film outing, *Cairo* (W.S. Van Dyke, MGM, 1942), was an improvement in that it gave her more to work with. She was billed third after the stars, Jeanette MacDonald and Robert Young, as Macdonald's faithful, warbling maid Cleona Jones, who gets to do a couple of songs and even finds a love interest of her own in Dooley Wilson. In *Cabin in the Sky* (V. Minnelli, MGM, 1943), Waters got above the title star billing for the first time in what was a film adaptation of her Broadway show of the same title. It ran for 156 performances at the Martin Beck Theatre starting October 25, 1940. As Petunia Jackson, Waters was devout and devoted yet again, this time to her ne'er-do-well gambler husband, Joseph "Little Joe" Jackson. Dooley Wilson played Little Joe on Broadway, but was replaced by Eddie "Rochester" Anderson in the film version.

The most important precursor of Berenice Sadie Brown among Waters's previous film roles is no doubt Dicey in Elia Kazan's 1949 film *Pinky* (Twentieth Century–Fox). As a sort of "Aunt Tom" deeply devoted to her white mistress, the land-rich, money-poor, 80-year-old Miss Em (Ethel Barrymore), Dicey is a far cry from Berenice, but she contains the seeds of the later character in her dignity, caring for others, and ability to reflect on life and experience. Her performance garnered Waters her first and only Oscar nomination, which was only the second time an African American actor was so honored. Film debutante Mercedes McCambridge won that year for *All the King's Men*. Waters was unable to attend the ceremony, as she was in *The Member of the Wedding* on Broadway.[14]

Waters was a natural actress. By that I mean that she had learned to act by acting, rather than by training. She was a natural in that she had an intuitive understanding of her craft, though that is not meant to suggest that she didn't have a technique or technical expertise to build on. When she tried to verbalize how she acted, she would often return to a type of proto–Stanislavskyan theory of affective memory. Waters thought of acting as "reliving" and added, "To relive in a part, as I do, costs. It costs me." She explained, for example, that in enacting her monologue on her husband Ludie's death in *The Member of the Wedding*, "it wasn't a man I grieved for. It was my precious little grandmother, Sally Anderson."[15] Waters's maternal grandmother had been chiefly responsible for raising her and passed away in 1914, when Waters was 18.[16] She thought of her grandmother as the most important influence of her childhood: "My great regret is that she didn't live long enough to share some of the money and the comforts my work in show business has brought me."[17] Reflecting further on her acting in her second volume of autobiography *To Me It's Wonderful* in 1972, Waters wrote, "Other actors may approach their parts in other ways, but aside from the fact that like everybody, I've got to memorize lines, I don't prepare in any way." She attributed her fine diction not to any formal training, "No one taught me to speak or sing this way," but to the fact that she had a "short tongue."[18]

Donald Bogle wrote of Waters in 1988, "In her hands, the mammy stereotype had been transformed into the black mother earth figure."[19] This is true of Dicey in *Pinky*, even more true of Berenice and, for that matter, also true of Dilsey in the 1959 film adaptation of William Faulkner's novel *The Sound and the Fury* (M. Ritt, Twentieth Century–Fox). More recently Bogle has written "Waters' great gift as an actress was that regardless of the script or character or the contrivance of the movie itself, she exhibited ambiguities and contradictions that seemed to come from her own personal experience. Unlike previous screen mammies, she was never emotionally one-sided, neither all Christian resignation (like Louise Beavers) nor all rage and indignation (like Hattie McDaniel)."[20]

As performed by Ethel Waters, Berenice in *The Member of the Wedding* emerges as one of the first universal African American characters in mainstream American culture. By universal, potentially a difficult and dodgy term to use, I mean that Berenice does not stand forth primarily as a representative of her racial, religious, gender or otherwise defined and limited group allegiance or minority status, but rather as a representative of the human race. Her individual human experience of love, loss, and suffering are presented as a lesson that not only Frankie can and should learn from, but the film's audience as well. In the novel, Berenice wears an eye patch that marks her as being disabled, in addition to being marginalized by her race, age, and gender. This eye patch only makes its appearance in the first scene of the film, though. Its disappearance serves to decrease the distance between Berenice and her potential audience and, also, symbolically to prove that there is no limit to her vision, however physically impaired.

Certainly, there have been many films since *The Member of the Wedding* to focus on

In a film which has vision and blindness as one of its themes, Berenice Sadie Brown's eye patch in this initial scene from *The Member of the Wedding* (Stanley Kramer Productions, 1952) would seem to take on a heavy symbolic significance. Yet Ethel Waters's Berenice (center) soon discards the patch and turns out to be the wisest and most far-sighted character in this intimate domestic drama about large existential questions. In Fred Zinnemann's cinematic version of a Broadway hit play by Carson McCullers, all three leading players had the opportunity to preserve their sterling performances for posterity. On the left, Julie Harris as Frankie Addams; and on the right, Brande De Wilde as her cousin John Henry.

the African American experience in the United States and stories of African American life. Yet there is no classical Hollywood film I can think of to have represented the African American experience as universal experience during a time before the segmentation of the American movie audience, when every Hollywood film was intended to appeal to every potential audience member.

By the time Waters finished playing Berenice Sadie Brown, arguably the most important role of her career, she had already achieved all the worldly fame and material success she would ever have. By 1952, she had crossed boundaries and set records, she had made and lost large sums of money, she had conquered every available artistic medium and there was really nowhere for her to go but down. She said herself 20 years later: "Mountains are high, a diamond is sparkly and brilliant, but a diamond is cold and so is the air on the top of that mountain. Cold. Show business is climbing the mountain and then coming back down. Nobody can stay at the top."[21]

By the end of *The Member of the Wedding* (Stanley Kramer Productions, 1952), tomboy Frankie Addams (Julie Harris, right) has become quite the little lady and is ready to free herself from mammy Berenice's apron strings (Ethel Waters, left), as boyfriend Barney (Danny Mummert) looks on.

Ironically, then, while *The Member of the Wedding* was an artistic triumph and a huge commercial success, it marked the beginning of the end of her career as a professional artist. In Stephen Bourne's phrase, "she gave up show business for Jesus."[22] Waters became a familiar presence at the evangelist Billy Graham's crusades. Starting at a revival in New York City in 1957, for the last 20 years of her life Waters' performances at these services were her chief artistic outlet and her most important work. Ethel Waters died in 1977.

Dowager Deluxe: Helen Westley in *Splendor* (1935)

"I am really the original for the Sphinx. Am I not like some rare exotic marble, for ages standing in an ancient, desolate mood, overlooking some fathomless desert?"[1]

Helen Westley was the most distinguished character actress of her generation. Lucile Watson might conceivably challenge that position because she lived and worked longer, but Westley was the more versatile actress and played a more central role in American cultural life as a founding member of the Theatre Guild. Dress her up, dress her down, Westley could be as loud and bumptious as a stevedore and as high and mighty as a duchess. On her death, it was estimated that she had acted in 40 productions for the Guild alone and she remained a member of its board of directors until a year before her passing.[2]

The actress who would be known as Helen Westley was born with a name as imposing as her face, Henrietta Remsen Meserole Manney, in Brooklyn on March 28, 1875.[3] She was the younger of the two children of drug store owner Charles Palmer Manney and Henriette Meserole Manney. Her older brother, Charles Fonteyn Manney, born in 1872, would become a respected composer, choral conductor, and chief editor of the music publishing house Oliver Ditson Company of Boston.[4] Westley was educated at the Brooklyn School of Oratory, Emerson College of Oratory in Boston, and the American Academy of Dramatic Arts, having wanted to become an actress from an early age. She made her first New York stage appearance on September 13, 1897, at the Star Theatre, as Angelina McKeagey in *The Captain of the Nonesuch*.[5]

Westley once said, "I put my youth behind me at an early age because youth is the age when thinking and feeling have their largest hold, and I wanted to be doing."[6] After some years spent touring and in stock, she married the actor John Westley on October 31, 1900. He had been born John Wesley Wilson Conroy in New York City in 1878 and would be seen in a number of shows on Broadway between his debut in *Cyrano de Bergerac* in 1899 and his final bow there in *Work Is for Horses* in 1937, including Rachel Crothers's *The Three of Us* (1906–07), Oliver Goldsmith's *She Stoops to Conquer* (1912), George S. Kaufman and Marc Connelly's *Dulcy* (1921–22), Owen Davis's Pulitzer Prize–winning *Icebound* (1923), and George Farquhar's *The Beaux' Stratagem* (1928). He also made a handful of films before his death in Hollywood in 1948.[7]

On March 8, 1907, the couple had their first and only child, a daughter, who was named Ethel. As Ethel Westley, she was also briefly on the stage, making her Broadway debut in 1925 as Julesa in Molnár's *The Glass Slipper*, where her mother played Adele Roma-

jzer. Ethel was also seen as Madeline Arnold in the Theatre Guild's celebrated original production of O'Neill's *Strange Interlude* (1928–29). During the play's long run at the John
Golden Theatre, she married fellow actor Alexander Howard Ross Cann. The marriage
ended in divorce. Ethel married twice more and died in San Francisco in 1983 at the age
of 75.[8]

"During her twelve years of marriage," writes William Lindesmith, "Helen Westley
subordinated her career to the demands of domesticity."[9] She and John Westley went their
separate ways in 1912. She was 37 and ready for the major phase of her acting career to
begin. Basing herself in Greenwich Village in a narrow, four-story red brick townhouse,
which still stands at 104 Washington Place, just off Sixth Avenue and across the street from
the converted church that is now NYU's Islamic Center, Helen Westley became a vibrant
part of New York's intellectual and artistic community in the teens and 1920s.[10] "Miss
Westley lived downtown in those days, and was a familiar Village character — a swart-
skinned, aquiline, burning sort of woman, slim and with something of the look of the
fanatic in her gray eyes."[11] With the likes of Sinclair Lewis, Theodore Dreiser, Susan Glaspell,
and Lawrence Langner, she was a member of the Greenwich Village's Liberal Club.

With Langner and others, she founded the Washington Players in 1915 and returned
to the stage at the Bandbox Theatre on February 19, 1915, as the Oyster in their production
of *Another Interior*. A number of other plays for the Players followed, at the Bandbox and
later the Comedy Theatre, until the group disbanded in 1918. "A direct, honest, and often
outspoken woman, she was unswerving in her quest for perfection. Neither the size nor
showiness of a role was important to her; whether or not it was good theatre was her main
concern."[12] The *New York Times* wrote at the end of Westley's years with the Washington
Players, "[W]ith every successive appearance before us it becomes more certain that she is
an artist of very unusual range and intelligence."[13]

"Despite her interest in the histrionic," wrote the *New York Times* in 1917, "it is an
interest which comes second to her passion for books, and it was necessity rather than choice
which sent her upon the stage."[14] A much later interview suggested that her forebears "were
canny about property and are said to have left her independently wealthy."[15] When asked
by Djuna Barnes in 1917 why she had become an actress, Westley responded, "Probably it
was the easiest thing for me to do.... Perhaps this is not the great thing I was cut out for;
the next five years will tell."[16] They did, indeed. In 1918, she became one of the founding
members of the Theatre Guild, which was formed to produce non-commercial works by
American and foreign playwrights. Starting with the production of *The Bonds of Interest* at
the Garrick Theatre in late April 1919, Westley would only appear in Guild productions for
the next 15 years, the richest of her stage career. "A brilliant character actress," the *New York
Times* wrote on her death, "she drew critical acclaim in virtually all of her Guild roles."[17]
Westley herself had a casual attitude to her own talent and artistry and was not above poking
fun at herself: "Give me despair, and I am at my best. Give me sorrow, and only then are
my shoulders worthy of me — at renouncing, for instance. Where have I learned this trick
of the half-turned shoulder, the cold, drooping eyes? Through sorrows and difficulties.
There's nothing like it for developing the figure and making one supple; it's better than
dancing or swimming. Oh, yes, I can face all things."[18]

Among the many highpoints from her Guild years were playing Mrs. Clegg in *Jane
Clegg* (1920) with Margaret Wycherly in the title role; Nurse Guinness in Shaw's *Heartbreak
House* (1920), one of the Guild's early successes, with Elisabeth Risdon as Ellie Dunn; Lady
Marden in A.A. Milne's *Mr. Pim Passes By* (1921/1927), another hit and starring Laura Hope

Crews; Mrs. Zero in Elmer Rice's *The Adding Machine* (1923); "Mama" in *The Guardsman* (1924–25) with Alfred Lunt and Lynn Fontanne; Ftatateeta in Shaw's *Caesar and Cleopatra* (1925), with Helen Hayes cast against type as the Queen of the Nile; Mrs. Higgins in *Pygmalion* (1926–27) to Lynn Fontanne's Eliza Doolittle and Reginald Mason's Professor Higgins; Mrs. Amos Evans in O'Neill's *Strange Interlude* (1928–29), her biggest commercial success, with Lynn Fontanne as Nina Leeds; Martha in Goethe's *Faust* (1928); Lady Britomart Undershaft in *Major Barbara* (1928–29); Amelia Light in O'Neill's *Dynamo* (1929) with Claudette Colbert; Frau Lucher in Robert Sherwood's *Reunion in Vienna* (1931–32), another big hit with Lunt and Fontanne; and Mrs. Wells in John Wexley's *They Shall Not Die* (1934) with Ruth Gordon. Westley also supported Eva La Gallienne in Molnár's *Liliom* (1921) and Margalo Gillmore in *He Who Gets Slapped* (1922), Shaw's *The Doctor's Dilemma* (1927–28), and Ben Jonson's *Volpone* (1928).

Helen Hayes recalled in her 1968 spiritual autobiography *On Reflection* the time back in 1925 when she starred in the Guild's production of *Caesar and Cleopatra* with Westley in the "grim, sardonic, and immense rôle"[19] of her nurse Ftatateeta. Seeing that Hayes was peeking through the stage curtain, Westley had chastised her for "counting the house." Hayes explained that she wasn't counting the house, but rather looking to see if a certain young man she was interested in was in the audience. "Someone special?" Westley asked, "raising her wonderfully hooded eyes, simultaneously dropping the purple bags beneath them." She was duly impressed that he came to see the play every night. When Hayes admitted that, so far, he hadn't come at all, the older actress suggested she send him a ticket or call him. Hayes preferred to wait, she said, to which Westley responded: "If *I'm* after a man I call him up until he moves." Hayes describes Westley as "as casual a performer as I ever worked with." The man in question, by the way, was Hayes's future husband Charles MacArthur.[20]

During her Guild years, Westley was acting with many talented players she would meet again later in Hollywood, among them Spring Byington, Dudley Digges, Catherine Doucet, Helen Freeman, Beryl Mercer, Phyllis Povah, Claude Rains, Selena Royle, Edward G. Robinson, Joseph Schildkraut, Gale Sondergaard, Franchot Tone, Henry Travers, Lucile Watson, Cora Witherspoon, Margaret Wycherly, and Blanche Yurka. Biographer David J. Skal writes that when Claude Rains was "ordered" by his first movie director James Whale "to start seeing at least three movies a day in the days before he left for California," he "found a willing movie companion in his Theatre Guild friend Helen Westley."[21] Maybe this was where the seed was planted for Westley's own move to Hollywood in 1934, the year after Rains.

Westley once said, tongue in cheek, "The theatrical profession for one of my facial attainments is hardly all it should be in way of accessibility." She continued,

> I am too far away from the public they can't appreciate my full value. Every line, every muscle of countenance is worthy of study. Yes, I shall have to take up something confidential with the public, that as they lean forward to say "Would you really advise this or that?" they will become acquainted with the peculiar worth of my extraordinary and individual features."[22]

She could hardly have known when she said this in 1917, that 17 years later the "something confidential" that would bring her even closer to her public would be the movies. For years she refused to have any traffic with Hollywood. Then, finally, she succumbed on what was more or less a whim. Money was not incentive enough, but when someone at a party suggested she should ask the producer who was pursuing her for her own train compartment on the journey to Los Angeles, he responded, "You can have the whole train, if you'll only come" and that sealed the deal.[23]

Westley's permanent removal to California took place in 1934 and, though she returned to Broadway for one last hurrah in early 1939, the remainder of her acting career would be spent in Hollywood. During her eight years there, she lent her myriad talents to no less than 38 films, always in named, credited roles. She was usually among the top six players in the credits, as a sign of the respect in which she also was held in the movie industry and the significance of the parts she was given. Let me mention a few favorites.

In her first scene as Loretta Young's imperious, "suffering no fools gladly," paternal aunt Margaret "Maggie" Ridgeway in *Café Metropole* (E.H. Griffith, Twentieth Century–Fox, 1937), she accuses the Metropole's proprietor Monsieur Victor (Adolphe Menjou) of being a "charlatan" when he can neither provide wild strawberries nor visiting royalty at his restaurant. Her second, equally barbed remark refers to Russian Prince Alexis (Tyrone Power) asking Young to dance via intermediary Menjou: "Sounds like a royal pick-up to me." When she hears Alexis is a Russian, she responds: "Then why isn't he driving a taxi?"

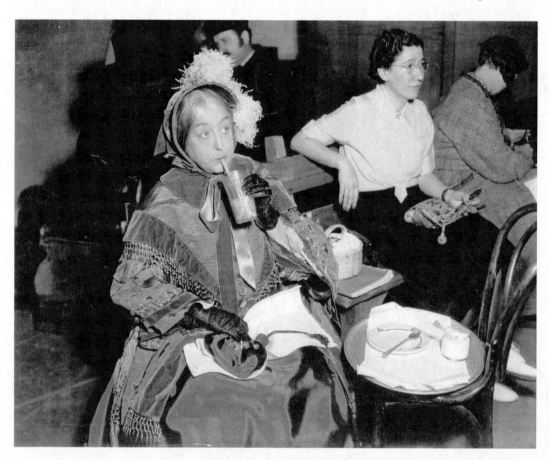

Helen Westley supported Shirley Temple four times at Twentieth Century–Fox. Here she is seen taking a break from filming *Dimples* (1936), set in mid–nineteenth century New York. Westley is sipping iced tea, the caption informs us, and plays "a pre–Civil War widow" who wants to adopt the street urchin portrayed by Temple. No stranger to costume dramas both on stage and screen, vastly versatile Westley was equally at home in modern roles.

And so it goes on. Westley's purpose is clearly to provide sardonic remarks on the evolving plot. She certainly does not function in the customary aunt role of chaperone or advisor, as even parental authority is nil in this film in which Young only follows her heart. As the plot brings the Akron, Ohio, aunt and niece in contact with the criminal underworld, Westley develops a fine line in gangster lingo. When Power disappears, she guesses that "he's taken it on the lam." Later, when Westley and her love interest Gregory Ratoff are apprehended on the train by the French police, accused of being impostors, she proclaims: "Well, I guess they got us at last, Smartypants." She also avers, "I'm his moll. Where he goes, I go."

Wife, Husband, and Friend (G. Ratoff, Twentieth Century–Fox, 1939), starring Loretta Young and Warner Baxter as the New York high society couple Doris and Leonard Borland, is a mixture of *Dinner at Eight* (upper-class wife oblivious to husband's company's dire financial situation) and *Doubting Thomas* (upper-class wife nurtures artistic ambitions, which husband is dubious about). As Young's amateur operatic mother, Mrs. Blair, Westley is more stylish and modern in dress here than was often the case in her other dowager roles. She wears a remarkable mink coat with a large shawl collar, which may be the same one as in *Café Metropole* two years previously. According to her beleaguered husband, Major Blair (George Barbier), his wife's town hall concerts have failed annually for 27 years. Her function is basically to support her daughter in her "folly" and be an antagonist to her son-in-law (Baxter). Mrs. Blair repeatedly accuses him of being out of his mind and has a relationship that can only be described as adversarial with her husband. The "friend" being referred in the title is Binnie Barnes in Baxter's case and singing teacher Cesar Romero in Young's case. Interestingly, while the romantic angle in the Barnes-Baxter relationship is heavily emphasized, there is no parallel suggestion of hanky-panky in the Romero-Young relationship.

Westley's penultimate film role as Emma Harper in *Bedtime Story* (A. Hall, Columbia, 1941) had some interesting parallels to her own life, as she plays the character woman in Fredric March and Loretta Young's stage troupe. At a dinner party early in the film, where they are discussing how the stage is making Young miss out on other things in life, Westley proclaims: "I've raised four children and never missed a cue." After March and Young have split, Westley appears to tell Young that March wants her back because he loves her, not just to put on his new play. She then has to break the bad news to March that Young has married the straight-laced, stuffed-shirt banker played by Allyn Joslyn. Westley, March, and crony Robert Benchley respond by going on a bender. All is, of course, well in the end.

Westley was often wasted, though, in terminally dull aunt, landlady, grandmother, or other generic old lady roles, like Marilla Cuthbert in *Anne of Green Gables* (G. Nichols Jr., RKO, 1934), Therese in *Chasing Yesterday* (G. Nichols Jr., RKO, 1935), Aunt Sophie in *Alexander's Ragtime Band* (H. King, Twentieth Century–Fox, 1938), and Blanche Brunot in *Lady from Louisiana* (B. Vorhaus, Republic, 1941). John Springer and Jack Hamilton explain that when Westley went under contract with Twentieth Century–Fox in 1936, "she was tossed into everything that called for a gruff or supercilious oldster, whether or not the part was any good at all. Usually, it wasn't. She had her moments like *Café Metropole* and *Wife, Husband, and Friend* but more often she had to stooge for Shirley Temple, Jane Withers or even Joan Davis."[24]

While it is far from her most critically acclaimed or popular film today, Samuel Goldwyn's *Splendor* (E. Nugent, 1935) gave Westley her most splendid dramatic role during her years in Hollywood. Alexis Carrington and Angela Channing, stand aside! Forty-five years before *Dynasty* and *Falcon Crest*, there was Emmeline Lorrimore, matriarch of the New York

The acting challenges given to Helen Westley in Hollywood were seldom daunting, but in *Splendor*
(Samuel Goldwyn Company, 1935) she was given a role she really could get her teeth into. As Emmeline Lorrimore, she is willing to go to any length to preserve the family manse, even to the extent
of prostituting her sweet, innocent young daughter-in-law (Miriam Hopkins). From left: David
Niven, Joel McCrea, Katharine Alexander, and Westley.

Lorrimores, who will go to any length to halt the family's declining fortunes and salvage
their eminent social position. "It's an old family," she tells her new daughter-in-law, Phyllis
Manning Lorrimore (Miriam Hopkins), "and has been a great one." As the film opens, the
Lorrimores are entombed alive in their white elephant of a Fifth Avenue mansion, which
Mrs. Lorrimore wants to retain at any cost. Besides Mrs. Lorrimore, there is her wastrel son
Clancey (David Niven), her promising, good-hearted son Brighton (Joel McCrea), and her
unmarried daughter Martha (Katharine Alexander). The family is in desperate financial
straits. Mrs. Lorrimore has been served a summons for an unpaid dress bill in her own
home, the telephone has been cut off, the butler is doing all the housework, and Martha
has to be the family's housekeeper. "I'm hanging on with everything in me," Westley tells
her three children.

When the hope of the family, eldest son Brighton, marries poor Southern girl Phyllis
on a trip to sell the family's land, it is a "calamity" and they don't mind telling her. The
hope was that Brighton would marry Edith Gilbert (Ruth Weston), a sausage heiress from
Kansas with $20 million, who in her own account has nothing to do "but wear a hat all
day." Weston gives a marvelous performance in this unsympathetic role. Mrs. Lorrimore's
attitude is that the family should "wait with diplomacy" to see how Brighton and Phyllis's
marriage develops. Later, seeing that her children are helpless to improve the situation, she

proclaims, "I shall do something myself now." This "something" consists of throwing Phyllis into the eager arms of the family's rich bachelor cousin, Martin Deering (Paul Cavanagh).

Despite the family's impoverished state, Westley is got up in the grand dowager style with all the trimmings. When Deering says to her at dinner "You're a grand old war horse, cousin Emmeline," she doesn't seem to mind. Neither does she mind being compared to Queen Victoria by her daughter, after Brighton's new position with Deering's firm allows her to buy a new hat. In this wicked company, McCrea is a big babe in the woods and a bit of a cipher in his role as the hero. He doesn't seem to fit into the family at all, but maybe that is the point. He finally redeems himself, though, by taking matters into his own hands and selling the Lorrimore mansion over his mother's head. Her only concern is "What will become of me? Where shall I go?" Phyllis Lorrimore gets a job in an upscale department store selling dresses and Edith Gilbert faithfully comes and buys one every week.

Miriam Hopkins and Westley already knew each other well from a successful Theatre Guild production of a play called *The Camel Through the Needle's Eye* at the Martin Beck Theatre in 1929. *Splendor* was the only work by the Broadway hit playwright Rachel Crothers to have been written directly for the screen. Starting out as a writer of feminist-inspired problem plays like *The Three of Us* (1906) and *A Man's World* (1910), Crothers segued into a highly successful creator of comedies of manners, such as *Nice People* (1921), *Expressing Willie* (1924), and *As Husbands Go* (1933). Several of her plays were turned into films, including *Old Lady 31* (1916 and 1940), *Let Us Be Gay* (1930), *When Ladies Meet* (1932), and *Susan and God* (1937).

André Sennwald wrote in his *New York Times* review of *Splendor* that Crothers had originally "planned to make this devastating social criticism in one of her plays of fifteen years ago, but she was deterred by the stark and ruthless nature of her material." Unfortunately, Sennwald continued, the movies had been dealing with the need for even the upper classes to go to work in Depression times "for a good many years, a circumstance which robs *Splendor* of some of its novelty.... The film is managed with impeccable intelligence and good taste, but it is to be feared that Miss Crothers and Mr. Goldwyn are sacrificing their heavy artillery in a cause that is not worth the trouble." He thought the Lorrimores were "acted with poisonous effectiveness," including Westley as "the embittered dowager."[25]

After three years in Hollywood, Westley told the *New York Times*, "I live a simple, centered and rooted life." She traveled widely ("London and Milan are almost as familiar to her as New York and the Pacific Coast cities"), liked gingerbread and milk, rainy nights and wild birds: "She insists that one reason she stays on the West Coast is because they grow such excellent lettuce out there."[26] In 1939, legendary producer and director George Abbott lured Westley back to Broadway for what would prove the last time. *The Primrose Path*, which premiered at the Biltmore Theatre on January 4, 1939, was a new play by Robert Buckner and Walter Hart. Westley played the central role of the grandmother in a matriarchal family of women working in the world's oldest profession. The critic for the *New York Times* noted, "Miss Westley has most of the good lines and most of the good action of the play, and who is there to say that she sometimes appears to be putting it on a little thick?"[27] *The Primrose Path*, in altered form and minus the definite article of the title, was turned into a film starring Ginger Rogers and Joel McCrea in 1940. Queenie Vasser made her screen debut aged 70 in the role of Grandma and, like Westley, "stole the show."[28]

After the 166 performances of *The Primrose Path*, Westley returned to Hollywood and completed 11 further films, including *Lillian Russell* (I. Cummings, Twentieth Century–Fox, 1940), *The Captain Is a Lady* (R.B. Sinclair, MGM, 1940), *All This, and Heaven Too* (A.

The Captain Is a Lady (MGM, 1940) was a character actress extravaganza. Helen Westley was the sympathetic head of a retirement home for ladies, where Beulah Bondi and her aged husband, Charles Coburn, seek refuge when they lose their home. (From left): Clem Bevans, unidentified actor, Billie Burke, Francis Pierlot, Dan Dailey, Westley, Virginia Grey, unidentified actor, Cecil Cunningham, Charles Coburn, Helen Broderick, and Beulah Bondi. The actor barely visible behind Cunningham and Coburn is unidentified.

Litvak, Warner Bros., 1940), and *Lady with Red Hair* (C. Bernhardt, Warner Bros., 1940). Her health "first gave serious concern" in January 1942, when she was completing work on *My Favorite Spy* at RKO. In May, her daughter Ethel brought her back to Middlebush, New Jersey, to care for her in her home. Westley died there of coronary thrombosis on December 12, 1942, at the age of 67.[29] Her philosophy of life was "Let the world go by and watch it going, that's all," she said to Djuna Barnes in 1917. "We take it too seriously. After it is all over and the procession has passed, there remains just exactly what remains after a carnival: a little more dust, a broken bottle or two, and some colored confetti."[30]

Appendix: The 100 Top Performances by Character Actresses in Hollywood, 1930–1960

The list is alphabetical and no ranking is implied.

SARA ALLGOOD as Beth Morgan in *How Green Was My Valley* (John Ford, Twentieth Century–Fox, 1941)

JUDITH ANDERSON as Mrs. Danvers in *Rebecca* (Alfred Hitchcock, Selznick International, 1940)

EVE ARDEN as Ida Corwin in *Mildred Pierce* (Michael Curtiz, Warner Bros., 1945)

FAY BAINTER as Aunt Belle in *Jezebel* (William Wyler, Warner Bros., 1938) and as Stella Hadley in *The War Against Mrs. Hadley* (Harold S. Bucquet, MGM, 1942)

ETHEL BARRYMORE as Mary Herries in *Kind Lady* (John Sturges, MGM, 1951)

FLORENCE BATES as Edythe Van Hopper in *Rebecca* (Alfred Hitchcock, Selznick International, 1940) and as Mrs. Manleigh in *A Letter to Three Wives* (Joseph L. Mankiewicz, Twentieth Century–Fox, 1949)

LOUISE BEAVERS as Nellie LaFleur in *Bullets or Ballots* (William Keighley, Warner Bros., 1936)

CLARA BLANDICK as Helen Livingstone in *Shopworn* (Nick Grinde, Columbia, 1932)

MARY BOLAND as Effie Floud in *Ruggles of Red Gap* (Leo McCarey, Paramount, 1935) and as the Countess De Lave in *The Women* (George Cukor, MGM, 1939)

BEULAH BONDI as Emma Jones in *Street Scene* (King Vidor, Samuel Goldwyn, 1931) and as Lucy Cooper in *Make Way for Tomorrow* (Leo McCarey, Paramount, 1937)

ALICE BRADY as Angelica Bullock in *My Man Godfrey* (Gregory La Cava, Universal, 1936)

HELEN BRODERICK as Madge Hardwick in *Top Hat* (Mark Sandrich, RKO, 1935)

BILLIE BURKE as Millicent Jordan in *Dinner at Eight* (George Cukor, MGM, 1933)

SPRING BYINGTON as Penny Sycamore in *You Can't Take It with You* (Frank Capra, Columbia, 1938)

MRS. PATRICK CAMPBELL as the pawnbroker in *Crime and Punishment* (Josef von Sternberg, Columbia, 1935)

CONSTANCE COLLIER as Melissa Pilson in *Shadow of Doubt* (George B. Seitz, MGM, 1935)

GLADYS COOPER as Mrs. Henry Vale in *Now, Voyager* (Irving Rapper, Warner Bros., 1942) and as Mrs. Railton-Bell in *Separate Tables* (Delbert Mann, Hill-Hecht-Lancaster, 1958)

ELLEN CORBY as Aunt Trina in *I Remember Mama* (George Stevens, RKO, 1948)

JANE COWL as Emily Hedges in *Payment on Demand* (Curtis Bernhardt, Gwenaud, 1951)

LAURA HOPE CREWS as Mrs. Phelps in *The Silver Cord* (John Cromwell, RKO, 1933) and as Aunt Pittypat Hamilton in *Gone with the Wind* (Victor Fleming, Selznick International, 1939)

HENRIETTA CROSMAN as Hannah Jessop in *Pilgrimage* (John Ford, Fox, 1933)

CECIL CUNNINGHAM as Aunt Patsy in *The Awful Truth* (Leo McCarey, Columbia, 1937)

JANE DARWELL as Ma Joad in *The Grapes of Wrath* (John Ford, Twentieth Century–Fox, 1940) and as Jenny Grier in *The Ox-Bow Incident* (William A. Wellman, Twentieth Century–Fox, 1943)

JEAN DIXON as Molly in *My Man Godfrey* (Gregory La Cava, Universal, 1936)

MARIE DRESSLER as Carlotta Vance in *Dinner at Eight* (George Cukor, MGM, 1933)

MILDRED DUNNOCK as Mrs. Ellis in *The Story on Page One* (Clifford Odets, Twentieth Century–Fox, 1959)

MAUDE EBURNE as Aunt Maggie in *Ladies They Talk About* (Howard Bretherton and William Keighley, Warner Bros., 1933)

ISOBEL ELSOM as Leonora Fiske in *Ladies in Retirement* (Charles Vidor, Columbia, 1941)

HOPE EMERSON as Rose Given in *Cry of the City* (Robert Siodmak, Twentieth Century–Fox, 1948) and as Evelyn Harper in *Caged* (John Cromwell, Warner Bros., 1950)

BLANCHE FRIDERICI as Kate Halsey in *The Office Wife* (Lloyd Bacon, Warner Bros., 1930)

MARJORIE GATESON as Pat Lawton in *Cocktail Hour* (Victor Schertzinger, Columbia, 1933)

GLADYS GEORGE as Jacqueline Fleuriot (Madame X) in *Madame X* (Sam Wood, MGM, 1937)

GRACE GEORGE as Vinnie McLeod in *Johnny Come Lately* (William K. Howard, William Cagney Productions, 1943)

CONNIE GILCHRIST as Frankie in *Presenting Lily Mars* (Norman Taurog, MGM, 1943)

MINNA GOMBELL as Else Taylor in *After Tomorrow* (Frank Borzage, Fox, 1932)

MARY GORDON as Ma O'Hara in *The Irish in Us* (Lloyd Bacon, Warner Bros., 1935)

ETHEL GRIFFIES as Mrs. Hobley in *Waterloo Bridge* (James Whale, Universal, 1931)

LOUISE CLOSSER HALE as Powers in *The Barbarian* (Sam Wood, MGM, 1933) and as Mother Hallam in *Another Language* (Edward H. Griffith, MGM, 1933)

ESTHER HOWARD as Mrs. Kraft in *Born to Kill* (Robert Wise, RKO, 1947)

JOSEPHINE HULL as Veta Louise Simmons in *Harvey* (Henry Koster, Universal, 1950)

ALMA KRUGER as Amelia Tilford in *These Three* (William Wyler, Samuel Goldwyn, 1936)

ELSA LANCHESTER as Mrs. Smerrling in *Mystery Street* (John Sturges, MGM, 1950)

JESSIE ROYCE LANDIS as Clara Thornhill in *North by Northwest* (Alfred Hitchcock, MGM, 1959)

DORIS LLOYD as Martha Bowley in *Vigil in the Night* (George Stevens, RKO, 1940)

HELEN LOWELL as Tillie in *Side Streets* (Alfred E. Green, First National, 1934) and as Nettie Putnam in *Party Wire* (Erle C. Kenton, Columbia, 1935)

ALINE MACMAHON as Bertha Krasnoff in *Side Streets* (Alfred E. Green, First National, 1934)

MARJORIE MAIN as Mamie Fleagle Smithers Johnson in *Murder, He Says* (George Marshall, Paramount, 1945)

HATTIE MCDANIEL as Malena Burns in *Alice Adams* (George Stevens, RKO, 1935), as Mammy in *Gone with the Wind* (Victor Fleming, Selznick International, 1939), and as Minerva Clay in *In This Our Life* (John Huston, Warner Bros., 1942)

BUTTERFLY MCQUEEN as Prissy in *Gone with the Wind* (Victor Fleming, Selznick International, 1939)

BERYL MERCER as Mrs. Midget in *Outward Bound* (Robert Milton, Warner Bros., 1930)

JUANITA MOORE as Annie Johnson in *Imitation of Life* (Douglas Sirk, Universal, 1959)

AGNES MOOREHEAD as Fanny Amberson in *The Magnificent Ambersons* (Orson Welles, RKO, 1942) and as Madge Rapf in *Dark Passage* (Delmer Daves, Warner Bros., 1947)

MARY NASH as Miss McDaid in *The Rains Came* (Clarence Brown, Twentieth Century–Fox, 1939)

MILDRED NATWICK as Aunt Amarilla in *Yolanda and the Thief* (Vincente Minnelli, MGM, 1945)

UNA O'CONNOR as Emma Lory in *This Land Is Mine* (Jean Renoir, RKO, 1943)

EDNA MAY OLIVER as Aunt Betsey in *David Copperfield* (George Cukor, MGM, 1935)

RAFAELA OTTIANO as Russian Rita in *She Done Him Wrong* (Lowell Sherman, Paramount, 1933)

MARIA OUSPENSKAYA as Baroness Von Obersdorf in *Dodsworth* (William Wyler, Samuel Goldwyn, 1936)

LEE PATRICK as Effie Perine in *The Maltese Falcon* (John Huston, Warner Bros., 1941)

ELIZABETH PATTERSON as Aunt Kate Barnaby in *Go West Young Man* (Henry Hathaway, Paramount, 1936) and as Eunice Habersham in *Intruder in the Dust* (Clarence Brown, MGM, 1949)

ALICE PEARCE as Lucy Schmeeler in *On the Town* (Stanley Donen and Gene Kelly, MGM, 1949)

JESSIE RALPH as Mrs. Burley in *San Francisco* (W.S. Van Dyke, MGM, 1936)

MARJORIE RAMBEAU as Mrs. Manley in *Slander* (Roy Rowland, MGM, 1957)

THELMA RITTER as Birdie in *All About Eve* (Joseph L. Mankiewicz, Twentieth Century–Fox, 1950)

FLORA ROBSON as Jessica Newcome in *We Are Not Alone* (Edmund Goulding, Warner Bros., 1939)

MAY ROBSON as Apple Annie in *Lady for a Day* (Frank Capra, Columbia, 1933) and as Granny Leslie in *Reckless* (Victor Fleming, MGM, 1935)

ALISON SKIPWORTH as Mabel Jellyman in *Night After Night* (Archie Mayo, Paramount, 1932), as Mrs. Rasmussen in *The Song of Songs* (Rouben Mamoulian, Paramount, 1933), and as Mrs. Pampinelli in *Doubting Thomas* (David Butler, Fox, 1935)

GALE SONDERGAARD as Mrs. Hammond in *The Letter* (William Wyler, Warner Bros., 1940)

JO VAN FLEET as Kate in *East of Eden* (Elia Kazan, Warner Bros., 1955)

EVELYN VARDEN as Mrs. Burns in *Hilda Crane* (Philip Dunne, Twentieth Century–Fox, 1956)

QUEENIE VASSAR as Grandma in *Primrose Path* (Gregory La Cava, RKO, 1940)

ETHEL WATERS as Berenice Sadie Brown in *The Member of the Wedding* (Fred Zinnemann, Stanley Kramer Productions, 1952)

LUCILE WATSON as Lady Margaret Cronin in *Waterloo Bridge* (Mervyn LeRoy, MGM, 1940), as Fanny Farrelly in *Watch on the Rhine* (Herman Shumlin, Warner Bros., 1943), and as Mary Kimball in *My Reputation* (Curtis Bernhardt, Warner Bros., 1946)

HELEN WESTLEY as Emmeline Lorrimore in *Splendor* (Elliott Nugent, Samuel Goldwyn, 1935)

MAY WHITTY as Mrs. Bramson in *Night Must Fall* (Richard Thorpe, MGM, 1937) and as Lady Beldon in *Mrs. Miniver* (William Wyler, MGM, 1942)

MARY WICKES as Miss Preen in *The Man Who Came to Dinner* (William Keighley, Warner Bros., 1942)

CORA WITHERSPOON as Mrs. Williamson in *The Mating Season* (Mitchell Leisen, Paramount, 1951)

MARGARET WYCHERLY as Ma Jarrett in *White Heat* (Raoul Walsh, Warner Bros., 1949)

LILLIAN YARBO as Mattie Harriet in *Café Society* (Edward H. Griffith, Paramount, 1939)

BLANCHE YURKA as Madame De Farge in *A Tale of Two Cities* (Jack Conway, MGM, 1935)

Notes

Introduction

1. David Thomson, "The Lives of Supporting Players," Movie Acting, the Film Reader, ed. Pamela Roberston Wojcik (New York and London: Routledge, 2004), p. 208.

2. Gilbert Seldes, "The Itsy-Bitsy Actors," *More Character People* by Arthur F. McClure, Alfred E. Twomey, and Ken D. Jones (Secaucus, NJ: Citadel Press, 1984), p. 15.

Clara Blandick

1. John Springer and Jack Hamilton, *They Had Faces Then: Annabella to Zorina, the Superstars, Stars and Starlets of the 1930's* (N.p.: Castle, 1974), p. 33.

2. www.imdb.com (accessed February 27, 2010).

3. Information on Blandick's parents and early residence from www.wikipedia.com, based on U.S. Census information (accessed February 27, 2010).

4. Information in this paragraph from www.ibdb.com (accessed February 27, 2010) and the entry on Blandick at www.wikipedia.com.

5. "Miss Blandick Dies; Film Actress Was 81," *New York Times* (April 16, 1962), p. 23; Allan R. Ellenberger, *Celebrities in the 1930 Census* (Jefferson, NC: McFarland, 2008), p. 36.

6. Springer and Hamilton, *They Had Faces Then*, p. 33.

7. Ruth Gordon, *Myself Among Others* (New York: Atheneum, 1971), p. 84.

8. *Life Begins* was remade as *A Child Is Born* in 1939 with Spring Byington taking over Blandick's role as Mrs. West.

9. See the biographical article on Blandick at www.tcm.com (accessed February 27, 2010). Robson and Blandick had been seen together in the Janet Gaynor version of *A Star Is Born* (W.A. Wellman, Selznick International, 1937), where Robson was the nurturing grandmother and Blandick the nay-saying spinster aunt.

10. Murphy quoted in Aljean Harmetz, *The Making of* The Wizard of Oz (New York: Delta, 1989), p. 121.

11. See Harmetz, p. 121, and the entry on Blandick at www.wikipedia.com.

12. Harmetz, pp. 126–37.

13. As Karen M. Stoddard laconically points out in *Saints and Shrews: Women and Aging in American Popular Film* (Westport, CT: Greenwood Press, 1983), p. 45.

14. My account of Blandick's suicide is based on "Miss Blandick Dies," p. 23; Springer and Hamilton, *They Had Faces Then*, p. 33; and the entry on Blandick at www.wikipedia.com.

15. Charles G. Norris, *Zelda Marsh* (New York: E.P. Dutton, 1927).

16. All information from the MPAA/PCA Collection at the Academy of Motion Picture Arts and Sciences Library (AMPAS), as quoted and discussed in the notes on *Shopworn* at www.tcm.com (accessed February 27, 2010).

17. Axel Madsen, *Stanwyck* (New York: HarperCollins, 1994), p. 72.

18. Al DiOrio, *Barbara Stanwyck* (New York: Coward-McCann, 1983), p. 77.

19. Toomey quoted by Al DiOrio in *Stanwyck*, p. 77.

20. See notes on the film based on the MPAA/PCA Collection file, AMPAS Library at www.tcm.com.

21. See Madsen, *Stanwyck*, p. 73.

22. See DiOrio, *Stanwyck*, p. 77.

23. See DiOrio, p. 77.

24. Mordaunt Hall, "Notorious Kitty Lane," *New York Times* (April 4, 1932), www.nyt.com.

Helen Broderick

1. Quoted in Donald Bogle, *Heat Wave: The Life and Career of Ethel Waters* (New York: HarperCollins, 2011), p. 219.

2. Arthur F. McClure, Alfred E. Twomey, and Ken D. Jones, *More Character People* (Secaucus, NJ: Citadel Press, 1984), p. 39.

3. Alfred E. Twomey and Arthur F. McClure, *The Versatiles: Supporting Character Players in the Cinema 1930–1955* (New York: Castle Books, 1969), p. 52.

4. Melissa Vickery-Bareford, "Helen Broderick," *American National Biography*, ed. John A. Garraty and Mark C. Carnes (New York and Oxford: Oxford University Press, 1999), Vol. 3, p. 590.

5. Vickery-Bareford, p. 590.

6. John Springer and Jack Hamilton, *They Had Faces Then: Annabella to Zorina, the Superstars, Stars and Starlets of the 1930's* (N.p.: Castle, 1974), p. 43.

7. John Parker, *Who's Who in the Theatre: A Biographical Record of the Contemporary Stage* (7th ed.; London: Pitman, 1933), p. 303.

8. Springer and Hamilton, *They Had Faces Then*, p. 43.

9. Springer and Hamilton, p. 43. MGM made a one-off attempt to rekindle the old Marie Dressler–Wallace Beery magic when they teamed Broderick with Beery in

the western *Stand Up and Fight* (W.S. Van Dyke, 1939). The result was less than captivating, and cosmopolitan Broderick was about as much at home in the western genre as Billie Burke or Mary Boland. Her most frequent male co-star was short, dumpy, and balding Victor Moore in no less than six films: *Swing Time* (1936), *We're On the Jury* (1937), *Meet the Missus* (1937), *The Life of the Party* (1937), *She's Got Everything* (1937), and *Radio City Revels* (1938). Springer and Hamilton write that Broderick and Moore "never scored nearly as well as a team as did a Mary Boland and Charles Ruggles, or Aline MacMahon and Guy Kibbee" (p. 43).

10. Roger Ebert. "*Top Hat*: Those charms about you..." *Chicago Sun-Times* (October 23, 2005), www.suntimes.com.

11. Ebert, "*Top Hat*."

12. Alan Vanneman, "Fred and Ginger Hit Their Highest Peak in *Top Hat*," *Bright Lights Film Journal*, no. 31 (January 2001), www.brightlightsfilm.com.

13. Ginger Rogers, *Ginger: My Story* (New York: HarperCollins, 1991), pp. 138–39.

14. Ebert, "*Top Hat*."

15. Vanneman, "Fred and Ginger."

16. André Sennwald, *Top Hat* review, *New York Times* (August 30, 1935), www.nyt.com. *Variety* is quoted as saying that Broderick's "material isn't what it should be" in Vickery-Bareford, "Helen Broderick," p. 591.

17. Ebert, "*Top Hat*."

18. Springer and Hamilton, *They Had Faces Then*, p. 276.

19. www.findagrave.com (accessed March 4, 2010).

20. Vickery-Bareford, "Helen Broderick," p. 591.

Constance Collier

1. "Constance Collier, Actress, Dies; Leading Dramatic Coach Was 75," *New York Times* (April 26, 1955), p. 29.

2. John Springer and Jack Hamilton, *They Had Faces Then: Annabella to Zorina, the Superstars, Stars and Starlets of the 1930's* (N.p.: Castle, 1974), p. 65; Emanuel Levy, *George Cukor, Master of Elegance: Hollywood's Legendary Director and His Stars* (New York: William Morrow, 1994), p. 90. It is arguable that Collier had a greater influence on Hollywood films as a speech coach than as an actress.

3. William J. Mann, *Kate: The Woman Who Was Hepburn* (New York: Henry Holt, 2006), p. 395.

4. Information on Collier's unorthodox marriage and her relationships with Max Beerbohm and Phyllis Wilbourn from Mann's meticulously researched biography of Hepburn, *Kate*, pp. 396–97, 421.

5. "Constance Collier," p. 29; Springer and Hamilton, *They Had Faces Then*, p. 65.

6. Springer and Hamilton, *They Had Faces Then*, p. 65.

7. Noël Coward, *The Letters of Noël Coward*, ed. and with commentary by Barry Day (New York: Alfred A. Knopf, 2007), pp. 311–12.

8. John Gielgud, *Gielgud's Letters*, ed. and with an intro. by Richard Mangan (London: Weidenfeld and Nicolson, 2004), p. 109.

9. See Christopher Silvester, ed., *The Penguin Book of Hollywood* (London: Viking, 1998), p. 404.

10. Daniel Blum, *Great Stars of the American Stage: A Pictorial Record* (New York: Greenburg, 1952), Profile 47.

11. "Constance Collier," p. 29. Collier had supported Bob Hope in *Monsieur Beaucaire* (G. Marshall, Paramount, 1946).

12. "Constance Collier," p. 29.

13. Springer and Hamilton, *They Had Faces Then*, p. 65; Mann, *Kate*, p. 403.

14. "Constance Collier," p. 29.

15. "Rites for Constance Collier," *New York Times* (April 27, 1955), p. 31.

16. Richard Abe King, *Jane Cowl: Her Precious and Momentary Glory* (Bloomington, IN: 1stBooks Library, 2004), p. 121. King's biography contains many mentions of Collier.

17. Mann, *Kate*, p. 403.

18. Mann, p. 397.

19. Frances Marion, *Off with Their Heads! A Serio-Comic Tale of Hollywood* (New York: Macmillan, 1972), p. 247.

20. Her second film at MGM, an uncredited appearance in *Anna Karenina* (C. Brown, 1935) with Garbo in the lead, followed directly on *Shadow of Doubt*. Her third and final film at MGM was the turgid 1940 adaptation of Rachel Crothers's hit play *Susan and God*; Joan Crawford was entirely out of her depth in the lead role of reformed socialite Susan Trexel. Collier is only visible in one short group scene 80 minutes into her close friend George Cukor's film, as the painfully jolly leader of a spiritual reform movement that has infected Mrs. Trexel with the desire to "give, give, give." In some of her films, the names of Collier's characters were more substantial than the parts themselves! Her Lady Constanzia Lorridale in *Little Lord Fauntleroy* (J. Cromwell, Selznick International, 1936) is one good example of this phenomenon. In other films, she was little more than a glorified hat rack. In *The Dark Corner* (H. Hathaway, Twentieth Century–Fox, 1946), for example, she played a wealthy art collector with nothing to do but act as an admiring chorus to Clifton Webb (e.g. "*So* like you, Harvey!").

21. This film would prove Oliver's final one at RKO before she was lured over to MGM for *No More Ladies* and *A Tale of Two Cities* in 1935.

22. Frank S. Nugent, *Shadow of Doubt* review, *New York Times* (March 11, 1935), www.nyt.com.

23. Denis Meikle, *Vincent Price: The Art of Fear* (London: Reynolds and Hearn, 2003), p. 54.

24. Nugent, *Shadow of Doubt* review, www.nyt.com.

Jane Cowl

1. Joseph Verner Reed, *The Curtain Falls* (New York: Harcourt Brace, 1935), p. 221.

2. Daniel Blum, *Great Stars of the American Stage: A Pictorial Record* (New York: Greenburg, 1952), Profile 74; Richard Abe King, *Jane Cowl: Her Precious and Momentary Glory* (Bloomington, IN: 1stBooks Library, 2004), p. 104.

3. See Blanche Yurka, *Bohemian Girl: Blanche Yurka's Theatrical Life* (Athens: Ohio University Press, 1970), p. 75.

4. King, *Jane Cowl*, p. 85.

5. See Alan S. Downer, "Jane Cowl," *Notable American Women 1607–1950: A Biographical Dictionary* (Cambridge, MA: Belknap Press of Harvard University Press, 1971), Vol. 1, p. 392.

6. "Jane Cowl Is Dead; Star of the Stage, 65," *New York Times* (June 23, 1950), p. 25.

7. Quote from Downer, "Jane Cowl," p. 392; see also Jeannie M. Woods, "Jane Cowl," *Notable Women in the American Theatre: A Biographical Dictionary*, ed. Alice M. Robinson et al. (New York: Greenwood, 1989), p. 169; and King, *Jane Cowl*, p. 298.

8. Blum, *Great Stars*, Profile 74.

9. Downer, "Jane Cowl," p. 393.

10. "Jane Cowl Is Dead," p. 25.

11. See John Parker, *Who's Who in the Theatre: A Biographical Record of the Contemporary Stage* (7th ed.; London: Pitman, 1933), p. 424 and www.findagrave.com for the 1890 date. Downer, "Jane Cowl," p. 391, gives Cowl's birth year as 1883 based on her birth record in Boston City Hall. Cowl's *New York Times* obituary ("Jane Cowl Is Dead," p. 25); Cynthia M. Gendrich, "Jane Cowl," *American National Biography*, ed. John A. Garraty and Mark C. Carnes (New York and Oxford: Oxford University Press, 1999), Vol. 5, p. 612; Woods, "Jane Cowl," p. 167; and www.imdb.com all give the year as 1884. Though Richard Abe King's well-intentioned biography is both interesting and valuable (and gets us as close to Jane Cowl the woman and artist as we are likely to get at this late date), its haphazard organization and impressionistic style means that Cowl's *New York Times* obituary and the encyclopedic article by Alan S. Downer in *Notable American Women* (1971) cited above (based on official records) remain the most reliable sources of information about the facts of her life and career.

12. King, *Jane Cowl*, p. 38.

13. Reed, *The Curtain Falls*, p. 220.

14. Downer, "Jane Cowl," p. 391.

15. King, *Jane Cowl*, p. 32.

16. Downer, "Jane Cowl," p. 391.

17. Downer, p. 391.

18. Downer, p. 392, based on Cowl's and Klauber's marriage record in the New York City Dept. of Health. Her *New York Times* obituary mistakenly gives the date as June 19.

19. King, *Jane Cowl*, pp. 62, 194, 396.

20. "Jane Cowl Is Dead," p. 25; Woods, "Jane Cowl," p. 168; Reed, *The Curtain Falls*, p. 166.

21. Yurka, *Bohemian Girl*, p. 72, incl. quote from Cowl.

22. Reed, *The Curtain Falls*, pp. 162, 166.

23. Reed, p. 162. Drama critic Vernon Rice once compared interviewing Cowl to "interviewing a well-dressed cyclone" (quoted in Blum, *Great Stars*, Profile 74).

24. King, *Jane Cowl*, p. 371.

25. Yurka, *Bohemian Girl*, pp. 70–71.

26. One future star who worked with Cowl on Broadway was Katharine Hepburn, who played her daughter in *Art and Mrs. Bottle* by Benn W. Levy. Joseph Verner Reed, who co-produced the play in 1930, has an amusing description of their desperate search for a younger actress sufficiently plain to meet with Cowl's approval and how she later accused Hepburn of making her forget her lines through casting an evil spell (*The Curtain Falls*, pp. 211–15). For another comic account of Cowl's foibles, I strongly recommend the chapter entitled "Jane Cowl and the Arabs" in character actor Harold J. Kennedy's hilarious memoirs *No Pickle, No Performance: An Irreverent Theatrical Excursion from Tallulah to Travolta* (Garden City, NY: Doubleday, 1978), pp. 29–32. Without giving too much away, I can reveal that the episode deals with the fallout from Cowl's suspicions that the Amherst College football players chosen to abduct her in Shaw's *Captain Brassbound's Conversion* were "pansies." In this anecdote,

maybe not conducive to endearing Cowl to the boys in the band, she vowed that "no pansy is going to take me to the mountains" (p. 30), but lived dearly to regret her prejudices.

27. See Charlotte Chandler, *The Girl Who Walked Home Alone* (New York: Simon and Schuster, 2006), p. 295.

28. See James McCourt, *Queer Street: Rise and Fall of an American Culture, 1947–1985* (New York: Norton, 2004), p. 502.

29. Barbara Leaming, *Bette Davis* (London: Orion, 1992), p. 222.

30. Ed Sikov, *Dark Victory: The Life of Bette Davis* (New York: Henry Holt, 2007), p. 286.

31. Leaming, *Bette Davis*, pp. 220–21.

32. Sikov, *Dark Victory*, p. 288.

33. See the "Notes" on the film at www.tcm.com (accessed January 7, 2011).

34. Though they had no scenes together in *Payment on Demand*, Sullivan and Jane Cowl had been in a play together in New York in 1941. *Ring Around Elisabeth*, Cowl's penultimate Broadway show, lasted only ten performances at the Playhouse Theatre (King, *Jane Cowl*, p. 433).

35. Cowl also acted in at least one silent film, *The Spreading Dawn* (L. Trimble, Goldwyn, 1917), in which she starred with her frequent Broadway leading man Orme Caldara (Parker, "Jane Cowl," p. 424; "Jane Cowl Is Dead," p. 25; Downer, "Jane Cowl," p. 392; www. imdb.com). Blanche Yurka mentions Cowl working on a film in Fort Lee, New Jersey, while they were rehearsing her play *Daybreak* in New York in 1917 (*Bohemian Girl*, p. 71).

36. King, *Jane Cowl*, p. 433.

37. King, p. 456.

38. King, p. 457.

39. Bosley Crowther, *Payment on Demand* review, *New York Times* (February 16, 1951), www.nyt.com.

40. Davis quoted in Chandler, *The Girl Who Walked*, p. 295. Davis's memory served her well. The exact line is: "Be careful, Joyce. When a woman starts getting old, time can be an avalanche and loneliness a disaster."

41. King, *Jane Cowl*, pp. 360–62. The birth year given for Klauber is usually 1879, though Downer claims he was born in 1869 ("Jane Cowl," p. 392).

42. King, pp. 364, 412–13.

43. King, p. 468. Her assets amounted to only $3,000 and her debts to $15,000.

44. "Jane Cowl Undergoes Operation," *New York Times* (June 20, 1950), p. 22.

45. "Jane Cowl Is Dead," p. 25.

46. See www.findagrave.com (accessed January 7, 2011).

47. Chandler, *The Girl Who Walked*, p. 182; Sikov, *Dark Victory*, p. 287.

48. "*Payment on Demand*," *Variety* (January 1, 1951), www.variety.com.

49. Crowther, *Payment on Demand* review, www.nyt.com.

Henrietta Crosman

1. Bret Wood, "*Pilgrimage*," www.tcm.com (accessed January 10, 2011).

2. Strictly speaking, Henrietta Crosman worked mostly for Fox Film Corporation, which merged with

Twentieth Century to become Twentieth Century–Fox in 1935. According to her obituary in the *New York Times*: "From 1932 to 1936 she was in Hollywood under contract to Fox Films." See "Miss Crosman Dies; a Leading Actress," *New York Times* (November 1, 1944), p. 23. Three other character actresses at Fox before, during, or after Crosman's brief tenure there are Jane Darwell, Helen Westley, and Sara Allgood.

3. Crosman may have given the impression she was born in 1865, as this is the year given in John Parker, *Who's Who in the Theatre: A Biographical Record of the Contemporary Stage* (7th ed.; London: Pitman, 1933), p. 433. All other sources consulted, starting with her obituary in the *New York Times*, give 1861 as her year of birth.

4. Quoted in Daniel Blum, *Great Stars of the American Stage: A Pictorial Record* (New York: Greenburg, 1952), Profile 15.

5. Campbell also directed Crosman's last silent film, *Wandering Fires* (1925), starring Constance Bennett, where Crosman played the mother of Bennett's shell-shocked, amnesiac fiancé George Hackathorne. John Springer and Jack Hamilton claim that Crosman was "one of the earliest of the big stage stars to try out the movies," when she starred in *The Unwelcome Mrs. Hatch* (A. Dwan, Famous Players) in 1914. See John Springer and Jack Hamilton, *They Had Faces Then: Annabella to Zorina, the Superstars, Stars and Starlets of the 1930's* (N.p.: Castle, 1974), p. 281. Mrs. Fiske had created the role of Mrs. Hatch, who loses custody of her daughter after a messy divorce, on Broadway in 1901.

6. Biographical information in this paragraph from "Miss Crosman Dies," p. 23; Blum, *Great Stars*, Profile 15; Robert J. Dierlam, "Henrietta Foster Crosman," *Notable American Women 1607–1950: A Biographical Dictionary* (Cambridge, MA: Belknap Press of Harvard University Press, 1971), Vol. 1, pp. 412–14; Stephen M. Archer, "Henrietta Foster Crosman," *American National Biography*, ed. John A. Garraty and Mark C. Carnes (New York and Oxford: Oxford University Press, 1999), Vol. 5, pp. 785–86.

7. Blum, *Great Stars*, Profile 15.

8. Dierlam, "Henrietta Foster Crosman," p. 413, incl. quotation from Crosman's speech.

9. See Frank Capra, *The Name Above the Title* (New York: Vintage, 1985), p. 149.

10. Axel Nissen, *Actresses of a Certain Character: Forty Familiar Hollywood Faces from the Thirties to the Fifties* (Jefferson, NC: McFarland, 2007), p. 159.

11. Springer and Hamilton, *They Had Faces Then*, p. 281.

12. Lewis C. Strang, *Famous Actresses of the Day in America: Second Series* (Boston: L.C. Page, 1902), p. 26.

13. "Miss Crosman Dies," p. 23.

14. John Ranken Towse, *Sixty Years of the Theater: An Old Critic's Memories* (New York and London: Funk and Wagnalls, 1916), p. 422.

15. "Miss Crosman Dies," p. 23.

16. Strang, *Famous Actresses*, pp. 37, 40; Towse, *Sixty Years*, p. 422.

17. Towse, *Sixty Years*, p. 422.

18. Scott Eyman, *Print the Legend: The Life and Times of John Ford* (Baltimore: Johns Hopkins University Press, 2000), p. 141.

19. Tag Gallagher, *John Ford: The Man and His Films* (Berkeley: University of California Press, 1986), pp. 93, 94.

20. Quoted in Eyman, *Print the Legend*, p. 141.

21. Her face and neck often look preternaturally smooth on film, which may suggest she was adept at the subtle arts of "taping," a kind of temporary face lift favored by actresses before the advent of extreme makeovers. On the other hand, taping was hard to get away with if you weren't wearing a wig. Maybe Crosman just had very good skin.

22. Had the film been made some years later, the role would no doubt have gone to Jane Darwell. She arrived at Fox in 1933, but did not receive top billing at the studio until *Star for a Night* in 1936. Darwell would not work with John Ford until *The Grapes of Wrath* in 1940. A film like *Pilgrimage* might not have been made at all by the early 1940s.

23. Joseph McBride, *Searching for John Ford: A Life* (London: Faber and Faber, 2003), p. 198.

24. Mrs. John Drew actually died in 1897, long before any of her grandchildren pursued a film career.

25. Bret Wood, "Pilgrimage," www.tcm.com.

26. See A.D.S., "Henrietta Crosman Scores in *Pilgrimage*, Which Has Premiere at the Gaiety," *New York Times* (July 13, 1933), www.nyt.com.

27. McBride, *Searching for John Ford*, p. 194.

28. Wood, "Pilgrimage," www.tcm.com.

29. "Pilgrimage," *Variety* (July 13, 1933), www.variety.com.

30. A.D.S., "Henrietta Crosman," www.nyt.com.

31. Based on votes at www.imdb.com (accessed January 10, 2011).

32. Information in this paragraph from "Miss Crosman Dies," p. 23; Blum, *Great Stars*, Profile 15; www.findagrave.com (accessed January 10, 2011).

Cecil Cunningham

1. What about uncles? Well, American film history doesn't really give us much to compare with the aunts. I'm hard put to think of a single really high-profile uncle, but that may be my faulty memory. An unmarried, childless, older man, who acts protectively or aggressively towards the hero or heroine? Surely a more "iffy" situation than an old spinster or maiden lady giving us her two cents worth or making sympathetic noises in the background. Old bachelors are dubious, spinsters are just pathetic. And so it goes.

2. Richard Barrios, *Screened Out: Playing Gay in Hollywood from Edison to Stonewall* (New York and London: Routledge, 2003), p. 155.

3. Barrios, p. 155.

4. John Springer and Jack Hamilton, *They Had Faces Then: Annabella to Zorina, the Superstars, Stars and Starlets of the 1930's* (N.p.: Castle, 1974), p. 283.

5. Information on Cunningham's early life and career from Springer and Hamilton, *They Had Faces Then*, p. 283, and www.ibdb.com. Information on Jean Havez from Robert Edwards, "Jean Havez," www.findagrave.com and www.imdb.com (accessed January 11, 2011).

6. "Jean Havez Sues for Separation," *New York Times* (August 17, 1917), www.nyt.com.

7. Springer and Hamilton, *They Had Faces Then*, p. 283.

8. "Jean Havez, Song Writer," *New York Times* (February 13, 1925), www.nyt.com.

9. David Quinlan, *Quinlan's Character Stars* (London: Reynolds and Hearn, 2004), p. 106.

10. www.findagrave.com (accessed January 11, 2011).

11. Springer and Hamilton, *They Had Faces Then*, p. 73.

12. Ken D. Jones, Arthur F. McClure, and Alfred E. Twomey, *Character People* (South Brunswick and New York: A.S. Barnes, 1976), p. 60.

13. Alan Vanneman, "'If I were different, maybe things could be the same, only different': Leo McCarey's Screwball Classic *The Awful Truth* on DVD," *Bright Lights Film Journal* 46 (November 2004), www.brightlightsfilm.com.

14. Stanley Cavell, *Pursuits of Happiness: The Hollywood Comedy of Remarriage* (Cambridge, MA: Harvard University Press, 1981), p. 255.

15. As Cavell points out in *Pursuits of Happiness*, p. 255.

Esther Dale

1. John Springer and Jack Hamilton, *They Had Faces Then: Annabella to Zorina, the Superstars, Stars and Starlets of the 1930's* (N.p.: Castle, 1974), p. 77.

2. Dale's *New York Times* obituary mistakenly gave Noël Coward as the star of *Crime Without Passion*. See "Esther Dale, 75, Movie Actress," *New York Times* (July 24, 1961), p. 23. Coward and Dale never acted in the same film, though it would have been well worth seeing!

3. David Ragan, *Who's Who in Hollywood, 1900–1976* (New Rochelle, NY: Arlington House, 1977), p. 588; Springer and Hamilton, *They Had Faces Then*, p. 77; Alex Barris, *Hollywood's Other Women* (South Brunswick and New York: A.S. Barnes, 1975), p. 171; James Robert Parish, *Hollywood Character Actors* (New Rochelle, NY: Arlington House, 1978), p. 151; David Quinlan, *Quinlan's Character Stars* (London: Reynolds and Hearn, 2004), p. 109.

4. "Esther Dale," p. 23; www.findagrave.com (accessed January 13, 2011).

5. Blanche Yurka, *Bohemian Girl: Blanche Yurka's Theatrical Life* (Athens: Ohio University Press, 1970), p. 169.

6. "Esther Dale," p. 23.

7. "Esther Dale," p. 23.

8. "Esther Dale," p. 23.

9. Yurka, *Bohemian Girl*, p. 154.

10. Beckhard worked as a screenwriter on several films in 1935–36, including co-writing Shirley Temple's *Curly Top* (1935) in which Dale was billed sixth as John Boles's tony aunt, who becomes an adopted mother to Temple.

11. "Esther Dale," p. 23.

12. Bosley Crowther, *My Reputation* review, *New York Times* (January 26, 1946), www.nyt.com.

13. Clare Jaynes, *Instruct My Sorrows* (New York: Random House, 1942), p. 59.

Marie Dressler

1. Harold Lloyd quoted in Parish and Leonard, *The Funsters*, p. 221.

2. Rogers quoted in James Robert Parish and Ronald L. Bowers, *The MGM Stock Company: The Golden Era* (New York: Bonanza Books, 1972), p. 192; Cukor quoted in Gavin Lambert, *On Cukor* (London and New York: W.H. Allen, 1973), p. 66; Molly Haskell, *From Reverence to Rape: The Treatment of Women in the Movies* (New York: Holt, Rinehart, and Winston, 1974), p. 63; Lloyd quoted in James Robert Parish and William T. Leonard, *The Funsters* (New Rochelle, NY: Arlington House, 1979), p. 221;

Matthew Kennedy, *Marie Dressler: A Biography; With a Listing of Major Stage Performances, a Filmography and a Discography* (Jefferson, NC: McFarland, 1999), p. 225; Victoria Sturtevant, *A Great Big Girl Like Me: The Films of Marie Dressler* (Urbana and Chicago: University of Illinois Press, 2009), p. 3.

3. Kennedy, *Marie Dressler*, p. 197. Emanuel Levy, *George Cukor, Master of Elegance: Hollywood's Legendary Director and His Stars* (New York: William Morrow, 1994), p. 72, says March 16.

4. Dressler's year of birth is sometimes mistakenly given as 1869.

5. John Parker, *Who's Who in the Theatre: A Biographical Record of the Contemporary Stage* (7th ed.; London: Pitman, 1933), p. 491; Betty Lee, *Marie Dressler: The Unlikeliest Star* (Lexington: University Press of Kentucky, 1997), pp. 24, 28–30; Kennedy, *Marie Dressler*, p. 29.

6. Lee, *Marie Dressler*, pp. 59, 134.

7. John Springer and Jack Hamilton, *They Had Faces Then: Annabella to Zorina, the Superstars, Stars and Starlets of the 1930's* (N.p.: Castle, 1974), p. 289; Kennedy, *Marie Dressler*, pp. 116–17.

8. Laurilyn J. Harris, "Marie Dressler," *Notable Women in the American Theatre: A Biographical Dictionary*, ed. Alice M. Robinson et al. (New York: Greenwood, 1989), p. 228. Betty Lee calls the show "the high point of Dressler's career in the legitimate theatre" (*Marie Dressler*, p. 78).

9. Lee, *Marie Dressler*, p. 174; Kennedy, *Marie Dressler*, p. 148.

10. Harris, "Marie Dressler," p. 229; Kennedy, *Marie Dressler*, p. 155.

11. Lee, *Marie Dressler*, pp. 2, 250.

12. Christopher Bram, "Marie Dressler: The Popular Star of *Min and Bill* on Alpine Drive," *Architectural Digest* 53 (April 1996), p. 186.

13. Sturtevant, *A Great Big Girl Like Me*, p. 10.

14. Kennedy, *Marie Dressler*, p. 66.

15. Harris, "Marie Dressler," p. 226; Kennedy, *Marie Dressler*, pp. 27, 29.

16. Springer and Hamilton, *They Had Faces Then*, p. 289; Lee, *Marie Dressler*, p. 149; Kennedy, *Marie Dressler*, pp. 108, 111.

17. The term is from Kennedy, *Marie Dressler*, p. 144, where the author gives a succinct description of the Dressler-DuBrey relationship. See also Lee, *Marie Dressler*, ch. 16–21. DuBrey was born Clara Violet Dubreyvich in Idaho in 1892, lived to be almost 101 and can be seen with Dressler in *Politics* (C. Reisner, MGM, 1931) and *Prosperity* (S. Wood, MGM, 1932) and in mostly modest parts in dozens of other films between 1916 and 1959. Not long before her death in 1993, she was interviewed by Dressler biographer Betty Lee. Lee also gained access to DuBrey's unpublished memoir of her years with Dressler in an incredible turn of events reminiscent of Henry James's *The Aspern Papers* (see Lee, *Marie Dressler*, pp. 275–77).

18. Lee, *Marie Dressler*, p. 169; Kennedy, *Marie Dressler*, p. 182. In a special issue of *Architectural Digest*, Christopher Bram devotes an article to Dressler's final home, which includes fascinating contemporary photographs. See Bram, "Marie Dressler," pp. 186–89, 288.

19. Bram, p. 288.

20. Levy, *George Cukor*, p. 71. Levy discusses two changes from stage to screen: Kitty Packard blackmails her husband into not buying up Oliver Jordan's failing company, as that would scotch her chances at an entrée

into the Jordans' select social circle; and Paula Packard decides to stay with her fiancé Ernest after Larry Renault's suicide (p. 72). The film also omits most of the downstairs part of the "upstairs-downstairs" plot, as *Variety*'s reviewer noted, including a love triangle between the maid, the butler, and the chauffeur and the revelation that the butler, Gustave, is already married back home in Switzerland. The cook Mrs. Wendel's debacle with an aspic centerpiece that lands on the floor remains.

21. Emanuel Levy has pointed out that in *Dinner at Eight* the "interplay between the actors' offstage and onstage personalities enriched the plot" (*George Cukor*, p. 74). According to Billie Burke's biographer Grant Hayter-Menzies, "Almost everyone in the film is playing a caricature of him or herself, using elements of their own lives to enrich the performance" (*Mrs. Ziegfeld: The Public and Private Lives of Billie Burke* [Jefferson, NC: McFarland, 2009], p. 151). This dynamic is particularly striking in the case of the two actors playing actors: John Barrymore and Dressler. Margot Peters describes how Barrymore played Larry Renault as a combination of his father-in-law Maurice Costello, his brother-in-law Lowell Sherman, and himself (*The House of Barrymore* [New York: Alfred A. Knopf, 1990], p. 352). On Barrymore's preparation for the role, see also Levy, *George Cukor*, p. 73.

22. Springer and Hamilton, *They Had Faces Then*, p. 289; Kennedy, *Marie Dressler*, p. 221.

23. Lee, *Marie Dressler*, pp. 43–44; Kennedy, *Marie Dressler*, p. 42.

24. Lee, *Marie Dressler*, p. 244.

25. Kennedy, *Marie Dressler*, p. 199.

26. Mordaunt Hall, *Dinner at Eight* review, *New York Times* (August 24, 1933), p. 18.

27. Levy credits Donald Ogden Stewart with creating this "classic exchange" between Carlotta and Kitty. See Levy, *George Cukor*, p. 72. For a detailed account of how the ending came about, including Stewart's involvement, see Kennedy, *Marie Dressler*, p. 198.

28. Maria DiBattista, *Fast-Talking Dames* (New Haven: Yale University Press, 2001), p. 97.

29. *Dinner at Eight* review, *Variety* (August 24, 1933), www.variety.com.

30. Ethan Mordden, *Movie Star: A Look at the Women Who Made Hollywood* (New York: St. Martin's, 1983), pp. 126, 127.

31. Sheridan Morley, *Tales from the Hollywood Raj: The British in California* (N.p.: Hodder and Stoughton/Coronet, 1985), p. 134.

32. Kennedy, *Marie Dressler*, p. 199.

33. See Sturtevant, *A Great Big Girl Like Me*, p. 162.

34. Information on Maxine Elliott from "Maxine Elliott, 69, Stage Beauty, Dies," *New York Times* (March 7, 1940), p. 29; and Diana Forbes-Robertson, *My Aunt Maxine: The Story of Maxine Elliott* (New York: Viking Press, 1964).

35. Morley, *Tales from the Hollywood Raj*, p. 132.

36. Maxine Elliott was known for her pet monkey "Kiki," who was even mentioned in her *New York Times* obituary.

37. The quotation is from Matthew Kennedy, "Dinner Is Served: The Return of MGM's Witty '30s Romp," *Bright Lights Film Journal* 48 (May 2005), www.brightlightsfilm.com. Information on Mrs. Patrick Campbell from "Mrs. Campbell, 75, Famous Actress," *New York Times* (April 11, 1940), p. 33; Morley, *Tales from the Hollywood Raj*, pp. 132–34; and Margot Peters, *Mrs. Pat: The Life of Mrs. Patrick Campbell* (New York: Alfred A. Knopf,

1984). While Dressler may have modeled Carlotta's look on Stella Campbell, Constance Collier was more similar in appearance to stately Maxine Elliott, with her hooded eyes and patrician profile.

38. As fate would have it, too, Mrs. Patrick Campbell and Maxine Elliott both died in France within weeks of each other in the spring of 1940.

39. See Lee, *Marie Dressler*, p. 242. Ferber and Kaufman's hit play ran for 232 performances at the Music Box Theatre, closing in May 1933. By then the film version was already in the can, which explains why none of the Broadway cast members were asked to reprise their roles. After their Broadway run, the cast, including Constance Collier as Carlotta Vance, took the show to Chicago for nineteen weeks, ending there on October 21, 1933. See "*Dinner at Eight* Tour to End," *New York Times* (October 6, 1933), www.nyt.com; Charles Collins, "The Season in Chicago," *The Best Plays of 1932–33*, ed. Burns Mantle (New York: Dodd, Mead, 1933), p. 12; and Charles Collins, "The Season in Chicago," *The Best Plays of 1933–34*, ed. Burns Mantle (New York: Dodd, Mead, 1935), pp. 17, 19. The play was also staged in San Francisco during the summer of 1933 with Hedda Hopper as Carlotta Vance. See Edwin Schallert, "The Season in San Francisco," *The Best Plays of 1932–33*, ed. Burns Mantle (New York: Dodd, Mead, 1933), p. 20.

40. Cukor quoted in Sturtevant, *A Great Big Girl Like Me*, p. 162.

41. *Dinner at Eight* review, www.variety.com. Quoted in Lee, *Marie Dressler*, pp. 244–45.

42. Hall, *Dinner at Eight* review, p. 18.

43. Kennedy, *Marie Dressler*, pp. 151, 152.

44. "Marie Dressler, Noted Actress, Dies," *New York Times* (July 29, 1934), p. 22; Daniel Blum, *Great Stars of the American Stage: A Pictorial Record* (New York: Greenburg, 1952), Profile 37.

45. Quoted in Kennedy, *Marie Dressler*, p. 117.

46. On Dressler's height, see Blum, *Great Stars*, Profile 37; on her weight, see Lee, *Marie Dressler*, p. 2, and Kennedy, *Marie Dressler*, p. 2. Lee, *Marie Dressler*, p. 13 and Kennedy, *Marie Dressler*, p. 2 claim she was 5'7".

47. Sturtevant, *A Great Big Girl Like Me*, p. 168. Matthew Kennedy writes that "she carries each bauble and pelt as tribute to one or another romance from the youthful past" (*Marie Dressler*, p. 199).

48. Quotations from Parish and Bowers, *The MGM Stock Company*, p. 192; and Bram, "Marie Dressler," p. 186.

49. Lee, *Marie Dressler*, p. 242, incl. Cukor quote.

50. Springer and Hamilton, *They Had Faces Then*, p. 289.

Isobel Elsom

1. Helen E. Hokinson's delicious *New Yorker* cartoons from the 1930s and '40s would seem to indicate as much. Collected in books with titles such as *The Ladies, God Bless 'Em!* and *My Best Girls*, her entertaining drawings nearly always had naïve, blinkered, or pretentious older women as the butt of their jokes.

2. John Parker, *Who's Who in the Theatre: A Biographical Record of the Contemporary Stage* (7th ed.; London: Pitman, 1933), p. 516.

3. *Illegal* (W.C. McGann, Warner Bros., 1932) was Elsom's first American film in the sense that it was produced by Warner Bros., but it was shot at Teddington

Studios in England. The film is included in the wonderful collection of Warner Bros. films at the Wisconsin Center for Film and Theater Research at the University of Wisconsin, where I viewed it on June 21, 2007. Elsom got "above the title" star billing in this no-holds-barred melodrama about a single mother who gives all for her ungrateful daughters, including her reputation, by opening an illegal gambling joint to support her family. Evelyn Dean was a Gladys George or Barbara Stanwyck type of role and the film is a poor cousin to *Madame X, Stella Dallas, Mildred Pierce,* and other tales of motherly self-sacrifice combined with murder and mayhem. The film was made in England to satisfy the requirement that a certain percentage of films shown in Great Britain had to be made there.

4. Kaier Curtin, *"We Can Always Call Them Bulgarians": The Emergence of Lesbians and Gay Men on the American Stage* (Boston: Alyson, 1987), pp. 105, 108.

5. Curtin, p. 7.

6. See Curtin, pp. 107, 109.

7. See Curtin, p. 110.

8. Quoted in Curtin, p. 112.

9. "Maurice Elvey, Director of 300 British Movies," *New York Times* (August 29, 1967), www.nyt.com. Elvey directed no less than thirty-three silent films between 1913 and 1916 with another British actress who would show up in Hollywood films in her later years: Elisabeth Risdon.

10. "Isobel Elsom, 87, Dead, Stage and Film Actress," *New York Times* (January 16, 1981), p. D17.

11. Axel Nissen, *Actresses of a Certain Character: Forty Familiar Hollywood Faces from the Thirties to the Fifties* (Jefferson, NC: McFarland, 2007), p. 181.

12. Not to be confused with the 1940 film from RKO, *Primrose Path,* starring Ginger Rogers and Joel McCrea.

13. Edward Percy and Reginald Denham, *Ladies in Retirement* (New York: Dramatists Play Service, n.d.), p. 5.

14. Percy and Denham, p. 9.

15. Percy and Denham, p. 9.

16. Percy and Denham, p. 9.

17. According to a poll at www.imdb.com (accessed January 17, 2011).

18. Incidentally, Tierney and Elsom would end their film careers in the same film, *The Pleasure Seekers* (J. Negulesco, Twentieth Century–Fox, 1964), one of those marvelous 1960s "fun in the sun" films, this one with three young heroines: Ann-Margret, Carol Lynley, and Pamela Tiffin. Elsom plays the mother of a playboy (Anthony Franciosa), who chews him out when one of his conquests mistakenly thinks she has been invited to meet her prospective mother-in-law; and Tierney plays the wife of an adulterous newspaperman (Brian Keith).

19. For further discussion of the decline of the dowager in the 1960s, see Nissen, *Actresses,* p. 127.

20. "Isobel Elsom," p. D17.

21. "Isobel Elsom," p. D17.

22. www.findagrave.com (accessed January 17, 2011).

Hope Emerson

1. Boyd McDonald, *Cruising the Movies: A Sexual Guide to "Oldies" on TV* (New York: Gay Presses of New York, 1985), p. 21.

2. Quotations from Burns Mantle, "The Season in New York," *The Best Plays of 1929–30* (New York: Dodd, Mead, 1969), p. 5.

3. J. Brooks Atkinson, *"Lysistrata* Here with Broad Humor," *New York Times* (June 6, 1930), p. 26; Mantle, "The Season in New York," p. 5.

4. Mary C. Henderson, *Theater in America* (New York: Harry N. Abrams, 1996), p. 131.

5. Atkinson, *"Lysistrata,"* p. 26.

6. Blanche Yurka, *Bohemian Girl: Blanche Yurka's Theatrical Life* (Athens: Ohio University Press, 1970), p. 153.

7. Emerson "only" weighed 190 lbs. in later life, but in her prime she weighed as much as 230 lbs. On her height and weight, see "Hope Emerson, 62, Actress Is Dead," *New York Times* (April 26, 1960), p. 37; and Alfred E. Twomey and Arthur F. McClure, *The Versatiles: Supporting Character Players in the Cinema 1930–1955* (New York: Castle Books, 1969), p. 90.

8. Sumshee Urszula Kirken, "A Tribute to Hope Emerson," www.sumshee.com/hope-emerson.html (accessed January 19, 2011). This website contains a wealth of fascinating photographs from Emerson's life and career.

9. "Hope Emerson, Film Star, Dies," unsourced, undated clipping at www.sumshee.com/hope-emerson.html (accessed January 19, 2011). See also "Hope Emerson," p. 37.

10. Kirken, "A Tribute to Hope Emerson," www.sumshee.com/hope-emerson.html.

11. Kirken, "A Tribute to Hope Emerson," www.sumshee.com/hope-emerson.html.

12. "Hope Emerson's Rites Wednesday," unsourced, undated clipping at www.sumshee.com/hope-emerson.html (accessed January 19, 2011).

13. Twomey and McClure, *The Versatiles,* p. 90.

14. The quote is taken from the heading of the show's review in the *New York Times.* See Brooks Atkinson, *Swing Your Lady* review, *New York Times* (October 19, 1936), p. 22.

15. Atkinson, *Swing Your Lady* review, p. 22. Emerson studied under a woman blacksmith in Greenwich Village in preparation for her role ("Hope Emerson," p. 37).

16. This and the next quote from *The Best Plays of 1936–37,* ed. Burns Mantle (New York: Dodd Mead, 1937), p. 420.

17. Quotes from Atkinson, *Swing Your Lady* review, p. 22.

18. Quotes from Atkinson, *Swing Your Lady* review, p. 22.

19. Lewis Nichols, *Chicken Every Sunday* review, *New York Times* (April 6, 1944), p. 27.

20. Brooks Atkinson, *Street Scene* review, *New York Times* (January 10, 1947), p. 17.

21. All quotations on the play from Brooks Atkinson, *The Cup of Trembling* review, *New York Times* (April 21, 1948), p. 33.

22. Both Anderson and Moorehead had done one film each before playing their signature role: *Blood Money* (1933) in Anderson's case and *Citizen Kane* (1941), no less, in Moorehead's. My point is that they, like Emerson, quickly found their feet in film and were fortunate in getting such rare opportunities at the beginning of their film careers. In all three cases one could argue, though, that they only seldom found such challenging roles in film again.

23. A.W., *Cry of the City* review, *New York Times* (September 30, 1948), p. 32.

24. McDonald, *Cruising the Movies,* p. 25.

25. In the episode of TV's *This Is Your Life* which aired

on January 13, 1954, Richard Conte recalled "how gentle and sweet Hope was in real life" and how when it came time for the scene of near strangulation, "she had trouble throwing herself into the part" (Kirken, "A Tribute," www.sumshee.com/hope-emerson.html).

26. McDonald, *Cruising the Movies*, p. 26.

27. A.W., *Cry of the City* review, p. 32.

28. McDonald, *Cruising the Movies*, pp. 24, 25, 26.

29. "Hope Emerson," p. 37.

30. "Hope Emerson, Film Star, Dies," www.sumshee.com/hope-emerson.html.

31. David Quinlan, *Quinlan's Illustrated Directory of Film Character Actors* (2nd ed.; London: B.T. Batsford, 1995), p. 116.

32. Kirken, "A Tribute to Hope Emerson," www.sumshee.com/hope-emerson.html.

33. William J. Mann, *Behind the Screen: How Gays and Lesbians Shaped Hollywood, 1910–1969* (New York: Viking, 2001), pp. 136, 326.

34. Mike Connolly, "Mr. Hollywood: Mike Talked to Hope Right Up to Her Untimely Death," unsourced, undated clipping at www.sumshee.com/hope-emerson.html (accessed January 19, 2011).

35. Kirken, "A Tribute," www.sumshee.com/hope-emerson.html.

36. Richard Barrios, *Screened Out: Playing Gay in Hollywood from Edison to Stonewall* (New York and London: Routledge, 2003), p. 219n2.

37. Connolly, "Mr. Hollywood," www.sumshee.com/hope-emerson.html.

38. "Hope Emerson," p. 37; Connolly, "Mr. Hollywood," www.sumshee.com/hope-emerson.html.

39. "$75,000 Left to Emerson Friends, Kin," unsourced, undated clipping at www.sumshee.com/hope-emerson.html (accessed January 19, 2011).

40. "Hope Emerson," p. 37.

41. "Hope Emerson, Film Star, Dies" and "Hope Emerson's Rites Wednesday," www.sumshee.com/hope-emerson.html; www.findagrave.com (accessed January 19, 2011).

Mary Forbes

1. Maureen Stapleton and Jane Scovell, *A Hell of a Life: An Autobiography* (New York, Simon and Schuster, 1995), p. 73.

2. See www.imdb.com (accessed January 21, 2011). The year 1880 or 1883 is often given as Forbes's birth year. See "Mary Forbes, Actress, 91; Played Hollywood Roles," *New York Times* (July 24, 1974), p. 44; John Parker, *Who's Who in the Theatre: A Biographical Record of the Contemporary Stage* (7th ed.; London: Pitman, 1933), p. 564; and www.ibdb.com (accessed January 21, 2011). The place of Forbes's birth is also a bit of a mystery. Her *New York Times* obituary gives Hornby ("Mary Forbes," p. 44), while at www.ibdb.com it is Horney (accessed January 21, 2011). Hornby is a tiny place in Bedale, North Yorkshire, while there is no such place as Horney (in England, at any rate). Hornsey would seem to suit Forbes's patrician image better than Hornby or, certainly, Horney...

3. Information on Forbes's stage career from Parker, *Who's Who in the Theatre*, pp. 564–65 and www.ibdb.com.

4. David Ragan, *Who's Who in Hollywood, 1900–1976* (New Rochelle, NY: Arlington House, 1977), p. 616.

5. Flowers and Forbes were in a total of twenty films together between 1934 and 1958, including *The Awful*

Truth, Ninotchka, and *You Can't Take It with You.* They were in many of the same (party) scenes, too, however much in the background, as they both cleaned up well.

6. "Mary Forbes," p. 44.

7. "Ralph Forbes Dies; Stage, Film Actor," *New York Times* (April 1, 1951), www.nyt.com. Mother and son were seen in two films together: *Shock* (R. Pomeroy, W.T. Lackey Productions, 1934), where Ralph Forbes starred and Mary Forbes had an uncredited role; and *Stage Door* (G. La Cava, RKO, 1937), where they both perform in the play within the film, budding actress Terry Randall's stage debut. Katharine Hepburn is Terry Randall and Forbes is her mother in the play, standing right behind her when she opens with the infamous line "The calla lilies are in bloom again."

8. Mel Gussow, "Brenda Forbes, 87; Played Quirky Characters," *New York Times* (September 13, 1996), www.nyt.com. Mother and daughter also worked on two of the same films: *The Perfect Gentleman* (T. Whelan, MGM, 1935) and the expatriate British World War II extravaganza *This Above All* (A. Litvak, Twentieth Century–Fox, 1942), starring Tyrone Power and Joan Fontaine.

9. "Mary Forbes," p. 44; www.ssdi.com (accessed January 20, 2011).

10. Frank Capra, *The Name Above the Title: An Autobiography* (New York: Macmillan, 1971), p. 241.

11. Ed Sikov, *Screwball: Hollywood's Madcap Romantic Comedies* (New York: Crown, 1989), p. 142.

12. Roy Chartier, *You Can't Take It with You* review, *Variety* (September 7, 1938), www.variety.com.

13. "News of the Screen," *New York Times* (January 5, 1938), p. 17.

14. "News of the Screen," *New York Times* (April 9, 1938), p. 11.

15. Capra, *The Name Above the Title*, p. 243.

16. Chartier, *You Can't Take It with You* review, www.variety.com.

17. Sikov, *Screwball*, p. 143.

18. Chartier, *You Can't Take It with You* review, www.variety.com.

19. Frank S. Nugent, *You Can't Take It with You* review, *New York Times* (September 2, 1938), p. 21.

20. Donald C. Willis, *The Films of Frank Capra* (Metuchen, NJ: Scarecrow Press, 1974), p. 108. See Capra, *The Name Above the Title*, p. 241 for the original discussion of Mr. Kirby's role.

21. Sikov, *Screwball*, p. 142.

22. Joseph McBride, *Frank Capra: The Catastrophe of Success* (London and Boston: Faber and Faber, 1992), p. 382.

23. Willis, *The Films of Frank Capra*, pp. 109, 113n2.

24. McBride, *Frank Capra*, p. 384.

Marjorie Gateson

1. Alex Barris, *Hollywood's Other Women* (South Brunswick and New York: A.S. Barnes, 1975), p. 17.

2. B.R. Crisler, "Random Notes on Pictures and Personalities," *New York Times* (July 4, 1937), p. 3.

3. John Springer and Jack Hamilton, *They Had Faces Then: Annabella to Zorina, the Superstars, Stars and Starlets of the 1930's* (N.p.: Castle, 1974), p. 118.

4. "Mrs. Daniel T. Gateson," *New York Times* (March 17, 1934); Springer and Hamilton, *They Had Faces Then*, p. 296.

5. "Mrs. Daniel T. Gateson," www.nyt.com.

6. "Marjorie Gateson, Actress, 86, Dies," *New York Times* (April 19, 1977), p. 40; "Mrs. Daniel T. Gateson," www.nyt.com.

7. "Marjorie Gateson," p. 40.

8. *The Dove of Peace* review, *New York Times* (November 5, 1912), www.nyt.com.

9. "*Have a Heart* Is Bright and Tuneful," *New York Times* (January 12, 1917), www.nyt.com.

10. "*Fancy Free* Brings Clifton Crawford," *New York Times* (April 12, 1918), www.nyt.com.

11. Alexander Woollcott, *Little Miss Charity* review, *New York Times* (September 3, 1920), p. 6.

12. "*For Goodness Sake* Brisk," *New York Times* (February 22, 1922), www.nyt.com.

13. "*Sweet Little Devil* Liked," *New York Times* (January 22, 1924), www.nyt.com.

14. J. Brooks Atkinson, *Oh, Ernest!* review, *New York Times* (May 10, 1927), p. 24.

15. *So This Is Politics* review, *New York Times* (June 17, 1924), www.nyt.com.

16. J. Brooks Atkinson, *Hidden* review, *New York Times* (October 5, 1927), p. 30.

17. J. Brooks Atkinson, *The Great Necker* review, *New York Times* (March 7, 1928), p. 28. On first reading the play's title, I was uncertain if "The Great Necker" would have been understood in the same way then as it would be today or was possibly a biographical play about the French eighteenth-century finance minister Jacques Necker. Fortunately, I found enlightenment in Brooks Atkinson's review, where he writes that the title is "more physical than geographic" (*The Great Necker* review, p. 28).

18. In 1947, Gateson made a triumphant return to Broadway, after an absence of sixteen years, in a successful revival of the musical comedy *Sweethearts* starring Bobby Clark at the Shubert Theatre. As Madame Lucy, Brooks Atkinson wrote, she "plunges vigorously and humorously into the business of being chatelaine to a group of nubile young ladies" (*Sweethearts* review, *New York Times* [January 22, 1947], p. 31).

19. Gateson would work the most and the longest for Paramount, where she made thirteen films from her debut film *Beloved Bachelor* (L. Corrigan, 1931) to her last big screen appearance in *The Caddy* (N. Taurog, 1953). She made twelve films at Warner Bros. and eleven at Universal.

20. According to information at www.imdb.com, Gateson was 5'4" (accessed January 23, 2011).

21. Springer and Hamilton, *They Had Faces Then*, p. 118.

22. André Sennwald, "On a Swan Song," *New York Times* (May 19, 1935), p. X3.

23. James Robert Parish, *Hollywood Character Actors* (New Rochelle, NY: Arlington House, 1978), p. 221.

24. Mordaunt Hall, *Cocktail Hour* review, *New York Times* (June 2, 1933), p. 22.

25. David Ragan, *Who's Who in Hollywood, 1900–1976* (New Rochelle, NY: Arlington House, 1977), p. 156.

26. "Marjorie Gateson," p. 40.

27. www.findagrave.com (accessed January 22, 2011).

Louise Closser Hale

1. W. David Sievers, *Freud on Broadway: A History of Psychoanalysis and the American Drama* (New York: Hermitage House, 1955), p. 223.

2. "Mrs. Louise M. Closser," *New York Times* (April 30, 1932), p. 15; "Louise Hale Dies; Actress, Novelist," *New York Times* (July 27, 1933), p. 17; www.findagrave.com (accessed January 25, 2011).

3. "Minute Visits in the Wings," *New York Times* (November 29, 1914), www.nyt.com.

4. "Among the Authors," *New York Times* (October 6, 1912), www.nyt.com.

5. "Louise Hale Dies," p. 17.

6. "Walter Hale Dead," *New York Times* (December 5, 1917), www.nyt.com.

7. *Arizona* review, *New York Times* (September 11, 1900), www.nyt.com. Hale was still being billed as "Louise Closser."

8. John Parker, *Who's Who in the Theatre: A Biographical Record of the Contemporary Stage* (7th ed.; London: Pitman, 1933), p. 661; "Louise Hale Dies," p. 17; www.ibdb.com (accessed January 25, 2011).

9. *The Blue Bird* review, *New York Times* (October 2, 1910), www.nyt.com.

10. Alexander Woollcott, *Malvaloca* review, *New York Times* (October 3, 1922), p. 30.

11. *Candida* review, *New York Times* (December 9, 1903), www.nyt.com.

12. Alexander Woollcott, *Beyond the Horizon* review, *New York Times* (February 4, 1920), p. 12.

13. Alexander Woollcott, *Miss Lulu Bett* review, *New York Times* (December 28, 1920), p. 17.

14. Louise Closser Hale, "Miss Hale Is Resting," *New York Times* (February 6, 1921), p. XI.

15. John Corbin, *Peer Gynt* review, *New York Times* (February 6, 1923), p. 14.

16. John Corbin, *Expressing Willie* review, *New York Times* (April 17, 1924), p. 22.

17. "Walter Hale Dead," www.nyt.com.

18. "Louise Hale Dies," p. 17.

19. "Louise Hale Dies," p. 17.

20. "Walter Hale Operated On," *New York Times* (May 13, 1917), www.nyt.com; "Louise Hale Dies," p. 17.

21. Walter Hale's death notice, *New York Times* (December 6, 1917), www.nyt.com.

22. David Ragan, *Who's Who in Hollywood, 1900–1976* (New Rochelle, NY: Arlington House, 1977), p. 635. Hale lived with her German maid, Theresa C. Alzeo, in a home she owned at 6766 Wedgewood Place in Whitley Heights, Hollywood. See Allan R. Ellenberger, *Celebrities in the 1930 Census* (Jefferson, NC: McFarland, 2008), p. 115.

23. "Louise Hale Dies," p. 17.

24. "Louise Closser Hale Very Ill," *New York Times* (December 18, 1932), www.nyt.com.

25. "Louise Hale Dies," p. 17.

26. "Louise Hale Left $63,627," *New York Times* (February 17, 1934), www.nyt.com. In 1922, Hale had inherited $10,000 from a cousin, Annette K. Rankine. Mrs. Rankine, who had "disappeared while deranged on April 1, 1921, and whose body was found in the East River," had left an estate of $554,944, "chiefly in stocks and bonds." See "Mrs. Rankine Left Legacies to Charity," *New York Times* (May 13, 1921) and (incl. quotes) "Mrs. Rankine Left $554,944," *New York Times* (July 6, 1922), www.nyt.com.

27. All information on bequests and quotations from Hale's will from "Louise Hale Aided Nine Institutions," *New York Times* (August 3, 1933), www.nyt.com. One of her closest friends was Josephine Hull, whose husband, actor Shelley Hull, died only a year after Walter Hale. Hull later wrote of her husband and Louise Hale in death:

"She and Shelley are the only two of the dear dead I have ever seen who changed not at all." See William C. Carson, *Dear Josephine: The Theatrical Career of Josephine Hull* (Norman: University of Oklahoma Press, 1963), p. 144.

28. "Louise Closser Hale Honored," *New York Times* (April 23, 1934), www.nyt.com.

29. Beal and Hamilton made their screen debuts in this production. For Hamilton her role as Helen Hallam had also been her Broadway debut.

30. Helen Hayes with Katherine Hatch, *My Life in Three Acts* (New York: Simon and Schuster/Touchstone, 1991), pp. 64, 65, 70.

31. Mordaunt Hall, *Another Language* review, *New York Times* (August 5, 1933), p. 9.

32. Kenneth Barrow, *Helen Hayes: First Lady of the American Theatre* (Garden City, NY: Doubleday, 1985), p. 114.

33. Hale quoted in Barrow, pp. 114–15.

34. Hall, *Another Language* review, p. 9.

35. Hall, *Another Language* review, p. 9.

36. Hall, *Another Language* review, p. 9.

37. John Springer and Jack Hamilton, *They Had Faces Then: Annabella to Zorina, the Superstars, Stars and Starlets of the 1930's* (N.p.: Castle, 1974), p. 126.

38. Philip Wylie, *Generation of Vipers* (New York and Toronto: Farrar, and Rinehart, 1942), pp. 185, 189.

39. Edward A. Strecker, *Their Mothers' Sons: The Psychiatrist Examines an American Problem* (Philadelphia and New York: J. B. Lippincott, 1946), pp. 13, 30, 32, 37, 75.

40. Sievers, *Freud on Broadway*, pp. 76, 77, 275.

41. See Sievers, p. 77.

Esther Howard

1. "Actor Ends Life in Hotel," *New York Times* (October 21, 1926), www.nyt.com; Arthur Albertson's Certificate of Death, October 20, 1926 (Dept. of Health of the City of New York, Bureau of Records). Albertson died at 6 P.M.

2. "Actor Ends Life in Hotel," www.nyt.com.

3. Though the *New York Times* claims Albertson was thirty-three when he died in 1926, modern sources give 1891 as his year of birth. See www.imdb.com and www.ibdb.com. Albertson's certificate of death also states that he was thirty-three, presumably on the information of Esther Howard, but no date of birth is given.

4. All factual information and quotations in this paragraph from "In the Spotlight," *New York Times* (August 14, 1927), www.nyt.com.

5. "In the Spotlight," www.nyt.com.

6. After "her energy gave way under the strain" of playing the main role, Grace George was replaced by Minna Gombell before the opening of *The Indestructible Wife*. See *The Indestructible Wife* review, *New York Times* (January 31, 1918), www.nyt.com.

7. Alexander Woollcott, *Civilian Clothes* review, *New York Times* (September 13, 1919), p. 9.

8. "In the Spotlight," www.nyt.com.

9. "*Sweetheart Shop* Breezy," *New York Times* (September 1, 1920), www.nyt.com.

10. See "Theatrical Notes," *New York Times* (August 24, 1922) and "In the Spotlight," www.nyt.com.

11. "Theatrical Notes," *New York Times* (August 12, 1921), www.nyt.com.

12. "*Wildflower* Is Melodious," *New York Times* (February 8, 1923), www.nyt.com.

13. "*Tell Me More* Is Bright Musical Play," *New York Times* (April 14, 1925), www.nyt.com.

14. John Corbin, *Gringo* review, *New York Times* (December 15, 1922), p. 29; John Corbin, *In the Next Room* review, *New York Times* (November 28, 1923), p. 14.

15. Tad Mosel with Gertrude Macy, *Leading Lady: The World and Theatre of Katharine Cornell* (Boston: Little Brown, 1978), pp. 88, 89. One reviewer wrote of Howard's performance: "[T]he 'real class' as one might say, of the female roles was Esther Howard as Olive. This young woman is a real actress" (quoted in Mosel, p. 88).

16. Mosel, p. 207.

17. On Cornell and McClintic's unconventional marriage, see the Mosel biography *Leading Lady* and Lesley Ferris, "Kit and Guth: A Lavender Marriage on Broadway," *Passing Performances: Queer Readings of Leading Players in American Theater History*, ed. Robert A. Schanke and Kim Marra (Ann Arbor: University of Michigan Press, 1998), pp. 197–220.

18. "In the Spotlight," www.nyt.com.

19. *Allez-Oop!* review, *New York Times* (August 3, 1927), www.nyt.com. Bobby Watson (1888–1965), born Robert Watson Knucher, whom film historian Richard Barrios calls "the unsung pioneer of screen sissies," was on Broadway from 1923 till 1928, before embarking on a screen career which lasted until 1962. See Barrios, *Screened Out: Playing Gay in Hollywood from Edison to Stonewall* (New York and London: Routledge, 2003), pp. 66–68. Watson played Adolf Hitler in *The Miracle of Morgan's Creek* (1944), where Howard also had a small role.

20. "Premiere of *Nize Girl?*" *New York Times* (April 7, 1928), www.nyt.com. The title was changed to *A Lady for a Night*.

21. The Casino was right next door to the Knickerbocker Theatre, where Howard made her musical comedy debut in *The Sweetheart Shop*. Both theaters on the same block of Broadway (between 38th and 39th) were demolished in 1930 to make way for two huge office blocks. Thus, *The New Moon* was one of the last shows at the Casino.

22. According to the ratings and votes at www.imdb.com (accessed January 28, 2011).

23. Howard sometimes had to see herself bested, though, by another Sturges favorite, Elizabeth Patterson, who got showier roles in *Remember the Night* (1940), *I Married a Witch* (1942), and *Hail the Conquering Hero* (1944).

24. See "Notes" on *Born to Kill* at www.tcm.com (accessed January 28, 2011).

25. Director Wise had wanted to keep the original title, "but having Lawrence Tierney in the part, the studio thought it was important to get something more striking in the title." Looking back on the film towards the end of his life, Wise "thought a lot of it was just excellent." See Sergio Leeman, *Robert Wise on His Films: From Editing Room to Director's Chair* (Los Angeles: Silman-James, 1995), p. 78.

26. In the novel, this change of heart is motivated by Helen threatening to harm Mrs. Kraft's daughter, Rachel. This spinster daughter turned femme fatale is not in the film, which simplifies the plot and the character gallery of the novel to some extent. In the novel, Mrs. Kraft is called Mrs. Krantz. See James Gunn, *Deadlier than the Male* (Lexington, KY: Blackmask/Disruptive, 2007).

27. www.findagrave.com (accessed January 30, 2011). The logical inference from this final word on Esther

Howard is that one of her parents, probably her mother, was still alive at her death.

Josephine Hull

1. "Josephine Hull, Actress, Dead; Stage Career Spanned 50 Years," *New York Times* (March 13, 1957), p. 31. Her biographer, William Carson, claims she didn't get "above the title" star billing until her final Broadway show, *The Solid Gold Cadillac* (1953). See William C. Carson, *Dear Josephine: The Theatrical Career of Josephine Hull* (Norman: University of Oklahoma Press, 1963), pp. 278, 283.

2. Incidentally, Streep's two films both get a 7.7 rating in the Internet Movie Database's poll, while Hull's films both get 8.1 (www.imdb.com, accessed January 29, 2011).

3. "Josephine Hull," p. 31.

4. Carson, *Dear Josephine*, p. 7.

5. Carson, pp. 7, 14.

6. Carson, p. 5.

7. "Josephine Hull," p. 31.

8. Daniel Blum, *Great Stars of the American Stage: A Pictorial Record* (New York: Greenburg, 1952), Profile 111.

9. Carson, *Dear Josephine*, p. 14. He writes: "No one ever loved good, rich food more than Josephine Hull" (p. 128). On her weight problems, see also Carson, p. 132.

10. Quotation and Hull's reaction from Carson, p. 280.

11. Quoted in Carson, p. 282.

12. Blum, *Great Stars*, Profile 111.

13. Carson, *Dear Josephine*, p. 29.

14. Blum, *Great Stars*, Profile 111. Part of Hull's motivation for keeping her age a secret, apart from it being "one of the sacred family traditions" (Carson, *Dear Josephine*, p. 6), may have been because she got such a relatively late start in her chosen profession. Agnes Moorehead, another college-educated performer who started acting in her late twenties, shaved six years off her age when she applied to the Academy of Dramatic Arts in 1927, saying she was born in 1906. She stuck to 1906 for the remainder of her life, though she was actually born in 1900. Hull may also have been reticent about her age, because her matinee idol husband would have been about six years younger.

15. Carson, *Dear Josephine*, p. 89.

16. Carson, pp. 97, 114.

17. Carson, p. 141.

18. Carson, pp. 46, 173; John Howard Lawson, *Roger Bloomer* (New York: Thomas Seltzer, 1923), p. 196.

19. Carson, p. 173.

20. See "Josephine Hull," p. 31; Carson, *Dear Josephine*, p. 181.

21. Last quote from John Springer and Jack Hamilton, *They Had Faces Then: Annabella to Zorina, the Superstars, Stars and Starlets of the 1930's* (N.p.: Castle, 1974), p. 140.

22. Quoted in Carson, *Dear Josephine*, p. 209.

23. Springer and Hamilton, *They Had Faces Then*, p. 139; see the notes on the film at www.tcm.com (accessed January 30, 2011).

24. Mordaunt Hall, *After Tomorrow* review, *New York Times* (March 7, 1932), www.nyt.com.

25. Springer and Hamilton, *They Had Faces Then*, p. 140.

26. Carson, *Dear Josephine*, p. 211.

27. See "Josephine Hull," p. 31; see also Carson, *Dear Josephine*, p. 211.

28. Carson, pp. 210–12.

29. W. David Sievers, *Freud on Broadway: A History of Psychoanalysis and the American Drama* (New York: Hermitage House, 1955), p. 414. Hull biographer William Carson tells a different story of the genesis of *Arsenic and Old Lace*, claiming that Kesselring "aspired to write a farce" and in thinking of his grandmother came up with the most unlikely thing she might do to create the incongruity that is the basis of farce (*Dear Josephine*, p. 233).

30. Carson, *Dear Josephine*, p. 234.

31. Frank Capra, *The Name Above the Title* (1971; New York: Vintage, 1985), p. 309.

32. Carson, *Dear Josephine*, p. 244.

33. Carson, p. 234.

34. Carson, p. 55.

35. Carson, p. 164.

36. Bosley Crowther, *Harvey* review, *New York Times* (December 22, 1950), www.nyt.com.

37. Springer and Hamilton, *They Had Faces Then*, p. 303. Penny Sycamore in *You Can't Take It with You* (1936) was Hull's first major dizzy dame role. Columbia made a film adaptation of Kaufman and Hart's comic classic, with the role of Penny played by Spring Byington. When the film premiered at the Astor in New York on September 1, 1938, Hull was still playing the zany would-be dramatist Penny at the Booth Theatre right across the street. It was a rare thing for a film to premiere before the Broadway run was over, but *You Can't Take It with You* had been running since December 14, 1936, and would end in December 1938. It was Hull's longest run to date, though it would later be far outdone by *Arsenic and Old Lace* (1444 performances) and *Harvey* (1775 performances). While Hull stayed for the whole run of *You Can't Take It with You*, she was replaced by Laura Hope Crews and Patricia Collinge in *Arsenic* and Marion Lorne in *Harvey*.

38. Carson, *Dear Josephine*, p. 255.

39. Carson, p. 270.

40. Carson, pp. 270–71.

41. Carson, p. 160.

42. Blum, *Great Stars*, Profile 111.

43. Jessie Royce Landis, *You Won't Be So Pretty (But You'll Know More)* (London: W.H. Allen, 1954), p. 183.

44. Windust quoted in Carson, *Dear Josephine*, p. 235.

45. Carson, p. 131.

46. Carson, p. 286.

47. "Josephine Hull," p. 31.

48. "Josephine Hull," p. 31.

49. www.findagrave.com (accessed January 29, 2011).

Patsy Kelly

1. J.T.M., *Private Number* review, *New York Times* (June 12, 1936), www.nyt.com.

2. John Springer and Jack Hamilton, *They Had Faces Then: Annabella to Zorina, the Superstars, Stars and Starlets of the 1930's* (N.p.: Castle, 1974), p. 305.

3. James Robert Parish and William T. Leonard, *The Funsters* (New Rochelle, NY: Arlington House, 1979), p. 360.

4. Alex Barris, *Hollywood's Other Women* (South Brunswick and New York: A.S. Barnes, 1975), p. 83.

5. Judith Roof, *All about Thelma and Eve: Sidekicks and Third Wheels* (Urbana and Chicago: University of Illinois Press, 2002), p. 192n1.

6. Roof, p. 3.

7. Roof, p. 3.

8. Roof, p. 87.
9. Roof, p. 3.
10. Roof, p. 11.
11. Roof, p. 16.
12. Roof, p. 19.
13. J.T.M., *Private Number* review, www.nyt.com.
14. As in some eighteenth-century novel by Richardson or Fielding, the characters names really say it all. Richard Winfield's WASP background and Ellen Neal's innate nobility are indicated by their Anglophone names, while Gracie and Smiley's comic, working-class propensities are underscored by their more folksy nicknames. Gracie doesn't even have a surname.
15. J.T.M., *Private Number* review, www.nyt.com.
16. Roof, *All About Thelma and Eve*, p. 16.
17. Roof, p. 17.
18. William J. Mann, *Behind the Screen: How Gays and Lesbians Shaped Hollywood, 1910–1969* (New York: Viking, 2001), p. 136.
19. Mann, p. 138.
20. See Boze Hadleigh, *Hollywood Lesbians* (New York: Barricade Books, 1994), pp. 56, 62, 65–66.
21. Information on Kelly's parents and early life from Parish and Leonard, *The Funsters*, p. 357.
22. Springer and Hamilton, *They Had Faces Then*, p. 66; Parish and Leonard, *The Funsters*, p. 357.
23. See Hadleigh, *Hollywood Lesbians*, p. 66.
24. Information on Kelly's early performing career from Parish and Leonard, *The Funsters*, p. 358.
25. Flint, "Patsy Kelly," p. 28.
26. Quoted in Parish and Leonard, *The Funsters*, p. 358.
27. Parish and Leonard, p. 358.
28. Parish and Leonard, p. 359.
29. Quoted in Mann, *Behind the Screen*, p. 139.
30. Flint, "Patsy Kelly," p. 28.
31. See Hadleigh, *Hollywood Lesbians*, pp. 67, 68.
32. Hadleigh, p. 56.
33. Mann, *Behind the Screen*, p. 139.
34. Mann, *Behind the Screen*, p. 138. Richard Lamparski gives a fascinating account of the accident in his *Hollywood Diary* (Boalsburg, PA: BearManor Media, 2006), pp. 123–46.
35. Mann, p. 362.
36. Lee Israel, *Miss Tallulah Bankhead* (New York: G.P. Putnam, 1972), p. 291; Parish and Leonard, *The Funsters*, p. 363, incl. Kelly quote; Flint, "Patsy Kelly," p. 28.
37. Israel, p. 292.
38. See Israel, p. 292.
39. Hadleigh, *Hollywood Lesbians*, p. 69.
40. Mann, *Behind the Screen*, p. 362.
41. Barris, *Hollywood's Other Women*, p. 162.
42. Parish and Leonard, *The Funsters*, p. 365.
43. Barris, *Hollywood's Other Women*, p. 37.
44. Parish and Leonard, *The Funsters*, p. 366.
45. Quotes from Hadleigh, *Hollywood Lesbians*, pp. 56, 68.
46. Flint, "Patsy Kelly," p. 28.
47. Flint, "Patsy Kelly," p. 28; www.findagrave.com (accessed January 30, 2011).

Alma Kruger

1. "Alma Kruger, 88, Actress in Films," *New York Times* (April 8, 1960), p. 31.
2. Charles Plunkett, "The Drama," *New York Times* (April 17, 1898), p. MS6. Haverstraw is a town on the Hudson River in Rockland County, New York.
3. John Parker, *Who's Who in the Theatre: A Biographical Record of the Contemporary Stage.* (7th ed.; London: Pitman, 1933), p. 831.
4. "Melodrama Holds Sway at First Night Offerings," *New York Times* (May 17, 1903), www.nyt.com.
5. Parker, *Who's Who*, p. 831.
6. "Alma Kruger," p. 31.
7. *Hamlet* review, *New York Times* (June 8, 1909), www.nyt.com.
8. Parker, *Who's Who*, p. 831.
9. "What Brooklyn Theatres Promise," *New York Times* (November 3, 1907), www.nyt.com.
10. *The Stronger Sex* review, *New York Times* (November 24, 1908), www.nyt.com.
11. Burns Mantle, ed., *The Best Plays of 1935–36* (New York: Dodd, Mead, 1936), p. 406.
12. Brooks Atkinson, *Few Are Chosen* review, *New York Times* (September 18, 1935), p. 19.
13. "Alma Kruger," p. 31.
14. Brooks Atkinson, *Pride and Prejudice* review, *New York Times* (November 6, 1935), p. 32.
15. "News of the Stage," *New York Times* (December 2, 1935), www.nyt.com.
16. Emmett would also play Mrs. Tilford in the 1952 revival with Kim Hunter and Patricia Neal, directed by Hellman herself.
17. Lillian Hellman, *The Children's Hour* (New York: Alfred A. Knopf, 1936), p. 45.
18. Quotation from David Ragan, *Who's Who in Hollywood, 1900–1976* (New Rochelle, NY: Arlington House, 1977), p. 674.
19. Patricia White, *UnInvited: Classical Hollywood Cinema and Lesbian Representability* (Bloomington: Indiana University Press, 1999), p. 27.
20. White, p. 27.
21. Richard Moody, *Lillian Hellman: Playwright* (New York: Pegasus, 1972), p. 47.
22. Katherine Lederer, *Lillian Hellman* (Boston: Twayne, 1979), p. 29.
23. Harry Gilroy, "The Bigger the Lie," *New York Times* (December 14, 1952). Reprinted in *Conversations with Lillian Hellman*, ed. Jackson R. Bryer (Jackson and London: University Press of Mississippi, 1986), p. 25.
24. Mark W. Estrin, *Lillian Hellman: Plays, Films, Memoirs—A Reference Guide* (Boston: G.K. Hall, 1980), p. 15.
25. Axel Madsen argues that, despite the change in Martha Dobie's unrequited love object from her friend Karen Wright to Karen's boyfriend, the doctor Joe Cardin, Miriam Hopkins nevertheless plays the role as if it is Merle Oberon she is in love with. I don't see it. It would seem to me that the scene Martha and Joe have alone in the bedroom, where he falls asleep fully dressed on the couch, makes it abundantly clear where Hopkins's romantic interest lies. See Axel Madsen, *William Wyler* (New York: Thomas Y. Crowell, 1973), p. 133. Bernard F. Dick agrees with Madsen in his *Hellman in Hollywood* (Rutherford: Fairleigh Dickinson University Press, 1982), p. 39.
26. Carl Rollyson, *Lillian Hellman: Her Legend and Legacy* (New York: St. Martin's Press, 1988), p. 88.
27. Frank S. Nugent, "*These Three*, Those Five," *New York Times* (March 22, 1936), p. X3.
28. Frank S. Nugent, *These Three* review, *New York Times* (March 19, 1936), www.nyt.com. On the reception of the film, see William Wright, *Lillian Hellman: The*

Image, the Woman (New York: Simon and Schuster, 1986), p. 113; Rollyson, *Lillian Hellman*, p. 88.

29. The epithet is from Nugent, *These Three* review, www.nyt.com.

30. The only thing I find outrageous and egregious about this first film adaptation is the tacked-on Hollywood ending—"Wiener kitsch," as Patricia White has called it. It is really a gross and embarrassing example of an artificial happy ending: "[R]arely has heterosexual consensus looked so manufactured" (both quotes from White, *UnInvited*, p. 27). It is inconceivable that such an astute critic as Frank Nugent should have thought that the conclusion to *These Three* "is as effective in its way as the somber conclusion of the play" ("*These Three*, Those Five," p. X3).

31. J. Brooks Atkinson, *Daisy Mayme* review, *New York Times* (October 26, 1926), p. 24.

32. According to the poll at www.imdb.com (accessed February 2, 2011).

33. "Alma Kruger," p. 31.

34. www.findagrave.com (accessed February 2, 2011).

Aline MacMahon

1. Information on William MacMahon from "William MacMahon, Former Editor, Dies," *New York Times* (September 8, 1931), www.nyt.com.

2. Information on Jennie MacMahon from "Jennie MacMahon," *New York Times* (January 7, 1985), www.nyt.com. After her father's sudden death from heart disease in 1931, MacMahon encouraged her mother to take up acting. Jennie MacMahon subsequently attended the American Academy of Dramatic Arts. She began her professional acting career under the name Jenny Mac when she was fifty-three years old, appearing in small stage roles and in several films directed by her nephew S. Sylvan Simon. She died at her home in Beverly Hills, California in 1985, shortly before her 107th birthday, making her and Agnes Moorehead's mother, Mollie Moorehead, who died in 1990 at aged 106, the longest living mothers of any well known American actress.

3. "Who's Who On the Stage," *New York Times* (December 4, 1926), www.nyt.com.

4. "International Lady," *New York Times* (March 22, 1942), www.nyt.com; Alfred E. Twomey and Arthur F. McClure, *The Versatiles: Supporting Character Players in the Cinema 1930–1955* (New York: Castle Books, 1969), p. 151; John Springer and Jack Hamilton, *They Had Faces Then: Annabella to Zorina, the Superstars, Stars and Starlets of the 1930's* (N.p.: Castle, 1974), p. 314.

5. "Who's Who," www.nyt.com; Twomey and McClure, *The Versatiles*, p. 151; Springer and Hamilton, *They Had Faces Then*, p. 314.

6. "Who's Who," www.nyt.com; Twomey and McClure, *The Versatiles*, p. 151.

7. "Who's Who," www.nyt.com.

8. Both quoted in Bruce Lambert, "Aline MacMahon Is Dead at 92; On Stage and Screen for 50 Years," *New York Times* (October 14, 1991), p. B8.

9. "*Beyond the Horizon* Is Seen Again Here," *New York Times* (December 1, 1926), www.nyt.com.

10. J. Brooks Atkinson, *Maya* review, *New York Times* (February 22, 1928), p. 25.

11. "Theatre Padlock Invoked First Time," *New York Times* (February 25, 1928), www.nyt.com.

12. "Aline MacMahon Wed to Clarence S. Stein," *New York Times* (March 29, 1928), www.nyt.com.

13. "International Lady," www.nyt.com.

14. Paul Goldberger, "Clarence S. Stein, Planner of Garden Cities, 92," *New York Times* (February 8, 1975), p. 25.

15. David Ragan, *Who's Who in Hollywood, 1900–1976* (New Rochelle, NY: Arlington House, 1977), p. 267.

16. See "Old Ossining Farm Sold to Architect," *New York Times* (November 12, 1937) and "Plan Westchester Home," *New York Times* (December 27, 1937), www.nyt.com.

17. Information on Clarence S. Stein from "Aline MacMahon Wed," www.nyt.com, and Goldberger, "Clarence S. Stein," p. 25.

18. This was the last play at the Shubert-managed Garrick Theatre at 67 W. 35th St., no doubt because of the financial crisis. After three years as a burlesque house, this theater from 1890 was razed in 1932.

19. Quotes and other information on *Winter Bound* from Kaier Curtin, "*We Can Always Call Them Bulgarians*": *The Emergence of Lesbians and Gay Men on the American Stage* (Boston: Alyson, 1987), pp. 140–53. Curtin devotes an entire chapter to this production.

20. "*Winter Bound* Moves Along Devious Paths," *New York Times* (November 13, 1929), www.nyt.com.

21. Curtin, "*We Can Always*," p. 150.

22. Lambert, "Aline MacMahon," p. B8.

23. Lambert, "Aline MacMahon," p. B8.

24. Quoted in Lambert, "Aline MacMahon," p. B8.

25. "International Lady," www.nyt.com.

26. David Quinlan, *Quinlan's Character Stars* (London: Reynolds and Hearn, 2004), p. 280.

27. Springer and Hamilton, *They Had Faces Then*, p. 177.

28. "International Lady," www.nyt.com.

29. "International Lady," www.nyt.com.

30. Larry Swindell, *Body and Soul: The Story of John Garfield* (New York: William Morrow, 1975), p. 108.

31. "International Lady," www.nyt.com.

32. James Robert Parish, *Hollywood Character Actors* (New Rochelle, NY: Arlington House, 1978), p. 355. See also Quinlan, *Quinlan's Character Stars*, p. 280.

33. According to the poll at www.imdb.com (accessed February 4, 2011). In second place is *Gold Diggers of 1933* and in third place *One Way Passage*.

34. Ragan, *Who's Who in Hollywood*, p. 267.

35. John Gielgud, *Gielgud's Letters*, ed. and intro. by Richard Mangan (London: Weidenfeld and Nicolson, 2004), p. 109.

36. "International Lady," www.nyt.com.

37. Lambert, "Aline MacMahon," p. B8.

38. www.findagrave.com (accessed February 4, 2011).

Beryl Mercer

1. David Ragan, *Who's Who in Hollywood, 1900–1976* (New Rochelle, NY: Arlington House, 1977), p. 714.

2. John Springer and Jack Hamilton, *They Had Faces Then: Annabella to Zorina, the Superstars, Stars and Starlets of the 1930's* (N.p.: Castle, 1974), p. 179.

3. Alex Barris, *Hollywood's Other Women* (South Brunswick and New York: A.S. Barnes, 1975), p. 41.

4. "The Young 'Old Lady' of Mr. Barrie's Play," *New York Times* (June 24, 1917), www.nyt.com.

5. Mercer's date of birth is the same in all the sources I have consulted, starting with John Parker, *Who's Who in the Theatre: A Biographical Record of the Contemporary Stage* (7th ed. London: Pitman, 1933), p. 978.

6. Ken D. Jones, Arthur F. McClure, and Alfred E. Twomey, *Character People* (South Brunswick and New York: A. S. Barnes, 1976), p. 143; "The Young 'Old Lady,'" www.nyt.com.

7. Information on Mercer's early life and career from "The Young 'Old Lady,'" www.nyt.com (incl. final quote); Parker, *Who's Who in the Theatre*, p. 978.

8. *The Shulamite* review, *New York Times* (October 30, 1906), www.nyt.com.

9. "The Young 'Old Lady,'" www.nyt.com.

10. www.imdb.com (accessed February 6, 2011).

11. "The Young 'Old Lady,'" www.nyt.com.

12. Parker, *Who's Who in the Theatre*, p. 978.

13. "The Young 'Old Lady,'" www.nyt.com.

14. "*The Lodger* Proves Highly Amusing," *New York Times* (January 9, 1917), www.nyt.com.

15. "The Young 'Old Lady,'" www.nyt.com.

16. "Two Barrie Plays in His Best Vein," *New York Times* (May 15, 1917), www.nyt.com.

17. All quotes and information in this paragraph from "The Young 'Old Lady,'" www.nyt.com. Mercer had started as Lena Ashwell's understudy in 1904 (Parker, *Who's Who in the Theatre*, p. 978).

18. Death notices, *New York Times* (March 25, 1921), www.nyt.com.

19. "Thomas Ince's Widow Wed," *New York Times* (May 5, 1930), www.nyt.com.

20. Information on Herbert from James Robert Parish, *Hollywood Character Actors* (New Rochelle, NY: Arlington House, 1978), p. 370, and www.imdb.com (accessed February 6, 2011).

21. Parker, *Who's Who in the Theatre*, p. 978.

22. "Beryl Mercer, 57, a Noted Actress," *New York Times* (July 29, 1939), p. 18; Allan R. Ellenberger, *Celebrities in the 1930 Census* (Jefferson, NC: McFarland, 2008), p. 169.

23. John Corbin, *Queen Victoria* review, *New York Times* (November 16, 1923), p. 15.

24. *Outward Bound* was revived on Broadway in 1938 with Laurette Taylor as Mrs. Midget and Florence Reed as Mrs. Cliveden-Banks. The play has not been seen there since.

25. All quotations in this paragraph from *Outward Bound* review, *New York Times* (January 8, 1924), p. 26.

26. Springer and Hamilton, *They Had Faces Then*, p. 202.

27. According to the polls at www.imdb.com (accessed February 6, 2011).

28. Mordaunt Hall, *Outward Bound* review, *New York Times* (September 18, 1930), www.nyt.com.

29. Hall, *Outward Bound* review, www.nyt.com.

30. Quotes from Sutton Vane, "*Outward Bound*," *Sixteen Famous British Plays*, ed. Bennett A. Cerf and Van H. Cartmell (New York: Modern Library, 1942), pp. 482–84.

31. Hall, *Outward Bound* review, www.nyt.com.

32. See Ellenberger, *Celebrities in the 1930 Census*, p. 169.

33. Parker, *Who's Who in the Theatre*, p. 979. Information on the property from www.zillow.com (accessed February 6, 2011).

34. "Beryl Mercer," p. 18.

35. www.findagrave.com (accessed February 6, 2011). Mercer's former husband, Holmes Herbert, is also buried in Forest Lawn, with his third wife, the actress Agnes Bartholomew. He died in 1956 at the age of seventy-four.

Juanita Moore

1. "Classic Hollywood: *Imitation of Life* Anniversary Screening at Samuel Goldwyn Theater," *Los Angeles Times* (August 19, 2009), www.latimes.com; quote from "*Imitation of Life*: Production Notes," *Imitation of Life: Douglas Sirk Director*, ed. Lucy Fischer (New Brunswick, NJ: Rutgers University Press, 1991), p. 185.

2. "Classic Hollywood," www.latimes.com.

3. Sam Staggs, *Born to Be Hurt: The Untold Story of Imitation of Life* (New York: St. Martin's, 2009), pp. 20–21.

4. Staggs, p. 20.

5. For a detailed and interesting account of Moore's early life and career, see Staggs, ch. 2–3.

6. Alfred E. Twomey and Arthur F. McClure, *The Versatiles: Supporting Character Players in the Cinema 1930–1955* (New York: Castle Books, 1969), p. 162; Staggs, *Born to Be Hurt*, p. 28, incl. quote from Moore.

7. Twomey and McClure, *The Versatiles*, p. 162; Staggs, *Born to Be Hurt*, p. 36.

8. Twomey and McClure, p. 162.

9. "*Imitation of Life*: Production Notes," p. 185.

10. Staggs, *Born to Be Hurt*, p. 25.

11. Information on Moore's husbands from Staggs, *Born to Be Hurt*, pp. 29–30, 36–37.

12. Jeremy G. Butler, "*Imitation of Life* (1934 and 1959): Style and the Domestic Melodrama," *Imitation of Life: Douglas Sirk Director*, ed. Lucy Fischer (New Brunswick, NJ: Rutgers University Press, 1991), p. 297.

13. Donald Bogle, *Blacks in American Films and Television: An Encyclopedia* (New York and London: Garland, 1988), p. 116.

14. Lucy Fischer, "Three-Way Mirror: *Imitation of Life*," *Imitation of Life: Douglas Sirk Director*, ed. Lucy Fischer (New Brunswick, NJ: Rutgers University Press, 1991), p. 17.

15. Fischer, p. 28.

16. Thomas Cripps, *Slow Fade to Black: The Negro in American Film, 1900–1942* (New York: Oxford University Press, 1977), p. 266.

17. Cripps, *Slow Fade to Black*, p. 354.

18. "Success Won't Get You Happiness, Bub" (*Cue*, 1959), *Imitation of Life: Douglas Sirk Director*, ed. Lucy Fischer (New Brunswick, NJ: Rutgers University Press, 1991), p. 237.

19. Marina Heung, "'What's the Matter with Sarah Jane?': Daughters and Mothers in Douglas Sirk's *Imitation of Life*," *Cinema Journal* 26.3 (Spring 1987), pp. 29–30.

20. Staggs, *Born to Be Hurt*, p. 107.

21. Bogle, *Blacks in American Films*, p. 115.

22. Axel Nissen, *Actresses of a Certain Character: Forty Familiar Hollywood Faces from the Thirties to the Fifties* (Jefferson, NC: McFarland, 2007), p. 104.

23. Stephen Handzo, "Intimations of Lifelessness," *Bright Lights Film Journal* no. 6 (1977), www.brightlightsfilm.com.

24. Paul V. Beckley, "*Imitation of Life*" (*New York Herald Tribune*, 1959), *Imitation of Life: Douglas Sirk Director*, ed. Lucy Fischer (New Brunswick, NJ: Rutgers University Press, 1991), pp. 239–40.

25. Quote from Rainer Werner Fassbinder, "*Imitation of Life*" (1971), *Imitation of Life: Douglas Sirk Director*, ed. Lucy Fischer (New Brunswick, NJ: Rutgers University Press, 1991), p. 244.

26. Fassbinder, "*Imitation of Life*," p. 245.

27. Michael Stern, "*Imitation of Life*" (1979), *Imitation*

of Life: Douglas Sirk Director, ed. Lucy Fischer (New Brunswick, NJ: Rutgers University Press, 1991), p. 283.

28. Heung, "'What's the Matter with Sarah Jane?,'" p. 36.

29. Bogle, *Blacks in American Films*, p. 116.

30. Bosley Crowther, "Sob Story Back; *Imitation of Life* in Return to Roxy," *New York Times* (April 18, 1959). www.nyt.com.

31. Bogle, *Blacks in American Films*, p. 116.

32. *"Imitation of Life"* (*Time*, 1959), *Imitation of Life: Douglas Sirk Director*, ed. Lucy Fischer (New Brunswick, NJ: Rutgers University Press, 1991), p. 243.

33. Beckley, *"Imitation of Life,"* p. 239.

34. Bogle, *Blacks in American Films*, p. 424.

35. Donald Bogle, *Toms, Coons, Mulattoes, Mammies, and Bucks: An Interpretive History of Blacks in American Films* (4th Ed.; New York and London: Continuum, 2001), p. 192.

36. Crowther, "Sob Story Back," www.nyt.com.

37. "Classic Hollywood," www.latimes.com.

38. Staggs, *Born to Be Hurt*, p. 81.

39. "Classic Hollywood," www.latimes.com.

40. "Classic Hollywood," www.latimes.com.

41. Poitier quoted from a twenty-year-old interview in Susan King, "Classic Hollywood: Remembering Pioneering African American Actors," *Los Angeles Times* (January 31, 2011), www.latimes.com.

42. Fischer, "Three-Way Mirror," p. 22.

43. "London Critics Cool to *Raisin in the Sun*," *New York Times* (August 5, 1959), www.nyt.com.

44. Howard Taubman, "Theater: *The Amen Corner*, Baldwin's First Play," *New York Times* (April 16, 1965), www.nyt.com.

45. Staggs, *Born to Be Hurt*, pp. 13, 283.

46. "Classic Hollywood," www.latimes.com; "Juanita Moore," www.wikipedia.com (accessed February 9, 2011).

Marjorie Rambeau

1. "Miss Rambeau Denies Sending Love Wire: Mrs. Manton Ordered to Show Message Husband Got Was from the Actress," *New York Times* (February 25, 1926), www.nyt.com.

2. "Miss Rambeau Tells of Midnight Raid," *New York Times* (February 26, 1926), www.nyt.com.

3. "Miss Rambeau Tells," www.nyt.com.

4. For an account of the problems caused by Rambeau's drinking during the run of *Antonia*, see Patrick McGilligan, *George Cukor: A Double Life* (New York: St. Martin's, 1991), p. 51.

5. "Miss Rambeau Tells," www.nyt.com.

6. "Miss Rambeau Tells," www.nyt.com.

7. "Miss Rambeau Tells," www.nyt.com. Rambeau and Manton were in a play together, *The Valley of Content*, that premiered at the Apollo Theatre on January 13, 1925. Far from being the unskilled minion Rambeau's lawyer made him out to be, Manton was an experienced actor with nine shows on Broadway to his credit, starting in 1913. His last show there closed just a week before his wife's suit for divorce came to trial in late February 1926. At that time, Mrs. Manton alleged that he was earning $100–125 a week.

8. "Miss Rambeau Tells," www.nyt.com.

9. "Mantons Reunited; Actress Is Cleared," *New York Times* (February 27, 1926), www.nyt.com.

10. "Manton's Absence Halts Divorce Move: Court Reserves Decision on Application by Actor's Wife to Reopen Suit," *New York Times* (June 25, 1926), www.nyt.com.

11. "Mrs. Manton Wins Divorce from Actor: Naming Rambeau as Co-respondent, She Gets Custody of Children and $30 a Week," *New York Times* (December 3, 1926), www.nyt.com.

12. "To Mail Manton Papers: They May Also Be Nailed on Miss Rambeau's Door in $100,000 Suit," *New York Times* (February 20, 1927), www.nyt.com.

13. "Rambeau Case Is Heard: Attorney Says Actress Lacks Fare to Come From Coast," *New York Times* (February 19, 1930), www.nyt.com. The census taken on April 14, 1930 shows that Rambeau was living modestly at the St. George's Court Apartments at 1245 N. Vine St. in Hollywood with a lodger. See Allan R. Ellenberger, *Celebrities in the 1930 Census* (Jefferson, NC: McFarland, 2008), p. 196.

14. "Marjorie Rambeau Defaults," *New York Times* (April 18, 1935), www.nyt.com; Kevitt Manton's Certificate of Death, July 31, 1931 (Dept. of Health of the City of New York, Bureau of Records). Manton took an overdose of the barbiturate sleeping powder Veronal.

15. "Miss Yurka Wins Separation Suit," *New York Times* (March 5, 1925), www.nyt.com.

16. "Miss Yurka Wins," www.nyt.com.

17. Blanche Yurka, *Bohemian Girl: Blanche Yurka's Theatrical Life* (Athens, OH: Ohio University Press, 1970), pp. 105–12.

18. "New Mack Play at the Longacre," *New York Times* (December 5, 1914), www.nyt.com.

19. "Marjorie Rambeau Weds," *New York Times* (March 9, 1919), www.nyt.com.

20. "Apprenticed to a Pirate," *New York Times* (December 13, 1914), www.nyt.com.

21. "She Went A-Barnstorming in Cold, Far-Off Alaska," *New York Times* (December 5, 1915), www.nyt.com.

22. "Extravagant Farce by Avery Hopgood," *New York Times* (November 30, 1915), www.nyt.com.

23. "Cheating Cheaters Most Entertaining," *New York Times* (August 10, 1916), www.nyt.com.

24. *"Eyes of Youth* Go Crystal Gazing," *New York Times* (August 23, 1917), www.nyt.com; "Trailing the Elusive Talent," *New York Times* (September 16, 1917), www.nyt.com.

25. "Marjorie Rambeau in War Melodrama," *New York Times* (August 27, 1918), www.nyt.com.

26. Alexander Woollcott, *The Unknown Woman* review, *New York Times* (November 11, 1919), p. 11.

27. Woollcott, p. 11.

28. Alexander Woollcott, *The Goldfish* review, *New York Times* (April 18, 1922), p. 33.

29. "She Went A-Barnstorming," www.nyt.com.

30. "Some Thoughts on First Nights," *New York Times* (December 13, 1914), www.nyt.com.

31. "Some Thoughts," www.nyt.com.

32. "Extravagant Farce," www.nyt.com.

33. "She Went A-Barnstorming," www.nyt.com.

34. John Parker, *Who's Who in the Theatre: A Biographical Record of the Contemporary Stage* (7th ed.; London: Pitman, 1933), pp. 1122–23; Daniel Blum, *Great Stars of the American Stage: A Pictorial Record* (New York: Greenburg, 1952), Profile 62.

35. "She Went A-Barnstorming," www.nyt.com; Blum, *Great Stars*, Profile 62 (incl. quote).

36. "She Went A-Barnstorming," www.nyt.com.

37. "Apprenticed to a Pirate," www.nyt.com.
38. "She Went A-Barnstorming," www.nyt.com.
39. "Apprenticed to a Pirate," www.nyt.com; "She Went A-Barnstorming," www.nyt.com.
40. "Apprenticed to a Pirate," www.nyt.com; "She Went A-Barnstorming," www.nyt.com. See also "The Actor's Christmas," *New York Times* (December 19, 1915), www.nyt.com on how Rambeau spent the Christmas of 1906 in Alaska.
41. "Sues Willard Mack for Divorce," *New York Times* (March 6, 1917).
42. Information on Dillman from "Marjorie Rambeau Weds," *New York Times* (March 9, 1919), www.nyt.com; Ginger L. Pedersen, "Hugh Dillman and His Dream: Sandy Loam Farm," www.palmbeachpast.org (accessed February 11, 2011); www.ibdb.com (accessed February 11, 2011).
43. "Marjorie Rambeau Sues," *New York Times* (August 9, 1923), www.nyt.com.
44. "Marjorie Rambeau Gets a Divorce," *New York Times* (November 14, 1923), www.nyt.com. In 1926, Dillman married Anna Thompson Dodge, the widow of Horace Elgin Dodge Sr. and one of the richest women in the world. She was fourteen years his senior. The marriage ended in divorce in 1947. Dillman died in 1956, but Anna Dodge Dillman lived to be ninety-nine, dying in 1970, the same year as Rambeau.
45. "Marjorie Rambeau Weds Third Husband: Actress Is Bride of Francis A. Gudger in Ceremony at Yuma, Ariz.," *New York Times* (November 11, 1931), www.nyt.com; John Springer and Jack Hamilton, *They Had Faces Then: Annabella to Zorina, the Superstars, Stars and Starlets of the 1930's* (N.p.: Castle, 1974), p. 324.
46. Parker, *Who's Who*, p. 1123.
47. "Plans Return to Films: Marjorie Rambeau Signs Contract to Appear for Paramount," *New York Times* (December 10, 1932), www.nyt.com.
48. Mack died in Brentwood Heights, California, in November 1934, at the age of fifty-six. He had married actress Pauline Frederick in 1917 and after their divorce married Beatrice Banyard, who was twenty-four years his junior. The *New York Times* pointed out in his obituary, "His wives were all actresses who had co-starred with him in plays." See "Willard Mack, 56, Actor-Author Dies," *New York Times* (November 20, 1934), www.nyt.com.
49. David Quinlan, *Quinlan's Character Stars* (London: Reynolds and Hearn, 2004), p. 358.
50. "Marjorie Rambeau Dies at 80; Broadway and Screen Actress," *New York Times* (July 8, 1970), p. 43.
51. Frances Marion, *Off with Their Heads! A Serio-Comic Tale of Hollywood* (New York: Macmillan, 1972), pp. 207–08, 209.
52. Quote from Bosley Crowther, *Slander* review, *New York Times* (January 17, 1957), p. 32.
53. Social Security Death Index, ssdi.rootsweb.ancestry.com (accessed February 11, 2011).
54. www.findagrave.com (accessed February 12, 2011).

Evelyn Varden

1. There is no information on Varden or her connection with Oklahoma in the Oklahoma Historical Society's online "Encyclopedia of Oklahoma History and Culture," http://digital.library.okstate.edu/encyclopedia/index.htm l (accessed February 13, 2011).
2. Information on Varden's early career from "Evelyn Varden, Actress, Is Dead," *New York Times* (July 13, 1958), www.nyt.com.
3. "Evelyn Varden, Actress, Is Dead," www.nyt.com.
4. Quotes from "A Good Play Made from One Bad Egg," *New York Times* (November 23, 1910), www.nyt.com.
5. "Faversham to Direct the Elliott Theatre," *New York Times* (July 5, 1918), www.nyt.com.
6. "Skinner Wins an Ovation," *New York Times* (March 18, 1919), www.nyt.com.
7. "Blanche Hall Critically Ill," *New York Times* (August 14, 1926), www.nyt.com.
8. Quotes from Brooks Atkinson, *Our Town* review, *New York Times* (February 5, 1938), p. 18.
9. "Evelyn Varden, Actress, Is Dead," www.nyt.com.
10. Brooks Atkinson, *Romeo and Juliet* review, *New York Times* (March 12, 1951), p. 21.
11. "Evelyn Varden, Actress, Is Dead," www.nyt.com.
12. "Evelyn Varden, Actress, Is Dead," www.nyt.com.
13. The part was created on Broadway by Juanita Hall and later taken over by Diosa Costello and Odette Myrtil.
14. One of the few scholars to be interested in *Hilda Crane*, W. David Sievers devotes several pages to the play in his magisterial study *Freud on Broadway: A History of Psychoanalysis and the American Drama* (New York: Hermitage House, 1955), published only a few years after the play's Broadway run. He calls it "a moving study of a modern woman told with compassionate understanding of defense-mechanisms" (pp. 344–45).
15. Samson Raphaelson, *Hilda Crane* (New York: Random House, 1951), p. 19.
16. Sievers, *Freud on Broadway*, p. 345.
17. Brooks Atkinson, *Hilda Crane* review, *New York Times* (November 2, 1950), p. 38.
18. Bosley Crowther, *Hilda Crane* review, *New York Times* (May 3, 1956), www.nyt.com.
19. Quotes from W.A. Darlington, "London Letter: Report on Lesley Storm's New Play," *New York Times* (October 20, 1957), p. X3; Lesley Storm, *Roar Like a Dove* (London: William Heinemann, 1958), p. 17, 27.
20. The play flopped on Broadway in the spring of 1964, closing after only twenty performances. Jessie Royce Landis played Muriel Chadwick.
21. Darlington, "London Letter," p. X3.
22. "Evelyn Varden, Actress, Is Dead," www.nyt.com.

Queenie Vassar

1. "Mrs. Kernell Wants a Divorce," *New York Times* (March 11, 1892), www.nyt.com.
2. Information on Harry Kernell and quotes from "Harry Kernell Is Dead," *New York Times* (March 14, 1893), www.nyt.com.
3. "Harry Kernell Insane," *New York Times* (October 8, 1892), www.nyt.com.
4. "Actors Entertain Lunatics," *New York Times* (February 10, 1893), www.nyt.com.
5. "Harry Kernell Is Dead," www.nyt.com.
6. "Harry Kernell Is Dead," www.nyt.com. As Vassar lived to be almost ninety, we may assume her husband did not infect her with syphilis or that if he did, she was cured. Kernell's first wife, on the other hand, Kittie O'Neill, "the best female jig dancer in the world," died only a month after her ex-husband, aged thirty-eight, from an unstated disease. See "Kittie O'Neill Dead," *New York Times* (April 17, 1893), www.nyt.com, incl. quote.

7. "Queenie Vassar Gets a Divorce," *New York Times* (November 10, 1900), www.nyt.com.

8. "Queenie Vassar Gets a Divorce," www.nyt.com.

9. Quote from "Francis Wilson in *The Toreador*," *New York Times* (January 7, 1902), www.nyt.com.

10. Irwin is best remembered for performing the first onscreen kiss in film history. That was the "Kiss Episode" with John C. Rice from her 1895 hit show *The Widow Jones*, which was filmed in 1896. See Daniel Bloom, *Great Stars of the American Stage* (New York: Grosset and Dunlap, 1952), Profile 22.

11. "*Lady of the Slipper* a Very Lively Show," *New York Times* (October 29, 1912), www.nyt.com.

12. "Queenie Vassar to Wed Cawthorn," *New York Times* (June 1, 1902), www.nyt.com.

13. Information on Cawthorn from "Who's Who This Week in Pictures," *New York Times* (April 29, 1934), incl. quote; and "Joseph Cawthorn, Comedian, 81, Dead," *New York Times* (January 23, 1949), www.nyt.com. The articles give 1867 as his year of birth, while 1868 is given on his grave marker.

14. "Elsie Janis a Slim Princess," *New York Times* (January 3, 1911), www.nyt.com.

15. Allan R. Ellenberger, *Celebrities in the 1930 Census* (Jefferson, NC: McFarland, 2008), p. 53.

16. "Joseph Cawthorn," www.nyt.com.

17. "Screen News Here and in Hollywood," *New York Times* (October 23, 1939), www.nyt.com.

18. "Screen News Here and in Hollywood: Queenie Vassar to Make Debut," *New York Times* (October 27, 1939), www.nyt.com.

19. Frank S. Nugent, *Primrose Path* review, *New York Times* (March 23, 1940), p. 19. In the play, the grandmother is a gruff but basically benevolent figure, who tries to give her daughter a "happy ending" with one of her clients and disapproves of her granddaughter marrying a "stuck-up guy." See Robert L. Buckner and Walter Hart, "The Primrose Path," undated typescript, Performing Arts Research Collections — Theatre, New York Public Library.

20. Bosley Crowther, *Lady in a Jam* review, *New York Times* (September 11, 1942), p. 25.

21. "Queenie Vassar, 89, Dies: Musical Comedy Star of the Nineties — Seen in Films," *New York Times* (September 13, 1960), www.nyt.com; www.findagrave.com (accessed February 16, 2011).

Ethel Waters

1. Juanita Moore quoted in Sam Staggs, *Born to Be Hurt: The Untold Story of* Imitation of Life (New York: St. Martin's, 2009), p. 29.

2. Ethel Waters with Charles Samuels, *His Eye Is on the Sparrow* (1951; New York: Jove/HBJ, 1978), p. 235.

3. These career successes are documented in several of the books and articles on Waters. See, for example, Waters, *His Eye Is on the Sparrow*, pp. 223, 246; Elizabeth Hadley Freydberg, "Ethel Waters," *Notable Women in the American Theatre: A Biographical Dictionary*, ed. Alice M. Robinson et al. (New York: Greenwood, 1989), pp. 904, 905; Stephen Bourne, *Ethel Waters: Stormy Weather* (Lanham, MD: Scarecrow Press, 2007), pp. x, 9, 14, 41, 42, 87, 92–93, 96; Donald Bogle, *Brown Sugar: Over One Hundred Years of America's Black Female Superstars* (New York and London: Continuum, 2007), p. 87; Donald Bogle, *Heat Wave: The Life and Career of Ethel Waters* (New York: HarperCollins, 2011), pp. 229–30, 233.

4. Bourne, *Ethel Waters*, p. 81.

5. Waters, *His Eye Is on the Sparrow*, p. 274.

6. Bosley Crowther, *The Member of the Wedding* review, *New York Times* (December 31, 1952), www.nyt.com.

7. Crowther, *The Member of the Wedding* review, www.nyt.com.

8. Patricia White, *UnInvited: Classical Hollywood Cinema and Lesbian Representability* (Bloomington: Indiana University Press, 1999), p. 166.

9. White, p. 157.

10. Donald Bogle, *Toms, Coons, Mulattoes, Mammies, and Bucks: An Interpretive History of Blacks in American Films* (4th ed.; New York: Bantam, 1974), p. 82.

11. Bogle, *Toms, Coons*, p. 63.

12. Peter Noble, *The Negro in Films* (London: Skelton Robinson, n.d. [1949]), p. 210.

13. Thomas Cripps, *Slow Fade to Black: The Negro in American Film, 1900–1942* (New York: Oxford University Press, 1977), p. 384.

14. Bourne, *Ethel Waters*, p. 77.

15. Ethel Waters, *To Me It's Wonderful* (New York: Harper and Row, 1972), pp. 133, 134. See also Bourne, *Ethel Waters*, p. 82.

16. Bourne, *Ethel Waters*, p. 2.

17. Waters, *His Eye Is on the Sparrow*, pp. 10, 11.

18. Waters, *To Me It's Wonderful*, pp. 133, 152.

19. Donald Bogle, *Blacks in American Films and Television: An Encyclopedia* (New York and London: Garland, 1988), p. 480.

20. Bogle, *Toms, Coons*, p. 154.

21. Waters, *To Me It's Wonderful*, p. 147.

22. Bourne, *Ethel Waters*, p. xi.

Helen Westley

1. Helen Westley quoted in Djuna Barnes, "The Confessions of Helen Westley," *The Gender of Modernism: New Geographies, Complex Intersections*, ed. Bonnie Kime Scott (Urbana: University of Illinois Press, 2007), p. 44. This interesting interview, conducted by the future author of *Nightwood* (1936), was originally published in the *New York Morning Telegraph Sunday Magazine* on September 23, 1917. Barnes performed with Westley in the Theatre Guild production of Paul Claudel's *The Tidings Brought to Mary* at the Garrick Theatre in 1922–23.

2. William Lindesmith, "Helen Westley," *Notable Women in the American Theatre: A Biographical Dictionary*, ed. Alice M. Robinson et al. (New York: Greenwood, 1989), p. 919.

3. During Westley's lifetime, she was thought to have been born in 1879, but her birth certificate gives the year 1875. See Lindesmith, "Helen Westley," p. 920.

4. "Charles Manney, Music Editor, 79," *New York Times* (November 1, 1951), www.nyt.com.

5. John Parker, *Who's Who in the Theatre: A Biographical Record of the Contemporary Stage* (7th ed.; London: Pitman, 1933), p. 1409; "Helen Westley, 63, a Noted Actress," *New York Times* (December 13, 1942), p. 74. There are more details of Westley's earliest acting days in "Regarding Helen Westley," *New York Times* (December 16, 1917), www.nyt.com; and "Helen Westley Shows Her Mettle," *New York Times* (December 12, 1937), www.nyt.com.

6. Barnes, "The Confessions," p. 41.

7. "John Westley," *New York Times* (December 28, 1948), www.nyt.com.

8. On Ethel Westley Cann Burns Hjul, see "Ethel Westley Married: Actress in *Strange Interlude* Wed to Alexander H.R. Cann," *New York Times* (May 31, 1928); "Cann-Gilbert," *New York Times* (October 16, 1938), www.nyt.com; and www.ssdi.com (accessed February 18, 2011).

9. Lindesmith, "Helen Westley," p. 918.

10. Parker, *Who's Who in the Theatre*, p. 1410.

11. "Helen Westley Shows Her Mettle," www.nyt.com.

12. Lindesmith, "Helen Westley," p. 919.

13. "Four New Plays at the Comedy," *New York Times* (December 4, 1917), www.nyt.com.

14. "Regarding Helen Westley," www.nyt.com.

15. "Helen Westley Shows Her Mettle," www.nyt.com.

16. Barnes, "The Confessions," p. 43.

17. "Helen Westley," p. 74.

18. See Barnes, "The Confessions," p. 42.

19. Quote from *Caesar and Cleopatra* review, *New York Times* (April 14, 1925), www.nyt.com.

20. See Helen Hayes with Sanford Dody, *On Reflection: An Autobiography* (New York: M. Evans, 1968), pp. 145–46.

21. David J. Skal with Jessica Rains, *Claude Rains: An Actor's Voice* (Lexington, KY: University Press of Kentucky, 2008), p. 79. Westley and Rains acted together in four Guild productions, but only one film, *Lady with Red Hair* (1940), a biopic about Mrs. Leslie Carter starring Miriam Hopkins.

22. Barnes, "The Confessions," p. 45.

23. "Helen Westley Shows Her Mettle," www.nyt.com.

24. John Springer and Jack Hamilton, *They Had Faces Then: Annabella to Zorina, the Superstars, Stars and Starlets of the 1930's* (N.p.: Castle, 1974), p. 337.

25. Andre Sennwald, "Rachel Crothers and Samuel Goldwyn Collaborate on *Splendor*," *New York Times* (November 23, 1935), www.nyt.com.

26. "Helen Westley Shows Her Mettle," www.nyt.com.

27. L.N., *The Primrose Path* review, *New York Times* (January 5, 1939), www.nyt.com.

28. David Ragan, *Who's Who in Hollywood, 1900–1976* (New Rochelle, NY: Arlington House, 1977), p. 816.

29. "Helen Westley," p. 74; Springer and Hamilton, *They Had Faces Then*, p. 337.

30. Barnes, "The Confessions," p. 44.

Bibliography

Barrios, Richard. *Screened Out: Playing Gay in Hollywood from Edison to Stonewall*. New York and London: Routledge, 2003.

Barris, Alex. *Hollywood's Other Women*. South Brunswick and New York: A.S. Barnes, 1975.

Barrow, Kenneth. *Helen Hayes: First Lady of the American Theatre*. Garden City, NY: Doubleday, 1985.

Blum, Daniel. *Great Stars of the American Stage: A Pictorial Record*. New York: Greenburg, 1952.

Bogle, Donald. *Blacks in American Films and Television: An Encyclopedia*. New York and London: Garland, 1988.

_____. *Heat Wave: The Life and Career of Ethel Waters*. New York: HarperCollins, 2011.

_____. *Toms, Coons, Mulattoes, Mammies, and Bucks: An Interpretive History of Blacks in American Films*. 4th ed. New York and London: Continuum, 2001.

Bourne, Stephen. *Ethel Waters: Stormy Weather*. Lanham, MD: Scarecrow Press, 2007.

Capra, Frank. *The Name Above the Title*. New York: Vintage, 1985.

Carson, William C. *Dear Josephine: The Theatrical Career of Josephine Hull*. Norman: University of Oklahoma Press, 1963.

Cavell, Stanley. *Pursuits of Happiness: The Hollywood Comedy of Remarriage*. Cambridge, MA: Harvard University Press, 1981.

Chandler, Charlotte. *The Girl Who Walked Home Alone*. New York: Simon and Schuster, 2006.

Coward, Noël. *The Letters of Noël Coward*. Ed. and with commentary by Barry Day. New York: Alfred A. Knopf, 2007.

Cripps, Thomas. *Slow Fade to Black: The Negro in American Film, 1900–1942*. New York: Oxford University Press, 1977.

Curtin, Kaier. *"We Can Always Call Them Bulgarians": The Emergence of Lesbians and Gay Men on the American Stage*. Boston: Alyson, 1987.

DiBattista, Maria. *Fast-Talking Dames*. New Haven: Yale University Press, 2001.

Dick, Bernard F. *Hellman in Hollywood*. Rutherford, NJ: Fairleigh Dickinson University Press, 1982.

DiOrio, Al. *Barbara Stanwyck*. New York: Coward-McCann, 1983.

Ellenberger, Allan R. *Celebrities in the 1930 Census*. Jefferson, NC: McFarland, 2008.

Estrin, Mark W. *Lillian Hellman: Plays, Films, Memoirs—A Reference Guide*. Boston: G.K. Hall, 1980.

Eyman, Scott. *Print the Legend: The Life and Times of John Ford*. Baltimore: Johns Hopkins University Press, 2000.

Fischer, Lucy, ed. Imitation of Life: *Douglas Sirk Director*. New Brunswick, NJ: Rutgers University Press, 1991.

Forbes-Robertson, Diana. *My Aunt Maxine: The Story of Maxine Elliott*. New York: Viking Press, 1964.

Gallagher, Tag. *John Ford: The Man and His Films*. Berkeley: University of California Press, 1986.

Gielgud, John. *Gielgud's Letters*. Ed. and with an introduction by Richard Mangan. London: Weidenfeld and Nicolson, 2004.

Gordon, Ruth. *Myself Among Others*. New York: Atheneum, 1971.

Gunn, James. *Deadlier Than the Male*. Lexington, KY: Blackmask/Disruptive, 2007.

Hadleigh, Boze. *Hollywood Lesbians*. New York: Barricade Books, 1994.

Harmetz, Aljean. *The Making of* The Wizard of Oz. New York: Delta, 1989.

Haskell, Molly. *From Reverence to Rape: The Treatment of Women in the Movies*. New York: Holt, Rinehart, and Winston, 1974.

Hayes, Helen, with Katherine Hatch. *My Life in Three Acts*. New York: Simon and Schuster/Touchstone, 1991.

Hayter-Menzies, Grant. *Mrs. Ziegfeld: The Public and Private Lives of Billie Burke*. Jefferson, NC: McFarland, 2009.

Hellman, Lillian. *The Children's Hour*. New York: Alfred A. Knopf, 1936.

Henderson, Mary C. *Theater in America*. New York: Harry N. Abrams, 1996.

Israel, Lee. *Miss Tallulah Bankhead*. New York: G.P. Putnam, 1972.

Jaynes, Clare. *Instruct My Sorrows*. New York: Random House, 1942.

Jones, Ken D., Arthur F. McClure, and Alfred E. Twomey. *Character People*. South Brunswick and New York: A.S. Barnes, 1976.

Kennedy, Harold J. *No Pickle, No Performance: An Irreverent Theatrical Excursion from Tallulah to Travolta*. Garden City, NY: Doubleday, 1978.

Kennedy, Matthew. *Marie Dressler: A Biography; With a Listing of Major Stage Performances, a Filmography and a Discography*. Jefferson, NC: McFarland, 1999.

King, Richard Abe. *Jane Cowl: Her Precious and Momentary Glory*. Bloomington, IN: 1stBooks Library, 2004.

Lambert, Gavin. *On Cukor*. London and New York: W.H. Allen, 1973.

Lamparski, Richard. *Hollywood Diary*. Boalsburg, PA: BearManor Media, 2006.

Landis, Jessie Royce. *You Won't Be So Pretty but You'll Know More*. London: W.H. Allen, 1954.

Lawson, John Howard. *Roger Bloomer*. New York: Thomas Seltzer, 1923.

Leaming, Barbara. *Bette Davis*. London: Orion, 1992.

Lederer, Katherine. *Lillian Hellman*. Boston: Twayne, 1979.

Lee, Betty. *Marie Dressler: The Unlikeliest Star*. Lexington: University Press of Kentucky, 1997.

Leeman, Sergio. *Robert Wise on His Films: From Editing Room to Director's Chair*. Los Angeles: Silman-James, 1995.

Levy, Emanuel. *George Cukor, Master of Elegance: Hollywood's Legendary Director and His Stars*. New York: William Morrow, 1994.

Madsen, Axel. *Stanwyck*. New York: HarperCollins, 1994.

_____. *William Wyler*. New York: Thomas Y. Crowell, 1973.

Mann, William J. *Behind the Screen: How Gays and Lesbians Shaped Hollywood, 1910–1969*. New York: Viking, 2001.

_____. *Kate: The Woman Who Was Hepburn*. New York: Henry Holt, 2006.

Marion, Frances. *Off with Their Heads! A Serio-Comic Tale of Hollywood*. New York: Macmillan, 1972.

McBride, Joseph. *Frank Capra: The Catastrophe of Success*. London and Boston: Faber and Faber, 1992.

_____. *Searching for John Ford: A Life*. London: Faber and Faber, 2003.

McClure, Arthur F., Alfred E. Twomey, and Ken D. Jones. *More Character People*. Secaucus, NJ: Citadel Press, 1984.

McCourt, James. *Queer Street: Rise and Fall of an American Culture, 1947–1985*. New York: Norton, 2004.

McDonald, Boyd. *Cruising the Movies: A Sexual Guide to "Oldies" on TV*. New York: Gay Presses of New York, 1985.

McGilligan, Patrick. *George Cukor: A Double Life*. New York: St. Martin's, 1991.

Moody, Richard. *Lillian Hellman: Playwright*. New York: Pegasus, 1972.

Mordden, Ethan. *Movie Star: A Look at the Women Who Made Hollywood*. New York: St. Martin's, 1983.

Morley, Sheridan. *Tales from the Hollywood Raj: The British in California*. London: Hodder and Stoughton/Coronet, 1985.

Mosel, Tad, with Gertrude Macy. *Leading Lady: The World and Theatre of Katharine Cornell*. Boston: Little Brown, 1978.

Nissen, Axel. *Actresses of a Certain Character: Forty Familiar Hollywood Faces from the Thirties to the Fifties*. Jefferson, NC: McFarland, 2007.

Noble, Peter. *The Negro in Films*. London: Skelton Robinson, n.d. [1949].

Norris, Charles G. *Zelda Marsh*. New York: E.P. Dutton, 1927.

Parish, James Robert. *Hollywood Character Actors*. New Rochelle, NY: Arlington House, 1978.

Parish, James Robert, and Ronald L. Bowers. *The MGM Stock Company: The Golden Era*. New York: Bonanza Books, 1972.

Parish, James Robert, and William T. Leonard. *The Funsters*. New Rochelle, NY: Arlington House, 1979.

Parker, John. *Who's Who in the Theatre: A Biographical Record of the Contemporary Stage*. 7th ed. London: Pitman, 1933.

Percy, Edward, and Reginald Denham. *Ladies in Retirement*. New York: Dramatists Play Service, n.d.

Peters, Margot. *The House of Barrymore*. New York: Alfred A. Knopf, 1990.

_____. *Mrs. Pat: The Life of Mrs. Patrick Campbell*. New York: Alfred A. Knopf, 1984.

Quinlan, David. *Quinlan's Character Stars*. London: Reynolds and Hearn, 2004.

_____. *Quinlan's Illustrated Directory of Film Character Actors*. 2nd ed. London: B.T. Batsford, 1995.

Ragan, David. *Who's Who in Hollywood, 1900–1976*. New Rochelle, NY: Arlington House, 1977.

Raphaelson, Samson. *Hilda Crane*. New York: Random House, 1951.

Reed, Joseph Verner. *The Curtain Falls*. New York: Harcourt Brace, 1935.

Rogers, Ginger. *Ginger: My Story*. New York: HarperCollins, 1991.

Rollyson, Carl. *Lillian Hellman: Her Legend and Legacy*. New York: St. Martin's Press, 1988.

Roof, Judith. *All About Thelma and Eve: Sidekicks and Third Wheels*. Urbana and Chicago: University of Illinois Press, 2002.

Sievers, W. David. *Freud on Broadway: A History of Psychoanalysis and the American Drama*. New York: Hermitage House, 1955.

Sikov, Ed. *Dark Victory: The Life of Bette Davis*. New York: Henry Holt, 2007.

_____. *Screwball: Hollywood's Madcap Romantic Comedies*. New York: Crown, 1989.

Silvester, Christopher, ed. *The Penguin Book of Hollywood*. London: Viking, 1998.

Skal, David J., with Jessica Rains. *Claude Rains: An Actor's Voice*. Lexington: University Press of Kentucky, 2008.

Springer, John, and Jack Hamilton. *They Had Faces Then: Annabella to Zorina, the Superstars, Stars and Starlets of the 1930's*. N.p.: Castle, 1974.

Staggs, Sam. *Born to Be Hurt: The Untold Story of* Imitation of Life. New York: St. Martin's, 2009.

Stapleton, Maureen, and Jane Scovell. *A Hell of a Life: An Autobiography*. New York, Simon and Schuster, 1995.

Stoddard, Karen M. *Saints and Shrews: Women and Aging in American Popular Film*. Westport, CT: Greenwood Press, 1983.

Storm, Lesley. *Roar Like a Dove*. London: William Heinemann, 1958.

Strang, Lewis C. *Famous Actresses of the Day in America: Second Series*. Boston: L.C. Page, 1902.

Strecker, Edward A. *Their Mothers' Sons: The Psychiatrist Examines an American Problem*. Philadelphia and New York: J.B. Lippincott, 1946.

Sturtevant, Victoria. *A Great Big Girl Like Me: The Films of Marie Dressler*. Urbana and Chicago: University of Illinois Press, 2009.

Swindell, Larry. *Body and Soul: The Story of John Garfield*. New York: William Morrow, 1975.

Towse, John Ranken. *Sixty Years of the Theater: An Old Critic's Memories*. New York and London: Funk and Wagnalls, 1916.

Twomey, Alfred E., and Arthur F. McClure. *The Versatiles: Supporting Character Players in the Cinema 1930–1955*. New York: Castle Books, 1969.

Waters, Ethel, with Charles Samuels, *His Eye Is On the Sparrow*. New York: Jove/HBJ, 1978.

_____. *To Me It's Wonderful*. New York: Harper and Row, 1972.

White, Patricia. *UnInvited: Classical Hollywood Cinema and Lesbian Representability*. Bloomington: Indiana University Press, 1999.

Willis, Donald C. *The Films of Frank Capra*. Metuchen, NJ: Scarecrow Press, 1974.

Wright, William. *Lillian Hellman: The Image, the Woman*. New York: Simon and Schuster, 1986.

Wylie, Philip. *Generation of Vipers*. New York and Toronto: Farrar and Rinehart, 1942.

Yurka, Blanche. *Bohemian Girl: Blanche Yurka's Theatrical Life*. Athens: Ohio University Press, 1970.

Index

Page numbers in **bold italics** refer to illustrations.